# CHOCOLATE & DIAMONDS

## For the Woman's Soul

# "Timeless Treasures to Warm the Heart and Soothe the Soul"

**This book is for every woman, everywhere.**

# Chocolate & Diamonds for the Woman's Soul: Timeless Treasures that Warm the Heart and Soothe the Soul.

A Hot Pink Premier Anthology ™

2015-2016 All Rights Reserved

ISBN-13:

978-1508821748

ISBN-10:

1508821747

http://www.hotpinkpublishing.com

Co-Compiled by *Carla Hall and Laurie Grant*

Sponsored by *The Talking Jar Series* and *Belanie Dishong*

Foreword by Michelle Scism (Decisive Minds)

If you would like to know more about any of our authors, please visit

ChocolateAndDiamondsfortheWomansSoul.com

**THANK YOU FOR YOUR SUPPORT**

May you always
know love & freedom
in your heart ♡

*Linda Spencer.*

# Our Contributors

# 100+ Inspiring Stories

# Sisterhood of Support

Every woman in the world is a diamond. It doesn't matter where she was born, the color of her skin, or what mistakes she thinks she has made. Diamonds appear when the heat has sufficiently shined the facets.

She may not see her brilliance until she has gone through the fire of adversity and the heat of pain. She may not feel her brilliance until she has let go of the old and embraced the new. Diamonds are all around us if we only open our eyes. Inside this book, you'll meet over 100 diamonds who used writing as a technique to release their legacy through the Hot Pink Anthology Series ™

Chocolate is a universal elixir for women who want to relax and allow the smooth flavor to transcend anything not-so-good in their life at any particular moment. Imagine coming in from a snowy hike and sitting down in front of the fire with a nice cup of hot cocoa. The soothing richness penetrates your soul with warmth and comfort. There are many documented health benefits of chocolate, in addition to the emotional retreat enjoyed when consumed.

***Chocolate & Diamonds for the Woman's Soul*** is a transcendent treasure for the ages. Each woman who wrote in this book, released a deeply held inner story. Some are sharing for the first time rape, tragedy and loss, while others are simply allowing us to walk a mile in their shoes. Imagine life as you know it taking a complete turn after becoming blind within an instant at 23, or being born with Spina Bifida. Put yourself in the shoes of someone who is currently going through the flames of cancer. Allow yourself to find comfort and gratitude in your life, by reading the stories of these women.

Hot Pink Publishing and Anthologies is a premier publishing house for women writers. Our motto is "No Woman Left Behind" and we achieve this through our anthology program and membership site. Our options are affordable so all women who have a story, also have a vehicle to carry the story all the way to publishing.

It is our intention that you'll read this book and order several more copies for your family and friends. You'll help support women who are writing their way into a changed world. We believe women holding untold stories, remain in agony until such time as her story is birthed. Join us in our featured anthology and feel the rush of writing your own book.

# Belanie Dishong Sponsor

## *In Support of Women's Growth*

Belanie Dishong, Founder and CEO of *Live at Choice*, is an expert in experiential training techniques that empower her clients to create breakthroughs that lead to transformational and sustainable life changes.

Belanie's story is one of forgiveness, and began with the desire to empower others. Through a chilling and life-threatening experience, Belanie came to realize that SHE was the common denominator in every single problem in her life. This revelation led her on a journey of self-discovery, and became the foundation of her programs at *Live at Choice*.

For more than two decades, Belanie has led thousands seeking a better life through workshops and courses that show them how to connect their mind with their heart's desires. She now teaches others how to break free of the limitations that keep ideas, desires and dreams from becoming reality. The *Live at Choice* programs extend beyond the hearing realm to embrace the Deaf and Deaf-Blind Communities, uniting these cultures through shared experience.

Belanie and her team of *Live at Choice* Platinum Coaches know that when people become empowered at their core, limitations vanish, dreams are realized and possibilities are limitless.

# Chocolate & Diamonds Sponsor

## *A Message from our Sponsor, Jeanne A. Dexter*

### And The Talking Jar Series

If talking is so easy...

Why is it so hard to communicate?

The stories in Chocolate and Diamonds for the Woman's Soul will help you see the bigger picture. Jeanne Dexter and The Talking Jar Series and Hot Pink Publishing & Anthologies (President Carla Hall) share two powerfully similar missions focusing on the same BIG PICTURE. I have joined hands with Carla to support 100+ women who are releasing their legacy by unleashing their story. Some of the stories are being written for the first time so that the potential reader will not only read with their eyes but with their soul. The mission of Hot Pink is "No Woman Left Behind and I certainly did not want to be left behind from joining this book.

I simply ask you, as you open the pages to each of the stories inside, like a "message in a bottle", waiting to be discovered, *unwrap the story*, listen for the wisdom and gather the message from someone who has already traveled this road. Use it to empower your life and then share it with someone else. It won't take long for you to see why I sponsored this book. With Gratitude, I pray these stories and The Talking Jars serve you well.

**Jeanne A. Dexter "The Talking Jar Series Inc." To connect with Jeanne or find out more about future releases; "Up the down Escalator", a Series; Divorce, Grief, Bullying, Anger and "The Kid in the Middle" (Adults and Children) and "The Bully Bee", a story about Community. (Adults and Children) visit www.TheTalkingJar.com**

There is no greater *agony* than you bear an untold story inside you.

Maya Angelou

# DEDICATION by Carla Wynn Hall

First of all, I would like to dedicate in gratitude, this book to all women everywhere who have seen their life more as a chunk of coal, than a precious diamond. You are the reason this book exists. Secondly, I want to say to my family, I am honored to be walking this life with you by my side. To my sons, Logan, Joshua and Nickolas, I dedicate my story of child birth and food cravings. I want to say a special legacy shout out to my grandchildren whom I hope read this when they are grown. Humble appreciation to my executive team and sponsors who put their heart and soul into fueling our movement. Laurie Grant, who is the organized leader of our team, thank you so much for holding the space for me to create. Jeanne Dexter, the official sponsor of this book who has always seen the power of unleashing a story, to totally transform a life. To Denise Thompson for coaching the ladies in their emotional state during the early stages of writing, I am truly grateful. To my mother Janice for teaching me about persistence and my mother-in-law Regina Hall for unconditional, never-ceasing love.

Lastly, I want to dedicate this book to "Granny". Granny is my 92 year old Great Grand Mother (in Law) who told me a story about taking a bus ride from Alabama to Idaho when her first born child (my husband's grandmother RIP) – was just an infant. She told a beautiful story of having 50 cents to her name when she left to be with her husband.

# DEDICATION by Laurie K. Grant

I am grateful for the opportunity to witness the coming together in community and healing of the women who participated in this wonderful collection of stories. Stories of life challenges and struggles and how they proved to be resilient and able to overcome.

I want to thank Carla Wynn Hall for allowing me to provide organizational structure to the process and giving me the honor of being a partner and co-compiler in this anthology. To be part of a collective effort which united authors from Canada, the United States, the United Kingdom, Australia and South Africa to collaborate on this creation, shows the power of being connected.

I thank my son, Harley Jaymes for supporting my efforts by being the most fabulous chef and preparing my dinners so I could focus on this work.

Last, but not least, my heartfelt gratitude goes out to the women who entrusted us with their stories and the task to bring them to life in the hope they will uplift and inspire another woman who may be walking the same path.

**Remember to Be the Change You Want to See in this World and to Show that Change to the World.**

# Foreword by Michele Scism

Chocolate & Diamonds for the Woman's Soul is truly a masterpiece. As a 3rd generation entrepreneur, the journey to success has been sprinkled with advice from mentors regarding the process of writing a book. Simply speaking, all of my current mentors agree: "Having your own book is not optional". Having a book under your belt in business, firmly establishes you as an expert in your chosen field.

The brilliant facet of the Chocolate & Diamonds for the Woman's Soul program is the women who are being empowered to do more in their life and business as a result. I work with women (and men) on creating strategies for success from creating successful selling systems, to utilizing conversations which result in closing a deal. One of the main roadblocks to success for women especially, is the green-eyed monster called FEAR. Fear is in everything women do. The anthologies or collaborative books published by Hot Pink work to help women get past fear.

Personally, I have written three books and participated in book anthologies because I am convinced of their effect upon the success of a business. I host events each year that focus on success as it relates to business, making money, closing deals and creating "Decisive Plans" for implementation. Because I have written my books I feel my success has taken a new leap forward.

I offer my support through the life of this book, for the authors of Chocolate & Diamonds for the Woman's Soul. You may contact me to inquire about my programs at *http://www.DecisiveMinds.com*

TRANSFORMATION

# #BUTTERFLIES

she transformed

# Linda J. Spencer

### Ontario, Canada

## *Remembering Me and Breaking Free*

**Once you are awake, you can never sleep.**

**Once you remember, you can never forget.**

I vividly remember the day I started to wake up and remember who I am. It would inevitably be the day I embarked on my journey to freedom.

My life wasn't hard. I came from a very loving and simple family growing up on a farm, having my independence and freedom. As a child, I was free, artistic and crafty, smart as hell, but shy and naive. Even as an adult, my life was relatively simple.

I met my husband when I was sixteen, endured a long distance relationship while I attended college, and married him after I finished university. He was the love of my life and I would do almost anything for him, including forgetting who I was and becoming the person I thought he wanted me to be. Even with all the arguments, fits of jealousy and accusations of not loving him enough, I thought our marriage was ok, that this was how every marriage was. We endured for over twenty years through job losses and lost loved ones, through child bearing and child rearing, through illness and depression, through a miscarriage and a serious ATV accident.

It was when I decided to quit my public accounting job and started a new job in corporate that I began to remember who I was. I had spent years living my life according to someone else's plans for me. At 35, it was time to start living my life on my terms, which included more freedom. Not freedom from my life, my husband and children, but freedom to be me, and to be loved and supported AS me. I wanted to be free to dream my dreams and live them.

In the first year of my new job, I grew more confident in myself and made new connections. My love and passion for writing poetry was rekindled (after a ten year break) and my intuitiveness began to awaken. I thought the move to a corporate job was the best move for me and my family, especially since I had more time with them. But, my husband still seemed to resent my job (and my chosen career), in which working past 5 pm was normal and interacting with male counterparts was essential. He trusted no one and was perceptively threatened by my new friendships with my male coworkers. The arguments became more frequent and more intense, and the resentment grew even deeper, as did his jealousy. I felt completely unsupported by my husband, who seemingly wanted me home, while at the same enjoying the lifestyle that our joint incomes allowed. What felt worse was him criticizing my accomplishments and poetic endeavours. He would say things like, "What's the big deal", or "Why on earth would you write that" (and often insert profanity). Then, I would feel wrong about having my own thoughts and feelings. As a result, I stopped sharing with him, started keeping things to myself (ESPECIALLY my feelings) and once again started to suppress the true me, which led to a growing resentment inside of me that I hated.

A few years pass...as much as I loved my husband and tried to make a happy home for us, I thought for sure he would break me. Maybe my awakening scared him. He said many times he wished I would go back to being the way I used to be and to the way things used to be before we had kids. I started to question myself again. I questioned what I was doing wrong (he was really good at making me feel wrong in every way possible). How could I be a better person? How could I fix our marriage? My yearning for a solution led to a ton of self-help books, online research and self-help courses, and the help of a life coach. We even went to marriage counselling. But it wasn't good enough, in fact, things got worse. As I grew, he retreated. As I branched out, he became more resentful. I came to realize not only were we on completely different pages, we were in completely different books! There would be no catching up.

As a Christian woman raised in the Anglican Church, I couldn't bear the thought of giving up on my marriage. It created a lot of anxiety, around what my family would think, what my friends would think, AND what God would think.

It took a cosmic 2x4 (while on a spiritual retreat in the heart of Mexico in 2012, where I was so desperately hoping to find a solution to "fix" my marriage) to jar my memory of every argument, every put-down, every manipulation, and every act of anger and rage from my husband to wake up and realize that a life with him would continue on that very same path. However, once you are awake, you can never sleep. Once you remember, you can never forget. With that jolt of awakening, I could never again forget how he treated me. I could never again go back to the way I was before I awoke. Loving him was not enough. If this path with him continued, it would indeed break me AND my children. I wouldn't let that happen! My fear of a future with my husband became greater than any of my fears of separation and ending our marriage.

I remember the day I first felt emotionally free - it was two months after we agreed there was no hope of reconciling. We had a huge blow out the day before. He was very profane and degrading me in front of our children. It wasn't the first time, and wouldn't be the last, but it was certainly the last time it meant anything emotionally to me. The next morning as I drove to work, I realized any love I had for him was completely gone, he could no longer use love or guilt to manipulate me to give in to him. Tears streamed down my face at the release. My heart broke wide open, and I felt freedom deep within my soul. It was exhilarating!

Although for months I continued to live in fear of his anger and rage, and in fear for my children's emotional well-being, I knew the fear would come to an end, and the only thing left was to go through the mechanics of separation and divorce. But it was anything, but mechanical. The process was filled with emotion. My family didn't understand and tried to get me to patch things up. Many of my friends left (they were mutual friends of ours), and I felt abandoned. Thankfully, I had a wonderful support team in my community, my coworkers and my soul family. Without them, I would have felt completely trapped and alone.

The day came to reach a settlement. I had asked my guides and angels to guide me through this day, to do and say what was best. In the end, after much deliberation, consultation, guidance and meditation, I agreed to his terms, despite my reservations about his ability to provide proper care and emotional support to our children. Again, my fears of what would happen to them if I didn't agree were greater than my fears of what would happen if I did.

So I surrendered, not to him, but to my trust in greater powers beyond our conscious being. I was left with the knowing my children would know and experience great love, instead of intense anger and hatred. I'm truly grateful for everything that has happened in my life, INCLUDING the painful process of divorce, and what it has taught me is this:

- **The Universe truly does have your back, and the pain you feel is a signal to stop and redirect your path;**

- **True freedom comes with loving yourself, and others, so unconditionally that you are truly you no matter what;**

- **Love does in fact heal all wounds, in its own time, not yours; and**

- **It all comes back to love, and BEING the love that you were born to be!**

# Heather Burke-Huyghue

## Nova Scotia, Canada

### *A Weekend of Transcendence*

It was a beautiful Friday evening in mid-July of 1999. The sun was setting over the tree tops and it was emitting a beautiful pink glow across the front yard and into the den where my hubby and I were relaxing. Folks in the little fishing village of Nova Scotia, where I grew up believed this indicated the following day was going to be a good one. The old wives tale goes something like this: "Pink sky at night, sailor's delight!"

It was a rare occasion, all four kids were away and we had the entire weekend to ourselves. I recall sitting at my computer desk with my feet crossed and stretched out on the edge of the sofa while my hubby was lying peacefully on the sofa with arms comfortably behind his neck. We were listening to Solfeggio frequencies, which make up the ancient 6-tone scale thought to have been used in sacred music, including the beautiful and well known Gregorian Chants. The chants and their special tones are believed to impart spiritual blessings when sung in harmony.

Each Solfeggio tone is comprised of a frequency required to balance your energy and keep your body, mind and spirit in perfect harmony. We were listening to the tone of 528 Hz, which is believed to create transformation, healing, and miracles. What happened next is my true story. It's nothing short of a miracle in the spiritual sense.

As I was gazing off into the distance, I felt my body shudder as I had a vision of my celestial Guardian Angel. I had seen her before while doing past life regression so I recognized her immediately. I could see her, but not as you would. I was using my mind's eye as I am a Clairvoyant and Psychic Medium. She was wearing a long flowing light blue gown with large bell sleeves. She is tall and svelte, with very long wavy flaxen colored hair. She has large, oval shaped emerald green eyes and her entire aura sparkles – like a million Swarovski crystals.

We were communicating telepathically. She was stating how proud she was of me and she loved me very much. She told me I was on the right path and this pleased her because I was destined to help many people via the path I chose. I felt her start to pull away and my back began to tingle as it does when spirit is leaving my etheric body. Before she left, I asked her what her name was because I didn't know it. She said, "Sabetha". Then she was gone.

What appeared to be seconds in Earth Time, were many hours in Celestial time. It is my belief in the Angelic realm there is no time at all. It is only Earth that has time limitations because we are here for the "*Earth Experience*". Our time is monitored and limited until the "time" we return to our place of Origin. Some call this "Heaven". Others call it "Universal Consciousness". Whatever the case may be, it is my belief we are Spiritual Beings having an earth experience – similar to an Avatar.

I explained my vision to my hubby as I sometimes do and we quickly forgot about it as we were both deeply relaxed. I usually have my visions when I am wide awake and alert, but in a deeply relaxed state.

The following morning was Saturday. I awoke early to the sounds of the birds singing. I decided to do some Reiki on myself as I am a *Reiki Master*. I recall standing on my knees at the edge of the bed as I performed my ritual. I recall feeling a vibration deep within my root chakra (located at the base of my spine). It went up through my naval, solar plexus, and heart chakras, and exited via my throat chakra. As it did, I made a primal, guttural sound. My hubby was still in bed, observing me. He was actually shocked and pulled his covers up to his chin as his eyes popped open and his mouth dropped. He remarked, "That was NOT your voice!" As I finished my ritual, I felt a great heaviness off my shoulders, so to speak.

On the third and final day, Sunday, I awoke early again and as I lay in my bed I had yet another vision. It was my Guardian Angel once more. I was standing beside her on the side of a grassy knoll. We were gazing out towards what appeared to be a large body of water. I could smell the dampness in the air. I could see the clouds gently rolling by as I watched a bird fly overhead. I could hear young people splashing in the water down below us. I could see a floating dock behind the bushes that were dividing us from the water below.

My Guardian Angel beckoned me up the grassy knoll. The slender golden wheat grass gently swayed back and forth as I followed her up the side of the rolling hill. There was a meticulously mowed two foot wide path that led us straight up to the apex. Ascending upwards I thought to myself, "Who mowed this path?" It was out of place in my rational mind, but who was I to question my vision?

As we arrived at the top of the hill and the mowed path ended, we came to a tomb made out of what appeared to be grey slate. It was completely stone. I sensed it was ancient by its worn appearance. It had a door shaped opening in the center. I stood at the entranceway and peered down the stone stairs into its damp, dark cavern. There, to my astonishment, was a young girl, age 17, kneeling at a sarcophagus on a stone pew. I knew her age to be 17. It was imprinted in my subconscious mind. The sunlight had cast a beam of sunshine upon her as she kneeled before the sarcophagus.

She was wearing a cream colored outfit -- similar to a South Asian *Sari*. She was also wearing a shawl made out of the same sheer fabric as her outfit. It was draped around her neck and head. I could see her long, slender arms and flawless face. I could also see her ash blonde short hair peeking out from her scarf. She was weeping in deep mourning. I felt a strong kinship to this young lady. My heart went out to her. She glanced up at me, but there was no acknowledgement of my presence – as if she was not aware of my existence. I quickly glanced behind me -- to see where my Guardian Angel was, but she was nowhere to be found. In that instant I was shot back to my etheric body with a powerful shudder.

I told my hubby once again about my vision. He suggested I write it down in my journal, along with a drawing of the tomb, grassy knoll, and anything else I felt was pertinent. After writing my experience in my journal, I decided to go downstairs and research the name "Sabetha" as I felt strongly my Guardian Angel was trying to tell me something important. I just had to solve the riddle and I had an overpowering urge to do so.

I grabbed my housecoat and made my way downstairs to my laptop, which was sitting on the bench adjacent the kitchen counter. I proceeded to type in the word "Sabetha" on my laptop, assuming I would get the names of various Angels. Instead, I was directed to a small Christian church in the town of Sabetha, Arkansas, in the United States. I scrolled down quickly through the article. I stumbled upon a picture of a tomb that looked uncannily similar to the tomb in my vision.

I thought to myself, "What a coincidence!" This caught my attention. I continued to scroll. I came upon more information that caught my eye. It was about a young lady by the name of Joni Earickson, who, as a teenager enjoyed riding horses, hiking, tennis, and swimming. On July 30, 1967, at age 17, she dove into Chesapeake Bay while on a raft. After misjudging the shallowness of the water, she suffered a fracture between the fourth and fifth cervical vertebrae and became a quadriplegic, paralyzed from the shoulders down.

During her two years of rehabilitation, according to her autobiography, she experienced anger, depression, suicidal thoughts, and religious doubts. However, despite her disability, Joni learned to paint with a brush between her teeth, and began selling her artwork worldwide. To date, she has written over forty books, recorded several musical albums, starred in an autobiographical movie of her life, and is an advocate for disabled people and people who have doubted the existence of God.

Joni wrote of her experiences in her 1976 international best-selling autobiography, *Joni: The unforgettable story of a young woman's struggle against quadriplegia & depression*, which has been distributed in many languages. The book was made into a 1979 feature film of the same name, starring her. Her second book, *A Step Further*, was released in 1978.

I had never heard this woman, but I could certainly relate to her story, because I, too, at that very moment in time, was experiencing suicidal thoughts and doubts about God's existence. You see, I had been abused horribly as a child and wife. These experiences left me jaded and hurt. I was actually angry with God because I questioned why he would allow such horrible things to happen to me.

I decided to look for a picture of Joni at age 17. I needed to know what she looked like. After several minutes of searching, I came across a photograph of Joni just prior to her accident. To my shock and surprise, she was the young lady I saw in the tomb! Needless to say, I fell off my chair and began crying uncontrollably. My hubby came downstairs and asked me what was wrong. I explained to him what my Guardian Angel had shown me. He just held me and told me it was God's way of renewing my sense of faith.

What I've learned is bad experiences teach us COMPASSION for our fellow man and woman. More involved than simple empathy, Compassion commonly gives rise to an active desire to alleviate another's suffering. *Compassion is ranked a great virtue in numerous philosophies, compassion is considered in almost all the major religious traditions as among the greatest of all virtues.*

# Martine M. Mayas

New York, United States of America

## *Becoming Natural*

**"One of the lessons that I grew up with was to always stay true to yourself and never let what somebody else says distract you from your goals. And so when I hear about negative and false attacks, I really don't invest any energy in them, because I know who I am."**
**— <u>Michelle Obama</u>**

Becoming natural was never an option for me, not even a thought. It all happened by accident, after experiencing a series of nuisances for a couple of years. The pain started as headaches, then turned into terrible migraines. These migraines affected my eyes, vision and concentration. I experienced muscle spasms in my right arm and hand, and could not write legibly. After several Cat-Scans and MRIs, my doctors requested for me to diminish on relaxing my hair. I abided to the suggestion, and as the days and years passed, I realized my migraines were diminishing, until I didn't suffer from migraines or headaches anymore.

Right now, I've been natural for five years, including two big chops during my transition. The transition was actually easier because I wore braids throughout the entire process. I covered my hair with braid extensions since I noticed my hair was breaking from excess usage of chemicals. I wore many hairstyles, such as Kinky Twist, Senegalese Twist, and Cornrows. Once I was satisfied with the length of my hair, my mind automatically began to think about how I was going to manage the maintenance of my natural. My personal plan wasn't to cover my hair for the rest of my life - I had to find a way to wear it in its natural state and be comfortable with it.

So I began looking at different natural hairstyles to see where I could identify myself and my hair. I saw my hair type with dreadlocks and Afros. I enjoyed all the dreadlock styles. I decided to get my hair twisted in an attempt to begin my dread journey, but unfortunately, I didn't like that style on me. I wore it for two weeks, covered with a wig. Then, I decided to get crochet braids with kinky hair and once again, I didn't like the style on me, wore it for two weeks, and then cut it all off on my own. That's when people started noticing that I actually transitioned into being natural and started asking me questions, as well as, making comments.

The responses I received varied; many loved my new look, but a handful disliked it. One person actually told me: "You don't have the right hair texture to go natural." With great astonishment, I kept calm with a smile and didn't even reply to that comment, but listened and observed. That one comment became the set off to my natural hair journey. I simply asked God to show me the way. Once I surrendered, I started to familiarize myself with my hair type and style. As I took the time to learn and identify myself to my natural state of being, I began to realize this natural hair journey is bigger than anyone can possibly imagine.

It's more spiritual than anything. Natural hair is a lifestyle intertwine with power, confidence, attitude and challenges. You have to be willing to give up something or maybe even a few things to maintain your natural self. Being natural isn't about being perfect or looking the way people perceive you to look. It's about looking the way you are composed by your Creator. Being natural begins with your mind. It's about healing and finding oneself in its physical, psychological, spiritual, personal state and being proud to flaunt it.

My natural hair is actually 4C according to the hair chart, however I believe it may even be more like a 4D due to the tightness of its curl. Each strand of my hair is kinky and curly with coils in between. It is the perfect Afro texture. The look of my strands varies from day to day, from straight to curly to kinky to frizzy, regardless I love them all. To me, being a natural is the beauty of imperfection. It is creativity, nothing, but an art. 4C hair is the biggest challenges because of its thick coarseness. However, the reality is it's achievable to wear it daily, like I do. My biggest challenge was to embrace my imperfection and not allow others' opinions to dominate my mind and life. It wasn't easy. But, I did it by affirming myself, my hair, my beauty and charm on a daily basis.

The more I affirmed, the more I rose to perfection in the eyes of my Creator for accepting myself as I am. Writing and saying affirmations are a powerful tool- use them with care because your request do come true. Affirmations have helped me improve my outlook on life, change my mind to see the same things through better eyes, accept all that is, and work with what I have. Affirmations have also helped me in affirming the softness and manageability of my hair, as well as conditioning it on a weekly basis. 4C hair is not a struggle, if you affirm and believe it's soft, manageable and beautiful.

As I made the decision to wear my natural, I gained confidence and total happiness with myself. My poise and etiquette has illuminated me - people are always wondering, "Who is that woman?" and just walk over to me to compliment me on my hair. I must say it's been the best decision I've ever made for myself. The point of this story is as a Naturalist, you must wear a style that fits you as a person and your personality to enjoy your natural hair journey with excitement, joy and creativity. Natural hair is about tapping into your Divine with compassion, forgiveness, uniqueness and style.

I've learned God doesn't make errors. All is done for a reason. It's just up to us to embrace it as such, instead of questioning everything. Being a Naturalist denotes bravery, self-love, self-discovery and self-acceptance. I am so happy to be natural and very thankful of the ultimate thickness and coarseness of my hair. I am thankful for my experiences to be and to make a change. My natural hair has healed my pains and doubts about myself. I've achieved total freedom in all areas of my life, broken barriers and faced many fears. Everything has changed for me for the better – I am always happy with a vibrant and captivating spirit, ready to explore and just be me. I am so proud to have found this new level of happiness within me.

# Nicole M. Small

### Florida United States of America

## *Rolling With the Punches of "Spina Bifida"*

As I entered into this world in August 1989, my parents were in for the shock of a lifetime. It was at the exact moment my mother pushed for the final time they received the news I was born with a birth defect, Spina Bifida to be more specific. Over the next twenty four hours, I would undergo a handful of the first of eighteen operations I would need to maintain my condition to the best of the doctor's ability.

My parents were filled with a wide range of emotions which resulted in happiness, shock and fear. Happiness because they had just brought a beautiful baby girl into this world, shock because at the time the term Spina Bifida was foreign to them, they didn't know what it entailed and lastly, their minds were filled with fear of the unknown...will I die right here right now or be able to live a somewhat normal life considering what was just handed to my parents in a matter of minutes.

Thankfully, I was airlifted to All Children's hospital in St Petersburg FL for the first set of my 18 surgeries then I was admitted to Shriners Hospital for Children in Tampa which is a hospital that specializes in caring for individuals with Spina Bifida. Most individuals in my situation would say going in and out of surgery seemed to be the hardest part. I would have to say the surgery was the easiest out of everything. The hardest part for me, in my journey with Spina Bifida, was having to go to school each day and endure the countless stares and whispers amongst my fellow classmates.

I knew from the age of 9, I wasn't like the rest of them; I was completely different. When they were planning birthday parties and sleepovers, I was going in for another checkup or another surgery. I had a few friends who made small talk with me, noting their conversations were very shallow. I genuinely felt as if no one liked me, but I couldn't understand the real reason. I never really knew what they were thinking or feeling because they refused to get to know me.

I didn't have the opportunity of joining my fellow classmates on the playground because it was non-wheelchair accessible which only made them distance themselves even further away from me. We didn't share the common interest of being able to play on the swings or merry go round together. The feelings of distance were not only shared by my classmates, but I felt as though my teachers didn't take the time to really understand who I was as an individual, and not just someone with a physical disability. During my time in school I was going through a number of emotions and feelings with still trying to figure out who I was as a person and everything that came with my condition.

My classmates and teachers had one common interest, they didn't put in the time to understand who I was as a whole. The reason I wasn't just a great student is because I was always missing school due to a surgery and/or complication from the disability. If there was one thing I could tell individuals about others who have a disability it's *what is on the inside and not necessarily on the outside*. It wasn't until I was in my late teens that I came to terms with how everything turned out for me because I was in control of how I wanted my journey and my future to look like.

I learned early in life I was not going to let a disability or anyone else define me as a person. I feel as though I was put on this Earth because I deserved to live. The doctors told my parents I wouldn't see past my thirteenth birthday due to the severity of my Scoliosis, which is when your spine forms into the shape of an S. When your spine is formed into this shape this leaves little to no room for your lungs, which can cut off your breathing as you grow. My thirteenth birthday came and went and my parents noticed I was still happy and as healthy as ever. They breathed a sigh of relief because they knew everything would turn out just as God intended it to, just fine.

Years later I went on to graduate both high school and college, all of which were not an option considering the circumstances according to the doctors. Going through life's challenges both physically and emotionally really gave me the backbone and structure to handle any of the challenges because I believe I have conquered my first challenge in life which was the day of my birth. Some individuals may look at it as the worst possible day ever, but considering every milestone I've achieved and so much more despite the doctor's projection. I celebrate that day to the fullest extent because I deserve to.

I feel as though God had a plan for me when he created me twenty five years ago. There is not a day that goes by that I do not feel blessed because I was not made this way by mistake. Everyone is born just as they should be. In 2013, I decided I wanted to share my journey with Spina Bifida with others in my situation. My mission was to educate young parents who have children born with Spina Bifida, who feel they are at a loss for words and sometimes feel hopeless.

I've been writing about my journey through a blog. Some pieces are helpful, some are inspirational and some are both. I've found what I write is not just cathartic for me, but it really helps individuals having a difficult day whether they have a disability or not. The bottom line is, just because life presents you with a difficult problem, it's NOT your free ticket to curl up in the fetal position and give up, it's your opportunity to take LIFE into your own hands and make it however you envision for you and you alone.

In January, 2015, I started promoting events as a way of giving back to the Shriners because they gave so much to me at a time when we had nowhere else to turn. They never turn a family away regardless of the ability to pay and when you have a child with Spina Bifida, the bills can add up very quickly and become overwhelming in an already difficult situation.

In addition to Spina Bifida, I have a condition called Hydrocephalus. This is when excessive "CSF" which stands for "Cerebral Spinal Fluid" builds up in my brain and a shunt is implanted to drain the fluid and relieve the pressure from my brain.

Although I have Spina Bifida and Hydrocephalus, I am a stronger person. When you are in a difficult situation like mine, the key is to have a wonderful support system. If it weren't for my friends, family and family friends I think I would have given up. Instead, I keep "Rolling with the Punches".

# Nikki Brown

New South Wales, Australia

## *The Letter I Never Wrote*

### "Finding Myself"

As a young child, I always knew I was different. I felt it, I lived in a bubble and I didn't fit in. Being a child, who was socially awkward, overweight, shy and scared of others; I was always picked last for teams and played on my own at lunch time. I always, wondered why, but on another level, knew I didn't belong. Of course, this made me a target and the brunt of many jokes and taunting. This, for me, just cemented how I felt......So when you came along my world changed forever and I began to understand why I felt the way I did. You were the person who taught me so much and were meant to be the receiver of the letter I never wrote......

It was the end of my married life and I had moved to Sydney where my parents and sister lived, although I still felt like a ship without a rudder.

I took up some study and had two jobs. The first job was in a Solicitors office and the other in a lighting shop on the weekends.

My life was moving along nicely. I was exercising and eating well, although I was struggling with lung disease and had put on 20 kg with medication for my illness. Some friends of mine in Melbourne had joined a spiritualist organization and were encouraging me to come back to Melbourne to catch up and meet some of the other organization members. I took a little holiday down to Melbourne. I had arranged to meet up with all my old friends, as well as, the spiritual organization friends.

I entered the busy restaurant and sat at the table of around 15 people. The only seat available was next to stunning black South African women, whose name meant witness to God. As soon as I sat down next to her, she said "hello old friend, it's great to meet you again" I was gobsmacked what did this mean?

The chemistry and intensity of the moment completely took me by surprise. I had never met this woman before, but yet she was so familiar! For the next two hours I was in a new bubble with this woman, she was extremely charismatic and I was completely engaged by her. I felt things I didn't understand and yet seemed so natural to me. She was married with 3 children and told me her husband encouraged her to spend time with women, they had an open marriage, he knew their marriage was secure, but encouraged his wife to explore her bisexual side. I actually didn't really understand what this all meant, let alone how I was feeling. Yet I knew my life had changed in that instant and it would never be the same again.

When I got back, it was back to work and nightly phone calls after her children were in bed catching up on the day. The phone calls were not just mumbo jumbo, but rather educational. I learnt about intimacy and what it was. Past lives, which this was, I had had lives with this woman before! Chemistry, passion, and love which was unconditional. I learnt how to talk, and tap into the amazing depth of spiritual knowledge I didn't even know I had. I learnt I had feelings for a woman and finally understood why I had felt awkward around certain girls at school. I was bisexual. Wow! I had begun to discover who I was at last!

This revelation took a while to embrace, but yet seemed so natural to me. I had begun my journey of understanding myself and started to become aware my world wasn't really a bubble, but a place where there was so much to learn and engage with. I had ancient knowledge buried deep within me, I was only just beginning to understand. I read many books, became aware of energy, ego, the planets, my psychic senses, that I was unwell in the sense of I was still functioning from a needy, unworthy, co-dependent self. Because I had yet to discover who I was, how I fitted in and where I belonged. My life up until now had been emotionally immature. I was very naive.

Over the next 18 months whilst maintaining contact with my friend in Melbourne, I struggled with an unknown auto immune disease which involved my lungs, skin and muscles. The treatment involved steroids; my weight ballooned. I also fractured vertebrae and developed Osteoporosis. I would lose the weight, put it on again (25 kgs) and then lose it again only to get sick again. My life had become an emotional rollercoaster and I was the only one who really understood what it was like!

I was sad, miserable and had tried to forge a life for myself in a city full of people I couldn't connect with. So having lost my next lot of weight, I moved back to Melbourne and started an intimate relationship with my South African friend. I had previously joined the spiritual organization and now spent several evenings a week after work, visiting the Melbourne center studying the teachings.

During this time, I learnt so much about myself. I learnt I was smart, intelligent, that I could make friends, hold a relationship and live a relatively healthy life. This was until I became ill again with Polymyositis. I was again treated with steroids and place on an immunosuppressant. I finally saw hope.

Behind the scenes, however, a totally different scene was being played out. My South African friend had woven an intricate web of lies and I got caught up in it unwittingly. She had been the love of my life, but had tired of me, so the only way she could be rid of me was to concoct stories about me amongst other people she was also being intimate with! I had no idea! These people had also begun to concoct stories about me and so it went.

So the person who I had trusted, loved, and learnt so much from, had betrayed me and broken my heart. I was devastated and questioned everything I had been taught from this woman. Although at some level it had resonated, I began to understand that whilst one part of her had been true, there was another part of her which was dysfunctional in its own right and this was the part which had destroyed the love we shared. This was to be my earliest understanding of the ego and the shadow self.

Over the next 10 years, I managed to stay well, but became entrapped in a very dysfunctional relationship with a female partner who had a son on the Autism Spectrum, who had chosen to be un-medicated, in dealing with her bipolar and borderline personality disorder. Again, I was on a rollercoaster, of psychological abuse, emotional torment and ill health. I began again to self-loath and dislike who I was. I spent many nights alone during this relationship, crying myself to sleep.

After finding the courage to leave this relationship, I took up my spiritual practices once again, started doing psychic readings and Reiki healings in a little shop. Over the next 6 years, I met and loved three different women who I never had an intimate relationship with. They all told me they loved me and wanted to have a relationship with me, but at the last minute, some turn of fate had them, all saying they wanted to discontinue our friendships. I questioned again, what was it I had to learn from all of this? Why did this keep happening? There were most certainly lessons here in rejection and betrayal.

I began to understand my emotional wellbeing, how I saw myself had a lot to do with the illness and my relationship with others! I had my own shadow self and ego to deal with!

I had now been diagnosed with Lupus; I also had Fibromyalgia and Sleep Apnea. This new level of understanding about how I had sabotaged my own health and relationships through how I saw myself has brought me to where I am today! My understanding of how the past has defined who I am today, has led me on an amazing journey of self-discovery, with various practitioners.

I now have the most amazing group of friends, am as well as I can be and settled close to my parents. I happily operate a very busy holistic health practice, teach development and meditation. I am almost finished a Diploma in Counselling and a Diploma in Clinical Hypnotherapy.

The shy, socially, awkward girl, who had no friends, who was told she would never go further than year 11, who couldn't tie her shoelaces, read or ride a bike until she was 8, is now quietly confident, alive and ready for the next chapter. My own journey has shaped the very unique work I do with my clients and gives me the confidence to teach from my own experiences, today!

# Jamie Timmons

Maryland, United States of America

## *Birthed From Pain to Resilience*

The women in my lineage are some of the most courageous and resilient women I know. There is no wonder I am how I am today as I am cut from the same cloth. Each and every one in my lineage, going back to my great grandmother, have endured a great amount of physical, emotional and sexual abuse from their significant other. And their offspring became the inheritors of such abuse from the same men. Perhaps poverty and alcoholism played a role in our abusers' evil behavior. Consequently, just about every man the women in my lineage married or courted raised a violent hand, spoke a demeaning word, and sometimes sexually violated the women born in my family, including the little girls.

There was one man, the only man I will call grandfather. He was the man my maternal grandmother married and ultimately became widowed. He was the one man who actually showed me not all men are malicious. He never struck my grandmother, never cursed or yelled at her, but rather loved her until his very last breath. My grandfather was the kindest, gentlest, good-hearted man I've ever met. I believe it was with his passing that my grandmother eventually took her last breath. Though her medical records may state she passed from complications associated with bone cancer, I believe she passed from a broken heart. She just couldn't go on without my grandfather. Their love and connection was magical. After years of abuse, my grandmother finally found the one man who treated her like a human being; and living without him was simply unbearable.

As a child, I've witnessed countless fights with the men in my family violently striking their wives. But there's one occasion I recall that sticks out from the rest, when I knew my grandmother was the strongest woman alive!!! We lived in a very small rural town called Clarksdale, Mississippi. I was about four years old at the time. I was at my grandmother's home, a very small shack where you walk through the front door and you can see the back door. It looked like one big room, but she had it decorated where you could see the transition from the living room, to the kitchen, to the one bedroom, then back door. In my mind, as I try to recall details of the house, all I see is dark wooden panels. My grandmother was sitting at the kitchen table, which was a small round table with a plastic table cover and two wooden chairs. She was picking peas to cook for dinner. She had a big bowl in front of her, between her legs, she used to put the peas in and the podded peas lay scattered on her small kitchen table.

Sunny, my grandmother's boyfriend, walked in the door and, as usual, he was inebriated. Sunny had a wooden leg and walked with a limp. The children were told he had "sugar", a common term used for diabetes. So he walks in the house, pulls out his pocket knife, stumbles over to my grandmother, and begins to make small cuts on both of her arms. My grandmother does not flinch! She simply says, "Stop Sunny!" But she continued to pick the peas as he's slicing into her arms. Splatters of blood are everywhere, even on the peas in the bowl, but she continues to pick the peas. She doesn't push him away, she doesn't cry, she just picks the peas. I suppose he realized he wasn't getting the reaction he wanted; he walks away. My grandmother gets us, cleans up the blood and continues to prepare dinner.

How relieved I was to find out she never married Sunny. He died a lonely, miserable death. He was found naked in his hotel room, dead on the floor between the bed and the wall. My grandmother, even though they were separated at the time, went to his funeral. After all the hell this man puts her through, she still showed respect and never spoke about all of the beatings or arguments or bad instances she experienced with him. Over the years, those cut marks on my grandmother's arms were a constant reminder to me of that moment – I was there, and I saw it all with my own eyes.

Out of my grandmother's womb comes the next strong lioness, I am proud to call my mother. And again, there are many moments I remember my mother being violently attacked by both my father and then her next husband, whom I refuse to acknowledge as any relation to me. Her second husband, Johnny, was pure evil. Their marriage was filled with physical and verbal abuse, infidelity, complete lack of concern for my mother's health or feelings, and drunkenness. Johnny hated her children, me and my other two sisters, and the feeling was mutual. When this evil man would become extremely intoxicated, he went into belligerent and violent rages upon my mother. I was the only one, and the smallest in size, to come out of my room and fight him off of my mother. Today, I can still hear my mother's cry when she called my name and I came running with determination to turn his rage from my mother to me, as long as he wasn't hitting her.

When I was in middle school, there was an extended period of time I recall that actually still brings tears to my eyes just thinking about it. Johnny would come home drunk and force my mother in the car with him. I don't know where he took her, but when they returned, my mother's face was covered in blood. This happened which seemed like every weekend. He had a standing appointment to violently attack my mother for absolutely no reason at all, while intoxicated and filled with rage. I remember harboring such hatred for this man for all of the hell he put my mother through; so much hatred I would become physically sick at just the sight of him. But I wasn't afraid of him.

Johnny's physical and verbal abuse later turned towards me and my sisters, but mostly me because I fought back. My physical battle with this man carried on through my entire senior year in high school. I didn't participate in the normal senior activities most do, I was too busy fighting. No senior trips, or senior pictures, or hanging out with my friends; and my senior prom was a total disaster. All I did was walk the stage to accept my diploma, feeling a sense of hopelessness. After all, the whole year was trying to survive the physical fights. I knew there was no way I could win, but I was determined everyone would know he was in a fight! I kept long fingernails just to scratch his face. He would step on my neck, cutting off my air supply, and scream obscenities at me. My teen years were about survival, until after one semester at a local community college, my mother walked in the door with a U.S. Navy brochure. She signed me up to join the military at seventeen.

Did you know a single rope is made up of many strands of natural fiber twisted together? That is the women in my family. No matter how many times you punch us in the face, kick us in the ribs, spit on and demean us with your words, it only makes us stick together like a rope and become as strong as ever. Both my grandmother and my mother suffered years of physical and emotional abuse, but you couldn't tell they lived a terrifying life. They never talked about their abuse, but rather worked various jobs to provide for their children. We never went without food, clothing or shelter.

My story, which I didn't fully recall until I was in my early twenties, was a little different, but still on the same horrible and tragic path of abuse. My uncle sexually abused me while I was as young as five years of age. Visions of him standing in front of me, naked, with porn playing on the television behind him haunt me until this very day. Moments when there were other children in the room with me, his wife (my aunt) standing there, a video camera on the stand, and sexual escapades happening – things too explicit to write in this book. Children shouldn't be exposed to such lewd and perverted behavior, but it happened.

Those days of physical, emotional and sexual abuse are over now. My grandmother and mother both married the loves of their lives – kindred spirits. God truly saved the best for last! In my earlier years, I've watched my grandmother and mother suffer in silence; and in my later years, I've watched them laugh and love just as hard. Well, you know where I ended up – telling the story of triumph. I attribute my success to the women who came before me. Though we were bruised, we weren't broken. We eventually put that painful past, and the men associated with it, far behind us and now enjoy the "now". My grandmother's strength will always be with each and every woman in my family. Her tenacity will always shine through our darkest moments; and it was her love that brought us back together as a tight fitted rope!

# Jamie Crane-Mauzy

Utah, United States of America

## #MoCrazyStrong

Doing therapy is surprisingly very much like being a pro skier or a pro athlete in general. You have to set goals, work hard, accomplish more than you think you ever will, and believe you are going to achieve the unachievable. You also have to deal with the struggles, like still accomplishing when you've had a bad day, not feeling like you are accomplishing enough fast enough, and be open to see how far you've come, not thinking you haven't accomplished enough. It's inspiring if you are a pro athlete or recovering because you accomplish more than people expect.

Whoa, Pro skier? "What is she talking about?" Let me take the opportunity to explain who I am, and what happened to me recently. *My name is Jamie Crane-Mauzy and April 11, 2015, I sustained a Traumatic Brain Injury (TBI).* The other thing about me, that's important to know about this story, is I am a professional skier. I compete in slopestyle and halfpipe, which for slopestyle means I go off jumps and do off axis tricks and slide across apparatus, and for halfpipe there is a pipe made out of snow, which I ski across to reach a high amplitude, "catch air," and do tricks while up there. I was at the World Tour Finals in Whistler, Canada, when I fell so hard I ended up in a coma for eight days. For the first 72 hours they didn't know if I was going to survive or not. Luckily, I have no permanent brain damage. Basically, everything that could possibly be considered luck happened to me. Most people would say it was bad, horrible luck. But not me.

I think luck is very much attached to the attitude you bring into it. I speak from personal experiences. I have now accomplished two things most people think are lucky. I am a professional skier and a traumatic brain injury survivor. Being a professional skier takes tons more than luck. So much strength and so many struggles lead to the being a professional skier.

It's been my attitude of knowing how lucky I always am to even be able to put skis on that puts me and my competitors where we are. To be a TBI survivor is of course incredibly lucky. I am already able to drive and back to normal and I was just in a coma! With both of these, I definitely think my attitude plays the highest part in both of those. If you are light-hearted, confident, and believe you can achieve the impossible, well, then you can. It's all about your attitude that allows you to be lucky. Luck doesn't come on its own.

I was originally told I had leave the hospital by the end of August, now it's July and I am already back to being a normal person and writing this chapter! I have been pretty much blowing everyone's minds by how fast my recovery is and how well it's going. I believe I completely lucked out by how many people supported me when they heard I was in a coma. There's my family, friends, therapists, medical staff, and random people; they all supported me. I honestly believe I recovered so well and so fast due to their support.

That's why when I hear of someone else who's in a coma, I want to send my vibes toward them. When I was in a coma, my personal physical therapist made a pink bracelet that said #MoCrazyStrong on it. It was put on my right arm, because I hurt my right brain stem paralyzing my entire right side. Having it there actually helped get my right arm back to normal. Everyone who supported me wore one on their wrist as well. Now I give the #MoCracyStrong bracelets out to those recovering and those connected to those recovering, along with my love and support.

When I hurt my right brain stem, my entire right side of me was paralyzed. I don't remember when my entire right side was paralyzed, but I do remember when my right arm was paralyzed and when electric stimulators were put on it to get it to move again. It's been a hard process to get my right side to be equal to my left. My mom helped me with my recovery process tremendously.

She forced me to use it for eating when my mind couldn't comprehend why she was being so mean to me. When I was originally released from the hospital, I had to put coins into a jar, screw the tops on and off bottles, practice how to write, and my grandmother sent me a hand strengthening exerciser for my right hand. Most people who use it just want to strengthen their hands and arms, but I used it to help my right arm recover. Basically, I hated to use it, but the recovery I made with it was huge. When I started it was hard for me just to straighten my hand, and every single time I used it, I improved.

When I originally started recovering from my coma, I told everyone in my family a few times I had left the coffin. They asked me what the coffin was like and I said, "Cold and dark and stinky." I also talked about how I had seen angels, and the one I knew of, but had never met. She told me I could wake up and she couldn't and so I had to leave the coffin. My little sister Jeanee asked me if the angel was Sarah Burke, a pro skier that died in Park City, Utah, three years ago. I said yes, it was. I got hurt in Whistler, Canada, that's Sarah's hometown. She got hurt in Park City, Utah, that's my hometown. Every time Sarah was able to ski I was hurt, every time I was able to ski, Sarah was hurt. I never met her. But I know I owe how well and fast I am recovering to the guidance of angels, specifically the guidance of Sarah Burke.

Most people who've had a traumatic brain injury count it as the worst, most dramatic thing that ever happened to them. I honestly don't think so. I think my recovery, how fast it was, and my opportunities to get back to my normal made my TBI the luckiest thing that ever happened to me. My life goals are actually much more accomplishable now. For my entire life I wanted to be a public speaker and to write a book. I assumed it would take a long time, and I honestly didn't know what I would talk or write about, just I wanted to do it because I love talking and writing. Now I know what to say and write, and I am moving in the right direction tremendously fast. Every goal I've had for my whole life, and come across again, has been pushed along by the fact I was in a coma. Most people think it would be the most dramatic injury they could imagine. I think it was the luckiest, not worst, thing that ever happened to me.

So my experience over the last three months has been difficult, exciting, progressive and life changing. I've received help from all sorts of resources. High Fives, a non-profit foundation which sponsors winter mountain athletes financially, emotionally, and helps their athletes set goals and accomplish them to get back to competitive life, in either the original sport or a new one. It's been an incredibly challenging process. I don't remember the first month at all. I went from being in a coma to being awake, but completely dependent on others and still in the hospital. The second month I went from a dependent state in the hospital and not being able to remember anything to remembering songs, peoples' names, learning how to walk and eat by myself. The third month I became a lot stronger and agile, I learned how to drive a car, my right hand got back to normal, and I became extraordinarily similar to how I was before my crash. That's the journey I've been on recently! Loads of steps, some little, some huge, that I've made toward recovering completely and becoming who I was before I got hurt.

The doctors want to clear me to go back to full life, including being a pro skier. With my attitude, I will take my luck from my pro skier life that I put into my recovery experience, to create my new life as a Traumatic Brain Injury Survivor.

# Laraine Sacco

Florida, United States of America

## *Empowered Empty Nester*

The world beyond business and children is frightening and exciting as a new chapter is on the horizon. When I add up my children's ages, I've logged sixty-one years as a Mom and that's not counting twenty-five years day dreaming of the momentous day when a new life began which changed my soul and heart for an eternity.

It all started so long ago on a tree-lined street with a station wagon in every middle-class driveway. Growing up in a small family with a hundred close relatives who loved me unconditionally was magical at times. My parents worked hard and sacrificed to send me to private school and summer camp with the wealthy kids. The two lives were worlds apart. I wondered how one person could earn so much money to be able to afford luxury cars, European trips, a boat, and be members of 'The Country Club'. This was a curiosity that grabbed hold of me during my life.

I was always reinventing myself and redefining my goals to achieve a lifestyle where I worked smarter, not harder. Working in a corporate atmosphere provided a paycheck, but I wanted more so I would create a business and became energized. Motherhood changes everything.

*"The Right Mindset and a Plan Determine Your Future!"*

What were the three most important things to you when you were a child? Think for a moment. Cue the game show music...My burning questions were: Is it sunny outside? What's for dinner? –and– How did some people make so much more than others? The answer is: Every morning wake up with a positive happy attitude! Second, plan your 15 hour happy, fulfilled day to make the most of every minute. The answer to question 3 is still unknown, but what I have learned so far will be life changing.

*"Passion is Energizing and Contagious!"*

In the beginning there was the competition to "sell" or share the Girl Scout cookie. First rule of success is a positive attitude and an enthusiastic passion to speak with everyone at the age of five years old and break sales records. I broke the record for the most sold, ever. Recognized by my peers was wonderful, but success didn't always come without a price as I quickly experienced later that year when I won an art competition. As I walked among enthusiastic applause to receive my trophy, jealousy and envy roared like the 'Queen' of the jungle when Beth yelled "she cheated! I should win! She won the cookie contest!" The room became silent and I was frozen in fear! A flood of emotions came over me and I believe it was the first time I had an anxiety attack. Betrayal at five years old is a hard betrayal to overcome. My Mom said she wasn't a friend which stimulated trust issues. My mind was conflicted.

### *"You Are Important, Analyze Your Options!"*

The same year the boy down the block, Kevin, asked me to marry him and I excitedly accepted because I was concerned he might be the only proposal I would ever get and wasn't taking any chances. However, he tried to save me from a bee, even though I told him to leave it alone, the bee flew at me and stung my arm. The proposal was off. The scar on my arm is a twofold reminder to think about your choices and surround yourself with people who value you. The future did bring many possibilities!

### *"Negotiation Skills are Key to Success*

Why is it we can want something so incredibly bad, but give up? Has that ever happened to you? My entire life I wanted my own horse and continually begged my parents. What did I get? A rabbit. Actually, two so they wouldn't be lonely. They had each other and lived in a very nice duplex cage on the porch overlooking the pool. As a compassionate, caring person I felt my rabbits would be happier snuggling together because of the cold winter. You can learn a lot from rabbits. That's how we got six more which prompted the uncomfortable topic about the birds and the bees. Negotiating is an art in which I became an expert.

### *"Surround Yourself with Positive People who Lift You Up!"*

Have you ever wanted something, but changed your mind because of someone else's opinion and therefore changed your path to make someone else happy with their version of you? Why do we allow that? Is it to be accepted, please others? Growing up, my talents weren't always appreciated. At least that's what I thought. The way we hear comments can be in a positive voice or negative. I always heard it in the negative, until recently. My husband has always encouraged me to be whatever I wanted. After several business ventures and a family, I've finally learned to be me with the support of my husband and children, the right business associates and friends who encourage and lift me up to my true purpose.

### *"Envision Your Dream Life!"*

What is your dream? Write it down and let it flow. Give yourself permission to write down every goal big or small. Life brings many choices.

I've learned to 'feel' and if my heart feels conflicted, I follow the peaceful path. Every choice has benefits and consequences. What path is the right path? You get to decide. My dream was to have a family which I waited for a very long time and found the 'right' man. We were richly blessed with three sons. I also wanted to be my own boss and started several companies including a 'Cookie' Business in my late teens which stemmed from my love of cookies from age 5. Once again, passion needs to drive you. Transitioning is natural. I've won numerous awards throughout my business career and it's funny they mean nothing to me now. The most rewarding experience is my family.

*"Stay at Home Mom 'vs' Business Woman"*

Whether you are the CEO of your home and family or have a career and raise a family, it's a personal choice and a decision for you and your family. Before we had children, we decided I would stay home. After several years of loving every minute, I decided to start a part-time business to provide extras for the family. I spent a lot of time researching many business ideas until I transitioned into being a 'Concierge Real Estate Consultant' for over a decade. The passion to help others took over and my family life suffered. Yes suffered. My next big transition was becoming a partner in a skin care company. My 'role' is to chat with people and connect them to the right resource whether they are interested in the products or running their own 'virtual franchise' with a team. I am passionate about helping people with skin concerns because I know, first hand, as an adult having sensitive skin and acne my self-esteem plummeted, not to mention aging.

This business utilizes e-commerce to help others with a skin concern or work part-time or full-time to build a supplemental income with unlimited potential. This has allowed me to connect with amazing people and the ability to follow my inner talents of writing and art. Now, I spend a lot of time with my sons as they embark on their careers and spend more time with my husband, family, friends and pets.

Whatever your heart desires, listen. Being a stay-at-home Mom is an incredibly important role which many women feel unworthy. Do not ever think you are 'less than'. Running your own business… which could be a household… and being a mom takes planning, organization, intelligence and so much more. I've learned time is precious and your words and actions mean everything to your children. As two of my children will be graduating from college in a few months and one will graduate high school, I've now learned that time is going by way too fast and I can cry at any moment with the thought of losing them.

The process of becoming an 'empty-nester' is natural and has begun. Now is my time to continue making memories with my adult children. Happiness, feeling peaceful, healthy eating and exercising will allow me to live a more enriching life and enjoy every moment. I would love to hear from other women who are facing the challenges of staying-at-home or business women including women whose nest will soon be a little quieter.

# Vanessa Carter

Gauteng, South Africa

## *Things Happen For a Reason*

**"Things happen for a reason". I hear that often, I've heard it for most of my life and it's because people use it repeatedly as a way to show compassion.**

It doesn't mean I question the theory, I simply wonder why we need to go through such difficult experiences to achieve a higher purpose. We all base our life on it and isn't it strange how the theory gets us through? The thought we are going to get through everything and understand "why" in the end. I've had many difficult experiences, but my hardest times were from 2004 – 2014.

When I was twenty-five years old, I had a severe car accident in Johannesburg, South Africa which *damaged my face and body severely.*

I spent ten years reconstructing my face, trying to rebuild my life and accepting it. Besides the day of the car accident, there were six days during this decade that changed my life. These were those days:

### The first time I looked at my damaged face in the mirror.

I will never forget how scared I was to look in the mirror for the first time after the accident. I knew from the conversations around me the damage was severe. When I finally found the courage to look, my heart sank with the realization of what had happened. The hardest part was I had no idea where to begin fixing it. That day taught me when something is out of your control, sometimes the only choice you have is to stop burdening your mind with panic and to try work on one small solution at a time.

It took intense emotional and mental work, but to survive I had to keep my thoughts intact, let the fear go and move forward with my life. I had to accept I wouldn't know the answers immediately, it would take time. In the meantime, I had to learn to look past my distorted face and work on what I had.

**Deciding to start over after a superbug.**

I had spent five years in surgery. At the final stages, an implant was inserted to lift my cheekbone and my body rejected it. I ended up with an infection called MRSA, which destroyed a large portion of my face. Because MRSA is life-threatening, the doctors were forced to remove the implant before the MRSA entered my bloodstream. When I woke up from surgery, my facial bones had collapsed. I looked ten times worse than the day of the accident. I will never forget the doctor saying "You are lucky you survived. We managed to remove the MRSA because it was localized, but the damage will take years to fix". What I learned that day, was things don't always work out the way we plan. Bad things happen to good people. In fact, I have only ever heard of difficult journeys being handed to the strong.

As humans, we have to persevere and not allow our obstacles to stop us from believing in a good ending. I learned sometimes it's simply not the end.

**The day a world famous face transplant surgeon took time out to give me advice**

I spent years researching the internet and the failure of the last surgery had left me feeling hopeless. Most of our doctors didn't have informative websites so I battled to find anyone locally. I didn't understand the difference between the sub-specialties either. They all crossed over each other and the opinions I was getting were totally different. I was so confused. I emailed my medical history around the world and asked for help. At that moment in my life, I was ready to give up on myself and felt as if I had no reason to live such a difficult life, in pain, in isolation and with a severe deformity.

One day, a surgeon replied and took the time to Skype with me for half an hour. Those thirty minutes changed my life. He was working as a part of a world famous facial transplant team who was performing breakthrough surgery. He gave me a step by step guide of what I could do based on my type of injury. I had regained my hope from this and it probably cuts my journey down by several years, not to mention the complication which could have cost more of my face if I had to go through any more failed surgery. Besides the incredible team of Johannesburg doctors I ended up with, I believe a video consultation from thousands of miles away was a large part of what helped save my face. The lesson? Just when we think all hope it lost and we are ready to give up, is when the situation can turn around.

Following his advice, within eight months we had cosmetic success!

**The day I thought my face would be gone by morning.**

This was one of the worst days of my life. Four days after the successful bone surgery, I broke out with infection again. My face was on fire, I couldn't touch it because I was so scared I would infect somewhere and someone else. I had thoughts of how this infection was eating my face alive slowly and there was nothing I could do to stop it. All I could do was sit and wait for the test results to come back. Luckily, the tests came back as a minor infection and allergic reaction to a chemical used in theatre.

The lesson? Don't assume the worst, because sometimes it isn't as bad as it seems.

## Thinking I was not going to wake up the next morning.

Three months later my lower intestines collapsed. I had an adhesive bowel obstruction and it was caused by scarring inside from the accident. I couldn't eat or drink for two weeks, I was badly ill and in the most severe pain, I had pipes feeding food to my body. This was a part of my journey where I lay in bed thinking about what I had done in my life to pursue my dreams.

I thought about stupid material stuff like the nice sports car I always wanted, the overseas trip I never took, and the things most of us call living. I was only thirty-four and I was lying helpless in a hospital ward of ladies about eighty years old and my mind kept telling me how I shouldn't be there. It had been nine years since my accident and all I was finding in my life was hospitals, illness, medication, complication, isolation and reasons why I couldn't do the things I really wanted to because of an accident. Eight weeks later, I recovered with the mindset I would never waste another day of my life again.

## The day I spoke to the world's greatest minds in global medicine.

After I had made the decision not to waste another day of my life, I acted on everything I wanted to do. One of those things was to start awareness for people living with a facial difference. So I started a Facebook and a Twitter Page. Within a few months I was meeting people from around the world. In June 2014, I was invited as a guest to Paris to speak about my advocacy. I had never been overseas before, but I put aside all fear, boarded a plane and went. I spoke to a few hundred doctors from all over the world, including Stanford University. I was appointed an ambassador and invited back as an international speaker. I now represent my country as a patient voice for digital technology, specifically because I couldn't find access to help online. My lesson? Don't let your story dictate who you are, choose who you want to be. The only way to do that, is to listen to what it is you want in life and go for it.

Never put down your ideas of what you want to be, because if you have a higher purpose from all the difficulties you've been through, the only way you will ever know is to let go of thinking you can't achieve it. You may just deserve it too. Life isn't all hard. There are some incredible things, too. You just have to believe your experiences are leading you there.

# Chocolate & Diamonds

## Michelle Lowe

London, United Kingdom

### *Self-Preservation*

Crisis can be a beautiful thing — believe it or not. You see, I knew embarking on a different path and adapting to a new way of living was critical. I was very aware this would help me breathe again, as I was only experiencing the kind of breathing similar to when you dive in the water and hold your breath too long, you begin to panic and all you know is you have to get to the surface - quickly.

The kind of breathlessness which overwhelms you when someone scares you in the dark or the rapid breathing you endure when you know time is running out for you to accomplish something, when the fear sets in and begins to take over. I was in crisis mode, I had to act.

Prior to my life altering decision, I was living the "Sex in the City" lifestyle in New York. To outsiders, I had a perfect life. In fact a great life! Interesting theatre, gourmet restaurants, exciting bars, rocking nightclubs and well-appointed museums. I was surrounded by great friends, was financially independent on my six-figure salary and lived in an amazing condominium in a nice neighborhood. I was in love and married. The only missing element to complete the dream family was a baby. Outsiders saw this as ideal, but in essence, the very fabric of what I needed and wanted had been disintegrating around me "slow, slow, quick, quick slow" like the cha cha cha.

Let's be clear, this isn't a pity party story. I had a lot going for me. Separate to all the tangible stuff. I had personality, was attractive, sexy, vivacious, fun, and often, the life of the party with the English accent.

The truth is I lost me! For a marriage which was going nowhere, a job which was sucking me dry and the emotional strain of desperately wanting a child. I cannot emphasize enough how easy it is for any of us to go down this path of invisibility and loss of self.

I have a healthy ego, an extremely positive attitude, great intuition and I am a strong energy reader. At 38, I couldn't find a boyfriend, I wasn't looking very hard as I had a great support system. My cousin, my honorary big sister, my four "Sex and the City" girlfriends, a host of family in New York, my sister in Florida and my personal angel - my life friend in London. My main man was my best friend who's always there for me no matter what – I could ALWAYS count on him. My three bookends lived in the same building, (they took turns propping me up!) they rocked! Weekends and evenings they helped me hold it all together. It was "all good"!

Pre-Christmas 2001, I attended a party with a friend. He left early and there in my peripheral view, was my handsome, young husband to be. We danced the night away beginning a 7-month pursuit of cat and mouse.

In between was a brief interlude with a somewhat unavailable man abroad. Once that failed, I decided to see if I could seriously date a man 12 years younger. After 2 years of dating, we moved in. Things were fun. He was sensitive, slightly introverted, but appeared ambitious. He wasn't anything I wanted on "paper" but in real life, his actions showed he could replace my handcrafted fairy tale. He made me happy.

He was in school, but his education was taking too long. I encouraged him to give up his daytime job and go to school full time to fast track our home, baby and the life we wanted. It turns out the first part was our plan, the latter was to be my dream alone. He decided he needed better qualifications. He switched courses to become a PA (Physician's Assistant). I reluctantly agreed, his success meant our success – didn't it?

January 2006, we were married. It was a great day despite seeing three seasons in one day, most of which was heavy rain, but they say rain is good luck! Life changed in early 2006. I sold my apartment expecting to move into our larger apartment. The new build which we were anticipating with baited breath wasn't ready. It was thirteen months before we finally moved in. This tested the "theory of marriage" over and over again.

In addition, I experienced, 'severe mother-in-law syndrome'. She interfered constantly. The rift between my mother-in-law and I created a wound in my marriage that never healed, it festered and eventually infected our entire life. My job became increasingly hectic and time consuming. The stress of a new marriage, plus issues with the new build, all became too much.

On a memorably freezing day in early 2007, we finally moved into the new place. We were elated. Within 24 hours, we were unpacked and relishing the highly anticipated experience of "our home". We were happy. But it wasn't to last long. My work/life balance became non-existent. He was struggling and when I would enquire, he became agitated. How dare I question his quest for education?

I decided it's time to plan for the baby! This would be a great solution/distraction. I had been diagnosed with POF (premature ovarian failure). It had taken me time to accept, but I could consider egg donation as an option. We decided to go for it. I did all the research and communication with the doctors. He had to take three tests to my ten. My tenth test was so excruciatingly painful, it physically hurts now when I think about it. Following the pain and anguish, he backed out and decided he didn't want children yet. He wasn't ready. The question is why was I the last to know? Devastated by my reality… maybe I should have, could have left him then, but what's done is done and I believed in my vows, "for better or worse", so I tried to hold it together.

The 2008 economic crash came, no big bonuses, working harder and now co-managing a team of 26 people by default, not by choice. It was too hard to keep the cracks from appearing. I asked him to get a job, even a part-time job. He promptly responded, "You make enough money for the two of us!" That hurt – to the core. I had been the sole provider, now he was telling me, "so what!"

I was sensitive and tingling with anger, and distrust. The love turned sour, the hurt became a major pain. All were a catalyst for weight gain, hair loss and overwhelming stress. With little to no support at home came the desire to end it all. "What's love got to do with it", is the song that began to play in my head. Ever so slowly, it became my personal anthem.

D-day came one night around 11:30 pm. With my laptop in hand, hungry and looking like hell. I greeted him with a "hi" as I dragged my exhausted body through the door. Watching TV with his back to me, he barely raised his hand to acknowledge he had heard me and didn't even fucking turn around! What the fuck! Here I was killing myself for us, losing me and all for a backhanded hello? I tried to pick myself up off the floor with disgust and attempted to ask another question to get a more positive response. "Did you cook?" I asked in a somewhat hopeful voice. Again, he responded with his back to me "no, I was too busy". Right there, I decided "I could do better all by myself". At that moment, the shallow breathing began. In bed, (we slept apart at this stage) I was tossing and turning. Hungry, exhausted and struggling to breathe, I told myself tomorrow will be a different day.

But it wasn't. I felt more anxious and erratic. My energy and intuition kicked in saying, "you have to leave him". I didn't have a plan, but the universe kept saying, "Sista, it's now or never. You need to make this change NOW or it will change you forever." I would never contemplate suicide, I wasn't about to now, but I could fully understand what would make one pursue that door of no return. When you feel like you can't breathe, you can't move, you are in a dark box with water flowing fast and furiously. You can't stop it, you know you are drowning – you've only two choices; fight like hell to get out or surrender and drown.

Hell no! I couldn't drown, I had too much to lose – ME! I loved life too much. By December 31, 2010, I had left my husband, my home, my job and was on a plane headed home to London.

Currently, I am living a much smaller and happier life in London. I've had my struggles, but I've started my own business, embarked on a new relationship and found me again. Many people have told me I was brave and courageous. But, I can't accept that accolade; I can't wear that badge of honor. I can and do take credit for using my inner strength to do what I needed to, I began to breathe again – I did it for me – I did it for self-preservation.

# Judith Goldapp Richey

Texas, United States of America

## *A Blessing in Disguise*

**"I've quit my job and I've filed for divorce.
I want you to move out. I am done."**

These were the words I spoke to my husband in October 2008. At the end of my rope and frustrated beyond measure, I was at my breaking point. For three years I had told my husband how miserable I was in my $100,000+ a year career as a financial advisor. My marriage was in a shambles, my health was a mess. I had chronic migraines, insomnia, and I hurt all over. I just couldn't take my life the way it was one more day. I would rather live in a box, than continue to live the way I was.

What's really ironic is most people, looking at my life from the outside, would have seen success. I won every company award, trips around the world, had a significant income, launched my children into adulthood via college and seemingly had the "perfect" life. But, that wasn't the case. What I actually had was a complete and total meltdown.

I spent the next six months sitting on the couch in my front living room. And I cried, read, prayed, meditated, read and cried and cried some more. I went through counseling, both individual and group therapy sessions. I looked for answers as to how I got to this state. Being the prudent person I was, I had created an exit strategy for myself financially when I left my position as a financial advisor. Income was not an issue. My husband refused to leave me, much to my frustration, and I moved into the second master bedroom on the opposite side of the house. We didn't communicate much. I performed my duties as a mom in the most perfunctory of ways. Mostly, I worked on figuring out what had happened in my life that had gotten me to this point. I did find answers and I learned quite a bit during that six month period and since then, too.

I found I was harboring doubts, anger, fear, guilt, lack, low self-value and un-forgiveness. My first marriage ended when my first husband *called me on the phone* and told me "I don't love you anymore, I don't want to be married. I want a divorce." That catapulted me and my children into a several year drama which caused more pain than I thought anyone could stand. He ultimately terminated his parental rights to our children. I was a divorced mom with five children to raise on my own. More than that, my dreams of happily ever after were completely shattered and the fairy tale ending I thought my life would have, along with any 25th or 50th wedding anniversaries, went out the window. Everything I had dreamed of for my marriage—gone.

While I sat on the couch those six months (which was about 10 years after my divorce), I realized I hadn't truly forgiven my ex-husband for what he had done and what he had put our family through. I realized I hadn't forgiven myself for my role in my marriage falling apart. As I read and cried, I worked through forgiveness and released the resentment, guilt and anger I had been holding on to.

My poor second husband had become my whipping boy for all the negative emotions I had swirling around concerning my first husband. I expected perfection from him, and of course, he wasn't perfect. It's no wonder our marriage was in trouble, too. Fortunately for me, we were able to work through our marital issues and are still married-happily now. My meltdown was a wake-up call for my husband; he needed to attend to some of his own issues. As he described it, he's an ultimatum kind of guy and that two-by-four across the head of my announcement that day in October was just what he needed to make some needed changes in his life, as well.

From October 2008, I've been on a path of healing and self-discovery. I've learned who I am and what I want out of life. Up until then, I had acquiesced to others in my life, and had let them make the major decisions for me. My Mom and Dad encouraged all of us children to get teaching degrees, even though I didn't want to teach, that was what I went to college for. It wasn't a bad thing, but it really wasn't what I wanted to do.

My first husband moved our family from a city I loved to a small community for his job and I went along with it, because that's what wives were supposed to do. When I was dating my second husband, he encouraged me to leave my work on a master's in counseling to become a financial advisor, so I walked away and became a financial advisor. Somewhere I had developed a twisted thinking he wouldn't love me if I didn't go along. I gave up what I really wanted to have for the "security" of the relationship, even if it meant giving up on my own dreams.

As I healed through what I call my life time-out, I realized I didn't have to give up on my dreams, and I could even create new dreams. I met a coach through a conference who heard my past and asked me a question that forever reframed the way I looked at what I had been through. She asked me what had given me the *strength and courage* to do what I had done, to walk away from a highly successful, but miserable career and make the stand for a difference in my life. I had been operating from a place of weakness. She saw me as strong. Just that one question began changing everything in my life.

As I continued to discover what I wanted most out of life, I found there are people everywhere even more miserable than I am. And a majority of that misery comes from emotional blockages they haven't dealt with, or even have a clue they exist. I've been blessed to find healing aids for myself and now share them with others. One of those aids is essential oils. I work in emotional healing using essential oils to unlock and reveal hidden and buried emotions, so those blockages can be surfaced, revealed and released. The transformative power of the oils is truly life changing.

Even with all the work I've done for myself, I discover hidden feelings through the oils. I recently was using an oil to help me sleep. The first time I used it, I had a horrible nightmare about my ex-husband leaving me and the children in a burning house, to find our way out. I woke up yelling "Fire! Fire!". A week later, I used the oil again and had another nightmare. This one was about my current husband faking his own death and running away with another woman. Man! Not pleasant! The next morning I meditated and prayed as to the linkage between the two dreams and found I was holding on to issues of abandonment. I released those issues and have been free of them ever since. All because I used an essential oil for sleep.

I now work helping others find healing. That healing may come through the desire to find relief from a physical ailment or malady, or it may come through the realization that one's dis-ease is caused by trapped or buried emotions.

My true life's calling is as a helper and guide. I acted as my own guide when I spent time seeking answers on the couch, not knowing any other way to get help. I've connected with coaches, healers, other helpers and guides to form a network of caring, compassionate individuals like myself who've made it their life's mission to bring peace and understanding to others.

Life is a joy every day now I am perfectly in the realm I was always meant to be, for me. It's not without the normal bumps in the road. Just now, I am able to navigate from a place of peace and contentment, instead of frustration and stress.

Some would say, "What a pity you went through what you did." I say, "What a blessing I went through what I did, because now I am exactly where I am supposed to be.

# Marissa Thornberry

Arkansas, United States of America

## *Speak*

When I was a freshman in college, my history professor warned my class "the silent woman is a danger to herself and everyone around her." He paused, and as he said it again, the repeated rhythm invited me to listen even more carefully: "The silent woman is a danger to herself and everyone around her." I almost chuckled this time, realizing if he's right about that, then I had been living life on the edge for as long as I could remember.

The idea of me being dangerous was indeed a humorous one at the time. Until that August, I had lived in the same middle-of-nowhere town from the day I was born, and I had never thought of my life as anything spectacular or even very interesting.

These days, I know a little something about risk-taking. The four years between then and now have been full of traveling, often by myself, and often to places entirely new to me. I've chipped away at language and cultural barriers as I spent summers studying abroad and ministering to Honduran youth. I've thrown myself into an internship entirely outside of my field of study, as well as, my comfort zone, serving Chicago's homeless population. I've witnessed crime statistics come to life. I've seen homicide rates take on flesh, tears and human voices in the grieving and the fear that plagued neighbor after neighbor during my semester in Chicago. No longer am I one to back away from something frightening simply because of fear. However, my greatest barrier, and the real threat, is the one closest to home.

In my other lives, those outside of my small town of origin, I've become bold—not beyond the boundaries of my personality, of course, but bolder than I ever was before. I've changed. Demands, responsibilities, and encouragement have called me out of comfort. Strangers have transformed into friends. Challenges have morphed into fulfillment and purpose. I grew up when I left the place where I "grew up." In any other context—college, another country, a new city—I find it increasingly easy to make my voice heard.

But the coming back, mysteriously, makes me feel once again unable to do the things I wouldn't have done before I left. I've grown out of my perpetual silence elsewhere, but when I return to the place where it was born, it seems so much stronger than I am. I withdraw once again, even when I know my voice is called for. Somehow, my new and truer self is overtaken by the dangerously silent person I used to be.

What gives me, encouragement is I've become dissatisfied with letting this happen.

As a child, I would frequently feel paralyzed and unable to speak, even when I did have something to say, and even when I was invited to say it. Every day, it seems, I got in trouble for some instance of not talking when I was supposed to. Silence was my home, and I knew no other way. It always felt as if there was such a small window of opportunity through which to shove my words, and they just weren't ready yet. Or I wanted to keep them. Or I didn't want them to get damaged in the light of the day. Often, because I thought they would do no good anywhere else, I held on to them, protected them, kept them to myself.

Despite my inability or unwillingness to vocalize whatever was going on inside of me, I've consistently cherished a safer alternative. I could write it down; I could always write it down.

Although its permanence may hint otherwise, writing feels much safer to me than speaking. I have my words where I can see them, right under my nose, just a finger's length away. Because they are close and visible, I feel in control.

I've realized, however, in guarding my words so heavily, I am acting much like my own parents, who have tried their best to keep me to themselves. They have never wanted me to go too far away from them, but traveling has been one of the primary tools God has used to bring me to the freedom and joy I have now—that is, to the gradual formation my new self.

My parents have always wanted to keep me close and visible, and I appreciate their desire to see I am safe. But I know there comes a time when my purpose is elsewhere. Its then, stirred to move, but made to stay still, that I start to crumble. My word babies, too, will stagnate and wither if they are not sent out to where they need to be at the proper time.

So, like a mother, I am gradually, begrudgingly learning to let my words run and play and meet new people—and, more scarily, new sides of people I've known all my life. I am struggling and fumbling, but holding on to the desire to ask more questions, give more honest answers, and start conversations for no reason other than the pure enjoyment of the other person. Sending my words off day after day, removed from the shelter of my mind, is the most difficult thing I've ever attempted to do; but with each risk I let them take, the sending seems more worthwhile, and the silence more dangerous.

# Leigh Le Creux

Florida, United States of America

## *Write it Out*

As she looked up and met my gaze, I watched a single tear slide down her cheek and fall to the table. "I just don't understand what I did wrong, what I always seem to do wrong?" she paused, then asked, "What did I do to deserve this Leigh?" She shook her head and the tears came freely now. A quick, nervous glance to the coffee counter to our right, and she shrugged, no longer caring who blatantly stared at us. "I swear I've done everything I can to make this work, to change things...but I am just not strong enough to deal with it anymore."

She looked back down into her coffee, and she shakily lifted the cup to her mouth, her eyes bored into mine searching for me to give her answers. I reached over and touched her other hand with my own. "I wish I had the answers for you. I won't say I understand or know what you are truly going through because I don't. For me to even say such a thing to you would be an insult to you".

I wanted to cringe at the pain I saw in and around her eyes. If I had been one of the bystanders over at the counter I know I still would have felt it at that distance. "What I can tell you is this - I know a few other women who've been through similar situations to yours - not the same - it never could be - but still similar in a number of ways".

Pausing, I added, "Sometimes I wonder if God created women with bodies and the souls to be nurturers, but with hearts designed to be broken. It seems in my own experience there are more conversations about us as women trying always to learn to be stronger, how to cope and how to just love ourselves - let alone trying to love someone else." She nodded in agreement. "Perhaps that is where we must all begin then".

My friend's story is not a new one. Details are unique to her, yes, however the common feelings of loss, confusion and being unfairly judged were almost humorously expected. She had spent the better part of her life trying to re-unite with her mother following a messy divorce with her father taking parental responsibility when she was eight years old. As my dear friend now sat across from me; exhausted from sharing story after story and incident after incident of abandonment with her mother for the last fifteen years, she looked haggard and defeated. A few bouts of depression and loss of identity were the links that connected us and allowed us to be raw and vulnerable with each other allowing us both a place to heal.

The sounds of the cafe seemed to become louder as both of us were temporarily lost in our own thoughts. I smiled at the idea our thoughts were likely the same and she returned a half smile back. "How did you do it Leigh?" She asked, breaking our silence. "You know - get past the depression - the therapy, write a book and become a counsellor...all of it really. How did you do it?" I laughed and said, "Well, we don't have enough coffee for all of that - it would be a book in itself!"

She gave me a full out smile, then turned serious. "Well?" "Ok. Truth be told, it really can be summed up in three things - curiosity, NLP and writing". "NLP? I still don't really know what that is."

"Neuro Linguistic Programming. I didn't get into it right away though - it came later. Basically, I learned how my values and beliefs controlled my life and affected my emotions - that is what showed me the triggers to my depression and taught me how to cope and heal without drugs and other stuff."

I paused, "I guess what I mean is I learned to detach, to remove myself from the pain and confusion, so I look at it for what it truly was, and what it is doing for and to me. It basically took a lot of the emotional bullshit out of the way until I could find my way again. As hippy as it might sound, I needed to find myself."

"So what did you do first?" "Curiosity always comes first, then writing and finally the NLP. Journaling, to be specific." "I've never done that though people have told me I should". "I tell everyone they should. It's the cheapest and one of the most powerful forms of therapy."

"Really? How so? I don't get how keeping a diary would help me. The few times I've ever had one in my life, it hurt so bad to think about it, let alone write it down. I try to get past the hurt, but it plays over and over. I just can't." Her eyes began to fill again.

"First off, a journal isn't really the same thing as a diary. It can be I suppose, but journaling is more about your thoughts and feelings than a play by play of what happens every day".

Smiling, I added, "I won't lie to you either and tell you it's easy - it isn't at first. That's where some of the NLP can come in, but that's later. If you begin from a place of curiosity, then you see this as another experience that can help or stay the same. Those really are the only two possible outcomes - so just think, what would happen if it did help? Is it worth a short time of effort for a possible positive permanent change? For me the answer was absolutely, but some people aren't ready."

Shaking her head, she responded, "I know it worked for you obviously" as she gestured to us sitting at the table, "I am sorry, I just don't think I can 'fairy tale my life' as you say".

"Honey", I said, taking her hands in mine, "You need to know there is nothing more profound than actually living. Journaling, then writing saved my life. It allowed me to write about people who hurt me, whom I had hurt, my guilt, my shame and my terror...attempted suicide, cancer and the depression. I wrote about it all. I also wrote about the blessings and the love in my life.

And hell, yes, it was hard, it hurt and I wanted to stop. But after a week or so, I swear to you, I started to feel different, in fact, I began to actually feel again. I finally began to understand forgiveness and was able to not only give that to others, but to myself. It made me a better person, a better mom and wife, and a better friend. But it all starts with being curious enough to ask yourself some questions - even though you are unsure of what the answers will be and sometimes may not particularly like the ones you receive. Sometimes it's not what you want to hear or admit about yourself, but when you can, it heals." Now tears were running down my cheeks and I tightened my hands around hers.

"What matters is this not only helped me to heal and continues to do so, it's become a way of life for me. It's allowed my family and me to do things that we could only ever have imagined. It can for you too, but you must desire this and be committed to do it." I let go of her hands and nodded. "Yeah, so do you want to try?"

With a small smile she said, "But with everything that's happened, if I write about it, what will people think of me?" "Well, for now, you are just going to start writing for you, not necessarily a book", I laughed. "Seriously, just begin writing about your feelings - like I mentioned. Ask these questions, "Who has hurt you? Who may you have hurt? Who and what in your life has influenced you the most?"

Write about the good, bad and the indifferent".

After a sip of coffee, I continued, "It works this way. When you write all of these things down, it's like they become concrete and a part of them is removed from you. Same as when we write our goals and dreams. They become manifest on the paper and already begin to form in our reality making them stronger. Now with hurt and painful experiences it works the opposite way. When those are on paper in front of us, they lose some of their strength because now they are words, but not full out emotions within us. They are outside of us and we are then able to detach from it to see these experiences for what they are - experiences.

You then have the ability to gain wisdom from them and close those chapters to start to write new ones. You don't lose the memories, but you alter the emotional attachment and its effects on you. Hence, you then can 'fairy tale your life'.

The last sentence we said in unison and matching grins. We both stared at each other for a moment when she broke the silence. "Thank You." "My pleasure". As we rose from the table and walked to the door to leave, I stopped and said, "I am going home to write about our conversation today." A look of panic crossed her face.

"Don't be nervous I said, I would never share the details of your story nor your name. I don't have to. You see, I haven't met another woman yet who has not experienced pain, hurt, and depression and at some time second guessed her own self-worth. Those are the very things that connect us - our humanness. The same things remind us we are never truly alone. By sharing them, we help others heal and save lives." She nodded and embraced me. "I need to get going. I am already late and I need to stop on my way to pick up a journal". Now it was my turn to nod in silence. As I walked to my car I thought, I had better stop and pick up another journal as well.

# DeAnna Bookert

## South Carolina, United States of America

### *I am Not Broken. I am Better*

This was never the plan I had for my life. We were married January 3, 2000, my son was born and we decided to have another baby and here came our daughter. The plan was to raise our children, send them off to college, live in our dream home and watch them grow and become successful young adults.

**February 18, 2015, my life forever changed.**

It was six years ago when I was faced with depression. I now realize how detrimental not knowing who you are in Christ can be to you and your family. During this time I felt lost, alone, sad, angry and hopeless. I was having these feelings and didn't understand why. I was still working in ministry, trying to raise my kids and be a good wife. I couldn't explain my feelings to my husband or even myself. I remember talking with my pastor, Superintendent Dr. Warren D. Robinson and he told me "sometimes you have to be what you didn't have". I didn't have a father in the home. I didn't have a mentor and I didn't have a role model to encourage me to do more or have goals and dreams. Sometimes you have to be what you didn't have for someone else.

I began to pray and seek God for direction for my life. Why am I here? What is God's will for my life? What is my purpose? I never thought or considered I had a purpose. What I know now, as my purpose has been the thing that kept me going. See, I understand my purpose is to help others **Recognize, Develop and Apply** their God given purpose in their personal life, business and ministry. Sometimes you have to be what you didn't have. Purpose is that thing which you will do for free, it puts a smile on your face and you find yourself always thinking about it. I realized by knowing who I am and what my purpose in life is, made life easier to navigate even when the road got bumpy.

On February 18, 2015, I begin the journey on a different bumpy road. My husband and I left for work around 8 am and by 10 am I got this overwhelming sense I needed to speak to my husband. I called and called and didn't get an answer, just his voicemail. I called everywhere and everybody and no one had spoken to him. So I begin to pray, "Lord cover Michael, wherever he is; send your angels of protection, I plead the blood of Jesus over him NOW". It was around 4 pm when I received the call everyone hates to get. It's the hospital and all I remember is the lady saying, "Come to the hospital and bring a family member there's been an accident". My heart stopped. I knew I had to drive and get to the hospital safely, so I sat for a second to get myself together. I arrived to see my husband in a coma with doctors standing over him telling me, "It doesn't look good". I did what only I knew to do. I begin to pray and call all those I knew and told them to pray.

*Is any sick among you? Let him call for the elders of the church; and let them pray over him, anointing him with oil in the name of the Lord: James 5: 14*

I looked at my husband lying there in a coma, not responding, not able to open his eyes, not able to respond to pain in his hands and feet. I was faced with doctors telling me to take him off life support.

The doctors said, "He may always be the way I see him today". I had to make a decision, one that not only affected Michael, but me and the kids also. It was now time to walk out what I had been preaching and teaching to so many others. So, I decided to trust God. Not the doctors, not my family, but only God. I decided to trust God to heal my husband and bring him out of the coma.

Well, one week later, God did just that. Michael started breathing on his own and they took him off life support. Two months later, Michael was opening his eyes and at three months he began to smile and respond to pain in his hands and feet. See, it was then when I realized it was my faith that moved God. Not my tears, anger, frustration, sadness or worry. It was me waiting and trusting God completely without any doubt. This is where I found strength, courage and even a greater purpose.

*But they that wait upon the Lord shall renew their strength; Isaiah 40:31*

Knowing who I am in Christ and knowing my purpose has been the driving force that helped keep me grounded. I had built my company on helping others overcome adversity, move past barriers and apply purpose in their life. Now I am faced with adversity, I had to make a decision on what I was going to do. I decided not to be fearful or pitiful, but to be powerful. I found myself able to persevere through this life changing transition because of my faith. You never know how the things you go through maybe preparing you for your future. During my season of depression, I felt so alone and hopeless.

I had to learn what it really meant to put my trust in God because no one understood and I didn't know how to explain what I was feeling. Now, almost 6 years later I found myself reminded of the power I already have to overcome adversity. It's been through my faith and the power of God that I am able to solo parent our children, work a full time job, travel for speaking engagements, spend time at the hospital with my husband, operate in ministry at my local church and complete my Master's degree.

*Now unto him that is able to do exceeding abundantly above all that we ask or think, according to the power that worketh in us, Ephesians 3:20*

It's not been easy, but God has truly been faithful to me and the kids and I can only trust God that He will continue to watch over us as my husband continues his road to recovery.

# Jennifer Rychcik

Maryland, United States of America

## *Rollercoaster Ride*

### "A Journey to a Life of Abundance"

We are destined to meet the people who will support, guide, and nurture us on our life's journey, always appearing at the "perfect" moment. Some may stay for a lifetime, and others for just a short while, but our lessons learned are priceless treasures we can cherish in our hearts.

My journey has been filled with happiness, love, devotion, chaos, abuse, alcoholism, health challenges, hardships, and financial destruction. The road traveled has been far from smooth, testing my courage, strength, weakness, and faith. I lost the woman who possessed positivity, strength, hope, and gratitude and became completely entrenched with negativity and pity.

Often, I would think, "Why me?" It's an unbelievable story, and sometimes when I tell it, I can't fathom this was my life. Looking back, I've done many things hastily, in anger and desperation. I truly longed to be the author of a different story. I embraced the pain, and burned it as fuel to change the course. My heart is full of gratitude to be here today and tell this story to you in the hopes it will give you strength to continue on with your own journey.

Growing up, I was Daddy's little girl. My father was everything to me and I possessed a deep desire to please him. I never wanted to disappoint him; I just wanted his acceptance and love. I felt lost, insecure and lacked a sense of self. The name calling started at an early age. As a result, I felt I always had something to prove. Pleasing began as my personality style; I started to pay the price at a young age. My father's ritual after work was a can or two of Genesee beer before dinner. I tasted my first beer on my father's lap at age eight. From that point moving forward, I knew what alcohol could do for me.

In my teens, I continued to feel uncomfortable in my own skin. I became more familiar with the feeling alcohol could provide me. With each drink, I felt a warm tingly glow; I could conquer the world. Alcohol relieved me of the bondage of me. Despite being one of the best tennis players who began playing at an early age and part of the "in" crowd, I never felt I belonged. This behavior continued and exploded in college, which led me to relocating closer to home to finish my degree in nursing.

In an instant, my life drastically changed. My father had been complaining of neck pain and within twenty-four hours, he was diagnosed with non-small cell lung cancer and mesothelioma with metastasis to the ribs, pelvis, neck, left hip liver, and brain. His disease progressed despite aggressive therapy. He did maintain some quality of life, restoring his antique vehicles, but then pneumonia and a heart attack erupted. In just eight hours, he went into liver failure and became non-responsive. He awoke to voice one last request.

His words were, "Don't let me die here." He left us fifteen minutes after returning home. The guilt of making the wrong decision while caring for him nearly destroyed me, but no amount of guilt can change how the events unfolded. I thought by holding on, I was strong, but I learned the art of letting go of the guilt many years later was much more freeing.

Several years later, I relocated to Baltimore to practice as a nurse practitioner in surgical oncology at Johns Hopkins Hospital. I viewed this as a fresh start, since it was the ultimate "geographic cure," but my drinking resurfaced.

In the summer of 2000, I locked eyes with him on the escalator. The chemistry was intense; I had to meet him. The next eight years were an intense roller coaster ride with Curt. Our lives revolved around alcohol. On December 1, 2000, our relationship entered unchartered territory. This was the first episode of abuse. My hair was grabbed as I was dragged around the room and pushed down a flight of stairs to be thrown out at 5 AM on his porch steps naked. I pressed charges, but later dropped them.

The next three years, our disease exploded and brought extreme chaos into our lives in the form of multiple domestic disputes, emotional and physical abuse, and failed alcohol rehabilitation stints. Preserving this relationship was my uppermost mandate. I strived to be lovable and began squelching chunks of my personality, like setting boundaries or disagreements. I was unwilling to spend time with family and friends as this would mean time away from him. I lost the woman I had become due to my obsession over this individual and his journey.

It all changed September 1, 2003 as I entered the rooms of Al-Anon in search of answers to "fix" him. I learned my co-dependency and enabling was destroying him and interfering with his ability to fight the disease. My sponsor encouraged me to go to a meeting across the hall. This was the day of my last drink and I turned the focus on myself.

Curt lost his "best friend" in 2005 following two totaled vehicles and three DUIs. In one accident, our three dogs were nearly killed. His sobriety led us to building our dream home in the country, but it never lasted. The pain for him was just too much to bear, and he resorted to other substances. Prior to his incarceration for a hit and run, evading police, and possession of cocaine, he pulled a knife on me during one of his rages. During his incarceration, I embarked on forgiveness. Following his release, he was hospitalized on six separate occasions for alcoholism. On September 9, 2008, alcohol and Oxycontin took Curt's life. I attempted to revive Curt, but all efforts were exhausted. My worst nightmare had become my reality. This disease killed him.

Curt's death brought to light some revelations. These are concepts I was familiar with, but had lost along the way. It's important to live for today, as we never know what tomorrow will bring. Never lose sight of your goals as I did. Goal setting is important and propels us forward. It's not just about creating a plan for your life and holding yourself accountable, it feeds us the inspiration necessary to aim for dreams we never thought humanly possible.

I was left with over $250,000 in debt, along with a hefty mortgage and balanced two full-time jobs to sustain myself financially. Emotional eating ensued. I decided to consult a clairvoyant medium, as I thought I could "let go" if I talked to Curt. It was freeing to learn I couldn't have done one thing differently to have impacted his journey. During a session, I also learned I would meet an amazing man with a child when I was ready to receive them. Six months later, I met Dave on match.com. I am beyond grateful I've been blessed to experience true love twice in a lifetime and will marry my best friend in Disney celebrating our fairytale wedding.

But, still I was struggling. Health challenges ensued and my body completely shut down. I was exhausted, had no energy, and experienced discomfort everywhere. Exercising was not an option; I failed multiple attempts at finding a healthier path. After nearly collapsing from being on my feet all day at an amusement park, I realized I had to make a change. My future family deserved a better version of me.

October 4, 2013 was the day I made the decision to quit settling and start dreaming. I began a *nutritional cleansing program* and today have released over eighty pounds, gained limitless energy, and the discomfort in my body has dissipated. I created an unstoppable mindset and my passion and zest for life again, have been uncovered while empowering hundreds of women to change their course of health and wealth.

I have a beautiful life filled with abundance and possess no regrets. Curt made a lasting impression in my life and my heart while teaching me several valuable life lessons I will share with you. First, if we entrench ourselves with negativity, we can miss the amazing things life has to offer. Once we realize we have power over our mindset, we then begin to feel inspired to create a life we love. By focusing on our ideal life, we can create our own destiny. Second, when we begin to practice gratitude daily, our lives begin to shift, and it becomes extraordinary.

Our mental and physical health is impacted and our level of happiness skyrockets. Third, passion ignites our soul. Finding our passion is one of the greatest gifts we can give ourselves. Once we find our passion, we can begin to make a difference in other people's lives. We must always remember, life is a remarkable journey and it begins with a single step.

# Joumana Nasr

California, United States of America

## *The Greatest Gift of All*

I wish I could tell you that I've always known that I had intuitive gifts. But I can't.

I wish I could tell you that I've always known what I wanted to be when I "grew up". But I can't.

I wish I could tell you that my life today is the result of a well laid out and executed plan. But I can't do that either.

I can't tell you those things quite simply because they would be lies. The truth is that there was nothing in my life, in my childhood, in my upbringing, in my environment that gave me the slightest hint that this is where I would be today and this is what I would be doing. I didn't have any intuitive people, healers, life coaches, or entrepreneurs around me to guide me or inspire me to grow up to be "just like them".

Yet that is exactly who I am today: a medical intuitive, an intuitive healer, a life coach and an entrepreneur, all those things that I would've never thought of because I didn't know they existed so they were nowhere in my consciousness. But the Universe, with the help of a very special "angel", got me to where I needed to be to become who I needed to become, who I came here to become.

Before I dive any deeper into my story, here's a little background: Being from Lebanon, I come from a culture where education consisted predominantly of the "traditional" school subjects (Math, Languages, History, Geography, Science...) which means we had no Home Ec, Health, Drama, Music... You get the idea. And you can forget about after school programs. Our "after school" programs consisted of long (very long) hours of homework. If that alone wasn't enough to develop my left brain, as a teenager one of my favorite pastimes was solving Logic Problems.

This should give you a good idea of why all that "woo woo" stuff such as intuition, energy healing, Law of Attraction even meditation and visualization didn't exist in my world. No one around me talked about such things so it was very, very far from my sphere of awareness. I just didn't know what I didn't know and because I didn't know it, I didn't lose any sleep over it. Until I became desperate.

"Desperation is the mother of discovery" is my personal spin on the very famous saying "Necessity is the mother of invention" and it is. It is something I repeat over and over again to anyone who would listen because my own experience has taught me that in order to discover something so completely alien to us and to what we know, we have to either be open to it or desperate for it. And my advice is to always choose to be open because being desperate is truly painful.

For me, that desperation came at the beginning of 2009. I had gone through a series of major life changes over the previous two years that included moving countries because of war and then moving cities (more than once), my daughter moving away to college, my son starting high school, buying a home which was a tear down and then going through a total remodel from top to bottom in a very short period of time because I had family coming from abroad for the holidays in 2008 not to mention the birth of my niece's baby. I was stressed out and exhausted and my body was starting to send me signals, signals that I either missed or chose to ignore (or was I meant to ignore them?). I kept pushing myself to get one more thing done, then another and another. My logic was that when things go back to normal, I would have the time to take care of myself.

But that never happened. On December 28, 2008, my sister, Marilyn, left my home in the U.S. to go back to her home in Lebanon but she never got there. In true Hollywood fashion, on December 29, she passed away at the gate area in Paris waiting for her connecting flight. To say that the news came as a complete shock doesn't even begin to describe it. I really don't think there are words to truly describe such a situation. After that, it was running around renewing passports, going to Paris to pick up the body, going to Lebanon for the funeral, coming back to the States and then trying to make sense of the last couple of months while going through the grieving process and letting everything that happened sink in.

By that time, I had pushed my body way past any and all limits it may have had and it finally rebelled and stopped me in my tracks when I found myself battling depression. I would drive my son to school in my pjs because I didn't have the strength or the energy (or the desire) to get dressed. I would dread having my family come home in the evening because it meant talking and voices and watching TV and my nerves couldn't handle the noise. But it wasn't until I found myself fervently praying to get sick so I would have an excuse to avoid a family gathering that I knew I needed to find a way out of that darkness and I needed to do it fast. The only problem was that I was never big on doctors and medications yet that was all I knew. I knew that I wanted an alternative to the "traditional" route of doctors and drugs. But beyond that I had no clue what was out there.

This is where the magic started happening. It's like, once I made that decision, God/The Universe/Source/Infinite Intelligence (whatever you choose to call that benevolent power that is always there to support you) started showing me the way and opening the doors I needed to walk through to get to where I wanted to go.

At first, I discovered Reiki despite a lot of protest from my left brain. It not only opened my eyes but also gave me hope that I would be able to achieve what I wanted on my own terms. Then I won a ticket to a business retreat where the idea of creating a healing business that supported women in overcoming some of life's toughest challenges (including depression) was birthed. This led me to life coaching which then led me to meet a Lebanese medical intuitive at a networking event. As you can imagine, I was fascinated. I felt a very special kinship with her because of our similar background. This friendship opened me up to new possibilities so when I received an email out of the blue (is there such a thing?) about an introductory call on becoming a certified medical intuitive, I knew just enough to pique my curiosity and get me to sign up for the call. During that call, the host asked for my permission to give me a reading and before my mind had the chance to grasp the information she gave me, I had such a violent reaction in my body that I knew without a shadow of a doubt that it was true. I also knew that I had to sign up for that class despite my earlier belief that I didn't have a single intuitive bone in my body. You could say that my intuition guided me to the very thing I needed at the time to help me develop my intuition.

I will never ever know if I would have suffered from depression if my sister's death hadn't come after that 2-year series of stressful events in my life that had me exhausted and at the end of my rope. However, what I am absolutely sure of is that, without it, I would not have been guided to my purpose and my mission in life with that speed and that clarity. It truly was the greatest gift I had ever received from anyone. It is the proverbial "silver lining" in what has been the hardest experience of my life thus far.

On the other hand, what I do know is that we are all here for a reason and everything happens for a reason. Whether we choose to look for those reasons or not is entirely up to us and our willingness to go on those deep dives to uncover the treasures buried at the depths of our soul. I also know that we all came here with lessons to learn and a purpose to fulfill. For some this is very apparent early on. For others, more digging is required.

Today, July 2015, as I write these words, my family has some pretty dark clouds overhead. We are going through a challenging time. I haven't gotten to the silver lining yet but I know it is there somewhere. When will I get to it? What will be the lessons in it? I don't know yet. But I know they are there. They always are and that will probably be the subject of the next book.

# Dawn Shaw

Washington, United States of America

## *The Best Icelandic Horse Ever*

The moment I saw her, I knew something was wrong. She was laying in the stall and she was sweating. I met Askja for the first time while traveling in Iceland in September 2001. I had been shopping for a quality Icelandic mare to export, but none of the options I had been shown had resonated with me. The remainder of our trip was to be spent driving down the lesser developed eastern part of Iceland, circling back to Reykjavik past the glaciers in the south.

Then... two things happened. The first was the 9-11 attack, and then my husband Ian slipped a disk and ended up in an Icelandic hospital. This put a stop to the vacation half of our trip.

The significance of 9-11 to this story is *we were able to delay our trip home* by a week with no penalty. While they had news coverage in Iceland, we were shielded temporarily from the full impact of the tragedy back home. When we were able to make the drive back to Reykjavik, we stayed with friends there, one of whom was very connected to the Icelandic horse community. She made a few calls, and set up an appointment for me to meet a man who was selling a quality well-trained black mare.

What was I doing in Iceland shopping for a horse? Surely there are plenty of horses in the United States. Even Icelandic horses. But at the time, if you really wanted quality, you went to the source. But why an *Icelandic* horse?

I've always had an affinity for the exotic; for hobbies and interests outside of the mainstream. I wanted to play drums, but apparently didn't have the rhythm for it. Instead, I took up harp for a while until I discovered that while I love listening to music, playing music isn't my passion. I started martial arts in high school partially because it wasn't the normal every day extracurricular activity.

It is possible having a facial difference influenced my tendency toward uncommon activities. I was born with a rare type of tumor called a Teratoma. Unfortunately, this tumor had intertwined with my facial structure to such an extent that to completely remove it, the surgeons had to extract bone, nerve and muscle. The end result is the left half of my face is paralyzed and I've significant hearing loss in my left ear.

When you look different, standing out isn't a problem. However, I must have recognized, consciously or subconsciously, to be *attractive*, I had to be *interesting*. I didn't partake in activities merely because they were unusual. I chose them because I thought they would be something I would enjoy doing, and the fact they were exotic made them even more appealing.

So when it came to realizing my childhood dream of owning a horse, my preference would naturally tend toward a more unusual breed. But why specifically the Icelandic horse? I liked that they are short, but strong, so they are easier to get on, but still feel like there is plenty of horse under you. I liked that they have an extra gait - a smooth four beat gait known as the tölt which is a pleasure to ride. I liked the intelligent expression, and friendly curiosity. Plus, I was attracted to all the hair. Not just their thick wooly coats in winter, which sleek out for a few months in summer, but also those long thick year-'round manes and tails.

***None of this - my face, my hobbies, nor their own appearance - matters to a horse.***

Standing in her pen at the stables near Reykjavík, Askja was nondescript. She wasn't tall and didn't exude power and presence. She was also solid black, an attribute I didn't consider to be very exciting. Under saddle she came alive. Her tölt was fast, consistent and clear. She was energetic and responsive.

I purchased her because it made sense. Even after riding her I wasn't completely enamored with her, but that was largely due to inexperience. I didn't know how to recognize the quality I was looking at and experiencing.

I was also still working through fear and confidence issues caused by my first Icelandic. I had bought a horse which was totally wrong for me. He was fearful and inexperienced. I didn't have the skill or expertise to give him the confidence and leadership he needed to become a safe riding horse. He would bolt with me aboard and more often than not I would come off, mostly from the terror of being out of control. Though I was never seriously hurt in those falls, they were enough to shake my confidence pretty badly. I suppose I could have opted to sell him and quit riding, and that would have been a legitimate choice. But I decided instead to try to overcome my fear through education. I was passionate enough about the Icelandic horse to consider them worth my time, money, energy and devotion.

Because Askja was above my experience level, I raised my own abilities to fully appreciate and enjoy her. She had run off with me because she felt we weren't going fast enough (I had nicknamed her NASA), so I learned how to anticipate when she would take off so I could signal her to slow or stop. Despite her energy, she had common sense, and by learning to trust her, she helped restore my confidence. Horses seek leadership and thrive on having clear expectations. I had to learn how to be a fair and unambiguous leader. We performed in public breed demonstrations together, where her high flashy action turned heads. I bred her five times and got five lovely and talented offspring. Askja's talent, power and enthusiasm, which I didn't appreciate at first, eventually became my favorite attributes.

I wasn't too alarmed at her condition at first, seeing her there in the stall. I got her up and began walking her, as you do when you suspect colic, but when she kept trying to throw herself down to the ground again, I became increasingly worried. I called my friend over for support, and frantically tried to get a hold of a veterinarian. This proved challenging as it was the Friday before Labor Day weekend, and the vets weren't responding in a timely manner. One of my vets finally got back to me, but I would have to haul her in. I loaded her up, leaving her 2 1/2 month old filly behind, fearing the worst, but hoping for the best.

The 20 minute drive seemed like 20 hours. From the cab of my pickup, I could feel the trailer shake and hear the heavy thud as she went down, thrashing in pain. My heart wrenched. I was overcome with helplessness, fighting the temptation to drive ever faster

It didn't take long for the vet to reveal her findings. The generous dose of morphine did nothing to ease the mare's suffering. She was bloated and her gums were pale. She had severe colic, and had twisted her gut. Surgery wasn't an option- the vet doubted she would survive the trip to the surgical center, let alone the procedure.

The vet knew a landowner nearby. We hauled her over to an empty field, and it's there, we set her free from her pain. The landowner would come later and bury her. A part of me died with her that day. She left an indescribable hole in my heart. I still own two of her daughters and even though I love them and some of their mannerisms remind me of her, they do not fill the void. They aren't *her*.

I have a photo I took of Askja and her filly the day before. She was grazing happily, no sign of what was to come. When I had fed the horses that morning, nothing seemed amiss. New horse owners hear the horror stories of colic and wonder *will I know if something is wrong?* The answer is *Yes*. If you attend to your horses yourself, you'll notice when they don't behave normally unless you are completely oblivious.

Any time we lose a living creature we love, there's always the temptation to second guess ourselves and dwell on the "*what ifs*". What if I had been there that day? Would I have noticed her distress sooner? Before it was too late? The reality is, sometimes it comes on just that quick and the result is just as deadly no matter what you do. It's possible to run up thousands in surgery costs, only to lose the horse anyway. She spared me from having to make that choice.

They say you own a horse like her once in a lifetime. I don't believe that. One day I will find another horse as special as Askja. That horse cannot replace her, but "she" will have the energy, the talent and the attitude. She will be exhilarating to ride and I can show her off with passion and pride. She will make me feel special, like Askja did. Like I have the best Icelandic horse ever.

Yet regardless of who comes after, there is one thing I do know. When my time comes, it will be my black mare Askja standing there ready to carry me over to the other side.

# Christine Kay

British Columbia, Canada

## *Never Again*

It was the morning after the night before. My head was pounding. I felt slightly removed from the world. Staring into the small round mirror in the head of the 33ft sailboat which was our home, I didn't recognize the face as belonging to me.

One side of my jaw was swollen, I had bruising around my eyes and a lump on my forehead. I was feeling oddly calm and at peace with the world. I had made an irrevocable decision the marriage was over. I was out of there. It took me two years and it got worse before it got better.

However, I had learned one very important truth. ***It wasn't my fault.***

As usual, it had started from something trivial. Wham! Out of nowhere a stream of invective about how bad and terrible I was. Flight or fight? I chose to fight. Besides on a sailboat far away from friends and family, where could I flee to? As I was being held by my hair and having my head repeatedly rammed into the floorboards of the boat with a skewed upside down view of the cabin, this time I remember thinking in an oddly detached way, that's it, it's over.

I must have been screaming. I heard a male voice saying "What's going on? Stop that right away!"

It was a fellow sailor - dear old gentle Warwick - taking charge of the situation. He ordered K to take our dinghy and row over to his boat. Surprisingly meekly, K did exactly that.

Warwick turned to me and said "He has a problem, he needs help".

Bewildered, I opened my mouth to say, but it's not him, it's my fault and before I could form a sentence, the import of his words gradually dawned on me – a paradigm shift- *it's him, not me.* Wow. That really changes things.

Actually, it didn't really change much at all. In fact, things got worse before they got better. However, I was stronger for knowing in my mind it was over. I was so full of hope when we moved off the boat and moved into an apartment on the island.

I now realize the doctor had noticed signs of my obvious depression and had mentioned something to K who had brushed it off as PMS mood swings. One of his favorite phrases was telling me I was unstable.

The doctor invited us to see him. As he spoke to us, I realized he could see we had a deeper problem and I felt a glimmer of hope finally someone understood. He told K in his soft spoken Caribbean lilt to be more understanding of me. I was like a flower that needed nurturing. K nodded and seemed engaged. When we left, I truly felt confident things were going to be different.

That hope was dashed immediately. "What a load of mumbo jumbo I couldn't even hear what he was saying most of the time. Absolute nonsense." When his daughter came to visit was the absolute lowest time for me.

She obviously hated me. She had always wanted her parents to get back together. She treated me like dirt. K did nothing to defend me. One night I had hardly slept. When they went off for a morning swim, I made an excuse not to go and said I would have lunch ready for them.

I had a couple of hours of precious peace and quiet, so I made myself some lunch. It got later and later and there was no word from them. I got totally wound up because they couldn't even bother to call and let me know where they were. In my mind, it was deliberate, cruel and dismissive.

I was at the end of my tether. I called the doctor. I was sobbing hysterically. God bless him, it was a Sunday and he had a rare day off. He didn't hesitate. He came round to the apartment, spoke to me for a little while and gave me some Ativan which worked like a charm to calm me down.

This was my rock bottom – hysterical and Ativan were two words I or anyone who knew me well would never expect to see as a feature of my life. How could an intelligent, well-educated woman get herself in such a state? I used the medication sparingly as it made me a little foggy and, dealing with K, I preferred to keep my wits about me.

The knowledge I had reached out to someone for help and they had responded and I had an ally gave me strength. The only way was up. I wasn't so isolated anymore. I was building a network of friends. I wish I could remember exactly who said it. I do remember the words, though, "You could do his job."

Don't be silly, was my first reaction. Me, a scuba diving instructor? Then I thought some more Hmmm. Having a work permit in my own right would make me independent. It would give me an income, albeit a small one. I wold need to get my dive instructor certification

I found a perfect tiny house within walking distance of the dive school in Bonaire to rent for a month and off I went. So determined was I that this was a way to regain my independence and finally fulfill the vow I had made to myself over a year ago that I never had any doubt about what I was doing.

Here I was, almost 40, training with a bunch of kids in their 20s for a new career. I got stronger, fitter and leaner. More importantly, I had a new found confidence. No-one there knew K. They didn't know me as his wife, I was a person in my own right. I applied myself to the work, took on more responsibility, made new friends, worked as a team, forged alliances and found myself again.

The sense of achievement once we had our final certificates was incredible. Then I had my first wage cheque. That was the start of independence. Several weeks later, K decided he wanted to move. OK, fine, I said. I will stay where I am and you move. I don't think for a moment K thought I wouldn't actually follow him.

I negotiated with the landlord for a lower rent and got by. A couple of months passed. I decided to consult a divorce lawyer. He was served with the papers. He knew I was serious.

Contact Christine: **christine@christinheiteekaywellness.com**

# Chocolate & Diamonds

## Dr. Katherine T. Kelly

North Carolina, United States of America

### *The Day I Met My Father's Soul*

The day I saw his soul was also the day I met my own. It was Christmas day, 1990. Standing bedside on his right—my mother on his left—the priest arrived to offer his final blessing. My father had been admitted to the hospital for multiple organ failure 17 days prior—2 days after my 21st birthday. With failing lungs, he was immediately placed on a ventilator, leaving only his eyes to speak as he lay helplessly in the bed. But there was no need for words, for on that day his soul spoke volumes.

As my father looked past my mother to see him enter the room, he realized why the priest was there. He turned to look at me and as our eyes met, so did our souls. Frozen in the depths of the human condition—he in his, and me in mine—we connected in the most profound of ways. The entirety of what I saw through his eyes is impossible to explain, but the essence of the moment lingers even to this day. His immense fear in that moment penetrated me like no other experience, and yet, I also witnessed a contented release—one of retreat and resolve. He had fought a long battle. It was time to let go. He passed away quietly less than 12 hours later.

Seven years passed before I could honestly say I finished my grieving process. I remember casually speaking to someone about the fact it felt so strange that my father wouldn't be at my graduation when I received my doctoral degree. I went on to say he was the one who always supported my crazy career ideas—when I wanted to be a chef, he bought me a food processor; when I mentioned an interest in art, he bought me a paint set; when I started making crafts, he hand-delivered the tools to get me started; and when I told him I wanted to be a psychologist, he philosophized about the meaning of life. He "hired" me to help him with the paperwork in his own job and talked to me about "grown up" topics—many of which I hadn't a clue what they meant nor why they mattered. But the truth is, despite the many challenges of living with his long-term disability and illness, it all mattered. Everything.

As a therapist, many people ask me how long it will take for them to grieve or at least feel the sadness is not ruling their lives. I offer the honest answer in saying "I just don't know". For me, it ended the very instant I had the aforementioned conversation. It was the moment I realized the key role he had played in my life, one which allowed that last piece of grief to click into place so I could take what I learned and move on. That gem was the diamond in the rough—the light that freed me from my own dark passage in life.

But the light didn't stop there. Some 23 years later, another diamond would appear. This time, an even bigger one.

Having finished my degree as a psychologist, I went on to teach at a medical school, open a private practice, own a holistic health Center, and write a book. All of my career was geared toward health psychology, a specialty which emphasizes the importance of attending to the emotional aspects of physical illness and vice versa. In the midst of my work, I developed what I call The Soul Health Model, a blueprint for creating a balanced and healthy life that identifies 10 key elements of the human condition which, in both my personal and professional experiences, impact our ability to lead optimal lives. The model emphasizes if we deeply know and honor ourselves, live authentically, and use our soul—our inner ally—to inform our lives, then we would lead the most radiant and full life. When I wrote my book to explain the model, I knew it would be an important milestone; what I didn't know was it would uncover an even bigger meaning for my father's existence and heal the loss that much more.

During the promotion of *Soul Health,* I did over 70 radio interviews with both health and spiritual-based stations and podcasts. It wasn't until two-thirds the way through this on-air tour that the gem would arrive. Most of the interviews involved a description of the model and how to apply it to daily life. However, one announcer surprised me by asking a question about my own life. He asked when it was I had learned about the human condition and the soul.

I was dumbfounded. As a therapist, I am used to asking the tough and personal questions. It was particularly unnerving to be asked this as I knew thousands of people were listening on the other end. But the answer came quickly. It brought me right back to the day my father had his accident all the way up to the day he passed. It all flashed before me, my father's illness and subsequent death had opened my world to the soul. The experience of watching both my father and my family's human condition shift so dramatically as a result of his accident taught me not only about the multifaceted dynamics of life events, but it also showed me how one can lose themselves—and their soul—when buried under life's challenges. Had I not experienced those fateful years, I wouldn't be able to bring others back to their own soul, especially in their darkest of times. Essentially, I learned to bring others back to life because of my father's death.

No one can forget the moment they meet another's soul—especially when it marks the moment you meet your own. That shared experience of our separate, yet intertwined, human condition transformed me and the memory of that moment is forever etched in my mind. In this case, it was the ending of my father's life which marked the beginning of my own journey, not only as a person, but also as a healer—one which I wouldn't fully comprehend until more than two decades later.

We all learn in retrospect, and I now know that day in the hospital with my dad was the day I simultaneously understood both the human condition and the soul. When our eyes met, I learned to know your soul *is* to know true health. In my father's case, he had lost sight of himself and his soul years—perhaps decades—prior.

I had no idea my best training as a psychologist, author, speaker, and healer would be offered by my father's death. But once again, he became a teacher and primary supporter of my career path—this time, not so crazy ones.

Ann Landers said "The real trick is to stay alive as long as you live." To me, this means to stay conscious, aware, and always look for the golden nuggets that life has to offer. Consider these tips for opening your world to meeting your own soul:

- Know every ending provides a beginning. But sometimes you need the time, space, and assistance it takes to bring the understanding of the situation into full focus.
- Remember, there are always options…. Even when you are at a dead end. By opening yourself to your soul and its wisdom, your path will show itself.
- Understand fear always precedes transformation. Even when we feel immobilized, Forge Earnestly Ahead Regardless—F.E.A.R. and all will be well.
- Adopt the mantra: "To know my soul is to know true health—and in doing so, I will achieve radiant living." Your soul will soar higher and higher with each new awareness you gain by aligning with your most precious ally—Let your soul be your new best friend!

# Dr. Amy Cannata

New York, United States of America

## *Our Deepest Fear*

When women meet me, they see me and what THEY might see is this beautiful, doctor, who is all perfectly polished, put together, influential, woman of power wrapped up in a nice neat package. I am here to tell you that is not who I am.

### May 21, 2002

You can imagine how embarrassed, afraid, and humiliated I felt as this scene unfolded in front of my peers. This was only the beginning of the story. What followed were two more years of emotional and psychological torture I would endure during our divorce process. When he would plead with me, he had recovered and he would be different, and try to reconcile with me, I would stand my ground. Standing my ground came at a price. I would come out to find my windshield smashed or my tires slashed when I went to leave school.

Somehow I managed to persevere. I stayed focused on the vision I had for my future and the future of my daughters who were four and two years old at the time. When I was four years old, my brother was born. Since that time I've felt I was invisible to them. Basically, I've spent my whole life learning how to survive and how to transform my life. Working on my appearance and my emotions required me to step back and see the connection between the two.

That's why I am so passionate about sharing my divine gifts with all of you. It is my mission to help as many women as I can. Women who may feel invisible, who feel vulnerable or powerless, or who may be at a crossroads. To take control of their lives, to put yourself on the front burner instead of the back burner. I am here to be a messenger. To tell you, you matter, you are worth it. I am here to help guide emerging women of influence, to be your most shiny, sparkly, alive, empowered image of yourself that you can be so you can deliver your own divine gifts to the world.

# Dr. Markesha Miller

South Carolina, United States of America

## *Sometimes I Don't Wear Makeup*

I wish as a child someone had told me those years were solely a temporary thorn in my journey. I wish someone had told me I would be so much stronger because of them. I wish someone had told me my childhood would give birth to womanhood and endure the labor and pains of such. I wish someone had said, "Poopsey, you are beautiful and smart, always carry yourself like it and be a lady." Oh wait, someone did say it, my mom. Well, since my affectionate, childhood name has been disclosed, I guess I will tell my story.

My name is Markesha Miller, and sometimes I don't wear makeup.

Wait, let me explain.

Growing up in the small town of Pageland, South Carolina, I was taught at an early age the importance of BBP. Beauty, Brains and Personality!! My mother assured me that as a combination, this could be powerful, but one couldn't override the other. For example, beauty is great, but how far will it really advance you? After all, beauty is conditional and is only a temporary state; physical beauty that is. Of course, as a child, I hadn't discovered there was an alternative to physical beauty. I knew it was necessary to be smart, and to have goals.

This was modeled to me through my mother, as she was an educator for over 40 years. Let me be the first to say, growing up the child of an educator isn't an easy task. One could say you are expected to perform at a level of excellence: Let's just say I am glad this came easy for me. Of course, when all else failed, my parents instilled in me the importance of portraying a positive personality and being an individual who others would appreciate my presence and recognize my worth. I quickly learned my personality was mastered by who

I am and how I desired to be perceived. My attitude on the other hand, was developed by how individuals perceived me and responded back to me.

I think I've mastered the BBP, but this wasn't always the case. At one point in my life, I wasn't able to define beauty and struggled internally with my own self-image.

Many times we look at celebrities and ponder on their beauty and glamour. It is amazement which often strikes, wondering how someone could actually be this flawless. It's often this causes us to look at ourselves with comparison and sometimes ask the question, "What's wrong with me", or "How can I be like that woman?" I began this question very early in my life as a child and continued to seek the answer into my adulthood. However, I didn't gasp with amazement at celebrities, I compared myself to those around me. I felt I was marked at an early age, however, I just didn't realize the purpose of the mark.

I was born on February 24th, a healthy 10 lbs. 7 oz. baby girl to Roosevelt and Minnie Miller. If you were to ask my grandmother, Marguerite Blackwell, she would have told you "there is something special about that baby". I seemed like a normal, healthy baby, until I felt around the age of five that I wasn't. I had a birthmark which covered the right side of my face. This was a mark that would cast upon me, years of embarrassment, shame, low self-esteem, and bullying.

As a child I was asked if I had gotten into a fight. Many times going to the doctor, I felt suspicions of child abuse often arose. Nurses and doctors would take me into rooms away from my parents to inquire about "the black eye". I remember almost becoming robotic when responding, "It's my birthmark". There were times I would make this response before the question was presented. Let's just say... I knew what they were thinking.

"Don't make me give you another black eye." This was a statement I often heard from other children as a child. My mother had taught me to respond, "You didn't give me this one". That worked for a while, but soon, I began to ignore it more as I got older. I just didn't have the fight in me any longer. I guess I should add I grew up old school. My grandmother often would say it's not wise to argue with a fool, for bystanders may not be able to tell the difference after so long. It seems as I got older and began high school, my classmates saw my birthmark as part of me and questioned it less and could not find as much "bullying tactic" in it. Although the questions and comments ceased, the way I was beginning to feel about myself didn't. I think many people fail to realize the lasting effect of emotional scars.

I began wearing makeup at a very early age. My mother's idea was we could hide the birthmark with concealer. As a child, I was totally excited because I felt I could hide what brought me the greatest shame and also feel "grown". During my adolescent and teenage years, I realized the makeup only distracted, but didn't hide. I still entertained questions such as "what happened to that black spot on your face?'

My mother, at this time in my life, began to develop concern about my self-esteem and the development of it. During my time in high school, my mother made sure everything was in place to protect my self-esteem and to boost my confidence. I wore braces and underwent an oral surgery to secure "the perfect smile". At the age of fourteen, tumors were discovered in my breast. Thank God they were non-cancerous, but they had to be removed to prevent any complications. Now I know why one breast seemed larger than the other throughout my adolescent and early teenage years.

During my later teenage years, my mother entertained the idea of having the birthmark removed. I believe she knew the pain, self-doubt and embarrassment I had felt during my childhood because of "this mark". My mother is the type of woman who always had a way of making it better for me, or at least trying. While I underwent the surgery for my breast and the reconstructing process, the surgeon had explored with my mother the idea of removing my birthmark. My mother was definitely in favor and so was I! My father didn't typically give input on matters such as this, but my grandmother did! My mother's mom could be described as an outspoken woman with a wealth of wisdom. She told my mother it would be a bad idea to remove the birthmark. She stated, "What God gives, remains". Therefore, my mother was afraid to move forward with the process.

I continued to wear makeup throughout high school, college, and my graduate program. I realized my self-consciousness even followed me as an adult. I would never leave the house without makeup. I would not even go to the mailbox without makeup. In addition, I would sleep in my makeup because I didn't want to look in the mirror and see "that mark". I realized soon I became self-conscious in relationships. I always thought any man I dated could look past my makeup and see "that mark". I avoided hugs or anything that may cause a smudge or remove my makeup. After completing my PhD, I finally heard from God. All of these years, I had prayed and doubted in myself and my image. Where was my beauty? How could others be so flawless? Finally, after 30 years, I finally heard from God!

You see, I attempted to have my birthmark removed after the death of my grandmother. I knew she would have been against it and felt very strongly against the process. Therefore, I respected her wishes and didn't explore it anymore, until I began to have the feelings of "What would it be like to not have this mark on my face?" So, I made an appointment with a plastic surgeon and I underwent the process. How many of you all know it didn't work? Nope, failed attempt! So, guess what? We waited 6 months and did the process again.

Yep, you guessed it - it didn't work! By this point, my surgeon was confused. He had used the laser on the highest beam possible and admitted he was forceful with it. However, he felt the third time would be a charm. So, we tried it again! Surprisingly, it didn't work! By this point, my surgeon was totally baffled, but was determined to figure this out. So, he recommended we do a biopsy on my birthmark. This of course would require cutting on my face. It was at this time I heard my grandmother's voice, "What God gives, remains".

I knew I had to learn L.O.V.E. After all, what else is there to do with something that's a part of you? I had to "let go" of the painful childhood memories of my birthmark and the self-consciousness I was developing. I had to "overcome" the fear I was developing because of these memories. I had to allow myself to be "vulnerable" and exposed. I had to "embrace and empower" myself.

You may ask, why I am now telling this story. The response is simple. I feel on a daily basis all of us work to hide or cover up something we don't want others to see or know about us. There may be a woman out there right now going through an unhealthy relationship and has for years, but "she covers it up". There may be a woman right now living a full life of luxury, but feeling empty on the inside because she has worked so hard to "cover it up". You see, just as we work to cover those imperfections on our faces and our bodies, this is also how we work to cover those emotional and psychological scars. Remember, makeup does not take away, it only distracts.

I remember while growing up as a teenager, my mother would stress the importance of washing my face every night to remove the makeup. I couldn't see myself doing this because it would mean I would be reminded of my unhappy place. However, as I grew older, I began to see the effects that wearing makeup consistently had on my skin. After visiting my dermatologist, she immediately knew what the problem was..."I wasn't allowing my skin to breathe". So, I began to consciously wash my face every night while speaking positive affirmations to myself regarding my birthmark.

I studied it and truly can say I began to embrace it. I began to journal about my birthmark and wrote letters to it describing my childhood and how I felt it was responsible for much of my pain. Remember when I said I finally heard from God. During this point in my journey, I realized my birthmark was more than a "mark", it was a promise". I no longer saw this mark as what held me down, but what lifted me up. I became more confident in who I am as a woman rather than who I thought I should be. I knew my life was one of promise and fulfillment and what God says is for me cannot be taken away by man. Now I realize it, "the mark" is all over me, even in my name.

One thing I've realized as an adult, none of us are flawless. What "'L.O.V.E" have you poured into yourself? What physical, emotional, and psychological scars have you worked years to hide? Remember makeup isn't meant to be permanent, only to temporarily distract. Just as I was keeping my makeup on to protect how I felt emotionally, and at the same time damaging my skin; while we spend so much time trying to keep on the makeup physically, emotionally, and psychologically, we unintentionally harm other areas in our lives. Therefore, I decided not only to allow my skin to breathe.... but also myself.

My mother always told me I would look back on my life and say, "Mama you were right". Well, she was right! **My name is Markesha Miller and I am beautiful and smart. Sometimes I don't wear makeup, and I love it!**

# Linda Sherwin

Ontario, Canada

## *Do Ya Wanna Trade Your Salmon For My Tuna?*

It was a hot and sunny July day in southern Florida. The year was 2008. My friend, Jillian and I were meeting at an obscure location in Boca Raton. An enclave of sumptuous multi-million dollar mansions wasn't our destination. Neither was the pristine beach, nor the expensive boutiques.

No - we were travelling to a location which was certainly not on any promotional flyer or travel agents "must see" list. As I followed her car along the streets, I pondered what had brought me to this. I had run a successful business for years here in the USA after moving from Canada to be closer to my parents for the six months they spent in Florida. I started my business by doing what I had always done – meeting people, talking about what I did and acquiring clients. I lived in a lovely home just a mile from the ocean. I ran the beach every morning feeling grateful for the wonderful life I was living.

And then on December 1, 2006, my main client informed me – along with all the other consultants - they were cancelling all contracts. I've had contracts shortened before, but this complete sweep of all independent workers was a surprise. This was a large international company with offices around the globe and we all wondered what could possibly have happened. However, I was and always have been a survivor and set out to find more clients with a reminder to not put too many "eggs in one basket."

But something strange had transpired. Potential clients who had earlier talked about doing various projects were now putting them off until some undetermined time. Even worse – clients who had always paid on time were now delaying payment by 60 days.

What had happened? Little did I realize in south Florida with its crazy housing boom and inflated home values, we were feeling the effects of the Global Financial Crisis to come. I continued to work diligently to talk to current clients about payment, find new prospects and attempt to keep my life going.

Unfortunately, it meant using savings and any investments – which were dwindling in value – to make mortgage payments, pay for utilities and buy groceries. There was certainly no excessive spending of any kind. It was just the bare necessities that were being covered with no idea whether I would make it through the next month.

Not that misery really loves company – but I wasn't alone. Other independent workers were having the same challenges. Colleagues with full time jobs were either being laid off or told to pick up the slack of their fellow workers who had been "made redundant" as the politically correct term was used.

Then clients started delaying payment 120 or 180 days. Still others said they were unable to make any payments whatsoever. And this continued for almost 18 months. How could this happen to me, I mused? I've always worked very hard to overcome any obstacle in my way. In hindsight, did I really think I could have single-handedly overcome what many economists considered to be the worst financial crisis since the Great Depression of the 1930s?

So here I found myself following my friend who was in the same circumstances. As we travelled down the streets, I noticed the homes were much smaller, closer together and very few had cars outside. We parked a few blocks away and walked to our destination. We both had on big sunglasses and baseball caps – foolishly thinking we might be recognized and how embarrassing that would be.

As we approached the single story building, we saw a long lineup outside. People were talking to each other not quite as friends, but as acquaintances who had seen each other before. We had heard the doors would open at 11:00 am which was about 10 minutes away. As we joined the line, we purposely kept to ourselves and didn't join in the jovial banter around us. Furtively looking around hoping no one there would recognize us.

Promptly at 11 the doors opened. The line began to move forward in an orderly fashion. As we reached the door, Jillian and I were greeted with a smile and a "welcome" and handed two plastic bags with the suggestion if we needed more to just ask. The first table contained non-perishables – pasta, rice and cereal. The next table was laden with canned goods – vegetables, fruits, fish, meat and my personal favorite, peanut butter. The man in line ahead of us noticed our indecision and suggested we put these items in one bag and save the second bag for the fresh food. The people on the other side of the tables continue to fill the empty gaps as quickly as an item was taken away. The next tables had fresh fruit and vegetables and as directed, we put those items in the second bag. The line wound its way around the cavernous room and finally led back to the entrance where the line was even longer than when we had arrived. The whole process was extremely orderly and without incident.

Then, once outside, the most amazing things happened. People gathered in small clusters. Jillian and I just wanted to get out of there, but were hampered by these small groups. Three people came up to us – two men and a woman. "Hi, I am Joe," one of the men said to me. "I saw ya picked up some salmon. Do ya wanna trade your salmon for my tuna?"

We realized then what the clusters were. The people who had quickly filled their bags were now exchanging items for things they wanted, but perhaps weren't on the tables when they passed by. Joe, Peter and Marie were regulars at this location – this Food Bank. There I said it. As we exchanged items, they called out to others they knew and our little group grew. The camaraderie and kindness to each other was remarkable. Some even exchanged some simple recipes they had tried and wanted to share.

Without saying a word to each other, we both removed our sunglasses – no longer embarrassed to be sharing this moment with others. We didn't know who in the group were professional people like us who had been hit with hard times or who might have lived this way for a long time. We simply knew we had all been brought together by difficult circumstances and were doing what we could to make the best of it.

What a remarkable lesson? People who had little themselves and needed assistance for the most basic of things – food – were so generous and kind to one another. They weren't embarrassed that it was necessary for them to come here. They traded food, shared information and then went on with their day. As Jillian and I walked back to our cars, we didn't speak. As strange as it may sound, we were both grateful to have experienced the moment, whatever, the cause that brought us to it. I've never forgotten the lesson. In fact, any time I buy salmon, I think of Joe.

# Engracia Gill

Texas, United States of America

## *The Gift of Surrender*

Sometimes events in life appear to be overwhelming and yet, a silver lining shows itself in unexpected ways. I chose to surrender on this one occasion, not because I was so wise and so courageous. No, not at all. I actually surrendered because I was cornered, completely stuck. I made the decision to surrender half-heartedly. Then something marvellous happened.

Several years ago, I had been looking forward to a family vacation in my favorite spot on earth, a 400 acre farm in the Catskills Mountains. My husband and I had always enjoyed escaping to this bucolic setting when we lived in New Jersey. Our children always looked forward to the activities of fishing, hiking and looking for salamanders for the five years we lived in the region. The farm was stunning, set in the middle of 400 acres far removed from the nearest road with streams and fields alike surrounding the farmstead. This time we had moved far away. I was really looking forward to being able to go back and enjoy a week in August when the weather would be warm and the fields would be golden.

My husband asked that my father-in-law be included along in this week since we hadn't seen him in a while. I was rather hesitant because many times in the past my father-in-law had been quite rambunctious. He would often upset us by drinking way too much. Over the years, my husband had asked his father not drink in our presence anymore, which had often been a point of contention between father and son.

Often, I needed to protect my children and I would reluctantly need to enforce the same requests. I struggled with my husband's request to include his father. I was filled with fear because I could see while being in a pastoral setting was really fun for me and my family, my father-in-law may not share in such pleasures. I selfishly wanted what I wanted. However, my husband insisted and I could see no way out of the situation without a major rift between my husband

and me. I knew such a rift would be hurtful to him and my children. So I decided to give up my wish to have the farm to ourselves and to include my husband's father.

A few days after our discussion to include my father-in-law, I struggled restlessly through my feelings and thoughts. My thoughts kept turning to how difficult it was to be around my father-in-law, to the many times he had insisted on being in control of our get-togethers. I was not at peace at all. I knew I needed to change my attitude to have a good time. But I didn't know where to turn. I had about an hour reprieve before I needed to pick up my children from school. I turned on Oprah, something quite unusual for me to do.

Gary Zukav, author of the "Seat of the Soul", was on the show and explained the book's premise is everything is always about you - no matter what comes to you, in the end your attitude determines the outcome. As soon as I started to listen to Gary Zukav, time stopped! It was as if the coincidence of hearing exactly what I knew to be true at the moment I needed it so badly, cast a different light and feeling of the whole situation!

I suddenly realized I needed to change very deeply to bring the outcome, I desired, a week of fun and relaxation and love, deep, deep love. A love so big it would open my heart to my father-in-law without taking anything away from me, it was a pure gift so complete it came from another part of me. It was a stunning experience!

I remember going to my altar and kneeling in gratitude for the understanding of what my attitude needed to be. Then, completely at peace with myself, I let go without giving it another thought! I had been graced with a new attitude just as Gary Zukav was explaining to Oprah! The show had struck a chord with me. I understood my attitude was more important than what actually happened. I saw I could use whatever happened as a springboard to my own growth. As soon as I stopped resisting the learning, something magical happened. I totally understood changing me was the only thing that needed to happen in the situation. I knew I would establish a newer and deeper relationship with my father-in-law.

The days flew by. My sons were looking forward to their skateboarding camp near the farm. I couldn't wait for the magic of the streams and the quiet of the farm! Arrangements were made to meet my father-in-law at the airport and to drive together to the farm. I continued to feel at peace and grace! When we picked up our guest at the airport, I immediately sensed something wasn't right with him. He had been dealing with difficult health issues. I instantly sensed something about his health was off. I couldn't verbalize this thought at the time. I just registered it. My father-in-law was genuinely touched and excited to have been invited, a feeling soon very contagious to all of us.

What happened next truly amazed me. I couldn't have predicted the unfoldment in any way. The vacation was not tolerable, not average - it was great! I experienced a completely different side of my father-in-law I had never experienced in all the 20 years I had known him! A sense of harmony and fun permeated the gathering. We played games together and laughed riotously. This was an unbelievable unfoldment, a true miracle.

As the vacation drew to a close, our family gathered together outside to take family photos, a tradition in my husband's family. I had experienced such happiness and freedom in those days together. Gratitude flowed through me as we were about to say goodbye. My husband hugged his father. When it came time for me to say goodbye to him, this strong sense overcame my mind this was the last time I would see him. This sense overtook my mind and heart and I felt breathless. I had no idea what was brewing inside my intuition, but it felt so big it took my breath away. I reeled inside of me and looked deeply into my father-in-law's eyes and stated without reservation: "I love you, take good care of yourself". He gave me a great bear hug and turned around. I didn't speak of my inner sense and wordless thought to anyone.

Shortly after the vacation ended, some problems surfaced in my husband's family. One night, my father-in-law called and I happened to answer the phone. Once again, I felt this vivid sense of freedom and love with him. We had a real conversation and listened to one another respectfully with no strain at all.

Several weeks later, we had made plans to meet some dear friends at a camp about an hour away from home. On the way there, my husband's brother called, but he didn't leave a message or phone number where he could be reached. When we arrived at the camp, I had a nagging feeling my husband should call his brother back which I suggested to him. As I suspected, something was very wrong. My husband learned his brother had found their father, who had died three days earlier. I was so saddened to hear he had died alone, just weeks after we had shared such wonderful moments together. I was so incredibly grateful I had had the breakthrough which enabled me to love him so completely and freely, just weeks before his passing.

Deep inside of me, I knew nothing had happened by chance. I knew I had needed to confront my attitude. I also knew my deep desire to change myself happened with grace, as if my limited human understanding was momentarily suspended so I could attune to an effortless grace. I reflected back on the sudden, deep knowing I would never see him again. I reflected back on the wave of love that sprung forth through my heart as a love which sees behind the veil of circumstance and knows what we each crave for: to connect deeply.

# Robbi Hess

New York, United States of America

## 'Change Your Life: Before it is Changed for You'

As I read this quote it struck a chord. Why? Because my life was drastically, dramatically and forever changed at 4:45 pm on April 9, 2012. That date and time are etched forever in my memory, and on my body.

Why? Because it's the day I received the "you have breast cancer" pronouncement. I have the scars to show what I've been through and how I survived and am thriving. This was doubly devastating because I was going to turn 50 in less than 30 days. The weight of both of these was sometimes more than I could bear, but I persevered.

Phrases that hurt the most during this time were, "God only gives you what you can handle" and "You are so strong." First of all, how does God know what I can handle and why was I being forced to handle anything? Was it a test? Second, was I strong? I cried for hours. I would crumble into a weeping mess at sometimes the most inopportune times. That was strength? I was terrified. I still am. That fear never fully fades away. Well, perhaps it fades away in time, but I am three years, thriving and I am still scared.

### Life before

Prior to my diagnosis I was blissfully unaware I was working too hard, working too late at night, too early in the morning and missing too many important family events. Even when I closed the door to my office early and went to school functions or family parties, I was either thinking about work or working on my phone during these family events. I missed out on so much because I was never truly present. I was there physically, but mentally I was miles away. I always wondered "what's next" instead of enjoying "what's happening now." I was blind to it. I was driven. I was convinced this is what the solopreneur does; works all the time and is at the beck and call of clients.

## My transformation and transition

Losing my breasts was a huge deal. Those words don't even relay the depth of the loss to my self-esteem and to my very essence of being a woman. I did choose a surgery which allowed me to "wake up with breasts" and not have to go through implant surgery, but they weren't what I had before my 16-hour surgery. I know I needed to get the cancer out of my body, but even that rationale didn't make the process any easier.

I grieved the loss of my breasts. I grieved the loss of an unscarred body. I ranted and raved against God. I pleaded. I bargained. I cycled through the five stages of grief so often it made me dizzy.

During my treatments and surgeries, it quickly became apparent (not surprisingly) my oncologists weren't going to work around my "busy client schedule." Their driving goal was to get the cancer out of my body and get me on the road to wellness. It was while I was meeting with my medical oncologist I had a breakdown about my work, my clients, and my business where she brought it all into perspective by saying, "Would you rather have a life or a business?" Talk about a dash of cold water to the face. I wanted to live. I wanted to thrive. I wanted to see my children grow up and then see any grandchildren they might bless me with.

I learned to prioritize. I learned to say no to projects. I came to understand life is not for working 24/7, but for being with your loved ones. Working on your crochet projects. Reading a book. Taking a walk. Fighting for your life by doing whatever it takes to beat cancer.

Now, three years later. I am a thriving cancer survivor. I've clients I love working with. I've a business which helps support my family. I work normal business hours and I close the door at the end of the workday. When I am with my family or when I am watching a movie or taking a walk I make certain I am truly present. I don't worry about "what's next" because sometimes you just don't want to know what lies ahead.

I want to live in the now. I want to thrive in the present. I want my children and my friends and family to know when I was with them, I was truly with them.

I wish I hadn't waited to "change my life before it was changed for me" but since it did, I came to understand what a gift every day is. Yes, even crappy days when you step in dog poo and spill coffee on your white blouse and miss out on a potential new client, that day is still a gift because you are alive to experience both the good and the bad.

## My thoughts and hopes for you

If you receive a breast cancer diagnosis, allow yourself to grieve. Allow yourself to cry. Get angry. You are allowed to be scared. I also urge you to reach out to friends and family. Ask for help. I learned my friends and family were as scared as I was. They didn't know what to say or what to do. While I didn't have the strength to reassure them, I did discover sometimes all I had to do was say, "I don't know what you can do to help me, but right now I just need a hug." Believe me, that was something we all needed... to have that life raft in the midst of a storm.

Ask for help. Find a support group. There is a local breast cancer coalition, but I wasn't comfortable, and honestly couldn't talk without crying, so I found an amazing online group (if you would like to know more about the Booby Buddies, please reach out to me). I received support from women who "had been to the brink and back." I could cry, complain, voice each and every fear I couldn't have found the voice to say out loud to anyone else and I received support beyond measure. To this day I am involved in this group because of the newly diagnosed ladies who need to know that even though it seems you will never make it through, you will. I know. I've been there.

My new attitude about my work-life balance has changed me from a cancer survivor to a cancer thriver!

# Joan McGuire Pounds

## Colorado, United States of America

### *Struggle is Optional*

My sister was always the successful one. She's never had to make a resume in her life. The 2nd and last job she ever had was with IBM. She worked for them for 40+ years. Dad taught her to live beneath her means. Consequently, she never had to be concerned about not having enough.

I remember the conversation clearly. I was in my kitchen talking to her on the phone and relating some of the things which were going on at work. She asked me if I had ever thought about what I would do if my job was taken away. It was inconceivable to me. I told her I planned to retire from Hewlett Packard. HP had a culture of not laying off people.

When someone needed to move, they retrained them and ensured their success. They were very happy with me, I was making good money and getting consistent performance bonuses. She laughed at me! At first I thought it was cruel and as I look back on the conversation, I realize she was lovingly attempting to prepare me for my future.

One day at work during a large meeting, we were told about how the future of the industry was rapidly changing and we were each given the book, "Who Moved My Cheese", along with several other little gifts pertaining to the new company we had just become, Agilent Technologies. We were told it would be in our best interest to read the book because we would be having team discussions about it in the coming months. What they were really saying was, "We are about to move your cheese!" Less than a year later and two weeks after my last performance bonus, the entire team was laid off. It wasn't due to my performance. It was simply a business decision made in a corporate office with no regard given to how the decision personally affected me.

I was relieved because I was experiencing some stress reactions which were negatively affecting my health (I was internally hemorrhaging). My body was shutting down on me. I went on to lose my house. My kids weren't able to go to the nice schools they were attending. They had to move away from their friends. It was devastating. I wasn't able to find a job for a long time and a friend encouraged me to interview with Fast Company magazine to help me get some exposure which perhaps would provide a job interview. No job interviews came immediately from the article; however, I was contacted by an Indian recruiter about 6 months later who offered me my old job back at 50% less than what I had been making. I turned the job down on principal. This wasn't economics anymore, it was simply corporate greed! That was definitely not "the HP Way".

As I became employed and began to rebuild my life, I realized I was still very bitter over what I had been through. I was raised to believe you went to school, got a degree, so you could be successful with a company, work hard as if it's a chore and at the end of 40 years, you would retire and enjoy the rest of your golden years. The past years experiences created a huge shift in my thinking. It felt like the rug had been ripped out from under me and I was saddened when I saw Katrina refugees come to our area and be criticized for driving up rents, taking "our" jobs and generally mistreated when all those people were trying to do was to survive.

I thought with all the resources we have at our fingertips, there's **got** to be a better way! If I can connect to computers in Germany to start and stop equipment or monitor how much paper and ink a printer has when Germany is having blizzards, I am certain there is a way people can make a living and be able to sidestep a bad storm or attend to a sick relative without having their entire financial world turned upside down. About this time was when I first saw the movie The Secret. Everyone was talking about it so I wanted to see what the fuss was about. It sparked my curiosity. A lot of it was pretty "woo woo" to me, but some of it really made sense as I remembered what I had been taught in science classes over the years.

During the event, they were throwing T-shirts out into the audience and I caught a T-shirt which was practically thrown directly at me. I spoke to her after the event to thank her for inviting me and she inquired if I opened up the T-shirt yet. I hadn't. I went ahead and opened it up and the inscription on the T-shirt said "Struggle is Optional". I started to laugh and she said to me "You know, there are no accidents". *What she meant was the T-shirt was a message to me that my struggle was over.* My eyes began to leak then.

I went to that personal development class several times because of the revelations I received each time, along with the positive energy and people. I've learned a tremendous amount from the training and it's opened my mind to ideas and concepts I didn't even know existed before. I've learned most people who are better off than I am are not greedy, but rather are compassionate and willing to teach you what they know to help you to get to where they are. I was introduced to the concept of giving good value and being paid equitably for the value provided. I was introduced to the concept of having fun while I worked, which made the work more enjoyable and wasn't a form of goofing off.

The positive people I met were full of possibility and many had figured out different ways to be able to make a living, while traveling, while taking care of sick relatives, while avoiding catastrophes and having fun while they were still young enough to enjoy their lives. Every time I met someone who had figured it out, I made sure I took time to have a conversation. I was thirsty for this knowledge because they were already living the life I was searching for! I've made many good friends over the years who are scattered worldwide.

## My Quantum Leap

A friend of mine and I decided to take a deep dive into the personal development classes and we were able to study at an intense level at the feet of many millionaires which created our own personal Quantum Leap. We learned the practical skills along with the quantum science behind creating your own reality. As a result, we both created businesses which have helped us to have our money work for us. I now recognize many different resources I didn't recognize years ago. If I knew then what I knew now, my life wouldn't have included the struggles I went through because I wouldn't have been afraid of the unknown. I would have embraced the change before me. Along the way, I was able to meet and personally learn from many of the teachers in the movie, "The Secret" which I saw many years before. I never would have dreamed it would happen when I first saw it; however, now when I look back, it makes perfect sense.

As a lifelong learner, I am continuing my studies as I move forward and I am helping others along the way to discover "Struggle is Optional". I am now working as a website designer and digital media specialist for authors, speakers and coaches who want to make a profit from their passion. I've clients worldwide and I help them to create their own businesses, they can benefit from when they are traveling, taking care of family, or moving locations to avoid some of the wild weather occurring on our planet.

They traded the "security" of a job for the security of making a living and creating a life from what makes their hearts sing. They are able to be available to the people who mean the most to them. They have the ability to be paid in correlation to the value they create while creating wonderful experiences that wouldn't be possible if they were tied down to a job just waiting for their two weeks of annual vacation while they sit in fear of being laid off at any moment.

I am still pretty amazed when something good appears in reality that was just in thought form just days prior. I am excited knowing I was a conduit to make it possible. I love being able to provide my clients a step-by-step approach to creating the platform and products which ultimately lead them to the life of their dreams. I now consciously choose good thoughts to occupy my mind. Sometimes it's a minute by minute process as I proceed along my journey.

Instead of living in fear and stress beyond belief, while I desperately cling to a job I have no control over, I am now excited about the people I get to meet, the businesses I get to help build and the wonderful life that lies ahead of me. I am directing my own ship and the Wheel of Prosperity is my helm. The beauty of all this is you can do this too! When you are ready, I will be there to help you along your way! All you have to do is to reach out. I love my life!

# Shameka Andrews

New York, United States of America

## *Rollin through the Clouds*

How do you learn to accept yourself when you feel everyone has rejected you since the day you were born? How do you keep a smile on your face when all you want to do is cry? I've asked myself these questions many times, as I would lay awake at night and cry myself to sleep. How I got from there to here? One word, Faith. Faith my life wasn't always going to be this way; faith in something bigger than myself, faith, I could make it through the misery I felt almost on a daily basis.

I would describe my story as a dark black canvas with swirls of bright colored paint. I was born with Spina Bifida (Spina Bifida is a congenital defect in which the spinal column is imperfectly closed so part of the meninges or the spinal cord protrudes, often resulting in hydrocephalus and other neurological disorders). Prior to the 70s, the prognosis for people born with Spina bifida was death. At that time, the doctors believed I wouldn't live past the age of 5. *I am grateful to say this year I celebrated my 37th birthday.*

During the first few years of my life, I had a number of operations to correct secondary conditions such as hydrocephalus and clubfeet caused by Spina Bifida. Because of my disability, I've been in a wheelchair my whole life. During childhood, my disability created barriers in my life and in my relationships with other people. Lack of accessibility in my neighborhood caused me to be isolated the majority of the time. I remember I loved going to school and school events because that was usually the only time I was able to get out of the house on a regular basis.

Lack of accessibility is still a problem for me, but it has greatly improved over the years. It frustrates me when I cannot get somewhere because of the lack accessibility, but I know this will probably always be an issue. As an adult, I've learned to adapt and have managed to live a very active life. In 2003, I went through probably one of the most difficult transitions in my life moving out of my mother's house and moving into a community residence of nine people, while also learning how to navigate the system of disability services and going to college. I felt like someone opened a window and tossed me into this never ending black hole.

I went from living with five people in my mother's house to living with nine people in a community residence. I lived in the residence for three years and things were a little crazy at times. As you could imagine living with nine people could get a little crazy, but those nine people became like my second family. I still keep in touch with a few of them to this day.

In 2004, I found out about an organization called **Ms. Wheelchair America.** When they came to Albany, I volunteered in the hospitality suite. Ms. Wheelchair America is a week-long event where contestants participate in workshops, judging interviews, speeches and at the end of the week there is a crowning ceremony with entertainment, awards and the announcement of the winner. 28 women in wheelchairs competing for the title of Ms. Wheelchair America was very exciting to be part of. I had never seen such a thing before. I would describe it as fun, exciting and a bit stressful at times.

The next year with lots of convincing from other people in my life, I decided to try out for the competition. I was so nervous because public speaking has never been something I liked to do. I think I heard someone say once **people fear public speaking more than death** and I can see why. It can often feel like you are going to die standing in front of a crowd of people. I just remember saying to myself just don't get sick because I felt so nauseous.

I couldn't believe I was doing something like this. I felt so out of place going up against two who had accomplished more at that time than I thought I ever would in my lifetime. I was the second runner-up that night and after much thought, I decided to run again in 2006 and actually won the title of Ms. Wheelchair NY. I often say when I first got involved with the Ms. Wheelchair NY program, I felt like a little girl even though I was an adult. One of the things I was able to accomplish during my year as Ms. Wheelchair which I am very proud of was to get curb cuts put in on the street where I lived at the time which would allow me and the others to be able to stroll through the neighborhood.

I enjoy being able to stroll through the neighborhood, especially on a nice sunny day. During that year I had a slogan which I put on T-shirts and posters: **Disabled means Devoted, Intelligent, Successful, Ambitious, Beautiful, Loving, Educated and Determined** and that's me. I believe the Ms. Wheelchair NY program is one of the things that's helped me to become the woman I am today. It was a year of my life I will never forget. And now I get to pass that opportunity on to new women each year as the State Coordinator of the program. I feel like a proud mother every time a new woman joins the organization.

It's amazing how each person has grown as I have through the years. After my year as Ms. Wheelchair New York, I become a member of the AmeriCorps Program at the Self-Advocacy Association of NYS. The AmeriCorps team at SANYS provided disability awareness presentations in schools, boys and girls clubs and other community organizations. My favorite presentation working for SANYS was at a boys and girls club for 40 children between the ages of nine and twelve. It was so much fun being able to hang out with the children and after our presentation we raced around the gym and had lunch with them. I remember thinking I cannot believe I get money to do this! It was one of my favorite presentations that we did.

After two years of doing the AmeriCorps program through SANYS, I was promoted to Co-Director of Policy. That job came with lots of strolls to inaccessible bathrooms in the Capital and Legislative Buildings, but I've learned a lot and built lasting relationships working for SANYS. This past year I decided to cut back my work at SANYS to give me the opportunity to do some other things. In July of last year I was given the opportunity to work at the Independent Living Center of the Hudson Valley a couple days a week organizing health and wellness workshops for people with disabilities. This job opportunity came at a great time in my life as I had the personal goal of really taking better care of myself physically, emotionally and spiritually. After spending most of my life waiting to feel like someone accepted me for who I was, I decided it was time for me to learn to accept myself.

I know life will never be all rainbows and sunshine, but I plan to keep rolling until I reach the stars.

# Shefali Burns

Ontario, Canada

## *Attitude of Gratitude*

Have you ever looked at someone and thought, "Wow, they have had an amazing life!"? "They are so lucky!", "Life's so easy for them!". Have you ever had these thoughts about other people? I have, and I do still. And, I know other people have these thoughts about me and my life. My life is amazing. I do feel very lucky, and life is easy for me. But, it has not always been like this.

I thought I had the perfect life. I was married to a nice guy, I have 2 great kids, and I had a nice house, 2 cars, a dog, money in the bank, and a secure, steady government job with a good pension and quickly rising to the top. Everybody thought I had the perfect life. From the outside looking in, it looked really good. I have to admit I faked it quite a bit, you know the saying "fake it, till you make it". That can only take you so far. On the inside, I was miserably unhappy and dissatisfied with life. I wanted more, but I didn't know what I wanted. Interesting, isn't it? Do you feel like this? Do you want something, but don't know what it is you want?

One evening I went to see a movie in the theatre with my daughter, I am still surprised she went with me. The movie was Nights in Rodanthe with Richard Gere and Diane Lane based on the novel by Nicholas Sparks. It was a nice, romantic movie about finding love. One scene really touched me, or maybe it was the whole idea of finding love that touched me. As I watched them walking on the beach, having fun and falling in love, I realized I didn't have that, and I wanted it. I felt a yearning deep in my heart and soul, this is what I wanted, and this is what was missing in my life. Love. Being in love, loving someone, and being loved in return. Needless to say, that was the beginning of the end of my marriage. It was also the beginning of living life on my terms and choosing what was right for me.

I always knew my marriage was doomed to end, I was just waiting until the kids had graduated from university and were settled before I disrupted their lives. Now, it was like the Universe was telling me it wouldn't wait that long, I needed to change my life now. I told my husband I wanted to separate, he was shocked. We went for marriage counseling, and received lots of advice from family and friends. Unfortunately, nobody was listening to me, to my feelings. I didn't have any support, from anywhere, nobody was on my side. I had to fight with everyone, and I don't like fighting, I don't like confrontation at all.

We finally separated and my husband moved out. The kids stayed with me, of course, as well as, all of the junk in the house. I bought my husband out of the house, and he purchased a new house and bought all new furniture. I was a little jealous. I ended up with debt and old crap and he got a new house and a new car and new furniture. I became a single parent of teenagers. I am sure you can imagine what that's like. He had the support of family and friends, I was alone. I was a little nervous and stressed out. I was under a lot of stress, financial, emotional, and mental. How was I going to pull this off?

I was a life coach and Reiki master at the time, so I decided to use some of my tools to help me get through this difficult period. Here are the tools I used to raise my vibration, change my mindset, and keep my emotions elevated. I use these tools even now every day and I recommend this to my clients all the time.

We don't always have control over our situations, but we do have control over our thoughts, actions, and reactions. Are you thinking negatively or positively? Are you looking at limitations or possibilities? Do you know what the number one regret of the dying is? It is more like a wish, "I wish I had had the courage to live a life true to myself, not the life others expected of me".

This could be an opportunity for you as well, if only you can keep an open mind. How can you change your mindset right now to be more positive and open when you are going through a change or a stressful time?

Take action now by following these 6 guidelines and you'll remain in a more positive state and be able to handle anything that comes your way.

1. Be grateful for what you already have. Write down 3 things you are grateful for every day.

2. Meditate for at least 10 minutes every day.

3. Keep your thoughts and words positive.

4. Listen to inspirational, uplifting music or whatever makes you feel joy and happiness.

5. Exercise, walk, or do yoga regularly.

6. Drink more water and eat more fresh fruits and vegetables.

You are probably wondering if I take all of these actions regularly. I can honestly say, yes, I do, maybe not every day, but regularly. I am more positive and calm when I choose to follow these guidelines. I've more energy and I radiate peace and calm to those around me. I am able to go with the flow and see possibilities instead of limitations. I look to the future with expectation and joy instead of fear and anxiety. You can do the same. Try out any of these steps and you'll see a difference in yourself almost immediately

My #1 tool is gratitude. I write in my gratitude journal every day. This takes only 10 minutes to write down 3 things I am grateful for today. What does it mean to "have an attitude of gratitude"? What is gratitude? How can gratitude change your life? Gratitude to me is being grateful and thankful for everything in our lives. This includes the people in our lives, the lessons and challenges in our lives, the things that bring us joy and comfort, the basic necessities of life, etc. It means not taking anything for granted, accepting and appreciating what we have and who we are right now.

Having an attitude of gratitude shifts our awareness from what we are lacking to the abundance we already possess. With regular practice of gratitude, you'll feel more positive, balanced, calm, and peaceful. By practicing gratitude, we become aware we are part of a greater power. We expand our awareness and in the process become more humble. We become lighter and feel freer.

For myself, the most important benefit of practicing gratitude and having an attitude of gratitude is it keeps me positive and happy. Even on the tough days, there are always at least 3 things I can find to be grateful for, and if I am having a really bad day, I can read past entries in my journal to remind me of what's really important in my life and all the goodness I already possess. Being grateful instantly changes my perspective and I can go on and have a great day!

Now, several years later, I am married to the love of my life, living in 2 countries (Canada and Austria), am a transformational coach, healer, founder and host of Awaken To Happiness Now Telesummit. I am contributing on a global stage by facilitating change in thousands of people worldwide, generating revenue from multiple revenue streams, and truly living the life of my dreams. Creating my life as I choose by choosing what feels right for me. Life really is good and it can be for you as well! Wishing you an abundance of joy, love, happiness, and prosperity.

# LOVE

# #LOVE

## the truest of emotions

# Tandy Elisala

### Arizona, United States of America

## *Finding Roses*

### "A Beautiful Story of Life, Death, and Unconditional Love"

April 30, 2012, my mother was admitted to the hospital for pneumonia. With her COPD, congestive heart failure, asthma, diabetes, severe stage four-kidney failure, large blistering wounds accompanying severe leg swelling, and the rattling breathing sounds, she's in bad shape.

When my daughter Sarah and I visited my mom, she looked different. She appeared resigned, sullen, and quiet. Usually when she's in hospitals, she has a long list of things to bring from home. This time was different. As Sarah lay across her grandma's hospital bed, my mom started caressing Sarah's hair. As we left, my mom asked Sarah to do a quick dance and sing something for her.

You see, Sarah's always been the dramatic one who loves to dance and be the center of attention and laughter in o u r  h o m e . Her bubbly personality and contagious love for life brought joy to my parents. Sarah did a little dance twirl thing and my mom smiled and said, "Thank you, Sarah. I love you." Sarah said "I love you, too, Grandma" and gave her a hug. I gave my mom a hug and said, "I love you, Mom." She replied, "I love you more" to which I replied, "I love *you* more."

As I said that, we are in the hallway, leaving her room and, as I turned back, I could see her smiling. This was the last time I would hug her and feel her embrace, to see her beautiful smile and feel her unwavering love beaming from every ounce of her physical being. As we walked down the hall to the elevator, I was fighting back the tears. This was the second time in my life my mom said, "I love you more."

I couldn't help shake the feeling this time was different. Around 10:00 pm, I received a call from my mom's nurse saying she went into cardiac arrest. She was unable to breathe on her own. They put her on a ventilator and moved her to Intensive Care. They wanted me to be aware of her changing condition. Between calls from the doctors and nurses, and calls to my sister, Felicity, I didn't get much sleep that night. My dad was scheduled for gall bladder surgery the next day at another hospital. After letting him know of my mom's changing condition, he decided to proceed with surgery.

The next morning as I completed pre-op details with my dad's nurse, my oldest granddaughter Amanda called from my mom's hospital. She's crying and had a panic in her voice I had never heard before. She quivered, "You need to get down here right now, Mom. You need to be here now!" My mom's blood pressure was around 40/25. I told Amanda to tell my mom she needs to hold on until her babies get there. As Amanda told her this, my mom's blood pressure teetered around 70/50.

I started shaking and I could feel my pulse beating hard and my blood pressure rising. Leaning up against the counter in the next room to maintain balance, I immediately called Felicity and told her she needed to leave work and get to the hospital immediately. Leaving my dad's belongings with the nurse and relying on a friend to take care of my dad, I kissed my dad, told him what was happening, and, with a sad face, he said, "Tell her I love her."

I am so thankful Amanda was at the hospital with my mom as her condition went from bad to worse within hours. One hour we were talking hospice and the next we were reconciling with the fact she would die right there in the hospital room. Felicity, Amanda, Sarah, my son Steven, and I stood around her bed. I noticed all of us were touching her in some way. Over the next 5½ hours, we all watched her condition deteriorate. I did notice, however, when we would get up close to her head and talk to her, her vitals improved… for a few moments. During this time, we cried, we sang, we prayed, and we talked to her as we played some of her favorite songs.

When we played ABBA's song "Dancing Queen," her left foot moved through the song as if it was her way of dancing. Then, we each sat around her bed, held hands, and went around the room saying what we were thankful and grateful for about her.

We did this several times around the room. We told her it was okay to go. The hospital priest came and prayed with us several times. We talked about some of our funny moments with my mom. We would ask her questions as if she could answer them. We played songs which had messages of love as dedications from us to her.

Most songs we played for us *all* and sang too, were songs she loved. We all talked about memories we had of her over the years. We told jokes. We cried some more. It really was beautiful.

It was a serendipitous moment when we all looked at each other and felt complete. Immediately, my mom's remaining life force energy slowly sucked away. Nurses told us it was close and said to let her know when we were ready to turn off the machine. Felicity and I touched our mom, looked at each other across the bed, and gave the okay to terminate life support.

With the machine off, we all sat and waited and watched and cried. A few minutes later, my mom opened her glossy eyes, turned her head asking what was going on. The nurse came to her bedside and explained what was going on. Confused, she looked at me and I repeated what happened and gently told her she was dying. I asked her to shake her head if she understood what I was saying. She nodded and looked over at Felicity. Sobbing, Felicity told her it was okay to go and she would be okay. Mom turned her head back over to me and whispered, "Carmine."

I said Carmine (her cat) would be safe and taken care of. I promised her we would take care of him. She nodded. She then said "Bill." I've never heard my mom refer to our dad by his first name. Without skipping a beat, I asked if she remembered he was scheduled for surgery that day and told her he was in recovery and he would be okay. Her face softened and she leaned into her pillow.

In the moments before her death and with everyone she cherished most by her side, everyone touched and caressed her. What happened next was almost indescribable. We all felt the moment she left; the moment she left her body. Weeping sounds abound, I found myself screaming. I screamed at the top of my lungs. Crying and screaming, I felt every ounce of anger; rage, sorrow, love, and relief come out of my screaming mouth. I felt like a part of me was gone. I wanted her life force energy back. I needed my mom. Flashing before my eyes, on a screen running across my mind, it seemed like every single memory of us came whipping across my swirling head. I couldn't stop crying. I was inconsolable.

Time of death: May 2, 2012, at 3:25 pm. It was gloomy outside the entire day until the moment she died. Then, the sun came out and was beaming from her hospital window. Her soul was free. No more pain. What a beautiful thing. The day wouldn't have been so synergistic, beautiful, and peaceful had it been any other way. It was what happened after my mom's death that would demonstrate her unconditional love.

Days after her death, I was at a local spiritual bookstore and purchased a beautiful ceramic angel statue with the saying "A Mother's Unconditional Love" underneath. Days later was Mother's Day. My spiritual mentor, Tarra, emailed me and said my mom hopes I enjoy the flowers for Mother's Day. The kids got me an edible arrangement package in the shape of flowers. I thought that was what she was talking about. Then, I saw it...the very angel statue I just bought was of a mother putting her arms around her daughter and giving her a bouquet of roses. Wow. I got chills all over.

I treasure this statue and give thanks for the amazing spiritual connection I have with my mom. The day after solidifying this chapter title and story, I received a beautiful message from my aunt with a recording of her singing "The Rose" to me.

She said my mom and grandma kept insisting she sing this song to me and it would make sense. It certainly did! I love signs from the Universe.

# Grace Mauzi

Utah, United States of America

## *For the Love of Jamie*

It was a perfect spring day. We are visiting in Connecticut after a few days looking at schools for my youngest daughter. But there was something nagging me, something so deep in my soul I couldn't ignore it, yet I couldn't figure out what it was. The only thing I could possibly understand was one of my children was in deep serious danger of her life. We were at a deli and saw my oldest daughter's first boyfriend. He asked, "Is Jamie still so bossy?" And I knew Jamie was the child.

I got a text, "Jamie fell and it's bad" one moment after from her sister Jeanee (aged 18). But I couldn't say anything to anyone. I couldn't give that text any reality. I tried to believe it was her knee again. But I knew, it was her life this time.

An eternity passed. Maybe twenty minutes. My ex-husband, my stepdaughter (aged 35) and my youngest (aged 14) and I went to the beach. Somehow those three got to the water and I was standing alone. My phone rang. It was Jeanee's phone. The sister, who was with Jamie at the Free Ski World Cup Championships in Whistler, Canada, and who had texted me.

I don't know what she said to me. But the Doctor or paramedic got on the phone. I asked, "Is my daughter alive." He said, "Yes, at the moment." I screamed and fell to the ground. I was no longer present in my body. I was with Jamie. When the others got to me, I instinctively handed the phone to Amy. She's an anesthesiologist. The others made words as we went back to the car. I was being held by Jilly, my youngest, who is 4 inches taller than me and a hockey player. I don't know how Jeff made it to the car and I couldn't understand their words.

Through a great deal of confusion and fog, no passports, figuring out how to get them, Jilly and I arrived in Vancouver where Jamie, Jeanee, and Jeff were. The hours I was on the flight without phone service or internet were terrifying. I desperately wanted to be with her before she left us. I was truly terrified she would die before I got to her.

When I got to her, she was so dead looking. BUT she was ALIVE. And I knew there was only one thing I could give her. And that was every ounce of my love. She knew I was there. She sent me a message and the nurse also told me her monitors reacted to me. But I knew where it truly counts, in my heart.

All I knew was she was alive, in a coma, and I could love her in person, and that was it. The rest was completely unknown. I reinforced my decision. I would love my baby, my child, at any level of life she had in her. If she was in a vegetative state for life, then I would love her and care for her. And anything else she could do would be a gift of love and life from God.

The next 24 hours were more agony. She had a bolt in her head to measure the pressure and oxygen of her brain. We had our first speck of humor slip in. Her brain pressure went from -1 to 4. Some doctor type person said, "It's official, Jamie is a certified airhead. She must have had some extra air in there all the time since she still doesn't have any pressure in her brain." Humor, laughing, finding the lighter side to everything, looking for fun, and being acutely aware of how loving and love is directly related to each other were an integral part of our recovery process for Jamie.

I was adamant that not one single negative word or even thought be around or about Jamie. There was one intern in Vancouver who none of us liked. On his morning rounds, he told Amy and me, directly in front of Jamie while she was in her coma in Vancouver that she would take at least two years to be able to do anything. It would be very hard work, and ONLY if she were able to really try hard and struggle could she possibly be close to normal. She woke up slowly.

About a week after she was officially awake, she kept asking if she would ever be normal and saying all she wanted was to be normal. I kept saying, of course she would be normal. One time she replied, "But it will take two years and be so hard." That's when I said, "Oh Jamie we left that place and came here because we believe in you and we know we'll have fun reopening all your brain pathways. There's no date to when you'll recover fully. We are just going to dance, sing and love every minute of your recovery" "You mean it doesn't have to be hard? I don't have to struggle? And I can recover as fast as I want to?" And from that moment on Jamie has been all smiles, has known she can fully recover, and been utterly hysterical.

Besides love and laughter, I also made sure that as a family, we all brought out our strengths and expertise. We used supplements we knew were expressly related to brain healing and functioning, as well as, for general healing. On a daily basis, and for hours, her sister Janet did Reiki healing energy, sacral cranial work, and regular massage. We did cross midline movements with Jamie's limp body. We did specific aromatherapy. We had pictures printed and taped up all around her room. Jeanee was in charge of decorating every room she was in. Jeanee loves interior design, and by the time we were in rehab, Jamie's room looked like a college dorm room rather than anything close to a hospital room. We even had a hammock hung up on the overhead body lifter for patients who weren't able to move.

From the start, Jilly, the youngest sister instinctively took it upon herself to take care of Jeanee and me. She made sure we ate, a near impossibility, and slept, even harder, and even had moments to take walks and be outside. Without her care, neither Jeanee nor I could have maintained our strength and courage.

And Jamie's dad, my ex-husband, chose to be kind and gentle. To believe I would and could be able to give Jamie everything she needed to heal to her fullest strength. He chose to believe in Jamie. He was available to do any task or store run I felt was even the slightest bit necessary. When Jamie had an intense diaper rash, he literally ran out of the hospital to get her the Desitin when I asked him for it.

As soon as Jamie was able to eat real food, my sister and Janet made and brought to the hospital all the food Jamie and the whole family needed and wanted. We sat together for every meal in the community room and ate together as we always do. This family meal time was and is part of the basic practice and magic of our family.

I also knew there was magic to healing. And a certain kind of knowing brought things together. In the winter, about three months before Jamie's accident, I had a strong urge I must remember all the lullabies, I had to practice them, and I would be needing them. And I did. For hours at a time I would sing those lullabies, those sounds which were part of Jamie's first memories, sounds that gave her peace and solace in her first moments of life. In her rebirth, I know they gave her the same peace and solace, and some extra strength to know we were with her.

From this music came other music. Our dear family friend, who is a professional violinist, sent us many of his recordings. The first thing Jamie specifically asked for was his music. Then one day Jeanee and I played her music from just before her crash, Taylor Swift, as well as, others. Jamie didn't know her own last name, how old she was, or much of anything else, but she knew her songs. Every single word and tune. "Style", by Taylor Swift was her all time, ultimate favorite and we would play it for hours at a time.

In addition to music, there was movement. As I said, while she was in her coma and just coming out, we did lots of cross midline movement, and when she woke up, we walked, danced, did hours of Physical therapy. Movement was and is an integral part of her recovery.

And from movement came the world, the great outdoors. Even before she could stand on her own, I brought her outside, for the energy of life. We went to a park the first day she was able to walk that far, with a gait belt on, and I took off her shoes and socks to walk in the grass. She was clearly delighted by life.

Life for Jamie isn't complete without people. Long before she was awake, we encouraged friends and relatives to send us videos. We appreciated every person who sent love, prayers, magenta ceremonies, did snow dances, gave her positive energy, and wished her well. This passing of love in whatever form, purpose, and belief system without a doubt helped Jamie recover and blossom. We'll never know everything and everyone, but we all felt the massive amount of world love flow to Jamie. As soon as she wanted friends to come to the hospital, there wasn't a day without at least a half dozen spread out throughout the day.

Love, laughter, each of us doing our specialties, eating homemade food together, magic, music, movement, outdoors, and people were all integral to Jamie's healing. One without the others wouldn't have been enough. And all together gave Jamie the opportunity to be herself, to know that she was and will forever be the amazing, whimsical, loving, lovable, intelligent, athletic person she is. Now she'll forever also have the gift of life to share and inspire others. Where she leads us will be a journey of loving life and living love.

# Kristina Mendez Matejova

## *Vulnerability*

### London, United Kingdom

I sat down and cried. Tears were rolling down my cheeks and I didn't care to stop them. The therapy room felt cold and empty just like my heart. I felt abandoned, like a child curled up under a blanket waiting to be rescued. That's when my psychotherapist walked in to start our fortnightly session.

I explained how I felt lonely, abandoned, no one's priority. I have never been anyone's priority; and I suppose no one has been mine; my walls made sure of that. The walls I built around my heart to protect myself from all the hurt in the world. They were effective in keeping me in, but also in keeping everyone else out. I could not see that. Not until now.

The two weeks leading to this particular moment in time, to the breakdown in the therapy room, were rather challenging. Almost every appointment I had got cancelled. I felt deserted, crushed, scrunched up into an ugly ball that did not make it into the paper waste basket and no one could be bothered to pick it up.

A hug. That was all I needed. That's what I got, luckily. My therapist ensured my survival that day by a simple gesture of friendship, a warm embrace. She has suggested that people didn't take my needs into account because they didn't know what my needs were. It hit me. How right she was. I felt the truth of the suggestion resonating deep in my soul. I worked so hard on keeping people out, putting on a brave face and keeping my weaknesses to myself that I succeeded. I never asked for help, never reached out to others when I was in need, never told anyone what was important to me; that they were important to me. So how could they have known that if they cancel our arranged day out, it will cut me deep inside and make me feel rejected, lonely and abandoned?

My therapist suggested that from that moment on I allow myself to be vulnerable in the presence of my most trusted friends. To tell them of my fears and insecurities, to ask them for help when in need. "No fucking way", was my initial response. Everything within me rose like a swarm of bees poked by a stick on fire. She could not be serious! She was. Very. And she used that magic word that I am unable to resist. Challenge.

So there I was challenging myself in my usual fashion of 'all or nothing' and going right for it. The next day I spoke to my flat mate and closest friend. I felt so apprehensive I could barely get the words out. I told her that there might be times I feel hurt and lonely and I asked whether I could reach out to her in such times. Her response was so overwhelmingly positive that I was taken aback by it. There was not even a fraction of a second of hesitation before I got an 'of course, hun, I am always here if you need me' and a massive reassuring hug. She meant it, just as I mean it when I tell her I am there for her. I realised that it made me happy to help people, to be there for them in their hour of need. I also realised that if they did not reach out to me if they did not allow me to help them, I would be deprived of this pleasure. It occurred to me that I have been robbing my friendships of depth in connection because I required my friends to be vulnerable without allowing myself to be so.

Since that day, every friend I met up with I've had the same 'vulnerability' conversation. Every single time this caused more or less intense shift in our relationship, making our connection deeper, truer and more authentic. Instead of feeling lonely, I've been feeling blessed with the quantity and quality of my friendships. Most people responded to my openness by opening up themselves and admitting they struggle with asking for help, like me, for fear of rejection. We made pacts. Pacts of strong people making a solemn promise to each other to reach out, not withdraw and to be there for the other.

With each friend, the opening up got easier. I was not choking anymore, shifting my eyes uncomfortably, blushing or fidgeting in my seat. My openness, honesty and willingness to be vulnerable were met with compassion, acceptance and more of the same. I suppose that now I felt comfortable and secure in my friendships, being vulnerable did not feel like a challenge anymore, yet there was a feeling within that the work is not yet finished. The feeling was right. I met a man.

Why it is so much harder to be open, honest and vulnerable with whom you aspire to have the deepest and greatest connection there is, than it is with your friends and family?

I feel very attracted to this guy, he seems to be more or less exactly what I was looking for. I feel connected to him on a physical, intellectual as well as spiritual level. But instead of joy and pleasure I feel threatened and anxious. I feel scared that he might not feel the same and no matter what he says or does can change that, simply because I don't trust him to tell the truth. I don't believe he is willing to be that honest and vulnerable, because I am not. Projecting self onto others is a subject for a whole new chapter. Even just the idea of telling him how I feel scares the hell out of me. It's not like I want to go on one knee and pledge my love and life to him forever, neither am I asking him to respond in a certain way.

I don't need him to be as open with me as I want to be with him, although I do believe it takes two to tango in establishing a deeper connection. I just really want to share what is within me. There is so much inside of me that I feel like I am going to explode if I do not reach out, yet I am mute. Illogical and irrational fear has sealed my lips. My mouth is dry and my heart is trying to break through my ribcage just at the thought of saying: "I am confused. I feel disconnected. I am scared of the intensity of the feelings I have for you as they came as a surprise, completely unexpected.

The feelings of freedom, love and joy are mixed with the thoughts of 'shoulds' and expectations built in by my environment, society and upbringing. I think twice (or ten times) before every message I send, before every word I say. Is it the right time to say this? Is this the right wording? Shall I say this at all? Will I scare you away? Do I want you to stay?" We have known each other less than two weeks! A roller coaster of a ride. The highs are well worth it, the lows I keep hidden. Despite my promise to myself, despite my challenge, I am still not true to myself and don't share all of me despite a deep desire to do so.

Until now. I am brave. I am letting him read this. Now.

Through this experience, I've come to understand that willingness to be vulnerable, to expose our insecurities, is the ultimate act of bravery. If you can expose your perceived weaknesses, reach out to another in a time of need, tell someone how you feel despite not knowing how they might respond, then you are a hero. You are an inspiration to all humanity.

You are allowing the deepest of connections to happen with any human being you communicate with. You are allowing the other to be completely themselves in a safe and nurturing environment of your presence. By opening up and letting them in, you are allowing them to do the same. One by one, we can transform all our relationships and all our interactions with others. We can bring peace and compassion to the whole world one embrace at the time. But someone has to start this revolution. I am in. Come and join me. Go on. Be brave. Be you.

# Tahari Thomas

Texas, United States of America

## *Love Knows No Boundary*

**"Just when things look like they are falling apart, they are actually falling into place; the divine place they should be for everyone involved."**

**– Iyanla Vanzant**

I was, lying on the floor hurting, crying and broken. It was a familiar feeling, but there was a slight difference in me. I was no longer interested in blaming others; I decided to take a long look at myself. "Why do I keep finding myself in the same types of situations?" I asked. I was in the same familiar place, just a different catalyst. I realized this couldn't have been everyone else's fault. I played a role in this too, and if there was going to be a change, it was going to have to start with me.

I was "in love", or at least I thought I was. My heart was broken and I couldn't understand why I kept ending up with the short end of the stick. This wasn't the first time I felt like I was "in love" and it certainly wasn't the first time I had been heartbroken. My definition of love was warped and was based on the relationships I had observed my parents, family members, and friends have with others. Most importantly, my definition was based on what I was taught about God.

I had always viewed God as some sort of authority figure whose love I had to try to keep to secure my salvation and make it to heaven. I believed I was supposed to do everything God wanted of me or He would get upset with me, turn His back on me, or even worse, send me to hell for not obeying His Commandments. To make matters worse, I discovered I was a lesbian, and we all are aware of what the Bible says about homosexuality. I was actively struggling with this daily, believing I was going to hell because I was attracted to women and actively engaging in lesbian relationships. I didn't realize how much this affected me at the time, but it was one of the major turning points which have been a consistent part of my spiritual journey. I was taught my God either had or would abandon me because of who I was attracted to and chose to be in romantic relationships with.

On top of that, my biological father had also abandoned me, which was something my family didn't openly discuss. I didn't think it was a big deal because I have a father who has loved me unconditionally from the moment I was born and continues to do so now, but there was still the aspect of "not being good enough" for my biological father to want a relationship with me.

Both of these things deeply affected me and carried over into my romantic relationships. I was constantly wondering when the other shoe was going to drop for my lover - when was she going to realize I wasn't what she wanted me to be and leave? As a result, I was always trying to figure out what I had to do to make sure she continued to want to be with me and love me. This was the basis I was using in all my intimate relationships and many of my relationships with friends and family. I was a chameleon constantly trying to adapt to what others wanted me to do and be to be "loved". Recognizing this was a true eye opening experience. At this point in my life, I didn't know who I truly was or what I really wanted, but that was about to change.

I reached out to my cousin for some advice. I couldn't name it then, but I knew there was something different about her and how she approached life. She had had her spiritual awakening and she helped re-introduce me to spirituality. She advised me to focus on me and why I kept attracting the same experiences into my life. She introduced me to the book "In the Meantime: Finding Yourself and the Love You Want" by Iyanla Vanzant. I immediately dove into the book and this marked the beginning of my spiritual journey and awakening.

This book got me thinking about three important questions: *What am I feeling? What do I want? What am I feeling about what I want?* Those were questions I was determined to answer. For the next several months, I did quite a bit of soul searching, painstakingly trying to answer those questions for myself. Many nights I cried and cried. I felt lost and confused.

As I was reflecting on my life, I noticed I had a lack of confidence and self-esteem in my personal life. This led to me being very needy and I found myself smothering my partners because I was afraid they would leave me. I had serious abandonment issues that were being played out in both my intimate relationships and my friendships. These abandonment issues also resulted in allowing people to do whatever they wanted in my life, regardless of whether or not I was comfortable with it – basically being a doormat. I was living life as a victim of circumstances and people, which is the lowest level of energy a person could filter life through. I was often frustrated and broken, feeling I was being taken advantage of, but doing nothing about it. I realized I didn't truly love myself because I didn't honor myself and allowed others to dump any and everything on my life. I was determined to interrupt this pattern and make a major change in my life, starting with learning how to love me.

As I continued to read through the book, I was discovering things about myself I didn't know existed. I was finally able to leave the victim level, but jumped into anger, which is another low level of energy, yet slightly better than the victim energy. I became angry with everyone, even God. I then realized I wasn't really angry with God, but with what I had been taught about him. This wasn't serving me either, so I decided I was going to take responsibility for my life, start taking the steps necessary to heal all my past issues, and begin to grow into the person I was meant to be. In making this decision, I consciously moved to a higher level of energetic response to life, taking *responsibility* for my life.

I've spent the last few years living mainly at this level. I've experienced lots of personal growth and have learned to love myself. I've also spent time in some higher levels of energy such as servicing others and finding opportunities to grow in all situations in life. I am now in a loving relationship with the woman who originally made me question how I governed my romantic relationships and was the catalyst in starting my spiritual journey. Our time apart allowed us to grow and really learn what love was all about. The relationship we enjoy now has been built on a solid foundation with clear intentions on what love is about and how we will "show up" and be advocates for each other.

Throughout these trying times, I realized I wanted to assist other people in their personal and spiritual growth, so I decided to go to coaching school and become a certified life coach. When I am in a coaching environment or teaching a class about personal development, I feel alive and I know this was what I was put on this earth to do.

Currently, I am in the process of discovering my true beliefs about a higher power, possibly God and what, if any, place this divine being will have in my life. This is an extremely frightening task, as I've ripped the religious foundation I grew up with from under me. I am now embarking on a journey to discover the Divine for myself. As I look at how things in nature and the cosmos work, I can see there is a greater intelligence at play that we cannot fully understand. This leads me to believe there is a divine intelligence or energy at work in this world and in our lives, whether we chose to recognize it or not. Some may call it God, others call it the Universe or Divine Intelligence. The labels don't mean much to me, but it *is* my intention to learn more and find harmony and peace as I continue to live the life I was born to live.

# Karena Virginia

New Jersey, United States of America

## *Life*

Our father came to New York City from Italy when he was in his twenties. He didn't speak more than a word of English. Giulio Ferrari. How we all adored him. What courage, character, discipline and charisma this beautiful man carried through his life. His love expanded beyond limits, and it was shared with millions. Giulio was a passionate man who loved Opera, cooking, speaking four different languages fluently with his strong Roman accent. And, Giulio was a fun loving man who made everyone laugh all the time. We danced, sang, traveled and played games together growing up. Life was bright and beautiful. The easiest thing for daddy to say was "Do you know how much I love you?"

Our beautiful mother, Beryl James Ferrari, traveled by boat to America from England in her twenties. Her plan was to practice nursing while visiting the States. Mom's first stop was New York City. She worked at the hospital, I was born in, St. Luke's Roosevelt. Beryl is gentle. Her British accent is so proper and pure. I think our mother is the most honest woman I've ever met in my life. The truth is she has never once lied to us. While growing up at times we almost wanted her to fib just a bit, but mummy has always used honesty, honor and grace only. This isn't an exaggeration. Lovely Beryl, how we adore you.

Beryl and Giulio were the couple at the party everyone wanted to be with. Giulio's aura was so huge, when he walked into a room, the entire space illuminated. Mommy with her gentle and humble personality would often say with her English dialect, "Oh, Giulio, shhhh." But, daddy kept dancing. This dynamic they shared was mesmerizing to so many.

My childhood bedroom, bicycle, favorite dress and lollipop were always pink. I was what our daughter, Gabriella, would call a girly girl. Yet, there was always something in this pink shade that was recognized beyond the horizon in the sky. For, to me pink always symbolized love. It still does. There is a rose quartz in my left hand as these words manifest. My heart loves and has always loved so deeply. Yes...beautiful. But, if you are a softy, you know how emotionally challenging it can be to feel everything so deeply from the very depths of your being.

Here's where the duality comes into the picture. Growing up in a public school environment confused me, because from my deepest being I knew there was more than math, science and history. It was boring. What was in the sky so high beyond right and wrong, and transcending the human psyche? There was something so beautiful which this soul was longing to touch. The spirit remembered home in the heavens where all the angels danced and played music with love...yes, the same love I was carrying in my heart on this earth plane. Sometimes the urge to play with the angels was so powerful, math, science and history lessons were ignored.

The tall skinny girl with brown hair who wanted blonde hair had her head in the clouds. The teachers called mom and dad saying, "She is a very smart girl, but she is daydreaming all the time." Beautiful mommy and daddy were worried, and Karena, being the middle child, learned how to please her parents. Studying became a discipline. College was a necessity. How could we disappoint mom and dad after everything they were doing for us?

I was popular in high school, and voted all sorts of things from most understanding to funniest in the senior yearbook. I was captain of the cheerleading team, along with my two best friends. Yet, who knew this inner longing was felt so deeply in my heart? Hired at my first job at sixteen, mommy would drive me to the institute for severely mentally handicapped adults where I worked after school. Many of the patients residing in this home didn't speak or walk, and they were fully developed adults. While feeding them, bathing them and changing their diapers, I knew they comprehended more than the doctors thought possible. We connected so deeply energetically that ten years later when visiting one of the inpatients, Sally, using sign language, asked me for her applesauce. It was the treat I gave her every evening before the drive home. I just knew there was more to this thing we call life.

While in college studying and training in voice, movement and performance, I met a dear friend, Radha, who moved to New York from Berkley, California. She and I researched chakras, energy and mysticism. We ate tofu in place of meat, and meditated together to reach the pink sky which was residing deep within our hearts. Stillness. Yet, I studied and worked very hard at the earthly goals from this physical wavelength, as well. I needed to graduate college with honors to give back to my father who worked so hard his entire life to provide for his family. So, I did. Was it worth it? No. Did it bring me closer to the rose light in the heavens? No. Did I keep pushing myself? Yes.

After college, I moved to New York City to begin a career in acting and modeling. Giulio was so proud when he saw his daughter in commercials and on a Soap Opera. For, daddy did not think he was worthy of success. He came from a poor family in Italy, and lost his father at a young age. Our father had a difficult life, and we never really knew this until he passed away. He worked so hard every single day to move beyond insecurities, and no one ever knew he carried self- doubt.

I know this because the apple doesn't fall far from the tree. It looks like Karena has it all together on the outside. Yes, a beautiful husband and two healthy fabulous children. This is a divine blessing, and a blessing I hold sacred and dear from the very depths of my being. This house we live in is beautiful. It's like a castle. Charles works as a successful attorney in the Wall Street area of New York City. My closet is gigantic and it's filled with designer bags and clothes. I am being so truthful right now, and in no way is this being shared from ego. This openness and expression is flowing through me to acknowledge that no matter what we have externally, it will never fill the light in our heart. Only love fills this place. We share with the world very generously, and the gratitude in giving is so much sweeter than receiving anything of physical nature. I love giving...sometimes maybe even too much.

Yet, we must always honor our truth, and, the beauty in all of this as St. Francis of Assisi said is "It is in giving, we receive." I've experienced this observing others and myself. A dear friend of mine gave up everything in her large home to move into a small apartment. She just gave everything away...fancy furniture she purchased from a famous designer, crystals, linens, china, valuable gifts. We were all a bit overwhelmed when she was allowing everything to flow into the universe, including her husband! Well, this beautiful divine being is now by destiny in a job that pours in thousands of dollars a day. Does she share? Oh, yes. Does the flow continue? Of course.

This is one of the laws of the universal changes taking place on this planet today. Money is being used here as an example, because when we talk about prosperity it's often thought of as green. Yet, this is the way abundance works with everything in life. If you want a baby, give your motherly and fatherly love to another baby. Breathe deeply and have faith as you create the most beautiful gift for your friends' baby showers. The key is to give from a place of love so deeply in the heart. It can be challenging when we are afraid of losing everything, so we meditate and align ourselves with the grace of spirit. We take moments to reflect on gratitude, for being grateful is another way to enhance our abundance. Say "thank you." There is so much to be appreciative for in your life right now. Focus on the divine gifts all around you.

Taking a step back from the flow of the stream of consciousness at this moment, let me address the topic of true happiness. Of course, I don't have all the answers, yet one thing I know for sure is happiness comes from serving others. What happens in the glamorous performance industry? Yes...singing, dancing and acting for an audience is a lovely way to share. It is a magical form of energy exchange. Yet, the art in the acting is quite often lost in the mix of competition and doubt. Broadway acting can become just " a job." Film and television acting can become a monotonous and cold career of shooting the same thing over and over again. When modeling, you become an object...where is the soul in all of this? In my opinion...it's often lost, sad, repressed and very hungry for true connection and light. We have this unfortunate misconception that being a rock star makes life perfect. Having all the money in the world, and living in a grand home with beautiful objects around will fill the void. Yet, then when is it ever enough? Only when we become altruistic and we give more than we receive...well, that's my opinion.

Many of my girlfriends who are still working and living in New York City and/or Los Angeles as actresses never feel thin enough or attractive enough. Every facial line is analyzed. In fact, many of the most physically beautiful women you see are the most insecure. On the outside they may appear "perfect" or "not even real", while on the inside many hearts are aching.

We are being guided to recognize a very important lesson in this thing we call life. We must stop comparing ourselves to others if we want to find true happiness. We must understand the law of nature. The sun shines on all... all flowers bloom and all flowers die. Roses do not compete with other roses on the rose bush. They blossom from love, sunshine, nourishment and love. Roses are miracles which arrive from the vibration of love and light. We are as well. Life is short, and at the end of life, all that will really matter is how much we have LOVED.

# Alison Collins

New South Wales, Australia

## *Bloom*

**"And the day came...when the risk to remain tight in the bud was more painful then to bloom! Make today your day to BLOOM!"**

"Be careful what you ask for" was ringing in my head. At 29, a year after my first emotionally void, unhappy marriage ended (I was 19 when I married). I met the most beautiful man who treated me well, was loving, kind, gentle, and just all in all, a really great guy. He had all the wonderful qualities I craved in a man and a relationship.

However, unfortunately for me, I didn't believe I was worthy of such a love. Perhaps you have found yourself in this same situation...craving love yet feeling unworthy at the same time?

This relationship would end when I met a man who was a perfect match for me; a man who would enforce those already nega*tive beliefs, I held about myself!* These beliefs were formed early in my childhood as the result of trauma, living with an alcoholic father and a disempowered, suppressed and depressed mother...I had no real understanding as to what a "healthy" self-esteem or relationship was. After many years of heartbreak battling infertility problems, ectopic pregnancies, miscarriages and so many failed IVF attempts, my craving to be a mother was like a drug addict who craves heroin.

I thought I had hit the jackpot meeting this man. He was so charming, so handsome, so appealing <u>and</u> his wife had walked out on him and their three children...BINGO!

At last I found my family, at last I could take care of babies, and they were just babies, 12 months, 5 and 6 years old.

I spent so long consumed with my anger and judgement towards his ex-wife the children's mother." How could a woman walk out on her children, how could a mother leave her babies!!!" At the time because I was caught up in this,

I refused to see what was really going on; by the time I did, I was already madly in love with him and the children.

I came to understand my unmet need for love was so toxic (unhealthy) I missed all the warning signs. I just thought how wonderful that *someone, he, wanted me* to be with him 24/7. My understanding of love was warped; I thought the first time he acted jealous, *wow he must really love me!*

He was an extremely violent, jealous, possessive, intimidating, manipulative, mentally and sexually disturbed man. The reason his first wife, the mother of his children left her children was simply for survival. She was terrified he would kill her if she took them. She had left to stay alive. I would do the same, but it would take 11 years to do so.

They say a breakdown is an "opportunity for a "breakthrough", boy did I have a "breakthrough!"

I can still remember the day as if it was yesterday. It was 1999 (and no, I wasn't partying like it was 1999!!!). However, I was just about to experience one hell of an opportunity! I was living (or rather dying) inside this abusive 11 year marriage. By this stage, I had been stripped of all my power, self-worth, self-esteem; was isolated from all my friends and family, completely controlled, manipulated and abused sexually, physically, mentally and emotionally, yet somehow something inside of me wanted to live, but not like this.

On a morning after a particularly violent night, I was standing with my back up against the kitchen bench, staring blankly ahead, I was watching myself. It was as if I was standing outside of myself. Totally disconnected from myself, my body, and my feelings. As if I was made of glass. Suddenly I saw myself fracture into millions of small pieces all over the kitchen floor then, all those pieces disappeared down a big, black hole of nothingness.

I had no idea how long I stood there, but later I "found" myself standing in the shower with all my clothes on. I couldn't take my clothes off. I remember being terrified, have I lost my mind, why won't my body work, why can't I take my clothes off. I was later to understand the years of trauma caught up and my body/mind couldn't cope.

Looking back it was the best thing to ever happen really. It was as if I had to "fall apart" to come back together, in a new and different way. My life changed on Valentine's Day 14th February 2000. I received a phone call; my father had died. I hadn't seen my family for 3 years. I went to the funeral and cried and cried, but if I am totally honest, most of those tears were for me. I didn't want to go back to my marriage but I knew after the funeral I had to go back there.

After the wake I returned for what would be one last night. Something inside me knew this would be a life changing (or life ending night). I had begun to hide clothing and essentials and a little bit of money in the back of a deep cupboard and would pray he wouldn't find them. If you are in a domestic violence situation this is called your "Escape Plan" and it can save your life.

I was right. That night would end up one of the most violent nights I've ever endured. It was as if he knew I was going to leave him. I recall a "cold as steel" energy filled me that night. I remember looking into the madness in his eyes as he was over the top of me (with the telephone chord in his hands trying to wrap it around my throat). I made a declaration. I was getting out of here, even if he broke every bone in my body. It was if another part of me came to my rescue that night...something bigger than me...I am unsure but I will always be eternally grateful.

The next day was business and life as usual. We had a business together so we would go to work like "normal" people. No one ever realized the madness which was my life. When we arrived at work and opened for business, it was busy with many customers in our shop. I was serving one of them that morning, when I am sure an angel appeared to me in the form of a woman who pushed a card across the counter, underneath the card she was buying.

I turned over the card and read "Women's Emergency Refuge". By the time I looked up, she was gone. Just 5 minutes after I received the card, my sign, my proof this was happening, he leaned over and said "I am glad your father is dead" and laughed in my face I can't explain why this would become the defining moment...but I just knew it was mine. There were plenty of people around so I knew I was safe... he was a coward with everyone but me.

I went out to our office, picked up my bag, took some money from the safe (left most of it) walked past him (with smoke coming out of his ears and fire in his eyes) and walked outside. Mysteriously, a cab just "happened" to be right at the door. I asked the cab driver to take me home and could he please wait. I walked inside, opened the cupboard and took out the 4 storage bags I had hidden; filling them with as much as I could. I had to kick them down the stairs and out the front door to the lovely cab driver who was waiting to load them into the car.

I am sure he realised what was happening, he was so intent on getting me and my bags into the cab. He drove me to the train station and helped me put the bags on the train! I had so many earth angels help me get myself and those bags across train stations, upstairs and downstairs into another cab, then finally, 24 hours after I had left my Mother's home, 24 hours after I had buried my father, I was ringing her doorbell, leaving behind my marriage, my 3 step-children, my home and my business.

My life would change 360 degrees. I had begun to learn about the wounds from my past and how they impacted the inner beliefs I held regarding myself, life and love. I became an information junkie and threw myself into everything I could do to work through my pain, my grief, the loss of the children and my marriage. The memories of childhood molestation an 11 years of DV caused me to suffer PTSD "Post Traumatic Stress" Syndrome which also caused severe panic attacks. It was tough, painful, challenging and the grief was absolutely gut wrenching at times but I had such a passion and desire to live in the face of it all, I pushed through the pain. I now understand why I made the choices I made back then. I committed myself to working through my pain with Inner Child Healing, Breath work, counselling and a wonderful journey of inspiration, transformation and self-discovery. But mostly I learned, to love myself...I came to realize I was not only worthy, but I was pretty fabulous after all!

My passion and my purpose was birthed through this process...I was going to assist as many women as possible to own their own unique magnificence!

I've dedicated my life to teaching, empowering, supporting and nurturing women as they travel this path of healing self-discovery and self-love! Oh, and by the way, the lovely man I mentioned earlier? He arrived magically back in my life in 2002. A gift from the Universe. We married in 2003. **I now live with gentle love, deep respect, commitment and harmony, thank you John, you are my knight in shining armour. You were and are the love of my life!**

*And the day came...when the risk to remain tight in the bud was more painful then to bloom! Make today your day to BLOOM!*

# Barb Heite

Arizona, United States of America

## *Soul Wounds*

### "The Journey of Illusions of Separation to Universal Truths of Love"

How can so few words have such an impact on my soul? My skewed beliefs of my reality of me. I unwittingly, unconsciously, created a story of victimhood. Triggering myself, with careless words, creating miss communications within my own world. I automatically slip into my now unconscious habit of protecting my heart, reacting without thought. Creating an illusion of separation. It feels so necessary, my need to control the safety in my internal universe. Forming rifts, false beliefs, of myself instead of giving compassion. I stand in my self-righteousness of right or wrong, proving a point, no matter the cost of the love I hold ever present deep within the core of me.

All these feelings of unworthiness are held in check because of my twisted belief I am strong enough to stand alone. Creating walls, looking for evidence every day to fortify my fortress around my heart. My ego screams outwardly, "I don't need or want you." My heart sobbing inwardly, uncontrollably, with the understanding, recognition, of yet another missed opportunity to be seen and connect. My ego jumping in, pushing my heart aside, with unkindness's echoed inward, "You always screw things up with your neediness and clinginess." In an instant, my soul transforms back tapping into those long fought, battle-scarred opinions of myself of not mattering, not being good, smart, or pretty enough. My soul, sinks at the untruths of my ego. Feeling insignificant my heart whimpers and whispers back, "It's okay honey, you can run", and I do.

I run inward and hide in plain sight: A well paved path I created for myself. I know this pathway so well I am not even conscious of my movement toward isolation until I am there in my perceived darkness of my making. I sit in the misery, creating a safe place for the suffering of my soul with feelings of giving up, wanting to fade into nothingness, and not "BE" anymore. I inhale and anchor in deeply and feel it to my core with tears streaming down my face. Breathing in consciously through my perceived truth of heartache. I come to the awareness of my present reality, experience. In a blink of an eye, I realize this trigger of "less than" is my ticket inward to release the pain which lies dormant within me.

In these moments of giving up I am believing my emotions hold my truths. I am resisting and denying my authentic-self, creating fear through my well-practiced inner voice of self-doubt. I am prolonging unnecessary suffering out of being afraid of the unknown of letting go of false beliefs. Seeing the truth means taking responsibility and recognizing my part in creating and maintaining my role in my made up story. The actuality of my story is I know exactly how much time I've invested in protecting what I call soul wounds. I battled hard and long to collect my evidence to cement my soul wounds in the misery, beliefs, and details of my stories, that were meant to sustain the suffering. This current battle of my soul wound has seen many days on the battlefield and is one of my deepest wounds, a particular belief, I am hyper sensitive to. When I can see clearly I can call it what it is, my fear of rejection and abonnement.

I fight every step of the way toward healing to keep my version of my soul wounds in the forefront of my professed truth. My suffering becomes a place of identity on my path into ready-made darkness where I rarely shine light to explore. I become tangled in my messy thoughts and defensive words. I am so careless and become wrapped up in selfish behaviors as I struggle to hold onto what I know so well, the belief of not being enough. In these moments, of being selfish, I don't even question my reaction to my soul wounds. To me, in self-centeredness, it's much easier to stay on the surface of my soul and look outward and "scream" my victim mantras. When I take a breath and create space, and relax I can "see" the information and identify my behaviors I use to hide my pain triggers which I use to descend into my self-imposed suffering.

When my feelings are snarled and interwoven with a skewed belief of my worth, my soul wounds seem next to impossible to escape. It feels so real. I am influenced by the ego looking through the off-center lenses of self-doubt, looking for evidence to fight for the cause. My ego tells me I am not worthy or good enough and I don't matter. The ego creates a frenzy of confusion and crafts the "Illusion of Disconnect". The illusion is I am somehow disconnected from my own heart, my own core and my own soul.

Each false expression experienced is an ego won battle into diminishing of my self-esteem and confidence. I am creating a desperation of "clinging" to a belief of lack, which leaves me stuck in an ever downward spiral and not moving past the pain to acceptance. The question really for myself is, "how many battles am I willing to endure to staying miserable and resisting the echoes of my universal truths? Letting the pain bubble up through the shedding of my tears I identify the sheer exhaustion of the war between my ego and soul. I can no longer ignore, resist the battle cry of my soul, as I know my inherent truths and my inner voice will not be disregarded anymore.

Breathing with awareness, I relax into thoughts which gently guide me inward to find the questions of my heart. And a question drifts through my awareness, "WHO ARE YOU?" My Soul, without hesitation and with confidence echoes the answer that vibrates through me and roots deeper into the center of me. The answer sounds so damn simple. And I feel the question vibrate through me more intensely. WHO ARE YOU? And the answers springs forth louder and with surety. I experience a washing away, a cleansing, through a burst of light through me, and I not only hear the answer, I feel the answer. I know with certainty who I am. *I AM LOVE. THAT IS IT. THE REST IS JUST DETAILS IN A STORY.*

Experiencing what feels like epic battles within of my ego attempting to conquer my soul has brought me too many truths. One being, living consciously is a choice. A path which has brought me to an awareness within to stop, look, see, feel through the pain instead of being frozen in fear of my perceived suffering. As I go beyond old soul wounds that have healed on my path, I can now see with clarity these soul wounds are just subtle reminders of my past stories which have no meaning attached because of the conscious choice to feel the pain and come to acceptance. My gift of my sight inward gave me the Understanding that resisting and fighting "what is" was and is meant for my soul to experience complete wholeness.

The deep acceptance of my perceived pain and consciously choosing to rewrite the ending to my past stories has reinforced how I define and show up in the world through understanding my inherent worth of who I am. *I am conscious of the power I hold to shape the reality of my experiences to choose from fear or love.* I know I can feel pain, but don't have to create suffering. This enlighten state of BE-ing, linked to a universal truth, a knowing, I had the power all along. That I don't need to walk into to the light because I am the light.

I cannot escape soul wounds, it is part of my humanness, my experience. It is my choice to find the gifts and lessons and to remember WHO I AM. I know with each new trigger I am given, for whatever reason, to experience, is a washing of my soul. A letting go of resisting the truth. It's my call to action to go inward a little deeper and resume the work of shifting closer to my center, my authentic self. Coming to my "ahaha" moments, creating acceptance, a new reality, belief, magic within my world.

This remembering, waking of WHO I AM has brought peace to my inner battlefield. My ego surrendering knowing the war has been lost, though many battles won. The war was an illusion of my ego to feed behaviors to separate my soul from universal truths. Once you know something you cannot un-know it and that is where the war is won, in the truths, acceptance of "what is". I know to the core of me who I am, who we all are and my purpose. The answer is simple. It is LOVE.

# Kimberly Truitt

### Colorado, United States of America

### *Your Truth is On the Inside*

It's 1975. I am a tender six year old. My mom, 23 is a single mother of two. I was an innocent blonde-haired, blue-eyed, and highly sensitive girl with a BIG heart. I often felt sensitive and desired love and attention from my mom. Impatient and frustrated due to my mom's long work days which involved two full-time jobs, I announced I wanted to run away.

To teach me what she considered a valuable life lesson, my mom packed my little red suitcase, drove me to a random street corner, and dropped me off. As I sat on the street corner shocked, devastated and hysterical with tears streaming down my face, I felt deep regret for speaking my heart - I just my wanted my mommy's attention and love. Several minutes later through the blur of my tears, I could see her driving toward me. Although relieved, the reality overwhelmed me even more. As we drove home she asked: "Are you ok? No? Kimberly, do you now understand it's not safe nor ok for you to be alone? Running away from your problems isn't the answer." The lesson I learned was if I stood up for myself and what I wanted, I would be abandoned. My mother innocently started a spiral of people pleasing to avoid abandonment. The cost was significant.

This defining moment created an effect which would ripple unconsciously through the next 30 years. This trauma painted my perceptions, influenced my decisions, created my experiences, and ultimately - determined my reality, my misguided belief; I am insignificant.

I wish I could say I discovered my value with gentle nudges, patience, and loving kindness, but that wasn't my journey. I've experienced genuine loving gestures; however, I couldn't receive or embrace love without stirring up the devastation and pain I experienced on the street corner as a little girl.

I was 36 years old, married to the love of my life and just shy of our 10th wedding anniversary. My husband was the most honorable man I had ever known; Hollywood handsome, genius-level intelligent, stand-up comedian witty, fiercely loyal, devoted, committed, and deeply in-love with me. We were one of those couples who still had the energy of newlyweds. What was there to be unhappy about? I was living the life; I had the perfect husband, house, dogs, friends, extended family, cars, vacations, a successful career, we were a power couple, living the American dream. Life was good with just one thing missing, the baby. We had been trying to get pregnant for 7 long and difficult years. We were confident we would overcome this and create the family we dreamed of. Sadly, that wasn't our ending.

Devastated, heart broken, and more than $25,000.00 later, we didn't have the family we desired and adoption wasn't an option we could agree on. Little did I know, my denial of telling my husband I wanted to be a mom no matter what, would be the start of the unraveling of my beautiful life.

I poured myself into pursuing my dream of owning my own business by becoming a Certified Coach. This was the second time in my life I was following my desires. I felt so alive, scared, inspired and purposeful in a way I had never experienced. It's empowering when we are living on purpose and expressing our very essence. The first year my business was very successful. I was blissfully happy again. Unfortunately, that was to be short lived.

Just a year and couple months into my reality as a business owner. I was surprised when I started to feel an unsettling stirring at the core of my being with moments of feeling unsafe and insecure. I found it difficult to be in conversation with my husband's family about my business and my new found beliefs: what created TruHappiness. I was waking up at 3:00 AM regularly, unable to go back to sleep, with anxiety filled days where I wanted to peel myself out of my skin layer by layer. I started to feel disconnected from this beautiful life we created. One evening as my husband and I ate dinner, I suddenly burst into tears! He asked me what was wrong, I looked up with tears streaming down my face and said: "I feel like if you knew the real me, you wouldn't love me or want to be with me anymore." I didn't understand or know where those words, thoughts or feelings were coming from. Little did I know my deeply locked away secret – the belief I was insignificant was starting to bubble to the surface.

In my coaching practice, I decided I would focus on inspiring and empowering women to discover their purpose, to create a life which was an authentic reflection of their essence; to rebel against preconceived ideals in the 21st Century. My soul gave me a resounding YES, but I didn't realize my American dream wasn't in alignment with my company's vision. We cannot do for another that which we aren't doing for ourselves. I would need to start with my own life before I could create a thriving practice to do that for others. This began the rapid unraveling of my once beautiful life.

My aha moment came one day as I expressed my feelings of abandonment to my husband. I heard a whisper, "You…Kimberly…are the one who has been doing the abandoning." I realized out of fear of abandonment by those that I loved, I had been abandoning myself. I was convinced the only way to not be abandoned was to be whom and what everyone else wanted and needed. I had created a belief that my feelings, needs, and desires were insignificant relative to those I cared about. It was my life's mission (unconsciously) to prove my significance by creating happy environments, relationships, and events in my personal and professional life. I was operating from a core belief of fear, not love. I feared everyone would discover just how unlovable and insignificant I really was.

I believe the Divine is always speaking to us through our circumstances (Messages) and relationships (Messengers). The law of vibration is faithful, we attract that which we believe; not what we think or feel. For example: My husband's unwillingness to explore adoption translated to me that my feelings and desires to be a mom were insignificant.

There are countless other experiences which all proved my belief in my insignificance. My business was one attempt to prove my significance. If I could inspire and empower significance for other women that would somehow prove I was significant. I wish I could say it did. Unfortunately, it took another 7 years for me to finally realize that no amount of love, acceptance, and success from outside myself would heal and transform my belief.

By taking responsibility for my feelings, my desires, my beliefs and my life I have the power to be truly happy and whole. When I owned that I was the one who had abandoned my desires and my outward experiences were  a reflection of my inner belief, I empowered myself to change my experiences and, therefore, my reality. The power to change my belief was an inside job all along.

As a 42-year-old reflecting back on that random street corner with my mom I discovered what she had been teaching was, "Running away is not the answer to that which you seek." The only way to happiness is facing and walking through your unhappiness. I believe my mom and my ex-husband were earth angels to support me.

When I TRUST that life is for me and not against me, when I ask what is looking to be revealed, I always receive an answer. This practice is the golden key to transcending my life challenges, and illuminating the silver lining that already exists and is just waiting to be revealed. Learning to fully accept myself, my flaws and my significance is an ever evolving journey. I will never forget the price I paid for discovering **my truth was on the inside all along**. I walked away from my beautiful life with nothing intact. Not my marriage, my heart, my beloved four-legged babies, my financial security; or my belongings.

The irony is: my significance was discovered in facing my heart break alone, I had to lose myself, what I perceived to be safe and secure to find my true and purest self. I discovered it IS ok and safe to be alone. My mom and my husband were Divine Messengers with powerful and essential Messages. Our TruHappiness is unique to each and every one of us. There isn't a one size fits all happily-ever-after.

The Law of Vibration is ever faithful. I've discovered if I don't like the results in life, I am the one who has the power to change it. Now, instead of ignoring the gentle nudges of my soul; I ask, I listen, and I take ACTion in the direction of love which always leads to my TruHappiness. We don't get what we want in life, we get who we are.

*BE Love, BE Laughter, BE SIGNIFICANT, BE JOYfully YOU. Let your light shine brightly and always follow your Soul, it knows the way to Your TruHaPpInEsS.*

# PARENTING

# #PARENTING

the ultimate gift

# Carla Wynn Hall

Alabama, United States of America

## *Three Sons, Three Stories*

### "Chicken Nuggets, Egg Foo Young and Pancakes!"

I remember as if it were yesterday. "Carla. You are pregnant". This sound penetrated my soul in 1987. I was a senior at Etowah High School. I had transferred to Etowah from Gaston because it was a bigger school. I was madly in love, or so I thought, with my first love. He also attended Etowah. I never intended to get pregnant before graduating high school. I had big dreams of getting a scholarship in music. I played trumpet. I wanted to be a professional musician or a lawyer.

My parents divorced when I was 12. It caused tremendous anxiety in my family. I kept my mind focused on my education and band. The news I received would forever change the trajectory of my life. "How could I have a baby, I am still in school?" The stigma was too scary to think about. Looking back at my life, I clearly see patterns of young marriage, young pregnancies and failed relationship.

As the days rolled along, Logan Howell was growing in my womb. I began to notice my hunger increase. The patterns in my life involved stacked living arrangements, so it seemed perfectly normal that my husband, my soon-to-be son, and I would all live with my father as we are young and broke. Summer 1987, there's a TV commercial about chicken McNuggets. The cute little nuggets jumped off a diving board into a cup of barbeque sauce. As they entered the sauce, the sauce plopped to dance around the McNugget in a symphony.

I was 17 years old; the intense craving had to be met. Each day I would try my best to get some McNuggets. Fast forward. I went into labor with Logan early in the morning on February 1st, 1988. He was due January 27th. I had gained 60 pounds with him. For three days I labored and he wouldn't come forth. Caesarian Section was my option after I suffered high blood pressure for three days. When my blood pressure reached its apex, I was in full blown toxemia, a deadly condition where the blood pressure is so high, the body starts to shut down. I recall the gurney ride from labor to delivery. What was only a few doors down the hall, seemed like the longest ride of my life.

My oldest son, Logan was born on February 3rd, 1988. He weighed 8 lbs. 15 ozs. and 22 ½ in. He was a big baby. Today, he's a welding supervisor and drives a dirt track race car. He's the father of my three grandchildren Lilly, Chloe and Alexander.

Logan's father was killed in 1990. I remarried in 1995. I did not think I could get pregnant again due to the toxemia with Logan. I was wrong. We soon learned of my pregnancy with Joshua. Joshua was my natural baby.

We would often go to a Chinese Restaurant called "The China Doll". I had just been introduced to Chinese food. I remember when it hit me, I craved "Egg Foo Yang". My mouth watered when I thought about it. Did you have funny cravings during pregnancy?

During my pregnancy with Joshua, I developed Type II Diabetes. I had to take insulin shots daily to keep my glucose in check. I probably didn't need to eat all the Egg Foo Yang during my pregnancy, but my body craved the egg. So, as you suspect, I started begging to go to China Doll for this yummy protein dish covered in gravy. This craving was more intense than the McNugget craving.

My pregnancy with Joshua was uneventful. Today, he's the closest thing to a soulmate, someone could be blessed to have in their life. He's a balanced, athletic and compassionate spirit. Then the labor begins. Labor is a funny thing indeed.

My mom and I were looking around town for baby clothes and a bed for Joshua's. "Ouch", I yelled. What? How could I be in labor? I was 5 ½ weeks early? I got very scared. Since Logan came with induced, labor, I was shocked and terrified. I was taken to the hospital. My cervix was dilated to four which means Joshua was coming.

"Push it out, shove it out, way out". Imagine three grown men, my husband and his two brothers, doing this cheer in the hallway. This is how Joshua's entry to the world started. All I could think was "Oh God Please let this baby be born soon before they go to jail! "OMG" OWWWWWW!!!! The labor pains were picking up. I felt my water break. It went all over the floor. "Carla you are dilated to eight so we are taking you to the delivery room for prep". Yippee. I was about to have this baby. In the delivery room, the contractions came swift and became so painful. I knew he was coming. I couldn't not stop him. He literally was trying to climb out of my womb.

The nurse instructed me not to push. With no pain meds, my answer was clear "I AM NOT FREAKING PUSHING! THIS BABY IS JUMPING OUT! And a few words that were not so nice. Do you know what I mean? Natural child birth hurts. The doctor came in just in time. He said push, I pushed and Joshua the Great – was born. Oh the euphoria, the feeling of perfection, the moment the baby comes out of the womb. All the pain goes away instantly and is replaced with a big smile, a warm feeling inside and a sense of accomplishment. Joshua was born September 8, 1997 at 8 lbs. 5ozs.

It's a hot spring day in 2001. Sex wasn't something my husband and I were interested in as Joshua was growing up. Don't ask me why, but we just weren't intimate. However, one day we were. This is the day Nickolas was made.

Four weeks went by and no menstrual period. I was seven days late when I bought the test. As I walked to the bed to look at the results, about ten million emotions started to wash over me at once. Fear, happiness, anxiety, worry, excitement, confusion to name a few. I opened one eye, then the other. POSITIVE. Plop! I fell back on the bed. No one was with me at the time, except Joshua who was 4 years old, so no one really heard my scream. Now what would I do? Seriously. I have a 15 year old (Logan) and a 5 year old (Joshua) and they were both about to become big brothers.

I told my mother who seemed to already know because she says she knows everything about me. When Troy (their dad) got home, I told him. He was calm as usual and really didn't have too much to say. Nickolas and I had a love affair long before his birth. We were in love with pancakes.

This pregnancy was my sweet tooth craving. I wanted pancakes or waffles all day, every day. Yes, you guessed it. I would beg and beg for pancakes. Troy always made them every time I asked. I ate pancakes in the middle of the night. I loved to soak them with butter and let the savory syrup just run down my face. Troy would always laugh because I couldn't eat them without getting syrup all over me.

The pregnancy resulted in insulin shots, again. Pancakes were surely NOT on my list of acceptable foods. This time my weight climbed to 350 pounds. As Nickolas developed in my womb and I gained weight, I knew he wouldn't be natural like Joshua. I just had an intuition.

I was pregnant with Nickolas during 9-11. I remember it well. Logan, Joshua and I had all gone to the health clinic for my checkup. I was going to CVS Pharmacy for my insulin and shots. I walked into the pharmacy and heard the employees say "OMG" someone has bombed the Pentagon. There was also an accident right outside the pharmacy. People were starting to panic. I knew it could get bad so I filled up my gas tank and took my sons home.

Nickolas was born on November 20, 2001 via C-Section. I was having contractions, but the pain meds were making the contractions stop. My blood pressure started to go up and his heart rate started to drop, so they decided to do surgery. This time I was awake. My sister Kayla went into the delivery room with me. I could hear everything the doctors were saying as they cut my son out of my womb. I heard a snicker coming from the doctors.

I couldn't figure out what they were laughing at. Soon I realized they thought it was funny because his hair was orange like carrot juice. Welcome to the world Nickolas. Weighing in at 8 lbs. even and 5 weeks early, he was a big baby.

Motherhood brings a whirlwind of emotions from fear to elation. Raising three sons has taught me persistence. My personal mission in life is to release my legacy to my sons and grandchildren so they will one day follow my footsteps in entrepreneurship. Mothers, love your children, even if they are less than perfect in the eyes of others. You will never know how much you mean to your children.

I leave you with this one thought:

**"Every baby conceived is worthy of being born. Look at your children and give gratitude that a part of you, lives in them."**

# Michelle Galatoire

Texas, United States of America

## *I Could Not Be the Vessel*

Life was good. I had a wonderful husband. We shared a lovely home. We traveled extensively. We had good jobs, we were healthy and we were growing our savings for retirement.

People started asking…so when are you two going to have a baby?

I admit, having a baby wasn't something I dreamed about since I was a little girl, as some women do. I was honestly not focused on long term goals. I met life where life met me. And that was good enough. For a while.

But at thirty two and married four years, it was time to start thinking about it, to start trying. Naturally. And that was also good enough, for a while. The anticipation began to build along with the dreams of what our child would be like and look like. The fantasies began to tickle our imaginations. Would it be a boy or a girl? Which room would be the baby room? Would I be a stay-at-home mom or keep working?

Then a year passed. Then another with no pregnancy. The doctor visits began - blood work, examinations, tracking my cycle - still all good because there was no reason to think otherwise. Yet.

Another year. Fear started creeping in. Was there something wrong with me? The conversation with the doctors escalated to taking medication — Chlomid. That was horrid. I was a complete witch on this hormone altering medication. But after only five months I was pregnant! I was so happy! But in the third month, I doubled over in excruciating pain. I somehow made it to the hospital because there was no one around to drive me. As I walked down the hall to my doctor's office, people walked by shaking their head, saying "someone should be helping her!" as I held on to the wall to keep from falling over. I experienced a moment of ecstasy when an ultrasound allowed me to see and hear my baby's heartbeat. This moment ended all too quickly, replaced with horror as I was rushed to surgery because an ectopic pregnancy was rupturing. Tears of loss flowed down my face at the thought of the necessary surgery ending this little life. It was unbearable.

I spent the next year mourning the loss of the baby, all the while hoping to get pregnant again. Another year passed and the doctors said it was time to consider IVF. This started a whole new level of choices to navigate and opinions to deflect. Eventually, we delved into the world of infertility treatments. The demands were significant on our time, energy and peace of mind, and the cost was insane. There were endless appointments for blood work, examinations, ultrasounds – not the tummy ones – the doctor visits, the time off work, the scheduling. It was all extremely daunting, but with its promise of 60% chance of success, it would all be worth it.

The pregnancy test came back negative. My husband was in complete shock. He hadn't even considered failure a possibility. My God, we had put six embryos in! They didn't look promising, but we wanted this so bad we wouldn't only risk multiples, we would embrace them.

And so it went, for a total of twelve years....twelve long, painful and excruciating years. Each is etched in my mind, like the heartbeat of the first baby I lost.

And like the second loss which was a natural pregnancy during my acupuncture and herb cycles. Or the joy I felt over my brother having a child, while painfully conflicted with the jealousy which was natural, but felt horrible about so it doubled the distress. At the loss of my third pregnancy, I was almost inconsolable, and this was followed ten days later by the death of my father. And the visceral memories, like the heartache at another failed attempt, or the well-meaning comments "let go and let God" or "why don't you JUST adopt?" And the panic attacks at Babies R Us shopping for a friend's baby shower. Or the blood running down my arm as the tears ran down my face after yet another lab appointment. Would it ever happen for us?

Fast forward to eight inutero inseminations, five invitros, multiple surgeries, procedures and pregnancy losses and an insane amount of infertility drugs. The appointments, blood work, acupuncture, herbs, prayers and positive affirmations all began each month with rising hopes and then plummeted to despair and emptiness. It was an emotional rollercoaster ride. I don't like rollercoaster rides. It all became obsessive, to the point of self-abuse. And still no baby to love and hold.

The emotional, physical and psychological toll was long and deep. The strain on our marriage as my husband couldn't just fix this. The strain on other relationships, as well, because most often, when people tried to console, they inevitably said the wrong things. And what I made it all mean about me was the most painful of all – I am not worthy. I am not good enough. I am not a whole woman.

And, as life...God...Universe...The Divine would have it, beautiful blessings came in along the way to allow me to survive it all. I joined Resolve which supports, educates and advocates for couples going through infertility and adoption. I stepped up and out of my comfort zone to the role of President of my local chapter to fully immerse myself in what was available. I now see, it was divinely purposeful, as the women who served with me became my most treasured soul sisters. Working alongside each other and supporting women going through this crisis, we created community and immense support for each other.

My weekly visits with my acupuncturist and soul sister, Dr. Randine Lewis at her clinic became my refuge and her compassionate heart gifted me sanctuary during those stressful cycles. This led to working alongside her where we created amazing fertility retreat intensives and traveled the world to bring hope and healing to hundreds of women. Within this work, I met more amazing women who expanded my heart and my vision of my place in this world. Jewels of the journey.

These experiences led me to become a life coach – for fertility and self - care. My world expanded more. My spirituality reached new heights. My consciousness of allowing, rather than pushing through began to release me from the roller coaster ride of infertility treatments. I was ready to let go of trying to force a biological child into this world. I let go.

I chose to take one year off to heal and to allow the letting go to be fully expressed. I had known for years we would adopt, and I was committed to this option not being a band-aid to the real loss I was experiencing. During this time, I threw myself into personal development and read a lot...mostly on spirituality, learning to trust there had been divine orchestration in all that had happened over the years. I spent time in meditation, detoxing and cleansing on every level and practiced yoga and qi gong. I desired to be the best version of myself when that spirit chose to come.

We chose an adoption agency which placed at-risk children. We chose this for a number of reasons. Many friends had great success with this agency. Since I had witnessed so many women coming to resolution during my years with Resolve, I became familiar with both local agencies and international adoptions. We had spent our life savings on all the fertility treatments, so choosing an agency which I had seen have great success, find homes for children in need and where cost was insignificant, felt right.

The adoption process and the wait for placement took one year to the month. During that time we had several children (or sets of children) offered to us. Once, little twin boys were offered to us. I felt my heart close at this offer, and thought "What's WRONG with me?" Fortunately, I had a dear friend, and sister coach who helped me recognize my intuition was speaking loudly to me, and my choice was coming from a place of courage, rather than fear.

Then we got THE call. A precious, three day old baby girl was waiting at the hospital for us! It took only moments to say yes, and one day to complete the paperwork to pick her up. Eight years later, I am in complete awe of her. She is precocious, vivacious, deeply connected to spirit, open hearted, incredibly compassionate, empathetic, and immensely beautiful. I am certain my husband and I could not have created anything close to the remarkable being she is.

While it was by no means an easy road, I eventually traveled to a place of letting go of the form of how she came, letting go of not being the physical vessel from which she came through, and being open to the miracle that my heart and home is where my angel landed.

# Regina Hall

Alabama, United States of America

## *Grandmothers*

Every little girl grows up dreaming of becoming a grandmother. She just doesn't know it at the time. Most of the time, she thinks she just wants to get married to a tall, dark and handsome man, live in a big mansion, have lots of money and lots of kids. As she gets older and these things start happening to her, she realizes something is missing. There should be a final chapter in her life that all of these things were leading up to.

Getting married to the man of your dreams is great, but as time goes by, "Mother Nature" steps in and he, like yourself, becomes a little less tall, the dark hair turns gray, the handsome turns to wrinkles and a little bit of sagging where muscle used to be. You still love him the same, but now it's more comfortable and a little less romantic. And somehow that's the only way you would want it to be.

The mansion turns into a very lived-in house where there are scuffmarks on the walls from years of little hands, little feet, animals and parties. There are pencil marks on the side of the fridge to show how tall the kids have grown until the fridge becomes small in comparison. The furniture has a comfortable sag from years of being sat on, jumped on, wrestled on and even cuddled on. And always something needs to be repaired. And the funny thing is, you don't really care about the mansion anymore. It lost its appeal when your first child was born and you realized mansions don't have sandboxes or frogs in the dresser drawers or pudding cups under the bed that have been there since last week when you said, "No dessert if you don't eat all your dinner."

Being rich? Well, now that's the funny thing about life. Being rich doesn't necessarily mean having lots of money. Being able to pay your bills and maybe even go out to dinner or a movie once in a while becomes the default definition of rich. Paying for the braces and lost retainers, baseball gloves, ballet shoes, bowling balls, cub scouts and brownie uniforms, football and cheerleading fees and all the hot dogs and pizza you eat night after night because you wouldn't miss being there for every event or game; now that's being rich.

And of course there are the kids. They start out as newborns which are just the cutest, most precious things in the whole world. You are so proud of these perfect little bundles of joy. Then reality steps in. What if they have something wrong which causes them not to be so cute or precious or perfect? You get this overwhelming feeling maybe you should have waited until you were more ready for this special moment. Then everything turns out okay. They have nothing wrong with them.

That is, until you start messing with their life. Now comes the really hard part. What to do to make them the perfect adults you can be so proud of. Don't let them make mistakes you made as a kid growing up. Don't let them do without the things you had to do without. Don't put impossible goals on them like your parents did to you. Now you set your standards of what a parent is and how your child is going to turn out.

You aren't going to make any mistakes. Even though your parents are right there every step of the way telling you what to do. You don't have to listen, because you now know what to do. You are the adult and the sooner they learn that, the better off everyone will be. How would they know what to do? Have they ever been in your shoes? You called them at 3:00 in the morning because you needed the name of the doctor in town, just in case your child didn't stop crying by 8:00 a.m. He had been crying all night from a bellyache and you were just about to give him the warm bath and the fizzed out cola when they suggested it. It's not like you didn't know what to do. And you only ask your parents to babysit for you so they can get to spend time with their grandkids. You are doing them a favor, it's not for your benefit.

Even if it was a last minute call, they didn't have any plans anyway. If you are real lucky your parents will always be there just so you can compare how you raised your kids to the wrong way they raised you. All the boo boos, broken toys, wrecked cars, broken hearts, bad decisions and even the broken marriages somehow all lead back to the way they raised you. However, all the good decisions, good marriages, good kids and fine things in life, you did all this on your own with no help from them

These same children move away from home and sprout their wings. Sometimes they fly, sometimes they fall. The only thing which always stays constant in their life is the same parents that have been in the background, praying, wishing, hoping and worrying. They are not perfect parents and they didn't raise the perfect kids of their dreams.

Now comes the good part. The part of your life that always seemed missing. Grandkids. It doesn't matter if they are good or bad. Cute or less than cute. Grandparents are blind to their grandchildren's faults. And when a grandmother holds her grandchild for the first time, WOW! It's like no other feeling she's ever had. It's better than having your own child. It's all the joy with no pain involved. It's what you were hoping for. A perfect little child born from your child. The same one who didn't turn out quite so perfect. It's a second chance to help your child do all the right things you didn't do with them. They of course won't listen to you, any more than you listened to your parents. They think you are still trying to run their life. It would be funny if it wasn't so serious because you know what they don't know. You know all the pain, worrying and guilt that they are someday going to feel and there's nothing you can do to help them, except the same things your parents did. So what do you do?

I don't know the answer. All I know is, I am going to sit back and enjoy this little person completely. It's different from the way you enjoyed your own child because now all the responsibility is theirs and all the fun stuff is yours. And if a little "pay back" gets thrown, it just makes it all that much better. Being a Grandmother is what makes it all worth-while. Your own mother's name changes as you grow up from mama to mommy to mom to mother. It's not that way with Grandmothers. If you start out as Grandma, you end up as Grandma. And in their eyes you can do no wrong.

# Chocolate & Diamonds

## Haley Lynn Gray

### North Carolina, United States of America

## *Why I Became an Entrepreneur*

Most people who start a business have a reason for doing so, and I am no different. I didn't set out to start my own businesses because I thought it would be easier than working a normal, corporate job, but rather because I felt a calling and a bit of the need to change the world for each of the businesses I own now.

**This is my story...**

My parents moved to the area in 2005, wanting to be closer to family, and specifically to be closer to their grandchildren. What I discovered when they moved up here is neither one of them was doing terribly well. We had to start providing help to them nearly from the day they moved up here and bought a lovely 3200 square foot home. Because, you know, they needed the huge house to hold all of their stuff, and to rattle around in. They needed a lot of help getting their stuff moved, organized, hung, and where they wanted it in the house. That was just the first step, though.

Since Mom had Multiple Sclerosis (MS), Dad was her full-time caregiver. She couldn't or wouldn't cook, or prepare any of her meals, so she was fully dependent on him to prepare her food, just so - half a peanut butter and jelly sandwich with half a plate of cut up fruit for lunches, salad for dinner, and a small entrée. Almost everything about her was fairly high maintenance, and he was in charge of it.

Only - his health was declining. We noticed fairly quickly after they moved, Dad was having trouble with some tasks, like writing, and following complex conversations. He also complained a lot about back pain. We knew he had arthritis, but what we didn't fully appreciate was the severity of his osteoporosis, and how quickly his back was fracturing - and we didn't understand or appreciate the severity of the problem until after 2011 - years later. We took him to various doctors, orthopedists, a neurologist, a neurosurgeon, and another neurologist, neurosurgeon, and around and around. He was tested multiple times, wound up in the hospital, and was quickly discharged, with home health. Of course, we had no warning. The hospital and social workers just waved their hands, and told us home health would come by, take care of them, and everything would be OK.

The lesson I learned was everything wasn't just going to be OK, and there were assumptions on the part of the social workers that I was fully available to take care of my parents. This wasn't the case at all. I had four young children, who needed their mother. I also had a full time job I was juggling, trying to stay employed, and further my career during this time. To say it was hard would be an understatement. There were days I was literally in tears trying to balance it all, and the assumption I could do more, was frustrating almost beyond description.

We hired private duty home care for my parents at various intervals, and they would quickly let the caregivers go, because they didn't want to spend the money. See, people are conditioned in our country to think all care is covered by insurance, and if it isn't, then you must not need the care. That is certainly the truth with home care. It's not paid for by Medicare, so my parents thought they didn't need it.

Mom and Dad needed the help, but didn't want to admit it. They eventually agreed to have someone come in to prepare meals, and do some light chores for them, but not to have someone there all the time. It nearly took an act of congress to get them to keep a caregiver.

Let me tell you the story about the time when my mom had to go to urgent care, because she was having trouble breathing. They left the caregiver at home to let the maid in. Dad drove mom to the urgent care, where they promptly took one look at her, and told her she needed to be transported to the hospital. My dad called me at work (Imagine the screaming going through my head), to ask me to meet him at home, and drive my mom to the emergency room. Since the hospital was in the next town over, they needed me to take care of it, when they had perfectly competent help who could have driven them to the hospital. Mom spent over a week in the hospital for congestive heart failure, pneumonia, and flu. Then another 4 weeks in rehab, before being booted out for failing to eat. Actually, she didn't like the food, so she refused to eat anything they served, she certainly wasn't going to drink thickened liquids, and my parents wouldn't sign a waiver. So, her weight dropped to 85 pounds before she was sent home with 24 hour caregivers, who lasted about 6 weeks, before they decided they hated the loss of privacy.

Eventually Dad's health declined enough that he had to have a caregiver around the clock. It was at this point my eyes were truly opened to the home care industry. I got to see the good, the bad and the really ugly sides of the home care business. It was then I felt the need to change how things are done, by starting my own home care agency.

I got so many nudges along the way. Things like my dad being left unattended by a caregiver. A caregiver who never once, in two years of working as his caregiver, saw a supervisor during her shift, caregivers who poured kitty litter on top of the poop, and the crowning glory - the caregiver who gave him alcohol. So many things I could see needed changing, and are actually industry best practices, but so few people follow them.

I interviewed lots of caregivers, and found their pain points. Actually, almost all of my dad's good caregivers work for me now, because they are so passionate about providing exemplary care. Providing amazing care is what we do for our clients and we take good care of the caregivers too.

I decided I was going to start a business with solid foundations, and good business principles which takes good care of both the employees and the clients. This is what I've done. Over the last two years, I've slowly, methodically built what I believe is the best home care agency in my area. We take the best possible care of our clients- the way they want to be taken care of, and to their standards.

# Victoria Campbell

New York, United States of America

## *A Shape Shifter*

*I am a motherless fatherless child, abandoned at age 3 1/2 by both parents.* I've struggled a lifetime to understand who I am. A master of disguise, a chameleon, a shape shifter, depending on whose life I needed to fit in to. I learned very young, my thoughts, my wants, my desires, were not important. I had no rights. Having no identity of my own, I absorbed others identities and helped others fulfill their destinies, never my own.

Raised by my paternal abusive dictator of a grandmother, molested by my "father figure", the only place of refuge was my sibling's love for we shared the same fate. My sister cradled what was left of my heart. My brother, protected my soul as much as his small "child" hands could. Survival was our only hope.

I was an empty child, clay not yet shaped. I hardened myself to not absorb the lessons taught by my parents and others.

My sister, brother and I eventually escaped our "home" by running away. I was 14 years old. That was when I was given the choice of becoming a ward of the state or being emancipated. I chose to rely on myself. Emancipated at 14, a child with an unhealed fragile clay veneer, I was now left to fend for myself whilst still plagued with the internal identity of being unwanted, molested, beaten and alone.

But somehow, even despite all those things, I felt rich. For you see, I WAS NOW FREE. Those people could never hurt me again. The world, although not kind many times in the years thereafter, was still a respite from the hell I was used to. I learned to navigate this new place. My senses had been made keen. I had already learned what I DIDN'T WANT TO BE LIKE.

So, I polished myself. I hungered for the identity that was different than what my mirror showed. I killed my identity, "Vicky," and became Victoria, the person inside I knew was still there, hiding, protected by me. She is smart, she is kind, and she has the same opportunities as everyone else. My new parents became people of words which inspired me. People like Maya Angelou, Oprah Winfrey, Kahlil Gibran, Ralph Waldo Emerson, Thich Nhat Hanh, Dr. Wayne Dyer, Louise Hay, Tony Robbins and Eckhart Tolle. I absorbed every healing and inspirational word. Music and art became my solace. As I discovered the healing energy of the tones and the colors, it awakened my ability to desire.

I began to position myself in employment opportunities which could teach me the things I needed which I didn't get in my past world. I wore many hats through the years, bartender, waitress, secretary, executive assistant, office manager amongst many others. I surrounded myself with people I could learn from, and aspire to. I learned how to blend in. Working at a publishing company, I met my future husband of 23 years and I subsequently bore three children.

***My new title, Mother, would be the catalyst to my true healing.*** I wasn't ready for the love a child forces you to feel. I didn't realize that in the necessary life-preservation of hardening, I had also hardened against some very crucial necessities of life. Intimacy. The intimacy it took to be a mother to my children softened my clay veneer to once again be able to absorb the moisture of love.

I knew now I had to address my first instincts, which I couldn't trust to be a mother. They had been tainted by broken examples of such. I had to place myself in "school" once again, and reteach myself. And so, I embarked on yet another journey of healing, but this time, for my children's sake. I began reading every parenting book I could find. I watched parents who I admired and modeled my behavior after them, polishing myself as a future mother.

I was a stay-at-home mom for 17 years (a placement of myself that took courage, as I now had to confront my demons). A vulnerability I had to risk, to give my children the childhood I never had. I learned to be a mother, whilst healing my own inside child, a duality that at times was most difficult. In those 17 years, I guided 3 beautiful spirits and subsequently, those three beautiful spirits healed mine.

Through sharing their lives, I got to bake cookies, play outside in the rain, bang cups on camp tables, wipe tears, kiss boo-boos and give and receive many hugs. A childhood I never had, yet got to experience through them. I slowly healed. Sharing each day with my daughters, each minute, each milestone, healed my heart. It broke through my hardened clay veneer and exposed the tender underbelly of my soul. Each time they looked at me, touched my face, I was so filled with love, a love I had never felt before. I had never realized my own ability to give love. I worked to become a positive example in my community, so I could be an example of a mother that my children deserved. I became a community volunteer, and Girl Scout leader. I chaired on various school boards and was an active school volunteer and member of the PTA.

It wasn't until I held my first daughter that I realized I had never mourned the loss of my own mother. I had never allowed myself to realize losing her hurt me. The love my daughters needed from me somehow propelled me into realizing the love I had at some point, needed from my own mother. I finally understood my pain. Their innocence, their need for the love of their mother, taught me why I hurt so much inside. It explained my pain with the loss of my own mother and allowed me to finally heal the hurt little girl inside.

For you see, I once too, was a child who deserved a mother's love. I deserved to show my love to a mother, a father, a grandmother and to myself. Only I had learned, very early on, to shut those feelings down because it hurt too much, and caused pain in myself. But my children awakened my dead soul. They propelled me out of my own personal hell and into the mirror of myself. They breathed the life back into my unfeeling heart.

Today, my oldest daughter is a College Graduate with honors from a prestigious University. My middle daughter is currently in College and is on the Dean's List. My youngest daughter, a High School Junior, Honor Roll Student and National Honor Society inductee walks this life with me. My home is filled with music played by my children, art created by them and myself as well, displayed throughout. I am eternally grateful for all the lessons I was taught. I accept all of them as they have brought me to this healed space.

My identity as a motherless, fatherless daughter is one which has taken me a lifetime to accept and own with honor. For the scars I wear are only Scars. And I wear them with distinction.

**I AM a mother and I have three artistic, musical, kind, intelligent, wonderful daughters who honor ME and call me "Mother". Their identity is intact. And I can breathe, as ME.**

# Lisa Harris-McLean

Texas, United States of America

## *Legacy*

### "A Small Word with a BIG Impact"

So many people go through life never thinking about what their *legacy* will be; not conscious of what they will leave behind for others to learn. The belief life just randomly happens is not something I personally take stock in. In my experience; the pieces of the puzzle come together when one is actively engaged in putting them together. In other words, you must purposely participate in choosing the direction your life will take. Choices are available to make every day.

Thinking your choices are irrelevant to others, but in reality, all actions effect someone or something. The positive energy you expel when you smile can carry for miles. For example: a habit of always expressing a smile at people in passing, is a *legacy* which can begin the moment you smile at a passing stranger. This stranger in turn feels hospitality from your expression which is then carried with that person to his or her job.

Let's say for the sake of the example; the stranger is a teacher who works with young children. The teacher who was the recipient of your common, everyday practice of greeting people with a smile is inspired to teach a lesson on being polite to her class of twenty second grade students. The students in response to their teacher's lesson, learn the importance of a warm greeting. This seems quite average in perspective, but think about the impact when these children then practice this behavior throughout their lives and pass it on to their children. This is how a small gesture can have a huge impact on the world, hence creating your personal *legacy* of being kind to others by simply sharing a smile.

Being aware of how you impact others is not commonly on the forefront of your thinking in your youth, but I've encountered many young people mentoring youth and teens who poses the skills and practice of mindfulness from a very young age.

Mindfulness is a skill taught to us by others. Friends, family, caregivers all contribute to our emotional development or state of well-being in some form or another. People encounter many emotional experiences which foster a direct, yet individual reaction in another person. For instance, someone who is melancholy can make another feel depressed or sad without ever realizing their effect on others. Most people do not realize the power emotions play in an experience at the time of the experience, they realize the connection moments, days or years later.

Our personal experiences are what makes up our individual journey through life. For some of us, who are fortunate to live a long, full life of a half dozen decades or more our *legacy* is continuously evolving. Many are not dealt the gift of longevity, but are aware of the importance of their *legacy*. I was told by a family member who was diagnosed with a terminal illness, she felt appreciative of the awakening of consciousness due to her condition. She went on to explain she felt fortunate to live each day on purpose with no regret. Some people live their lives without purpose or urgency to complete task, take those family trips, and have those heart to heart talks with the people they love.

"Knowing my time is limited has granted me the gift of doing all of those things and I have no regrets." she said to me with a gentle smile. She talked about the memories she was making with her family and friends, the quiet times she spent just being content without bitterness or hast. Making me understand, it's not the time you are given, it's what you give to others during that time. It's been many years since that conversation, I can recall it as if it was just yesterday. The moments that seemed so ordinary in my life prior to speaking with her that day had been elevated into cherished memories of importance in the pause after each sentence she spoke.

My childhood memories included visiting her during family holiday celebrations with lots of laughter and embracing hugs filled with the scent of her perfume. Precious memories we sometimes take for granted were all gracefully transformed in my heart as she spoke to me. Her voice echoed in my head as I tapped the words out on my computer keyboard for this chapter. The thought of her advice still gives me a lump in my throat thinking about it. Her *legacy* consists of Love, Kindness, Beauty, Joy and living each moment to its fullest.

One's personal habits attribute to their *legacy*. Writing "Thank You" notes, being on time when someone is expecting you, offering a helping hand even though you are busy, looking someone in the eye when they speak, returning a smile to a stranger and even intentionally dropping a piece of your sandwich on the sidewalk for the stray dog you encountered on your walk to your office for work are all pieces of a person's *legacy.*

*"Your actions tell the world*

*who you want to be,*

*who you are,*

*and ultimately who you were."* - Lisa Harris-McLean

Resilience is definitely part of my *legacy*. A major part of teaching me to be resilient was played by a tiny green gecko. When I was about fourteen years old, I remember an evening we still laugh about today, but the story was not so funny given the circumstances years ago. My brother and I were making dinner which consisted of the last remaining two cans of meatless chili we could find in the bare pantry of the dilapidated rent house we lived in with our mom. Times were hard and food was scarce given our financial situation at the time.

Our mom was recently divorced supporting two kids to the best of her ability. We learned to be independent at a young age. Cooking was not a skill I had yet mastered, but I was doing my best to prepare a meal for my brother and me. As the electric skillet warmed up, the chili began to bubble like lava releasing an enticing aroma of tomato and spices throughout the kitchen.

We anxiously prepared our bowls accompanied with a fork and tall glass of sweet ice tea on the counter next to the skillet as we looked forward to filling our bellies for the evening before getting ready for bed. My brother was holding his plate waiting to be served when "it happened"! "It" was a tiny green lizard who appeared on the spice shelf just above the skillet. It sat gazing at us for a moment then with a blink of an eye it lunged forward propelling itself off the edge of the shelf plunging downward into the piping hot skillet which contained the last two cans of meatless chili we were patiently waiting to consume.

It landed in the center of the bubbling mass then slowly disappeared as if it was in quicksand until there was no trace of its tiny little green body. Turning to my brother with tears in my eyes I said, "I guess we are going to sleep hungry. I am sorry." To my surprise he resiliently said, "He landed in the middle the skillet, the chili on the sides is still okay." At that moment I realized no matter what circumstances you encounter, you always have a choice. You can choose to see the negative and succumb to the "impossibility frame of mind thinking" or you can choose to see all possible solutions to move forward.

"Encouraging all the women reading this book to be mindful, aware, and live your life in a way that leaves a lasting legacy to empower others."

# Samantha Karinna Dobler

### Alberta, Canada

## *Angel*

Angel is the only word I can think of when I even start to think about what happened.

November 2014. It was a Thursday night when I excitedly started a conversation (one of many) with my husband. "We need to get busy tonight! If we want to have a baby before the new school year". I had plenty of reasons why we needed to be on such a strict time line. When you are family planning, you try to take everything into account, your ages, your other kid's age, and time frames for summer vacations, holidays. Maybe some people just let things happen. I don't. I am a planner. I need to make sure everything I do is on a schedule.

We had been talking about having a second child for a long time now. We knew we definitely needed time in-between. I had a rough start with our first, learning how to be a new mom. I wanted to make sure we were all ready to invite a new baby into our very busy lives.

December 2014. Finally a POSITIVE! I knew pretty much from the first day we started trying, we were pregnant. We followed the ovulation calendar and made sure we were using the skip day method. We were overjoyed, and thoroughly shocked as it happened so quickly.

About Mid-December, my pregnancy symptoms were going nuts and I was having a large amount of abdominal pain. I couldn't keep any food down. Morning sickness was taking over my life. I went to the clinic and had an ultrasound completed as I was worried it may be an ectopic pregnancy.

The technician who performed the service was very quiet. She checked all my organs and became very quiet when she got to my uterus. I sat there waiting for her to tell me something, anything. "Well, it's definitely not ectopic, so that's really good news," she kept looking back and forth over two little blob looking things. I realized right away they were two separate sacs. I asked her, well, sort of told her, "Those are twins". She wouldn't even acknowledge me. In that moment I felt like something was very wrong. She advised she would have the doctor come in to speak with me.

When the doctor came in, he looked over the pictures the technician took and scanned me himself, as well. The air was stiff. I felt like I couldn't breathe. What was wrong? "I will send the results to your family doctor" and that was it, he left the room. The technician helped me clean up and hurried me out of the clinic. I felt so lost. All I knew was the pregnancy itself was where it should be and I knew there were twins. Whether or not they would confirm it.

A few days later, my doctor's office called, I needed to go in. He explained to me I was having twins. He also advised me he wanted a second ultrasound in a few weeks to confirm, as the ultrasound pictures showed some oddities which he couldn't explain.

Mommy mode kicks in. I am all over the internet, obsessing about twins, what it will bring, what to look forward to, what will be the challenges. What about oddities? Have to look that up too. What a mistake. Oddities. What a terrible word. Conjoined. All different areas of the body which could be conjoined. So right away I am looking up pictures and videos, trying to figure out if this is something we could handle. The answer was always yes. No matter how my twins came out, I was their mother and I could handle anything.

January 2015. My next ultrasound proved to be the toughest. I had already been transferred to my OBGYN, and he had a tech on-site. They wanted to date my pregnancy, as well as look into what was going on inside. Within minutes, my new technician held my hand as she took a picture of a beautiful 9 week old baby and beside the baby an empty sac. She looked into my eyes and explained the second baby didn't make it. She was unsure where the baby would have gone, I could have expelled it, or it could have been reabsorbed early on. I don't even remember everything she said. The technician told me as much as she could about the baby still inside. The love I felt for this little one was so strong. I wanted to be positive.

When I got home, I showed my husband the picture she printed for us. Showing our little baby, and the empty space above. I explained to him what I was told. We cried. This as parents was so hard to take in. Despite having a very healthy 4 year old already, and a very healthy looking baby inside, we lost someone. We lost our Angel. This baby would never get to join us. This baby would never come to be.

April 2015. Admitting to the world we lost a twin was the hardest thing I had ever thought I could do. We had already confided in some people. The mix of responses threw us into another whirlwind of emotions. "You are lucky you still have one", "Some people can't even get pregnant, you should be grateful", "There was obviously something clearly wrong with it, so it had to go".

Since when do any of those people get to decide what's best for us? How is it they could say something so cruel and heartless. We are grieving, we thought by opening up we could allow people in to help us move forward. We were so wrong.

June 2015 Today. We have 7 weeks to go before we meet our little boy. There isn't a moment that goes by I don't think about our Angel. We want to celebrate what could have been and what will be. We will grieve our son who never came to be, and we will celebrate what he taught us. We are so grateful we got to see him, even if he was just a small speck on a black and white picture, we'll always see a part of him in our son as he grows up.

Some Angels were meant to walk among us, while others were taken too soon, but all Angels will watch over us, guide us and keep us. Our Angel is my son. I will never forget you.

# Shavannah Moore

## North Carolina, United States of America

### *The Diamond of Being Mom*

I often ponder on how my life would have turned out if I had never had children, and quickly realized my life would be so different. See, at birth, I nearly didn't make it. I was premature. My mother was in the hospital for 2 months after I was born with a hard recovery.

I can only imagine what she went through giving birth to me. I can say my children are my diamonds and for them I intend to leave my legacy. I made a decision long ago that no matter how many obstacles tend to arise I will always keep going because there is no easy way to success. As Women, we make so many excuses with our children being one of the biggest. Just know they aren't obstacles, but instead they are blessings. Although having kids may delay the process of where you are going, remember your success was only delayed, not denied.

When I was 15 years of age, I had my first pregnancy. It scared the life out of me because I had no idea what I would do with a child at the age of 15. It was my choice to lay down and have sex, so I just knew I would have to face the consequences. I thought my life, for what I knew it as, was about to be over. Low and behold, a few weeks later I miscarried that baby. I felt as though a live human being had died and there was absolutely nothing I could do to stop it. This was one of the most heartfelt things I had experienced at such a young age. Although this was definitely a bitter sweet moment, a part of me was somewhat happy I didn't have to carry the responsibility of having a child at such a young age, needless to say.

As my life continued. So did the promiscuous side of me, which stemmed from being molested at a young age. I became pregnant again at the age of 18 and as a result, dropped out of high school. In my mind, I was still not ready to settle down, but this time I had no choice. Life had somehow thrown another curve ball my way and my first daughter was born. Even though I was young and had such a challenging childhood, she was actually the best thing to happen for me. For once in my life, I finally felt loved by someone other than my grandmother, who had been there for me heavily in my earlier childhood. This love was unconditional and couldn't be explained.

Although I was living a busy life, I knew I had a responsibility to take care of another person and it was no longer about me. The challenges started to come when her father and I went our separate ways shortly after she was born. My life unexpectedly took a turn for the worse. Not only had I dropped out of school, I ended up losing my job in the process, therefore I lost everything (car, apartment, etc.). I eventually had to let her go live with her father at the age of 3 until I got back on my feet. Once I finally got things together, he had a hard time giving her back to me because he had become attached to her. I allowed her to live with him for a little while longer, because it was a huge help with me getting back to work and going back to school. A few months turned into a few years and eventually ended up in court. This was one of the most difficult decisions I had to make at this time in my life.

Six years later I had my 2nd daughter and by this time had become a rising Entrepreneur. With overcoming all the obstacles and trials I faced as a young woman, I knew there had to be more to my destiny than me just working for someone for the rest of my life. At this time in my life, I had slowly started to tap into "who Shavannah was" and what my "purpose" was on Earth. It was to change the lives of girls and women worldwide by sharing my story and Empowering them to not only look back at where they came from, but to reach back and LEAD. I knew the gift I had inside was bigger than me and I had to share it with the World. After going through several businesses to see what was a good "fit" I finally knew my purpose was birthed through my pain. The pain I faced from childhood and throughout life. I am and will forever be grateful for my girls because had I not given birth to them, I wouldn't have become the woman I am today.

Shortly after having my daughter, I got married and thought my life was going great. Then I got pregnant with my son and life took another turn for the bad, my husband and I separated. Talk about a challenging life! At this point, I just knew I had to work harder than ever before. I felt my choice of men were all wrong and I had no luck with any of my relationships outside of the children that were being birthed from them.

I felt embarrassed, judged, and hopeless and felt things would never turn around for me. I came to the conclusion that enough was enough and no longer will I let life get the best of me. I wanted change, I wanted to live an abundant life, and I knew this would start with my determination. After days/nights of mediating and surrounding myself around more positive/ successful people my "SUDDENLY" hit me. Suddenly I woke up and realized I was an over-comer. My kids were not an obstacle, they were a blessing. My language started to change. My atmosphere stared to change. I started to think highly of myself and replaced the negativity in my life with positive thoughts ONLY.

Although my life had tried to get the best of me, because of the choices I made, I started to view things a lot differently. Every day when I woke up, I would speak positivity into the atmosphere, and instead of saying "How am I going to do this" I started to speak life to my situation "I got this" "I am unstoppable" "nothing can hold me back" I knew from that point on anything I touch personally or professionally, would positively flourish. "Shavannah, "You have to believe in yourself before anyone else will" is what I told myself numerous times throughout life from that point forward.

Today I stand on behalf of women like yourselves to be any and all that you can be. I speak to women all over the World and "Empower" them not only to look back at where you came from, but reach back and LEAD. I am now a happily married woman, an Entrepreneur, highly sought after Motivational Speaker and Author. I've officially accomplished everything "they" said I could never be. No longer will I believe the hype that because you have kids or have a troubled past you cannot become all that you were destined to be. You too can do the same. It's my prayer that as you have read just a part of my story, you make it your goal to allow your children to be the diamonds in your life. Keep pressing forward, turn your obstacles into opportunity and be all that you were placed on this Earth to be. You are an UNSTOPPABLE DIAMOND!

# Erica Antonetti

California, United States of America

## *The Courage of a "Mother's Love"*

My education is a product of the public school system along with all my family members. Never did I imagine I would eventually be "teaching" my children at home. Growing up, I understood homeschoolers were socially awkward and highly religious. WOW! Looking back, I now realize how judgmental, closed-minded, and just plain incorrect those assumptions were.

Due to being a military family, my son already had the experience of switching schools several times since the beginning of his education. Always being the "new" kid was severely difficult for him. It was even more difficult to make new friends while already knowing he would be leaving them behind to make new ones somewhere else. The bullying that comes along with each new school and set of children encountered was ever increasingly painful.

Collectively as parents, I feel many of us want our children to use this time to learn AND have fun. This is a time of growth in their lives where the reality of adulthood is not pushing them down with responsibility. It's a time for them to "play" with a bunch of different ideas and dreams, to figure out who they are and what interests ignite their passions. Educating our children is not about filling up blank space with dates and names they can never remember. Education is about introducing a new or different idea to another, inspiring one to make discoveries based on natural interests so they want to explore and understand the world around them in a bigger way.

It's about asking questions and the "trying on" of information to see and feel how it "fits", if at all, for each individual. Education is a process; a journey of collective experiences which brings you to higher knowledge just as many of us experience in spiritual journeys.

I realized receiving an education in our country should not equate to an experience one is required to suffer through because the law mandates attendance. My son refers to that definition as "prison". At this point in our experience, I have to agree with him. In my opinion, public school unfortunately doesn't allow for such exploration, so I felt several years of valuable learning and opportunity had already been wasted. I had finally come to the realization I would no longer expect my child to "make the best of it" while confronting issues at school during the day, then nurturing his spirit/self-worth by night.

We began the search for other options. Private school in one of the most expensive states to live in on a military income didn't feel like a real option. Nonetheless, we couldn't stay within a construct which was not working. Up to this point, I had never even entertained the idea of educating my children at home as being an option. I felt it had been created in society as somewhat taboo. Quite frankly, the thought of taking over responsibility for my child's education felt like an endeavor I was in no way prepared for. At least, that's what the "system" had been telling all of us.

For one month I immersed myself into the option of home education. I added myself to as many social media groups regarding the subject. I researched website after website of mom's who were doing it, the curriculums they recommended along with published research studies and articles. You know the platform that contains your family and friends "faces"? Well, it's one of the most helpful places a new parent can go to figure it all out and find support. I was a seriously concerned mom here! So I had managed to research endless hours upon hours, take notes, and ask questions, do legal research, ask more questions, begin to plan, become completely overwhelmed, and feel completely under-qualified!!

When the issues at school got to an all-time high, the decision was not even a question. My son made great grades. He's very smart and uniquely talented, just as every child I know is when given the opportunity to display it. *No matter how fearful I was about this decision, the pain of watching my child's imagination and self-confidence being crushed a little more each day was unbearable.* The bullying had leapt to a new level which had me thinking "it is no wonder these kids are shooting up schools!"

I began seeing another side to the institution I had entrusted my most precious gift. I had given permission to create the "playground" in which my son's brain would be engaged. As a result, he would participate in and bring value to the world he was an integral part of. That was the deal!

Another thing I started to notice was the failure in the system materialize from what was promised. I saw the failure in my parenting, not only to protect him at all costs, but also to protect the short amount of time that had been given to me to care for, learn about, impart knowledge, encourage curiosity, and above all, love my children to the best of my abilities. And to think I had so gladly handed my child over for the last five years when I barely spoke to his teachers. "His grades were great, no meeting required", they would say. I didn't know who they were or what background they had in the subject of education. I didn't know where they stood on the major issues which are discussed in the school setting these days like history, wars, different cultures, and sexuality.

What was I thinking?! Where did the decision to public school just become the only option?

It opened my eyes to ask, "How many other choices in my life had I made just because I was told to, because it was the mainstream choice, or because I wasn't aware of the other options available?" I realized our choices are still our own responsibility and ignorance is no excuse. I also see the flaw in viewing this situation as a parenting failure. It was truly just a lesson shining light on what needed correction.

As parents, I feel the vast majority of us love our children in such a great capacity that we wouldn't consciously send them to something which hurts or harms them. But what if we think we are doing the right thing despite the blatant signs that something surrounding this environment isn't. Many of us even have our own experiences which tell us nothing has changed much, yet we continue to send our most cherished because we don't see another option.

Between trying to pay bills and balancing the rat race, many people feel unhappy or like they can't slow down. You may feel you are not qualified, or the system knows better, or you just don't have the time. I am here to tell you this is a decision worth CHOOSING, or at least looking into.

I am a mother who honors all the different and tough choices each of us must make for the sake of our children's best interests. I am not making any judgment on public education as a conscious and informed choice. I know many who've gone on to be very successful from public, private, AND home education. I just wanted to share my personal experience as a journey from where we were to where we are now. To share how I feel this choice has been one of the single most important, courageous, and rewarding choices I've taken part in.

I will be the first to tell you I am not one of those moms who sits around baking cookies because being a mother is my greatest joy or accomplishment. I am one of those moms who LOVES my alone time more than anyone else I know. My patience can run thinner than some of the other "supermoms" I've observed, but I am also a mom who has learned so much more about my child than I ever thought was possible. Discovered were the details that had been skipped from my nurturing mission and the beautiful experience I gladly gave away to a stranger. Revealed was the joy and glow that became illuminated on my child's face when he really 'gets' how to solve an algebraic equation.

Educating my children from home is not easy, but it's really a mutual giving and receiving experience from you to your child and from your child to you. If you are a parent who finds whatever current education choice for your family is lacking in some way, but have the love, dedication, and courage inside of you to discover another path, please understand and be encouraged that you'll be successful in what you seek. Not to mention, you'll be teaching by example, the personality characteristics not often taught in schools, but needed to promote curiosity, exploration, and contented acquisition of knowledge.

Homeschooling is legal in ALL states of the U.S. Here are some websites you can go to and explore options for homeschooling in your current state.

# If you are a parent interested in educating your children from home, please use the resources below to learn more.

**Websites and Reference**

Homeschool Legal Defense Association

HDLA.org

**Donna Young**

www.donnayoung.org

**Homeschooling for Military Families**

www.homeschool-life.com   (for military families)

**Homeschool Curriculum**

www.cathyduffyreviews.com   (all about curriculum)

**New Approaches to Homeschooling**

www.homeschool.com/approaches   (all the ways to homeschool)

# Regina Hall

### Alabama, United States of America

## *A Letter to Mom*

When I was asked to write a story for this book, I was unsure of what to write. I thought of many things. I decided to write this letter to my mom who passed away in March of 2014. I hope you enjoy the story.

## ~Dear Mom~

Dear Mom,

I know it might seem to some, a little too late to be writing this letter to you. However I needed to do this to help me and maybe to help someone else who might be in a similar circumstance. I know we never had a great relationship. There were times when we didn't like each other. Times when we didn't speak to each other for years. Most of the time I was angry, bitter, resentful and even embarrassed at and by you.

You were feeling guilty, ashamed, unforgivable and even jealous. All of these emotions were very real to us at the time. What I didn't realize until just recently was there was a higher power which had a different plan for us. You had a very rough childhood growing up the eldest of five.

Your parents were not rich by any means. They were hard working people. They farmed and moved around a lot when you were young. Because you were the eldest, you were left to take care of your younger brothers and sister. You really didn't get to enjoy your childhood. You married young to get out of the house and didn't know how to act when you did finally leave home.

My dad was your first husband and not the nicest person back then. I've heard over the years, there was a lot of abuse both physically and mentally. He drank and smoked, but he was a hard worker. Your marriage ended when I was around three and my brother was eighteen months younger than me. I didn't remember my dad because of my young age and because the memories I did have, I locked away until later on in my life.

You then met another man and had three children with him. He wasn't a nice man either. He also drank and smoked and he was lazy and abusive to my brother and me. You stayed with him for about eight to ten years and then the marriage ended. All during your time with him, I had to take care of my younger brothers and sisters. I also was the eldest of five.

I couldn't wait to leave home and get out on my own. Away from the abuse and away from you. I blamed you for everything that happened to me. As I got older, I started blaming my real dad too, only he didn't know it. By the time he and I had a relationship, I was an adult with children of my own and he had changed his life around. He became a nice person and he wanted to be in my life. Your third husband was a combination of the first two. He drank, smoked and was physically and mentally abusive to you for years. He did change his ways later in life and became a nicer person.

You and I had a relationship for almost twenty six years after I moved to Alabama where you lived. It wasn't perfect, but it was a relationship. I had long since forgiven you for my childhood. You, however could not forgive yourself and we had many talks about this. I remember getting a phone call around Thanksgiving saying you were at U.A.B. hospital in Birmingham and I needed to come right away. This is when I learned you were in the fourth stage of cirrhosis.

You had taken so many prescription drugs over the years and your liver was damaged beyond its ability to repair itself. They only gave you one year to live. I had wasted a lot of years not doing things with you and when I found out you might soon be gone, I knew I had to make up for lost time. I started right away planning a Mother's Day trip for us. I had a friend at work who had lost her mother, so I asked her if she would like to go with us and help me out with you.

She agreed to go and we spent the week doing things I thought would be special to you. We went to the Aquarium and the World of Coke in Atlanta, Georgia. You had drank enough coke over the years to open your own World of Coke and we joked about it all the time. We had lunch at Johnny Rockets and it was awesome. We went to the Holy Land Experience and Medieval Times in Orlando, Florida and then on to south Florida to see your aunt and all your children and grandchildren who you hadn't seen in a long time. It was a wonderful trip.

You made it another year with only a few minor setbacks, so I planned another Mother's Day trip for us. This time we went to Mentone, Alabama and rented a cabin. Your mother was and is to this day, still alive so we invited her and your sister, your grand-daughter and great grand-daughter. Five generations of family and we had another wonderful time. I had members of the family and friends write letters to each member who went and we had a special dinner and alone time to read our letters. There were lots of happy tears.

Another year passed and you were still hanging in there. A little slower, but still able to make it on another Mother's Day trip. This time we went to Pigeon Forge, Tennessee and rented a house. We not only had five generations of family, but also my mother-in-law and friends with us. Twelve in all. We took lots of pictures and again had a wonderful time. I was already planning for the next Mother's Day. Here it's January, then February.

You were really having a bad couple of months. You fell a lot and seemed to be getting weaker. You got bad news on your last doctor's appointment. You now had a tumor on your liver and it was cancerous. You started begging my step-father and me to put you in a nursing home. This was something I had sworn I would never do. You were serious about it so we relented.

I had even thought maybe you would get rehab and be able to spend one more Mother's Day with us. It wasn't to be. On March 10th while my brother and I were holding your hands, you took your last breath. It was painful and sweet all in one.

The most wonderful thing I remember about our last years together was our Mother's Day trips. I missed you so much that next Mother's Day, I didn't feel like doing anything. I've since taken a trip with my daughter, her children, my new daughter-in-law and her children. We went to Myrtle Beach, South Carolina. Again it was a wonderful time, just different. They even convinced me to ride a three story sky wheel.

This is one tradition I would like to continue. And maybe the next generation will do it too. Family is important no matter how good or bad you may seem to think your life has been. I am glad I made time to spend with you, mom. I never have to look back and wish I could have done things different. I will see you again one day in heaven. Until then I will keep you in my heart.

Love your daughter,

Regina

"As of this writing, my grandmother "Grannie" is still living. She is a farmer at heart and a free spirit. Please take time today to forgive quickly. Our days on this earth are limited, so are our heartbeats."

# Chocolate & Diamonds

## Shequita Lee

### Virginia, United States of America

### *I Am Blessed*

As a single mother of two sons, I've asked myself many times "What will I do". Like you, I've felt scared and lost, and many times I stumbled and fell. Like me, you may have fallen to your knees and broke down in tears. Of course, I was wondering what's next. Thinking to myself and finally saying out loud, I can't take it anymore. I honestly couldn't do anything more, than what I've done already. I am at the end of my rope, what else can happen now. As a Christian, I knew I needed to have a conversation with God.

I let HIM know I had done all I could and needed HIS help. One of the scariest things I had to figure out was once you ask for help, it's not up to you to think of how you'll manage, and how you'll survive. Many times we face hard decisions, but we must remain strong. Make the decision to pray, God will continue to give you the strength, and the energy to keep moving forward. Stay on the path He has put you on.

In 2000, things took a turn. We are on our way to a wedding, and the road we were on was narrow, and rocky. Then the clouds suddenly opened up, and it started raining. The rain was coming down so hard, that even though the windshield wipers were on full speed, you could hardly see in front of you. It rained for an hour, and then it stopped. Once we turned the curb, we hydroplaned. He lost control of the car; we were veering head first towards another vehicle. As we collided with the other vehicle, I was thrown out of the passenger side window.

I know you are wondering, why I wasn't wearing a seatbelt, but earlier that day the seatbelt broke. Here I was lying unconscious on the ground, many feet away from the cars. In my unconscious state, I felt like I was falling. In that state I kept trying to grab a hold of something, but there was nothing there to grab. When I finally opened my eyes, there was a gentleman sitting on the ground next to me, he informed me he was a doctor. The doctor proceeded to ask if I was ok, and if I felt any pain. Not realizing what happened, I just stood up, but the pain set in, I couldn't breathe.

Then reality really sets in, and I realized what he was asking me. Again, the doctor proceeded to ask me questions to find out the location of the pain. All I knew is I wanted to stand-up. He advised me I shouldn't, I was just in a car accident and I was thrown from the car. The doctor started asking me a series of questions, to determine my consciousness; I answered all of his questions. Then asked where my husband was, and he pointed to him, we yelled to each other as we waited for the ambulance to arrive.

You never know how much you value your life, until a Priest walks into your hospital room, and offers to call someone for you. The only question I wanted him to answer is, "Am I about to die"? I pride myself with being a movie fanatic, and usually when a Priest comes to visit you in the hospital, this means bad news. However, the Priest visit was good news for me. He notified my family, and let them know where I was located. He was able to get the doctors into my room a little quicker. Some would still say this is kind of scary.

Many people would become distressed, if you got a phone call from a Priest, who was telling you your loved one has been in a head-on collision. By the time my family made it to the hospital, they expected to see me bandaged up to my head, but it was just the opposite. They were greeted with a warm welcome from me, as I was getting stitches to a cut on my arm. My breathing was labored, but I was still breathing. I had broken ribs, a collapsed lung, a punctured liver and internal bleeding, but I was still BREATHING.

After a couple weeks of therapy I was able to start getting back to normal. I still had a fear of someone driving me around in the rain. Yes, it took a little bit longer for me to be comfortable with this situation. At that time I started feeling like, this is another chance for me to get back on the right path, time for me to live on Purpose.

There was something in me, and I no longer wanted to be on the corner of sadness and unhappiness. I wanted more, but things had to change for me, I had to get away... remove myself from the situation. The hardest thing to do is to walk way. Walk into uncertainty, and trust God to guide your steps. But that's what I had to do, there were many times I was scared, and lost. I wondered "What will I do now?" I knew I was strong, that God would never give me more than I could handle, but I felt like maybe he is mistaken. Maybe I am not as strong as he thought I was. I won't be able to get past this.

After finally coming from the darkness, I realized God doesn't make mistakes. I started claiming my status of being Blessed! I survived and have further to go on my Journey!

# Jacqueline Miller

New Jersey, United States of America

## *Tell Your Dreams to God*

**"I am an empowered mom on a mission
to help other moms get to a higher place in life."**

Far too many women succumbed to the misconception that it's impossible to simultaneously follow their dreams and be a great mom. Does this sound like you? I am proof loss does not equal lost, your past can be someone else's present and motherhood isn't where dreams go to die. **I AM** living in the HAPPIEST place now than I've been in the last 13 years. Do you want to know how? I am a servant of God, who has been blessed with two amazing sons.

The oldest graduated college with honors and has just begun a career with his dream company; the youngest is a rising college sophomore, soon to be a published author himself. I took a leap of faith recently, formed my own company, became a bestselling author and am ready for the many exciting things I know are in store for me.

However, my life has not always been this "Pretty in Pink"

It was Super Bowl Sunday 2002. My husband didn't wake up. He suffered a massive heart attack in his sleep. To this day, the hardest thing I've had to do was to tell two young boys the man they idolized was no longer physically with us.

**Every emotion possible surfaced. Loss, guilt, disbelief and yes, anger.** How could I do this alone?

"God, why us? "I wondered. This major life event was clearly not a part of my plan.

I grew up in a home, with a Dad who was a hardworking man, but who was also a functional alcoholic. I truly believe alcohol was used to mask emptiness in his life. My Mom, who loved us dearly and worked harder than any other woman I know, was also a woman who gave up her dreams when she became a Mom. I learned everything I wanted to be as a Mom from my Mother. However, I also learned everything I *DIDN'T* want to be as a Mom – From My Mother. I knew as a Mom, I didn't want to be forced to sideline my dreams, simply because I decided to be a Mother, as she did.

Following the death of my husband, I was left feeling helpless and out of control. In response, I became consumed by the two things I knew I was good at -parenting and work. I felt as though since I had no control of what had happened in one aspect of my life, surely I would have control over these. I tried to balance it all. Executive by day and mom of all trades by night.

What I failed to realize was that in my attempts to be good at BOTH, I was barely functioning at a level which was reflective of my true abilities in either. It's very difficult to be good to someone or good at something, when you are losing connection with yourself. If you've been left a single parent, you certainly know how I felt during this time of transition.

At work, I was in charge of a strategic business unit. Outside of work, I became known by my children's name. Jacqueline, who? Rather than striving for perfection, I should have been striving for my personal brand of excellence. While I was blindly trying to be all things to all people, instead of being satisfied with my personal best, I transformed into a complete overall "hot mess."

I was being "Super Mom" at home and "Super Executive at work" so that illusive and highly sought after activity called "Self-Care" simply was non-existent.

My weight fluctuated regularly. I developed a variety of health issues and because I was so preoccupied being all things to all people, I put self-care on the back burner and that unintentional ignorance, brought consequences my way.

Even despite having one of my sons say to me one day, "Mom, I hope you are OK, because you are all we've got!" – I ignored the signs that were before me. In all of my chaos however, I was wise enough to know I could be the best mom ever to walk the face of the earth, but I knew I couldn't replace their dad, or show them how to be men. I needed a village and thankfully was blessed to find one.

I was determined I wasn't going to lose my sons to negative outside influences, nor were we going to fall prey to the stereotype of what a single parent household means to so many, especially those headed by a mother of African -American descent.

"IF I HAVE FAILED AS A MOM, ALL SUCCESSES ARE MEANINGLESS," became my motto.

I CAN DO ALL THINGS THROUGH CHRIST WHO STRENGTHENS ME- Philippians 4:13 became my daily scripture.

I needed help, but I was oblivious to the fact that the help I needed, the change I needed to make, was right there before me. I was too consumed with being in control, or so I believed - to reach for it.

Just as I thought life was beginning to take on some sense of normalcy and I was becoming accepting of my new life as a single mom, my six-figure human resources job, and the corner office I had worked so hard to obtain, was gone.

The dreaded "D"- also known as downsizing. I was now a single UNEMPLOYED MOM and again, left asking God, "WHY?"

I volunteered, I got involved in community service, yet something was still missing. Frustration once again set in when nothing was happening the way I thought it should. Self-care once again was placed on the backburner.

Several weeks before my youngest son was to leave for his first year of college, I walked past a mirror and the reflection frightened me. Just who was this stranger in the mirror, because she did not appear to be the woman whom I've always known? It was at that moment, I realized I was lost in the wilderness of life.

Up until then, I had done what so many Moms do, lost sight of self. We forget about the woman we are and the dreams we had before we became Moms. At my lowest moments, I found myself more frequently on my knees, praying and asking God to define my purpose. What is my purpose Lord? I know I am blessed and highly-favored, but what is it that you want from me? I've so many dreams of helping other people, especially women, but I just don't know how. Please help me find the "HOW."

It was around this time I began to write my blog with a focus on women's issues. Writing was always my first love and is therapeutic for me. It was the only form of self-care I never stopped implementing. Shortly after I began blogging, I attended a conference in California, where I was inspired by motivational speaker Lisa Nichols. This amazing experience motivated me to form my business, write my last book, and take a leap of faith.

After years of searching and uncertainty, self-doubt, sleepless night and limiting beliefs, it took a trip to California to meet people I didn't know previously, for me to finally identify my passion and my purpose. I left the event with a clear sense of MY PASSION and MY PURPOSE. I finally arrived at a place where I better understood my past could somehow be a present for someone else. I finally allowed God to take the wheel and from there I began to feel unstoppable.

THE LORD IS MY LIGHT AND SALVATION, WHOM SHALL I FEAR? Psalm 27:1

I encourage you to TELL YOUR DREAMS TO YOUR GOD AND WATCH THE BLESSINGS FLOW. Tell your dreams to God, but be willing to do the work. Don't ask him to guide your steps, if you are not willing to move your feet.

I finally reached a place where I was willing and able to give myself permission to be more than a MOM and I needed to give myself permission to SOAR! I had to go from Victim to Victory and I had to realize Loss DOES NOT equal LOST. It was ok to begin living for ME and in doing so; it didn't make me a lesser mom.

I needed to find a place of healthy harmony in my life, between SELF, FAMILY and CAREER. Something I didn't believe was possible before. I needed to find ways to celebrate ME, so I could truly be the role model my kids needed to see. I needed to believe I was good enough. A good enough woman, a good enough Mom, worthy of these blessings.

My pain, my loss, my obstacles, my adversity, all had their own purpose. God used me so I could serve others and I am grateful to be living my life by design, not default.

My signature coaching program, **"My Journey Back to Me"** was designed to empower Moms to get clear about what they really want in life and gain the tools to live without limits, all while being a great mom. I help Moms reconnect with their dreams, so they can live their best lives and be able to inspire their children to follow their dreams, too. How can a Mom encourage her children to follow their dreams, if she isn't following yours?

I ASPIRE to INSPIRE Moms Who Want to Be The Stilettos In a Room Full of Flats. Unapologetically.

# Roz Bazile

Texas, United States of America

## *It's A Good Day!*

October 11, 2014 - Today was a good day! I woke up refreshed, rejuvenated, and looking forward to the day ahead. I attended an all-day training session and received valuable information to help me achieve some of my personal goals. My sister was texting me this morning, excited about a workshop she wants us to attend which is sure to impact our futures for the better. She is so convinced that she goes ahead and purchases our tickets. I head home later this evening anxious to share what I learned and even more anxious to hear about this workshop that has her giddy about her future, our futures.

I walk in the house, put my bags down in my room and hurried to the family room to hear all about everyone's day and this exciting opportunity. My sister and mother are sitting quietly. I greet them as usual. My mom asks, "Did you get Rhonda's text." I said, "No, what text?" She said, "Mother just died." There is a long silence. I finally sit down. Mother, as she is so affectionately called by everyone, is my mom's oldest sister, the oldest of the four siblings, the matriarch. She was 93 years old. She's one of three girls and one boy. My mom is the youngest. Only she and my uncle are left.

There's an old saying that deaths come in threes. I don't know what statistics there are to prove or disprove it, but this is the third one in our family in the last 6 months. First it was my Aunt Olea, my mom's second oldest sister who was 90 years old. Then a few weeks later ,there's my cousin Benita, who was one of Mother's daughters and whose death was really unexpected at her age, and now today, Mother is gone.

I am reflecting and reminded death is part of this life which is what makes life so precious. For those of us who are still here that mourn and yet celebrate the life of such beautiful spirits as my cousin and aunts, we are sometimes challenged with how to continue living. How do you sleep at night knowing when you wake up the next day you wake up to the pain of losing your loved one? How do you manage to even make it through any day and think about anything other than your loved one? How do you smile? Will you ever smile again? And the hole in your heart, will it ever be filled?

I share this, not for pity or sympathy for myself, because as much as I will miss Mother's beautiful smile and gentle, but strong spirit, she lived an honorable, full, long life. My Aunt Olea, even at 90 years old, was as youthful and classy as she was in her younger days. She had a beautiful smile and spirit. My cousin Benita who died suddenly was only in her sixties. So I think it shocked me and my family even more because as you can tell our family line has a long life span in our genes and she was still very active in taking care of others as was her custom. She was finally about to retire in just a few months. She was the life of the party and started the party, if necessary. I miss her smile and laughter, her travel diaries, her good southern food cooked with a lot of love, and her genuine love and concern for others. She went out of the way to care for others. I miss her so much!

So, why am I sharing these tender memories with the world? To remind myself and possibly you, we only have one life to live so, live it well. My cousins who are the children of my now departed cousin and aunts, all have nothing, but wonderful things to say about their mothers and grandmothers. All three of them left such an indelible impression on their children and grandchildren, they feel so lost without them. In the Bible in the book of Proverbs chapter 31 verse 28 it says the children of a virtuous woman will rise up and call their mother blessed. What an honor to live in such a way that your children and children's children only have positive memories of your life.

I am challenged to consider my ways and my relationship with my own son and daughter who are now young adults. I am blessed to have the most wonderful relationship with both of them. We can talk about anything, and I do mean anything. We have a healthy respect for one another and dare I say we are friends. Not in the way some may think in that I am in their circle of friends, although they are comfortable hanging out with their friends even with me around. We are friends in the sense that we trust one another. We look out for each other's best interest. We cherish one another's secrets. We share our fears, insecurities, dreams, and our deepest thoughts without judging one another. We challenge each other to do better and be better human beings. I am grateful to say they call me Mom, but also a friend.

This wonderful relationship did not happen overnight. It was by design. It was intentional. When I was first pregnant, I knew what kind of mother I didn't want to be and decided what kind of mother I would become. Every lesson, every talk, every yes or no answer I gave them through the years were the building blocks for the relationship we now enjoy today. It wasn't always perfect as I am not perfect. There were some tough times and tough love, but it was all by design.

As a mother it can be easy to take the authoritative and dictatorship role. I cannot tell you how many times I've heard other mothers declare, "I am their mother. I am *not* their friend". My thought was always why can't I be both?

Who says I've to choose one over the other? What if the way to be a great mother is to become a great friend?

The question now is what will your children call you? What will they remember about you? What stories will they tell? What type of impact have you made in this life, but most importantly on the lives of others? Whether you have children or not, what will be your testimony, your story, your tribute to society, your legacy? Someone once said your legacy is not something you leave *for* someone it's what you leave *in* them.

A lot of people associate legacy with money or wealth. The money and assets you leave behind is an inheritance. The lessons on how to build wealth is a legacy. The legacy is not in that you were married for 50 years. The legacy is in teaching others how to remain committed in marriage and still love and respect one another after 50 years. The legacy is not that you were well known, but in what you were well known for.

You are creating your legacy right now whether intentional or not. Your decisions every day on how you live, how you treat others, how you manage your money, and how you spend your time are all the building blocks for your legacy. If you do not like the legacy you've created thus far, then change it. It's not too late. Begin to re-create your obituary, your testimony, your story, your legacy. Most of us have had less than admirable beginnings. As the saying goes, it's not how you start, but how you finish. So, no matter what you've been through or where you are right now, by God's grace get up, hold your head up, and LIVE! Live well because today is *still* a good day!

# FAMILY

# #FAMILY

the bond unbreakable

# No Woman Left Behind

**Hot Pink Publishing, Inc. is a publishing company devoted to growing strong women writers.** Our corporate vision is to create programs and services to bring in the thousands of stories held inside of women. To achieve this goal we have several options for women wishing to become published authors. Our focus is on **affordablity, sustainability and clarity** so all women have the same opportunity no matter the leval of skills, educational background or experience.

**If you are interested in writing a book or joining an anthology program just like the one you are reading, please visit our links below.** Our membership program is $27 a month and gives you a coupon code for 50% off all of our products as long as you remain a member.

HotPinkPublishing.com – Our Company

HotPinkMembership.com – Our Membership Site

ReleaseYourLegacy.com – Our Blog Site

HotPinkAttitude.com – Our Movement

# Laurie K Grant

Ontario, Canada

## *Don't Judge A Person – You Could Be Wrong*

"You can't judge a book by its cover", said my Gran, "You never know what's inside." I wish my adopted parents and all the specialists who worked with my adopted brother, Peter, would have heeded this message.

Let me tell you about Peter. Peter arrived at the tender age of 6 months. He's a quiet, reserved baby, except for a couple of interesting quirks, he cried at the sight of stiletto high heels and big, broad brimmed hats and he couldn't sit up by himself, he just flopped over every time. We knew very little about Peter, except he had been given up at birth.

He loved the garden, he loved music; however, he was slow to learn, to develop and to talk. In the early 60's no one knew much about neuroplasticity (the science of the brain's ability to reorganize itself by forming new neural connections throughout one's life) like we do now. It was thought Peter would catch up later.

Our great-aunt's house had a coal-burning furnace in the basement which you shovelled coal into to make the house warm. It was home to a few things, like spears, masks and tribal regalia from an African safari, but the basement jewel was an old upright piano.

Peter could listen to a song and play it back, note for note perfect on this old, out-of-tune piano. Our mother, trying to help Peter, arranged for a music teacher, however, she insisted on teaching traditional methods, which involved reading music and didn't develop Peter's innate ability, Reading music was a challenge for Peter, as was reading a book. It wasn't long before the piano interest died, never to be reborn. Thankfully, it didn't dampen his interest in music.

Peter ambled along, not developing very well. After many consultations with the few specialists practicing in a small town, our parents got a brilliant idea to send my brother to a school in Cobble Hill for children with challenges. It was only an hour's drive from our house, but our parent's decided Peter would be a boarder, only coming home on weekends. I discovered, after our parents died, my brother and I had been signed over to the Children's Aid Society. Our parents paid them $50 a month for each of us for our care.

When he was 15, Peter came home. He attended the local high school for grades 11 and 12. He never graduated as special education wasn't too advanced in Victoria in the 70's. The specialists informed our parents he was *developmentally disabled*, except that's not the language they used back then. Back then they called you "*mentally retard*ed". This label stuck with my brother like glue.

Spending time with me wasn't allowed. I was considered a bad influence because our mother couldn't control me, but she could exert great control over my brother. We found out year's later she was an undiagnosed *bi-polar disorder* with a mean streak. Was this because her father died when she was 12, or because her mother was slightly off balance as well – we'll never know, we can only surmise as all the parties are no longer here.

Peter's first job was working with Eric, who made door harps from exotic woods. Eric was incredibly patient with Peter and his challenges. Unfortunately, the job only lasted a few years and Peter moved on to another job in a copy shop.

During this time, my family decided to stop bringing Peter to family dinners. They liked to talk about politics, art, classical music and books – all the highbrow stuff. Peter got antsy because he was bored, no one talked to him about things he was interested in, like cars and gardening. The isolation of Peter had begun.

In his late 20's or early 30's, after our parents had left him alone at home while they went on a vacation, he started to have delusions. Delusions someone wanted to hurt him, to blow him up with a bomb and Saddam Hussein was coming to get him. Peter was admitted to hospital, determined to be suffering from *Schizophrenia* and put on a myriad of drugs. No one was told about our father's incessant obsession with news, watching four or five different news channels for three to four hours every evening or the fact that one of the biggest news concerns was about Saddam Hussein bringing his weapons of mass destruction to punish North America.

My brother was stabilized. He lived at home until our mother's health started to deteriorate. Our father moved Peter out and his own household to a condo. Peter lived on his own until 2002 when our mother died and I started coming home.

I was shocked by what I found. My brother, always an extremely slender child, was now a 6' 2" 250 pound sloth, stuck to an armchair watching wrestling all day with the mantra "**I CAN'T**". I found four electric razors all plugged in. "Why", I asked. Peter replied, "In case one dies while shaving, I've another one to use right away". There were five bottles of tire cleaner still in their bags, never opened. A Future Shop salesperson had convinced Peter to buy gold plated Monster Cables for his stereo system, except they were 40 feet long, when all he needed was maybe six feet. He had a cupboard filled with over 200 packages of incandescent light bulbs because he might need them if they were discontinued. His living room floor was covered in bags with the packaging and the receipts for his purchases in case he needed to return the item or have it repaired or replaced while under warranty. Great idea, except he never went back to check the receipt date and the pile grew. His clothes were old and tattered with sweat stains – apparently no one helped him to shop. He had been left to his own devices.

My family had been told by the specialists not to stress my brother out. They interpreted this to mean just let him come and go as he pleased with no expectations.

I started to work with Peter, on cleaning up his apartment, taking him shopping for new clean clothes, and building up his self-confidence hoping to change the "**I CAN'T**" mantra to "**I CAN**". However, living 3000 miles away in Toronto, it was difficult for me to really ascertain what was going on with Peter. I noted in many conversations with our father how Peter had similarities to my son, Harley, who had *learning disabilities* and an *auditory processing disorder*.

Fast forward a few years and our father's health is failing, but he wants to stay in his spacious condo to live out his days. I moved Peter in and he steps up to the challenge becoming chauffeur, grocery shopper, meal organizer and medicine dispenser. I was thrilled to see my brother is responsible, but due to Peter's diagnosis, our father was leaving his money in a trust to be managed by a trust company. Luckily for Peter, my cousin quit the job of executor/trustee and it became mine as I was the only one who would do the job.

Our father passed away in November 2012 and I left Peter living in the condo while I worked on the estate and the trust with the trust company. This didn't go so well, Peter blew $10,000. To this day, we don't know what he bought. Our family didn't pay much attention to him and the only programs the case manager found for him were like babysitting for seniors.

After moving Peter to Toronto, a psychologist recommended we admit him to the mental health hospital. Thanks to her influence, the hospital did a complete reassessment. Boy, am I glad they did, because it turns out my brother isn't *developmentally disabled* and he's not suffering from *Schizophrenia*. My brother is *learning disabled*, has an *auditory processing disorder* and a *delusional disorder* which is controlled with a small amount of drugs. Gone were all the heavy psychotropic drugs. We had an MRI done by a neurologist who told Peter the best thing he could do was to go out in the world and start learning.

It is two years since I moved Peter to Toronto. He has a job for the first time in over 15 years, he goes to literacy classes, he goes to cooking classes, he's learning to manage his money and to use a computer, he's lost 75 pounds and he's a real social butterfly. He has a life now, a life so much richer than before and now his mantra is "**I CAN**".

Please don't always believe what you see and hear. If it doesn't make logical sense, follow-up, get another opinion, because you never know, you might have a Peter in your life. My brother Peter is a perfect example of the effects of an incorrect misdiagnosis.

# Rhonda Townsend

Texas, United States of America

## *Created in Divine Perfection*

The word 'I' is a powerful word. I own my choices, my feelings and my POWER. During my journey of self-discovery, I learned to listen newly as if I had never heard it before. It's kind of like when you read the same Bible passage all your life and suddenly a light bulb goes off! Divine revelation is the term I like to use. Although there's nothing new under the sun, there are times when I get a light bulb moment. My journey to self-love is my light-bulb, my "AH HA", and is divinely inspired.

You see deep down inside, my self-talk says I have no value. I am worthless. I am not good enough. My life only matters to a few people. You say, "Oh Rhonda, how can you think such thoughts?" Well, it's because I gave meaning to things heard or unheard when I was a little girl based on my circumstances or what I was told. I work daily and constantly to negate the self-talk which impresses me to experience life through foggy and untrue filters. Because one thing I know to be true is I was created in perfection.

My momma would say, "If abortion would've been legal, you wouldn't be here". I was born in 1965 and abortions became legal in 1973 so I was about eight or nine when I started really processing it. The first time I heard it I honestly, immediately thought my momma doesn't want me. What I thought was I am worthless. I've no value. I am not worthy to live. I am not loved. I made choices in my life to support what I believed. I struggled with depression, with my weight, and choose food to soothe and fill the void of not being loved. I make unhealthy choices in my relationships with men.

I gave so much value to my momma. As a child and with naiveté, she was my God. I needed her love so badly. I remember giving her a hand-written birthday card when I was around nine or ten that said 'I want to be fat just like you when I grow up'. Truth is my momma does love me; her love showed up in ways I could not understand as a child because my love language is inherently different than how she shows it.

I am the baby of the family; the youngest of three. My sister is two years older than me and was my best friend and still is to this day. When we were little (okay yes, I was little at one time, yet still big for my age), my mother dressed us alike with the same hair style, same dress, and same shoes. People would always think we were twins, even though we looked nothing alike. My sister is extremely thin framed and petite; has caramel colored skin with copper undertones. Her wide ginger-tinted eyes with long black eyelashes and thick luxurious eyebrows slightly hide the slight freckles surrounding a tiny nose and full lips. She has a much chiseled jawline with defined cheeks. Her hair is jet black with curly coils and ringlets. She is strikingly beautiful! We are both born in the 60's and people still thought if you had European or American-Indian qualities, you are more beautiful than others. She is 5'2 (I am being generous with her height) and weighs about a 'buck-o-five' or 100 lbs. when soggy wet. She's still just as beautiful inside and out.

Now I am a generous mixture of sun-kissed brown skin with hints of warm and cool undertones. I was 'big-boned', tall for my age. My eyes are tight and Asian-looking. My dad endearingly called me Black Jap and had the biggest smile on his face when he said it; his face would light up and radiate warmth and love whenever we were in his presence.

Listen to me good! Those names didn't offend me whatsoever, so stop judging my now deceased father. I've much respect for him and even then I knew he loved me. You see, I was just a darker version of him. That man loved his girls and would kill for us (remind me to tell you that story). I looked just like my dad who was a 6'3", broad shoulders, bow-legged, red-boned stud of a man. I have a broader nose, a round face with a whole lot of cheek area. My eyelashes are short and my eyebrows are thin. My hair is dark brown, much coarser and thinner than sissy's. I developed early and by the time I was five or six, I was taller than my sister, thicker than my sister, and outweighed her by about a good ten pounds. Nowadays, I stand 5'9, well over 300lbs (sshhh, don't tell nobody!), and blessed with a large, voluptuous frame. I am a big girl, plus-size, curvy-girl, fat and fabulous, shapely.

Spiritualism is an overarching theme to combat and discredit the B.S. in my life. I respect whatever colloquialism you assign to your higher power i.e. the universe, or God you choose to believe. But my God is the God of the Bible. Now that we have this understanding, let's continue. On an intellectual level here are a few things I believe. God is love ($a = b$). God created me ($b = c$). I am love ($a = c$). Now I don't need you math scholars saying this isn't a good example of the transitive relative theory and my equation is incorrectly applied. Look, it works for me to help change and combat the negativity in my head; therefore, it is a solid theorem!

Almost 50 years and I recently discovered what love is or better yet what it isn't. I know on an intellectual level, I am love and am purposefully designed to love. But it was hard for me to love in a healthy way because of how I defined it.

Just know I adore love. I love the idea of being in love. I love to see people in love. I so earnestly want to be loved and have a life partner to accompany me on this earthly journey who would have my back through thick and thin. One who stays for the long haul regardless of the circumstances that may come in life.

One who supports my efforts, who appreciates how I was designed and accepts who I am without wanting to change me. A guy who says no matter what, "I am walking this path with you to spiritually lead you and we'll grow together." Doesn't that sound like a divinely inspired relationship? Well I've had that, but drop-kicked it to the curb and ran as fast as I could away. I didn't know what love was until now!

It's almost easier to define a thing once we know what it isn't. Love is honesty and open communication, trust, and friendship. Pretty simple stuff! So what's so hard about understanding it? I soon found out what love isn't.

Love isn't external; it doesn't come from 'out there' but comes from within. Love isn't caused by anyone or anything outside of you. You cannot and don't fall in or fall out of love. Love is not something that happens to you. Love is created by you, inside of you, and it's a choice! Love is an experience and you are either present to the experience or not. It's totally up to you to generate your experience. There are no different kinds of love; it's only celebrated differently. For example, the love I have towards my mother is celebrated differently than the love I have towards my life partner. When I *desire* a thing, I've a willingness and openness to have it. For almost 50 years, I believed love to be a failed insurance policy that was sold to me and I bought it at an expensive premium. I am love. I was created in love and placed on this earth to love.

Everything about you and how you are designed is perfect and intentional. Embrace your uniqueness and do not believe the lies about yourself. Your circumstances do not define who you are and what you can become. You somehow gave meaning to something that was said or not said about you. You gave value to that statement or to that person. Experience life in a new state of awareness, make new choices, and see new possibilities for your life.

# Mary Fortenberry

Arkansas, United States of America

## *Saying Goodbye*

**"All things are made beautiful at a timely hour," ~ Lailah Gifty Akita**

Mama and Daddy had a hard life for so many years. They always made us feel special. No one in the world could have convinced me that we needed anything else in this world that we didn't already have. Daddy worked hard. He ran a cotton gin during harvest time and we sharecropped. Mr. Edd owned the land and house. He paid for the lumber to enclose the hallway to the old house, to make more living space. Daddy fixed the house up.

There were no televisions, washing machines or dishwashers. We had no electricity. Mama washed clothes out back in a big black pot and hung the clothes on a wire that Daddy put up, from one side of the backyard to the other. I wore my sister's old clothes that Mama saved. All the younger kids out our way wore hand-me-down clothes.

Cooking flour was sold in cloth sacks which had flower designs. Mama made me a dress for church and told me how pretty I looked. She made me feel so beautiful in my flour sack dress. Mama ironed our clothes by heating an iron which she heated on top of the wood stove. She could play the piano and never had a single lesson. We lived on a gravel road called Deep Slew.

Cotton was the money crop. Mr. Edd paid for the seeds. Mama worked hard in the fields. Papa and Grandma lived close by, so Papa would pick cotton with Mama while school was going on. Daddy worked long hard hours during harvest time.

Mama always made sure she was at the house when the school bus ran. My brother, Billy, helped plow the fields with two mules. I remember running up and down the cotton rows. When the cotton was all picked, by hand, Mr. Edd got his seed money back, plus a portion of the crop money. Mr. Edd was a good man.

There was an old sweet black lady everyone called Miss Becky. She had a house full of grown boys. Some helped us pick cotton and her other boys worked at the cotton gin with Daddy.

Mama gave birth to eight children, all at home. It must have been so hard on her and Daddy. Three sons died right after birth. There were two more boys and 3 of us girls who lived. I was the youngest who survived.

In the summertime, we took our baths outside in aluminum tubs. The water was heated mostly by the sun. In the winter, the water was heated on the old wood stove in the kitchen. The house didn't have an inside bathroom, so we would go outside to the outhouse. We would pump our water outside and carry it inside.

I was born in 1940 on May 12th. December 7, 1941. World War II began. Germany was already at war with Italy. Then Japan bombed Pearl Harbor. The United States used the atomic bomb on Hiroshima and Nagasaki. Afterwards, Japan backed off. Hitler had already been trying to take over, but when Hitler was in hiding, he was killed. When the word got out Hitler was dead, the war was soon over.

There was a depression and it affected every family. Sugar and gas was hard for the United States to buy and they had to have it during the war. Families were handed out coupons for shares of sugar and gas. It was limited.

In the cold of winter, we stayed under the warm quilts until Daddy had the fireplace going and Mama had biscuits cooking in the old wooden stove in the kitchen. At night we sat on the floor around Mama's feet, listening to her read the Bible stories by the light of a coal oil lamp.

I never once heard Mama complain about anything. She kept us all clean, worked in the fields, raised a garden, and taught us to pray. All their hard work paid off. Mama and Daddy bought a house with 60 acres. No more sharecropping for us. Daddy was able to buy a tractor and told Mama, "No more field work for you!" Daddy bought a car and I could drive it.

Mama always showed Grandma and Papa (her parents) that she cared for them. When we moved to Sumner, Daddy built a little 4 room house for them, close to us. They were then living in a house out close to Aunt Ruth. Mama was so happy to have her Mama and Daddy back close.

Life continued to progress. One of my sisters and one brother got married. Another brother went into the army. My other sister went to college to become a school teacher. Then there was me, I had Mama and Daddy all to myself!

Mike, one of our neighbors came home from the army and 3 months later we eloped and got married. I had just turned 17. You never know when or how true love is going to change your life so quickly!

As the years went by, I had three daughters and one son. We bought a boat and went camping. Mama and Daddy always went with us. Most of the family would gather at the lake. We took Mama and Daddy to Disney Land in

California one year for vacation. Another year we went to Dauphin Island. We had such a wonderful time as we were busy making memories!

Wednesday was Mama's day. The kids and I would carry her to Clarksdale. We would go to Woolco, eat at McDonalds and get groceries before going home. The kids loved her. She was always making them laugh.

Then it happened. A truck hit two of my sister's sons on a motor bike and killed them. Not long after, Mama had a stroke and developed diabetes. She was in and out of the hospital so much, until she had to be put in the adjoining building of the hospital for long term care. Not long before this, we had moved to Arkansas. This was an eight hour round trip for me.

On September 11th, the family was gathering for Mama's birthday. By the time I got there, Mama had another stroke. Her right side was paralyzed and she couldn't talk anymore. When I walked in her room, a smile showed on the left side of her face, the side that wasn't paralyzed, and her left hand went up.

I sat by her bedside, holding her hand, and putting a damp cloth on her lips because she could not swallow and her lips were so dry. I got a little sleep, sitting in a straight chair, by her bed for four days while she kept having strokes.

The doctor said, she was dying and would be dead within a few hours. After hearing this, I left the room so Daddy could say his farewell to Mama in private. Then I went back in the room and my oldest sister stood at the foot of her bed. I caught hold of Mama's hand. Dr. Googe, a nurse, Aunt Ruth, her sister and F. L., Ruth's husband, were in the room. As Mama's blood pressure dropped so low, the nurse was crying as she gave her a shot. I squeezed Mama's hand and said, "Love you Mama, I love you" and she was gone.

Everyone left out, but Dr. Googe and me. It was so hard to let go of Mama's hand. Dr. Googe told me I had to leave and he stayed in the room until they came and got her. Tears still come in my eyes after all these years when I think of Mama and Daddy. It was so hard to say goodbye to someone you love as much as I loved my Mama and Daddy.

Some of Miss Becky's sons dug Mama's grave. As Mama was lowered into the ground, I heard my Daddy say, "Honey, it won't be long until I will be coming home to you." After a couple of years, Daddy got a bacterial germ in his blood that spread throughout his body. I could hear him praying in his room to go Home. He was ready to be united with his Lord and his beloved wife, my Mama.

The last time I went to the hospital to see Daddy, shaved his face and stayed until after dark. I hugged him and kissed his cheek. I told him, "Daddy, I love you." His last words to me were, "I love you too."

I made it back to Arkansas and crawled into bed. When the phone rang at 2 a.m., I knew Daddy's prayers were answered. He had gone and was with Mama.

# Mery N. Dominguez

Florida, United States of Amercia

## *Daddy's Little Girl*

I've always thought of myself as daddy's little girl. My dad has always made this clear to me. I literally walked into his life and I am not speaking figuratively, but that's definitely a worth mentioning and saving for another story. The story I want to share today is an excerpt of my life that has driven me to the place I am today. My mother has always been my biggest cheerleader and supporter.

Nonetheless, I've always lived with a throbbing quest to know I am good in his eyes. He has always encouraged me to be my best, to do my best and never hesitated to reprimand me if I wasn't. This constant reminder has left a resilient imprint in my life. His wisdom and advice has always rang loud in my ear. Time seems to change many things, but my love for him is inevitably reciprocal.

At this stage of my life, I reminisce on the times when I was growing up. How he always told me respect needed to be earned and that speaking the truth was imperative to keep someone's integrity. This has always been one of his biggest values, honesty. He shared stories about when he was growing up and how this was the way he was brought up. I knew since I was young, I never wanted to let him down. In fact, I wanted nothing more than to please him and bring him joy. At times this was a challenge. He was constantly working and always trying to build something to leave a legacy behind. I knew I too wanted to leave a legacy. Unfortunately, as a teenager for the first time I felt I failed at this wish.

I still recall the day I met the first sweetheart. I was fifteen and excited to have a young man as my neighbor. I knew having a boyfriend would be unacceptable, but I soon found out free will can play dirty tricks. I started talking to this boy behind my parents back. This was definitely the first time I totally disobeyed my parents.

*I felt miserable.* It was so much the case that after several months, I decided to call the relationship quits. That plan did not turn out as it had played in my head. We ended up having sex and I got pregnant. My world was shattered to pieces. Daddy's little girl had failed him. All his hopes were crumbling down. My life was falling apart. I took a chance and decided to keep my baby with the support of my baby's dad; but it hurt me so much to know how devastated my dad would be. Sure enough. This time of my life was the toughest. My dad has always been a disciplinarian.

My mom had to save me a few times from the whip of his leather belt whenever I did something wrong, so I could only imagine what he would do with something like this. I couldn't face him and eloped. At the time, I was turning 17 years old. When I called my parents that night, my mother cried on the phone and I could feel my dad grunting in the background. I felt he hated me and I would never recover that special love. The only thing I could do at the time was to promise myself I would succeed in life and make him proud of his daughter.

I have to admit my teen years were the hardest years of my life. Till then, I thought being a child was tough. I always felt bullied by kids from school because I was so skinny and bullied by my cousins because my skin color was a few shades darker than theirs. My parents seem to be the only ones who thought I was pretty. As a teenager, I didn't feel pretty at all. My boyfriend, who had become my husband thought I was pretty, but he didn't say it much. As a matter fact, as my body changed and grew, he often ridiculed me too. I would cry myself to sleep every day, hoping it was over. My dad at the time wasn't talking to me, due to his disappointment.

As my belly grew, my heart seemed to swell in agony. I remembered the time when my dad thought I lied to him and didn't talk to me for an entire day and I literally wanted to die. I felt the same pain until the day of my birthday, I was six months pregnant and my dad spoke to me again. I think that day I got my life back. My last three months of pregnancy were a lot more memorable, thanks to the fact I was able to feel again that I was still his girl. I gave birth to a beautiful little girl and since then what a blessing it is to have a child. My father was completely in love when he first laid eyes on her. This then propelled me to pursue my career goals as I had promised myself.

I truly wanted to fulfill my dad's dream. I finished high school and went on to a four year university to study education. My mother was a teacher too in Colombia and she made Spanish to be my first language, even though I was born in the United States. I developed a passion for my language at a very young age and decided to major in Foreign Languages. I got divorced after being married for three years. Think it's true when people say we were just too young. I married my second husband four years later and I have lived happily for nineteen years, thus far. In this marriage, I gave birth to my second daughter and who has inspired me in her teen years to pursue an even bigger aspiration.

I realized recently that through my life, I have continued to earn degrees and more titles, excited about my accomplishments, but always probably more thrilled about sharing the joy with my father. He has always had this penetrating look in his eyes and a beautiful grin when he is truly happy about something and I was able to give him that satisfaction whenever I shared a major accomplishment. As he has aged, I see him more fragile. I want to protect him and know he's healthy and active. It was difficult to see him nearly facing death a few years ago. It was during this time I realized my life was about to take a drastic turn. I had to surrender.

I put my dad in God's hands and my own life too. It was a wakeup call because during this time, I had recently started a business in direct marketing and I was focusing on growing personally. I was realizing what I was capable of doing was beyond a certificate and a title. I thought about those moments I had become busy doing odd jobs, chasing a dream which wasn't really mine. All this had taken time from my life where I could have spent quality moments with the people I loved, my family. I had given up countless hours to gain the ability to buy things to get more, to have more and this nearly caused me my marriage at one point. This very moment, as I prayed for my dad, made me understand that none of that matters if it isn't aligned with our values and purpose.

It became evident that if I could turn back time I would definitely stop and laugh more, have more fun, rest more, take time with my daughters to play and make them feel most important. I would take more time to have heartfelt conversations with my dad. For the first time, I was willing to accept God's will, even if it meant losing my dad. However, if he were to live, I was convinced I would follow a bigger dream. I would make him part of a legacy, not to prove anything, but to allow him the opportunity to live God's purpose as well. There was something we were meant to do together. Miraculously, surrendering is all I needed to do. The very next day, my dad came off life support. His organs which were failing, began to gradually recover. I not only got another chance with my father, but a chance to do life with him and not for him.

It has been an exciting journey. I have done some in depth searching. God and a good man, my husband have been by my side. My direct marketing business introduced me to a world of entrepreneurs which ignited my passion for my greatness within. My soul searched as if it had been thirsty in the dry desert for years. I realized my vision was huge and I was meant to help people. I paralleled that with finding my story and seeking my God given purpose. I knew all I had been through would bring me to something greater.

The sadness I felt during my teen years resonated with me loud and clear. I had been working so hard, just like I had learned from my father and had forgotten the most important lesson "remember where you came from" and I did. I decided to start a non-profit organization for pregnant teens and teen moms. I named it Academy of CLASS. I began to mentor a group of girls and immediately knew that my long years of experience as a teacher was training for this moment. Doing for a bigger purpose has become my ultimate and audacious goal.

I understand how important it is to have parents who love you and care for you. Not just to work hard to buy your stuff or pay for expensive education, but really to be there as a positive role model. This is so clear to me because I have seen it time and time again through the thousands of teens who I have encountered throughout my career. I even experienced it with my oldest daughter. I wish I could have done more with her and not just for her. She is a brilliant daughter, but I wonder if how many times she longed to feel like she was my little girl too. Although we have always been great friends and she is a college graduate, I wonder how much of that achievement was inspired by the need to over-achieve as I did to gain my approval. I pray, she always knows how proud I am of her and how much I wish only the best for her. I pray she always makes the right choices and recognizes the countless qualities which make her extraordinary in my eyes.

This feeling stirred me to start my life coaching business and work, particularly with parents of teens. This work has led me to be more aware how I show up as a parent to my own daughters. I have had to recognize they need me to be present. This includes putting my cell phone down and making the time together count by having random conversations and taking time to connect. I understand if I show her how much I value her, she will demand that level of value from those who surround her. Research, experience and endless studies have proven so many things I overlooked in the past.

If only I had known, what I know now. I have an urge to share this wealth of information with other parents. I know as a team, we can make amazing things happen. I want to be a partner to other parents to support them in making this time full of wonderful memories. Those I gave up on because of choices I made. I wrote a book, The Teen Commandments, to encourage teens to make the right choices by following simple and relevant guidelines. I have recently also written another book with my father. Yes, my dad! He told me, he always wanted to write a book and this became our project together, Enslaved Spirits. It has become an opportunity to connect on a deeper level. Wow, I get to do life with him and not for him. He has shared so many stories, thoughts, views and ideas I never thought possible.

I decided to incorporate my business into my life and not live my life recklessly in hopes of enjoying it later. I get to enjoy it now and do what I love. I share this simply to say I am following my own dream. I learned to let go and trust God. There are many people who live a lifetime hoping for a better life, a change, an opportunity to do more, be more and see more, but they are afraid to make the necessary changes to tell the difference. Many are enslaved to our own world, as my dad says in our book. Many of us live to please others in pursuit of happiness and fall short. I am pursuing my happiness as my heart dictates. My father sees this and he has told me how proud he is of me. He sees I am always doing something, but he knows it's all in good doing. I tell him he's part of my plan and he simply smiles.

Deep down and for the very first time, I've decided I am daddy's little girl, no matter what. There is nothing to prove, no word to say it just because I am sure he loves me. I am a champion of my present and the creator of my tomorrow. I am grateful for my present. I am honored to have two beautiful and dear daughters, who I adore, a husband who cares for me and who is worthy of my respect, a mom who melts me with her smile and a dad who makes me feel every day that I will always be his little girl. His love is not based on my achievements, it's based on how well I can fulfill my own expectations and how those can inspire others, as much as it has inspired him. I am truly fortunate because many people don't get this chance and I did. I am so grateful every day and hope the children I encounter feel the same in years to come.

# Debbie Reynolds

Utah, United States of America

## *The Name of Mother*

**"There is a name, a beautiful name,
Sweeter than any other.
Listen, I will whisper that name to you,
It is the name of Mother."**

My childhood summers were spent in the small town of Van Wert, Ohio. Those were carefree times, rocking on the white porch swing and watching the neighborhood activities or spending hours constructing dollhouses out of cardboard boxes and grandmas' material remnants. One of my favorite memories was a weekly trip to the local lake to catch a few fish with my grandpa.

The day began with a quick dig into the backyard compost heap. Lots of fat, juicy worms were the recipe for a good day's catch. Tackle box, cane poles, and the rusty bucket full of decomposing peels and worms was all we needed to "put dinner on the table."

Once at the lake, it didn't take long to get settled in, bait the hook and throw out the line. Some days the fish were as hungry as we were and it didn't take long for us to have a stringer full of fish. Other days, it seemed the fish were busy with more important fish life. That gave me the perfect opportunity to explore and look for one of the local residents of the lake, crawdads.

A crawdad is nothing more than a miniature lobster and the rocks were full of them. At first, I was very cautious. No one wants to get pinched by a crawdad. But practice makes perfect and soon I had a bucket full of crawdads. No fish. No worries.

Back home with the crawdads, I found an old metal washtub in the garage and filled it with rocks and water. A great new home for my summer pets. I learned two important truths that summer. Crawdads only move one way....backwards. And when you only move backwards, you end up in a circle with no beginning and no end.

My mother died on March 26th. Her cancer was diagnosed February 20th. Five weeks. I couldn't understand how this could have happened. She had just spent the Thanksgiving holidays with me. We decided to take a "bucket-list" trip to Vegas and the Grand Canyon. In Vegas, she stalked the casino patrons, waiting until they played their last quarter and then swooping in to pull the next winning handle. I had to walk away. As luck would have it, her system worked and she ended up with $205. Who knew?

Our Vegas trip ended with a visit to the M&M store. Next stop.....Grand Canyon. Unfortunately, the north rim was covered in snow that November, so we settled for a trip to Zions National Park. We stayed in a lodge and ate pancakes the next morning. Little did we know we had spent the night at the World Famous Bumbleberry Inn, home of the legendary Bumbleberry Pie and Bumbleberry syrup. A once-in-a-lifetime trip. Our entire drive home, we discussed whether bumbleberries were real.

When my mother died, I couldn't move forward. Every Saturday I expected the phone to ring for our weekly chats. My heart ached to hear her voice one more time. I thought of a million things that reminded me of her. And then one day it hit me. A mother's love is like a circle. It has no beginning and no end. And her legacy will be the reflection of her life in me.

Whenever I reach out to make a friend from a stranger, I will be following her example. When I was 16, I saw an old man walking along the side of the road in the dead of winter and offered him a ride. He had nowhere to go so I took him home. My mom made him a warm breakfast and gave him some of my father's clothes. We took him to the bus stop and paid for a ticket. For many years my mom would receive a Christmas card from him.

My love of antiques and the appreciation of past generations I learned from her. She was "The Keeper of All Things" and I will carry the torch for her now.

Every time I stop at a yard sale, I will wish she was with me. I would often scan the tables quickly and then grow impatient while she chatted with the sellers. More times than not, she would come to the car with a purchase I had somehow over-looked, but could not live without.

We had always made plans to go to Antiques Roadshow and meet the Keno brothers. Years later, my sister and I fulfilled that wish and even got a kiss on the cheek from one of the Keno twins.

When I pull over on the side of the road for a sickly dog or put out a bowl of milk for a lost cat, it will be because of the compassion for animals I learned from her.

No one will ever be able to make potato soup or potato salad like she did, but I will continue to use her recipes and her beloved potato salad bowl. Liver and onions and Harvard beets, anything lemon, pink wafer cookies, grapefruit boiled with sugar, Circus Peanut candy and black jelly beans will always remind me of her. She always had a row of jars along the back of her kitchen counter filled with pretzels and oyster crackers. I hope to keep a jar in my kitchen, too.

Whenever I visit a new destination, I will look for a small rock and slip it in my pocket to remind myself of her. Brown UPS trucks will always remind me of the many boxes she sent over the years filled with treasures for my children. I so wish I had kept all the hand-made Valentine cards and poems she authored over the years. Her thoughtfulness in sending cards is a tradition I hope to continue.

Because of her, I will always put a few coins into the Easter eggs I hide for my grandchildren and there will be a "golden egg" with a special prize.

*Playing a card game of Rummy, doing crossword puzzles, spending days on a 1,000 piece puzzle on a cardboard table, chocolate-covered cherries, and Christmas cookies in tins between layers of wax paper.....the list goes on and on of the simple memories that make up my mother.*

I remember the day I gave birth to my first daughter. I made a phone call to my mom before I even held her and we cried together as I announced her arrival and told her, her granddaughter would be her namesake.

Whenever I lose anything, I will always know to "look in Nellie's room." It was an expression I learned from an early age and never understood until years later. My mother lost her mother at the age of two and was raised by her grandmother Lou. Lou buried two daughters, Mable (my grandmother) and Nellie. When anything turned up missing, it was always said Nellie must have taken it with her to Heaven.

My mother's name was Delores Eileen Beams. D.E.B. As the youngest sibling and only girl, she was both protected and tormented by her three older brothers. She loved to tell the story of learning to ride a bicycle. Her brothers taught her to ride, but never taught her to stop so she would go round and round the block begging for them to help her stop. They would just laugh each time she passed by until she finally just crashed into the yard. She was often called home by her brothers shouting her name DELOR-ASS and it caused her a lot of embarrassment. When she was older, she used her initials to create a new name for herself....Deb.

"A mother's love is like a circle. It has no ending and no beginning. It keeps going around and around ever expanding, touching everyone who comes in contact with it." -Art Urban

**I am DEBra Lou. I am my mother's daughter. I am her legacy**

# Kali S. Steward

Massachusetts, United States of America

## *The Shadow of Sudden Changes*

~Matthew 13:32~

**"It is the smallest of all seeds, but when it has grown, it's larger than all garden plants and becomes a tree, so the birds of the air come and make nests in its branches"**

She is the bud of a seed growing in a womb where the odds of survival are against her. She is coming to the world three months early. Like a butterfly trapped in a cocoon ready to bloom, she will be born fitting into the palms of her parent's hands. Her parents were unwilling to accept they would go home childless because the mortality rate of being born premature in the 1970's and having congenital anomalies, in addition to respiratory problems, made it unlikely she would survive.

I am alive today, despite the health problems I experienced as a child and in opposition to what the doctors believed. I know God has a plan for me. A big plan.

My adolescent years in school offered a constant struggle. Trying to catch up in school because my learning development was delayed, was often a difficult task. Being born so small and premature caused me to learn a little slower. But that is ok.

As a child I just absorbed the aroma of roasted peanuts and green peppers & onions sizzling on a portable grill by the street vendors. The line was always long in this seemingly congested city. It was worth it all to get an Italian sausage on a soft crust roll. And, let's not forget the New York Hotdogs. I can vividly remember how delightful it was to get such a treat as a child.

My mother would be on a shopping spree, while my siblings and I would get lost weaving through the clothing racks as though it was some magical getaway, anything to silence the sound of honking horns. And not to mention the hearing pitches of voices ranging from high to low in conversations in taxi cabs which smelled like an old cigarette astray from the customers who rode before.

The Big Apple was full of mystery. Everywhere you turned there was something to learn about culture, like a melting pot of musicians, dancers and artist who came from all over the world to experience Stardom.

Lights, camera, action! The smell of the exhaust lingered in the air. Maneuvering through the crowded street packed like an airtight can of sardines, was super tiring to me. You could only anticipate your next destination. Tall buildings cascaded the sky, giving me a glimpse of what my life would become when I grew up working on Wall Street, crunching numbers while living the American Dream.

Dreaming kept me sane. I was so misunderstood as a child, bullied for no apparent reason. I felt back then it was because of my quiet temperament. I was a quiet child and often misunderstood. I never really felt the need to fit in. Everything seemed awkward to me in those formative years. I felt trapped in a world which restrained me from my creative ability to express myself. Without any hesitation, it appeared to be that I was entwined into a web, tangibly forced to conform into what I most disliked.

Her name was "Debutant Doubting Debbie". She always reminded me how much she disliked me simply because I was too quiet for my own good. Being bullied was considered to be the norm and part of the growing pains of adolescence. I suffered in silence. I had also conditioned myself to never show emotions toward the bullies. This time in my life and being a victim of bullying, would forever leave a lasting impression on me. I would often try to be invisible and blend in like a chameleon, camouflaged in the foliage that changed as the seasons came and went. The parallel journey of God walking beside me would be the very thing to break the barrier of my silence in 1992.

I remember so well the sunsets over the Everglades. The wonderful sounds of "Mother Nature" reminded me of the hot, sweltering summer in the Carolinas in the late 1980's. Oh, the constant sound of the annoying rooster who echoed from miles away. I gave him the name of Becker. I don't know why I chose that name. However, Becker was no match to the alarm clock my father gave me which could wake up the whole neighborhood. Something was different. The days were slow and the nights were long. I paced the floor all day long with anticipation that my dad would walk through the door. I realized he wasn't coming home because he passed away unexpectedly. I heard a thump on the door which was jarred open. I dropped to hear what was going on. All I can remember is my mother's painful cry for my father, as though the world had stopped at that very moment. The tick-tick of the clock on the wall was louder than ever.

My cat knew something was wrong. She sat beguiled as if she knew. She pranced toward her bowl, as my sister cried. My cat never left my sister's side that night. And my sister comforted the cat with strokes to make her purr. My mom who never wore her heart on her sleeve, was a stoic lady who was often expressionless, knew she would be burying her husband and our father. I wanted to just run until I couldn't anymore, then the pain wouldn't hurt as much. I needed my mother to comfort me reassuring me, it was only a dream and my dad would walk through the door to greet me asking me how my day was, the way he so often did.

Four years after his death, life was as though it was a cloud hovering over my head. My heart was like a river running on a drought, while my soul was held captive: just dead inside. Nothing mattered. Life itself was not the same. For the love of God I didn't even know who I was anymore, running basically on an empty tank of loneliness.

My sense of belonging was at an all-time zero. The battlefield of my mind was the devil's playground setting every booby trap to tear me down. I often wondered in those days of darkness, if I would ever come through. Then one day the "Voice of God" said to me (John 14:27) "Peace I leave with you. I do not give to you as the world gives. Do not let your heart be troubled and do not be afraid".

Not having closure has haunted me all of these years. See my dad had wanted my sisters and me to stay the night in the hospital because he was admitted three days prior to his death. He didn't know tomorrow wouldn't come. I pleaded with God to bring my daddy back and I would be obedient and ask for forgiveness. I told God, I was sorry for those times when I didn't listen. My dad was trying to protect me from people who were hurting me. I was so sorry.

While in college, a fellow classmate invited me to Bible study. That same year, I gave my life to God. I was now sure my voice would never again be silenced for fear of not being heard. My truth was to be a light for those who were in darkness. I soon became passionate about helping others who suffer in silence, to be aware of their symptoms so they too could escape darkness and soul entrapment. I had moved through the world like a chameleon. The world was bedlam. I would like to give you some advice as you move through your darkness or troubled time in life.

Speak your truth. Allow your words to flow. Not for anyone to read, but for you to speak with your own voice. You choose how to live your life. You can choose to live in your self-imposed treason, or you can choose to live in the light of God. You can defeat your enemies when you are strong in your conviction that God made you for a reason.

# Gwen E. Cover

London, United Kingdom

## *The Man with the Little Girl*

### "Acts of Love, Hardship and Adventure"

I would like to tell you a story about my Dad, Mr. Era Cover. A man with an unbroken spirit who was a true inspiration in my life. Nicknamed "The Soldier" by certain family members, this is my story.

My family was living on the warm, sunny shores of Jamaica when Dad was promised an apprenticeship as a tailor in Britain. As a child, I loved to see his face light up whenever he told the story.

"When you arrive in England, you'll have a brighter future and earn more money. You can always come back if you don't like it", said his sibling as they sat on the veranda listening to the night crickets and watching a glow fly whizz by.

Arrangements were made with the family's pioneers who had already made the journey to England. Since many signs in the windows of prospective landlords said "No dogs, No Irish, No Blacks", Auntie V invited him to stay with her until he found lodgings. It was clear hardships were ahead, but Dad remained determined to begin his new adventure.

From 1948 onwards, 125,000 people from the Caribbean Islands made the 8,000 mile journey aboard the SS Empire Windrush. Dad arrived by plane in September 1958 along with other Islanders who were invited to work and settle in Britain. These Caribbean immigrants were known as the 'Windrush Generation', making a significant landmark in British history.

A few years later, my mother and sister joined Dad, and I was born in the 'baby boom' era of the 60's, the second generation Black British of Afro-Caribbean descent. Most of the Caribbean Islanders were under the impression, London streets were "paved with gold", Dad, like others, were shocked to find life was much tougher than expected and dismayed when the Islanders were made to feel unwelcome by many British people.

**Dad showed me that a PURPOSE and a DREAM are the driving forces of WHY we do anything.** I realized it could be soul-destroying if you don't know the big WHY and WHAT you desire in your life and how you plan to leave a legacy. My dad was lucky to have family members support him through difficulties in spite of some occasional tension.

His dream of becoming a tailor was shattered. Dad had to work in the mines and expanding manufacturers. He soon learned about working with British white people. He laughed when he described the Brits' dry sense of humor, which he often didn't understand. Their love of animals was extraordinary and the drinking culture in the pubs was the key to meeting new folks, the British way of socializing. The latter led to much laughter when getting together with family and friends after a tiring fifty-hour workweek.

Persistence and determination were essential ingredients for the transition to living in a foreign land. Dad said he was grateful to earn an income, and live in a warm house, to see his nose and fingers in the fog and not get lost in the streets. I remember laughing when he told me this story. I couldn't imagine fog as thick as how he had described except for when I watched black and white Dracula movies with a foggy scene.

Then my Dad's big WHY and great dreams were suddenly re-written through unexpected events.

I was eight years old; Mum and Dad separated, now Dad's life had a new purpose as a single parent. Whilst I was in contact with my Mum and I know she loved me down to my little toes, my Dad was the main parent. He became known as "THE MAN WITH THE LITTLE GIRL", a title that initially irritated him though he never explained why. But I did notice he mentioned this phrase in the 1980's with laughter, rather than pain.

This episode in our life was very challenging and prepared me for dealing with prejudice, school bullying, emotional pain, feelings of shame for being different and using my wits to make intuitive decisions. I've since discovered I am Clair-sentient (the ability to sense or feel the presence of those who've passed or to sense the auras and vibrations of all living things). I am also a Clair-empathic (I can sense the emotional experience of a person, places, entities or animals although I struggle to name the feelings of the latter). It's no wonder I worked well using these emotional abilities with adult men and women in the criminal justice world, especially sexual offenders.

Aunty M, her husband and two daughters lived with us for a short period. It was so painful when they moved out to their new home. The emotional gap was unbearable. I filled this hole with food and this developed into an emotional eating addiction. To remedy this situation, I had to grow up quickly and became a mother to myself by the age of ten. Dad simply could not fill this gap. He was one person and could not be two parents, although he did his utmost to address all of my needs.

As a teenager, I was rude and angry at Dad and the world. I could not control my temper tantrums. Where on earth did Dad get his tolerance skills is beyond me? Yet he remained patient and spoke to me in a firm voice. I had grown into a woman with breasts and all the womanly things to go along with it. I looked to the school, friends and girly magazines for advice, but it was my astute Dad who spoke to me about menstruation, babies and men. My friends considered me lucky. Many had no such guidance from their mothers. I believe our discussion was an intimate and emotional time between Dad and I. He understood my transformation into womanhood better than I did. I felt loved, supported and strong. It was exactly what I needed at the time. I was getting inappropriate sexual attention in school and it was building rage within me. I found my inner strength to cope with it from the love and support of my Dad who was my solid rock.

In the 80's, Dad lost part of his left leg due to diabetes not helped by his incompetent doctor. This was another life changing event for both of us. How do you switch from an able-bodied world to a disabled world overnight? Well, Dad and I had to do this with no preparation. It was hard emotionally and physically for both of us to adjust to a new lifestyle. I constantly worried about Dad even though he was able to look after himself, walk with a prosthetic leg and drive a car. It was roughly ten years before he was comfortable enough in his body and mind to travel to the Caribbean Islands, USA and Canada to meet new family members. We had such fun!!

In 1998, Dad died of a heart attack. My own heart was literally broken. I found myself on a deep transformational journey which was difficult and confusing. The loss of my Dad, my rock, my world, triggered a spiritual awakening which changed everything. I found myself filled with an internal presence of the Holy Spirit and for weeks had no grieving pain. Eventually I came crashing down to Mother Earth and needed support. I couldn't look after my emotional and mental health on my own and it took guts for me to admit this first to myself and then to those who would help me. I don't like being vulnerable, but had to let go of my fierce independent streak. Thank God for my soul-mate, wonderful friends and family who supported and advised me through this time.

Today, deep feelings are evoked every time I think of Dad. In truth, the most satisfying role for my soul was being a daughter to him. I wondered if anything could ever come close to creating this kind of satisfaction. But recently, life took on an unexpected magical turn in many ways when I followed my intuition and surrendered to working with women leaders from all areas of life at a profound transformational level.

The Life Design Salon, a nurturing space for women deeply prompted to reinvent their lives, to stop suffering from emotional and mental harm, to seek fun, adventure and lifestyle freedom, was born.

I wish to end my story by saying you and I are soldiers as was my Dad. From his example, we can learn to persist in the face of rejection, hardship and change, and to live an influential life anyway. His spirit was unbroken to his death. England became his home in spite of every challenge, and he lays here resting in peace.

To you I would say, look after your emotional and mental health, indulge your joy by listening to the promptings of your inner world, and live your dreams.

# Sandy Parris

London, United Kingdom

## *C Is For Courage*

Although perfect wasn't quite the word I would use to describe my life, I had a lot to be thankful for. My business was thriving. I was enjoying a fabulous social life and looking forward to celebrating a milestone birthday. Life was pretty good and it would be fair to say, I was in a good place mentally and physically.

How could I possibly have known life as I knew it was about to change so dramatically?

After exchanging the usual pleasantries, the doctor fiddled with his notes, straightened his tie, adjusted his posture and cleared his throat before continuing with his diagnosis.

The words "biopsy- abnormal cells-endometrial-Cancer" tumbled from his mouth and hung heavily in the air. Although his lips continued to move, I couldn't hear anything else. He had said the 'C' word so everything stopped. Time stopped. My heart stopped. My breathing stopped. I felt as though I had been sucker punched by his words and dragged backwards through some kind of black gaping hole where nothing made sense anymore.

I had been holding mum's hand and as she loosened her grip and brought her hands towards her mouth, her head slumped against my shoulder as she gasped in shock. This couldn't be happening, I thought. This was just a routine visit. We were having afternoon tea later, so she can't have cancer!

Instinctively, I put my arms around her, hoping to hug away the shock of the devastating news we had just been given. The doctor's lips were still moving as he reached out to place his hand on mums shoulder "... endometrial cancer" echoed in my ears as he explained how lucky she was to be diagnosed at such an early stage and her treatment programme would consist of chemotherapy sessions followed by radiotherapy.

As the words swirled around in my head the initial shock quickly turned to anger. I was angry and resentful that this was happening to our family - my mother. Why was this happening to *my* mother? Cancer was something that happened to other people, not to us.

Through my years of organizing breast cancer awareness events I had been in contact with so many brave women who had battled, survived or were living with cancer. I was used to giving messages of encouragement, offering advice and supporting these incredible women through challenging times. Despite this, I couldn't quite comprehend what the oncologist had said, let alone ascribe the diagnosis '*endometrial cancer*' to my own mother.

But at least she was alive, right? She had a chance to beat this?

The coming days, weeks and months were shrouded in uncertainty as the family struggled to absorb the news which would certainly change our lives. Tears, prayers and difficult conversations took place as we entered what was unchartered territory. I had never known my mother to be ill and suddenly, I was faced with the very real threat of losing her. As my stomach tightened and began turning in on itself, I couldn't stop myself thinking about how much my mother meant to me; her laughter, wisdom, passion for life, her strength, resilience and values had hugely influenced me and shaped part of the woman I would become. Life without her was incomprehensible and I realized one thing - I had to step up and be there for her no matter what. I needed to find a way to quash the negative thoughts about my own mortality whilst channeling the fears that were steadily building inside of me.

We weren't going to take this lying down. I was up and ready for the fight. Mum was going to get through this and more than anything else in this world, I wanted to make sure I could be there, every step of the way. To be strong for her, I needed to strengthen myself.

Journal writing had never been a regular activity for me. It was something I had dipped in and out of in the past, but now, I felt compelled to commit my thoughts, fears and more importantly my gratitude to paper.

I had attended workshops, read books and articles about the therapeutic benefits of journal writing as a way of deflecting negatives and turning them into positives, and how writing can enable you to manage stressful situations. Now, I was putting the theory into practice.

By just turning up to write each morning and each evening I felt powerful, in control and connected with my thoughts and emotions. Sometimes, the page remained blank and nothing came. Other times, I wrote pages and pages.

The act of writing down my feelings and recording reasons for gratitude was energizing and transformative. My journal became a confidante who provided a safe space to untangle emotions, express myself or simply to vent without judging. Writing in my journal also offered me the chance to affirm ownership of my emotions, confront my fears and show appreciation for the many good things, which presented themselves.

Accompanying my mother to her first chemotherapy appointment was really tough. Whilst the nurses busied themselves attaching drips, catheters and monitors, I noticed how small and fragile she looked. She was always the bedrock of our family unit so seeing her hooked up to the machines was strange. We both put on a brave face.

Mum's sense of humor soon surfaced as she began telling the nurse that wearing the cold cap made her feel like a spaceman. Despite the awful circumstances, we found ourselves laughing and joking about how funny she looked. Laughter is a wonderful thing and it's infectious – the other patients began smiling, which lightened the mood.

As I wrote in my journal that night I knew we were going to beat this terrible disease.

'Dear Cancer,

Thanks so much for stopping by!

Your arrival was unexpected and unwelcomed, but you've taught me so many valuable lessons. Sometimes we need something like you to show up.

You taught me to believe in myself, to have courage and be strong. You reminded me of the need for humility and gratitude.

You almost had us beat, but because of you we are stronger, closer, wiser and thankful for the many simple opportunities which life presents.'

Time is one of our most valuable assets, yet it's one of the things that we least respect.

# Cynthia L. Ryals

Florida, United States of America

## *Beauty for Ashes*

### "Reclaiming Life and Love after Loss"

*"There are things that we don't want to happen but have to accept, things we don't want to know but have to learn, and people we can't live without but have to let go."* ~ **Author Unknown**

I often thought of my mother as the ultimate survivor, as strong as she was beautiful. As long as I can remember, there seemed to always be some major health challenge to overcome. There were times when doctors said she couldn't possibly survive, yet she always proved them wrong. Over the years, she lived through many major illnesses; yet, through it all, she kept her faith, hope, and sense of humor. No matter how dim the prognosis, there was never a time I doubted she would be just fine.

This time was different.

Upon hearing the news that she had been taken to the hospital, my internal world shifted. It was subtle, yet palpable; a storm brewing in the distance. She was tired, and my soul felt the weight of her weariness. I couldn't shake the sense of dread – a profound fear and sadness, punctuated with a growing anger. This couldn't be happening. I wasn't ready.

The weeks went by too quickly amid a flurry of doctors, nurses, family, and friends. The prognosis was hopeful, the words encouraging, the prayers uplifting; but my soul would not be soothed. My only solace was in the moments alone with my mother, as if we were the only two left in the world – the connection of love between us like a three-strand cord not easily broken.

In those final days, as activity slowed, I was finally able to be truly present with my mother. I observed everything with a sense of awe. I saw her beauty with fresh eyes. I realized how extraordinarily blessed I am to have come into the world through this amazing woman; fascinated that her body created and cradled my own.

Those days were profoundly precious. We talked while I fed her, and she smiled when I stroked her hair or kissed her face. She asked me about the Light in her room that only she could see. She spoke of those she loved who had passed on before her, who were starting to visit. I dared not tell her I was beginning to see them, too.

Then, there was the question which loomed like a dark cloud until my mother asked aloud: "Am I dying?" I reassured her she wasn't and everything would be fine, even as I struggled to find the truth in those words. My mother asked to hold my hand. Her eyes filled with sadness and love, as if she were longing to ease the heartbreak we both knew was inevitable. She gently rubbed my fingers, took a deep breath, and softly, with apology, announced she couldn't take any more. She was ready to go home.

It was her last day.

*"Grief wraps around people, takes them to a place they would not go otherwise."* — Patti Callahan Henry, *Between the Tides*

The morning my mother stepped outside of time, I returned to her home to find the carport covered in rose petals, her favorite flower. In the pre-dawn hours of the warm, autumn Wednesday, it was unexpected and jarring; simultaneously cruel and comforting. Every day until her burial, there was a fresh crop of red and white petals leading up to the door of the house.

My mother always had a flair for the elegant and dramatic.

It would be quite some time until I was able to ponder the meaning of the beautiful petals. After all, it's often hard to recognize the beauty on our path when we are covered in the ash of mourning. I struggled to wrap my mind around her departure. I became glaringly aware of my aloneness – no parents, no siblings, no spouse, no children – my sense of security, history, and belonging suddenly cut like a spiritual umbilical cord. There was no beauty beneath my feet; only clay and ash.

What would happen to me now? Who would I be now I was no longer anyone's baby? I was keenly aware I had lost the last person who would love me completely and unconditionally. The earth shifted and, suddenly, my journey was no longer safe; the road invisible. Love had been interrupted.

*"If you look deeply into the palm of your hand, you will see your parents and all generations of your ancestors. All of them are alive in this moment. Each is present in your body. You are the continuation of each of these people."* - Thich Nhat Hanh

In ancient times, there were cultures who marked the mourning of a loved one by anointing their own bodies with clay or ash. It was an act of humiliation – a stripping away of the comforts of the ego and flesh. Perhaps it was symbolic of the bitterness and barrenness of soul that comes with grief. The tearing away of the former self becomes the catalyst for our most profound journey of transformation. Ash becomes the remains of the fire that forms us anew; the very symbol of the ability to imbue our mortality with eternal meaning.

I have come to understand those days of roses as a lighting of my path – my mother's way of letting her presence be known, comforting me, and providing wisdom for the journey ahead. The abundance of fragrant petals were messages of joy – the trading of beauty for ashes.

*"GOD sent me to announce the year of his grace... and to comfort all who mourn, give them bouquets of roses instead of ashes, Messages of joy instead of news of doom..."* - Isiah 61, The Message.

This joyful message – this grace – is simply this: Love.

In the time since my mother's transition, her love continues to guide me into a clearer understanding of myself and my place in the world. She is helping me to understand Love never dies – any interruption is our own perception, not reality. Her love for me was, and continues to be, a reflection of beauty. I am coming to understand I am not only able to experience the unconditional, eternal love of my mother, but, more importantly, I am able to give this kind of love to myself.

I am learning to be my own soulmate, and define and live my life according to my own reflection of Truth and Light in the world. In this way, grief (in itself, a reflection of profound love) has become an ally – a guidepost on the path to becoming fully myself – the ashes from which beauty rises.

*"The only way to move from your reality to God's reality is through people who love you."*— Shannon L. Alder

There are many lessons and gifts on this journey. One of the most profound is the joy of selfishness. This is about radical, no-holds-barred self-care. Perhaps this is the hardest lesson to learn. Grief takes a toll on the body. In the first few months, I allowed myself to be carried away by stress and worrying about things that were out of my control. It caused major health problems, from which I am now recovering. I can now see this as a gift, because it forced me to be extremely mindful of how I care for myself.

As I reflect on all my mother endured in her body, she is teaching me to honor my own body – her gift to me. I now see it as the vehicle through which I give and receive love, and I honor it as sacred and precious. In doing so, I am able to move through grief and more fully into life, thereby honoring the life given to me. In this way, selfishness creates space for healing.

Walking this healing path requires gentleness, grace, and mindfulness. I have learned to nourish my body with whole foods, my mind with meditation, and my soul with laughter. I remember my worth by setting healthy boundaries, honoring my unique gifts and allowing in the expansiveness of joy moment by moment.

Most importantly, I am learning to reconnect to Love. Where there's Love, there's no real loss, for you cannot lose that which doesn't die. Love is a circular energy. The more you experience, the more you are able to give away and, therefore, the more you are able to experience.

*Comfort comes from knowing that people have made the same journey. And solace comes from understanding how others have learned to sing again* ~
**Helen Steiner Rice**

We grieve because we love deeply. It's the love inside the grief – the beauty that's calling us through the ashes – that longs to lead us into a deeper knowing of ourselves as Love. In this Love, we reclaim all of life.

# Chocolate & Diamonds

## Ayesha Hilton

### Victoria, Australia

### *Minnie*

I hold the letters in my hands. The envelopes are addressed in the cursive script taught in the early 1900s. I treasure these letters written to me over so many years. They are from the first person I felt most truly loved by. Her name was Margaret Roberts, but to me she was always Minnie to me. She was my mother's mother, yet I never called her grandma or nanna. Growing up I would spend as much time with her as I could.

Minnie may have been disappointed in my mother. Back in the 1970s in Australia, despite the apparently wild hippy days, it was still frowned upon having children out of wedlock, let alone be a single parent with four children to three different fathers.

I think my mother's marriage to my younger brothers' dad while she was pregnant may have been to please my grandmother. While Minnie may not have approved of some of my mother's choices, she did adapt to them and she loved us all dearly. When I was only four, my older brother was taken away from me and went to live with his father.

I felt like a part of me was missing and it would remain that way for the rest of my childhood. Often, the only time I would see him would be at Minnie's house in the school holidays. We grew older, it was often just my older brother and I who would meet at Minnie's, while my younger brothers stayed at home with my mum.

My brother lived in the harsh Australian bush in the middle of nowhere in a tent for many years. He would wear Australia military uniforms and the traditional slouch hat. So when he came to visit, it was odd to see how much he had changed and I really had no concept of his new life.

When we would visit Minnie at the same time, my brother and I would sleep in twin beds and have a wonderful time being spoilt by Minnie. We were both mini-adults with lots of responsibilities, so it was like a nurturing respite for our young souls.

In the morning, Minnie would wake us with hot chocolate and teddy bear biscuits. When we got up, we would have a two course breakfast of porridge followed by eggs on toast. Morning tea came quickly and involved a lot of sugar and cream. My favourite was Minnie's famous sponge cake filled with jam and cream. A close second, was her award winning hedgehog slice.

We would then have lunch with dessert, followed by afternoon tea, and then dinner with dessert again. It felt like we spent the whole day eating or planning our next meal. At home, I had very healthy food with little treats, so it was very exciting to be able to eat so much decadent food.

Minnie had been in her mid-forties when she had my mother and uncle. She was an older mother and grandmother in those days. She was born in England and migrated to Australia when she was about seven. She was one of only two girls in a family of thirteen children, so she was used to working hard on her family's farm and caring for the menfolk.

Despite growing up rough on the farm with so many brothers, Minnie was very much an English lady. Whenever we went out, she would wear her hat and gloves. It seemed to take her forever to get ready. She never learnt how to drive, despite her farming background, so we would catch the bus into town where she would spoil us, taking us out for lunch and buying us toys and clothes. I still have the first bra and pair of Levi jeans she bought me as a teenager. They don't fit anymore, but I like having them in my cupboard to remind me of the precious times we shared.

The best times of my life were spent visiting Minnie and I wanted to be with her at every opportunity, even when I was a teenager with an active social life. When my brother wasn't visiting Minnie, I would sleep in her king-sized bed. We would sometimes talk about her death. I wanted to be with her when she died. I had been bought up a Buddhist and I wasn't afraid of death, or talking about it. But I wanted to be with her when it happened.

I had planned it like this: I would wake up one morning and find Minnie lying beside me having passed away peacefully in her sleep. We would then say our last goodbyes.

When I was seventeen, Minnie's health deteriorated. We had just celebrated her 86th birthday the year before. Around this time, I wrote her a letter. I told her how much I loved her and offered to move in with her and take care of her. I even suggested finishing my education by correspondence. She wouldn't hear of it, of course, but I am so glad I made that heartfelt offer. We both knew and expressed how much we meant to each other.

One day at school, I was summoned to the principal's office. Minnie had suffered a heart attack and my mother had gone to be with her. My strongest emotion was anger – I was so furious with her for not taking me with her. I felt like I should have been there and I wasn't there when she needed me most. I decided to catch the train and go see her in the hospital. But before I could travel, we got the call she had died.

I can remember standing in my bedroom totally lost, sobbing my heart out. I was glad Minnie hadn't suffered for too long, but I felt like I had let her down because I hadn't been with her. The person I loved most in the world, and the one person who truly knew and loved me, was gone forever. Even as I write this, the emotions are so real twenty-four years later, that when I think about her, there is still a physical ache in my heart.

The day before the funeral, we went to view Minnie's body. She was laid out in a coffin with her hair and makeup done, wearing her best outfit. This was my first real death of someone close to me. I had seen a dead body when I lived in India as a child, but this was the first person I knew and loved who had died. It was traumatic to see Minnie so cold and lifeless in a coffin. She didn't look like herself.

I asked my mum if it was true they stuff cotton wool in the mouths of dead people. I have no idea where this trivia came from, but I know it was nerves and sadness 'made me say it. My mum was so cross and felt like I was behaving inappropriately. She kicked me out of the room and I didn't get to say a proper goodbye to Minnie. I still have some sadness and regret about this today, though I am sure Minnie didn't mind. And I know my mother was grieving herself and didn't mean to hurt me.

The funeral was a kind of torture to me. I looked at the coffin covered with flowers and I just wanted to open it up and have Minnie magically hop out and say there had been a big mistake. But there hadn't. She really was dead and it was hard to get my head around the finality of it. I thought about the last time I spoke with her and how I didn't realise at the time it would be the very last time I would hear her voice.

After the funeral, my mother gave me Minnie's engagement ring. I still wear it today. It is my most treasured possession. She wore it for more than forty years and I have worn it for more than half my life. I look at it on my finger, a beautiful small diamond in an antique setting, and I am reminded of her love for me (and my love for her).

I know being so loved by just one person can make all the difference. Minnie was that one person for me and after she died, I missed her so much. I made a lot of bad choices in my late teens and early twenties trying to recreate that love in relationships and encounters with the opposite sex. I confused sex with love.

I was so desperate to be loved, it makes me sad now to think about myself at that younger age. I feel a deep sense of compassion for the younger me and I cannot blame myself for what I did, knowing how much I longed to be truly loved. If I could go back in time, I would tell myself I am worthy of being loved and I am lovable. I think of all the years I spent yearning for love and the ocean of lonely tears I cried. It seems like a waste, but I have to be grateful for what has come to pass on my life's journey.

Only recently have I come to a place in my life where I have accepted myself fully, the light and the shadow, and now feel worthy of love. I suffered greatly through my bad choices and misguided search for love. But it was loving myself that changed everything.

Memories are strange creatures that exist only in our own minds. They aren't based on reality, but on one's perception. I have a version of my childhood I suspect no one else in my family would share. And yet, this is the only version I have. I have deep gratitude for the people in my life who have shown me loved and helped me love myself. And I give thanks for Minnie and the unconditional love she gave me.

# Marlene Pritchard

Mississippi, United States of America

## *Faith It Til' You Make It*

**"There is never a moment when God is not in control.
Relax! He's got you covered." ~ Mandy Hale**

I will bet you had to take a second look at my title looking for a typo. You are reading it correctly." Faith it till you make it" works better than "fake it till you make it!" This is what is taught in so many industries, especially the direct sales world.

When I first spoke with Carla about writing my story, we discussed my many paths I have taken to get where I am today. I have been down many different roads to find where my true passions lie. She and I both felt this is what my story should be. So we shall begin...

I think as women we go through many different phases in our lives. We begin as innocent daughters, develop into young women and usually join the workforce in some capacity before becoming a wife and mother. The role of grandmother will come to fruition if you live long enough. I' not there yet, but the good Lord willing, I will be blessed to have this title one day also.

I was raised in a very strong Christian family. Being raised in the "Bible Belt" of the south, we attended our local Baptist church every Sunday morning and Wednesday evening. Sunday school was just as important as regular school in our family and community. This was actually part of our social calendar also. This is how it is in the south. It's a great way to live...faith, hope and love as the Bible says.

Now that we have established my childhood was normal and I was raised with good values, we will jump to how I was finally able to get to the point I am at today. It has been quite the journey, but a good one I might add!

Both my parents are still living and are in very good health for their age. For this I give thanks daily. I am a wife of 28 years and have 3 healthy and happy grown children. All three graduated last May – 2 from college and my youngest from high school, so needless to say, we celebrated all month!

When I married the love of my life, I had to give up my job working for my family doctor due to relocating. I had been his personal nurse for 5 years. Loved this, but didn't really desire hospital work, so I decided I would try a different field altogether.

I went to work for Prudential. I studied and took my Series 7 so I could sell securities, along with disability, health and life insurance. This lasted about 1 ½ years, but I was not content. I wanted more, but I wasn't sure what it was.

I went back into nursing and worked in Outpatient Surgery and then transferred to the Heart Cath Lab. This is where I was working when I became pregnant with my son. I worked up until I delivered my first born, Miles, and I made my decision to stay home to raise my little boy, who I had been blessed with. This was a no-brainer for me. I couldn't bear the thought of leaving my precious Miles at a daycare.

We were enjoying life and I seemed content for the moment. When Miles was 8 months old, we decided to have our second child. I became pregnant with my only daughter, Tara. She has been nothing, except a blessing!

After Tara's birth, I quickly realized I needed adult conversation! Being with two children under two years old all day will do that to you! I decided I wanted to work again, but also desired to stay home with my two children. Alas, I came up with quite the career change this time!

This was the beginning of a life change for me! You will hear people say how certain businesses can be life changing… These words are a very true statement for me! I am going to share with you a story where I know my faith played a major role. My upbringing gave me the courage to travel and step out with faith onto territory I knew absolutely nothing about! My parents had always encouraged me and told me I could do anything and have anything in life that I wanted. What I needed was faith and desire… Fortunately, I had plenty of both!

I wasn't exactly sure what I was going to do until I went to lunch with my husband and a vendor he sold product for. The vendor asked if I wanted to rep for him and sell a few of his products. I quickly answered, "Sure, I will give it a try."

Long story short, I picked up a customer and was making around $600 a month and my business grew from there. He quickly started ordering additional products and then the referrals began. If you take anything away from what I just said, please hear this – **REFERRALS ARE KEY!**

My business took off very quickly. I was loving life! Here I am a young mother and wife, staying home with two wonderful children and running a business that was thriving! What more could a girl ask for! Right? How about another baby! I became pregnant with my youngest son, Nick. He has and will always be such a joy in my life! Blessed a third time!

My faith is really coming into play now. And I am keeping the faith! It's so important that you appreciate and have gratitude for what you have in life. Don't ever get complacent or take everyday life for granted. The day you do, is the day you will begin going backwards!

I want to share with you a couple of examples of how my home based business was exploding. I look back and just smile with unbelief. My husband, Tim, and I have quite the stories we will tell our children and grandchildren one day!

I had one particular customer who ordered a pallet quantity of a product. This product was very heavy and could not be unloaded by hand. In order to keep my supplier a secret from my customer, I would have to ship on two freightliners. My customer's order would come in on one trucking company and leave out on another. The problem is I was working out of my home so I didn't have a warehouse or loading dock. So again, what's a girl to do! The answer is "Get creative!"

I quickly made friends with both truck drivers. I always had a cold bottled water waiting for them after they did "the favor I asked." So what was the favor? They would back up their two 18 wheeler trucks at the end of my driveway. I lived on a corner lot so there was plenty of room. What a sight! But the beauty is when they did this every other week, my profit was $5,000 each time! I mean, how lucky can a girl get! I think I was a Mompreneur before anyone knew what this was!

The other story I would like to share is one of my customers moved to Mexico when Bill Clinton was in office and NAFTA was passed. I developed a relationship with a Mexican purchasing agent who called me on everything he was to order. He asked if I sold a certain product. I wasn't sure what the product was but me, myself and I (keeping the faith) always said "Yes, of course. How can I help you?" Orders were faxed back then, instead of emailed as they are today. He told me he would fax me an order for his next month's needs. I said "Okay, I will be looking for it."

Long story short, he faxed me a $112,000. 00 order. I didn't even know what the product was. Fortunately, a purchasing agent from another account of mine was able to direct me to one of the only two companies that had access to this product! Thank goodness I was able to get credit from this company and the story continues!

You can call it luck, but I prefer to call it faith. There are several nuggets to my story I would like to make sure you picked up on... **Take chances** when they are presented to you. Without saying yes, you'll never know what could have been! **Build relationships**...these are vital for business growth! And lastly, **keep the faith!** This has proven to be the most important of the three for me. Without faith, I would never have taken the chances or built the key relationships which allowed the life changing growth that happened in my business.

In closing, I would like to share, I've now developed a thriving health coaching business and have found my real passion! I have products and services which have been life changing for so many people including myself. I am once again blessed for keeping the faith!

# Kirsten Campbell

New York, United States of America

## *A Grandmother's Love*

As I watch my granddaughter sleep and cherish her powdery smell and the feel of her soft tiny fingers as they curl over my own, I remember my hopes and dreams at that tender age. At three years of age, I believed as most little children do; time goes on forever, and my parents would love and protect me forever. I had high hopes and never dreamed my little world would come to a crashing end.

I was born in Ankara, Turkey to my German mother and Jamaican father. It was 1960 and interracial marriage was frowned upon in the United States. Three months after my birth, we moved to the United States and soon my brother and sister were born. Right from the start, my life was full of heated negotiations. By the time I was three, physical memories were burned into my little soul. Do this and you won't be beaten with the belt or punched and put in a dark closet.

At four years old, I noticed we never had food in the fridge, but we always had plenty of Little Friskies cat food. The acrid smell of liquor floated through the house, along with cigarette smoke and weed. Pot parties were the norm and my mother and father put my siblings and me in a bedroom, while they smoked and drank their way into oblivion. At times we were lucky and they would pass out on the sofa. Sometimes, they yelled at each other, they fought and the sound of bodies thrown to walls permeated the air. Often, the door opened and large hands slammed me to the walls. I remember tasting blood for the first time at that age. Hospital visits were the norm as well. My life was not a dream. It had turned to a nightmare.

At five years old, my mother ran away from my dad, moved us away then moved back, once she figured out cat food wasn't a normal staple for children. On my sixth birthday, she took me to my Jamaican grandmother, Nana, and sat me on a couch in front of my father and asked me the most important question of my life, "Do you want to go with me or stay with your father?"

I was terrified of my father and when I looked into his eyes, I saw my answer, I had better say no. "I want to stay with my daddy," I said to her. My mother left. She didn't turn to say good-bye, but did promise to come back for me as she went out the door. I remember thinking how pretty she looked as she walked out the door in her beautiful red suit, matching high heels and hat. In my tiny mind I felt she would come back for us. Surely she didn't mean to abandon us…

A few months later, my father moved in with Nana. She was a religious woman who wouldn't stand for the smells my father brought into her house. "You get off the liquor and drugs or you leave," she told him. He left the very next day.

I became aware of real pain during the first year with Nana. My once vibrant world became full of grays and black. I was beaten mercilessly with an extension cord. Blood spilled copiously and she knocked out four of my teeth. She worked at a hospital and even though I was barely six, I had to get up and make her coffee and breakfast, iron her clothes and give her an insulin shot. She got ready for work and left me with a list of chores. I also had to dress and feed my little sister and brother. I fed them, dressed them and I even combed Vicky's soft blonde hair and wiped her face. I brought her to the babysitter and then dropped my brother to school. I went to school and cried and cried. I was so devastated with being abandoned by both parents. I told the teachers, but all they did was complain to Nana and she would then beat me-in front of them.

I missed my mother and father. They were not the best parents, but they were all I knew. At times, I did get hugs and kisses from them. Nana never gave me hugs or even a positive word. I was constantly kicked, punched and battered, then locked in a dark closet. When I got home from school, I washed dishes and did my homework. When Nana got home, she set her round marble table and prepared dinner. We sat at the table to eat and she prayed out loud that God would send her son. "Where's my son? Why did he leave this duplicate of Corina with me? I hate this girl! I hate her! Please take her before I kill her!!"

"Why does my Nana hate me?" I wondered. In my head Nana was a huge giant of a woman, who had stomped her way into my life. She grabbed my ponytail, slung me to the ground and stomped me, kicked me to the closet and then she sat my siblings in front of the television while she ranted on and on. "Why would he have to leave you here? Why? Why?"

I wondered the same thing. Why did my father leave me with a woman who tried to kill me? Why did my mother leave me with a woman who hated her? At times, I loved the closet. She forgot me and left me there, alone. I melted to the cold wooden floor and peeked out through the sliver of light under the door. I waited for my little sister's pudgy fingers to appear as she pushed them under the door. I rubbed her fingers and kissed them and fell asleep. She comforted me. Once I was released and Nana went next door, Vicky and I would stand at Nana's bedroom window and stare at the sky. We watched air planes as they flew overhead.

"She's on that airplane, right?" Vicky asked.

"She might be... She'll land the plane right there in the middle of the street," I said and smiled as Vicky's little face brightened.

At the time, I believed every word I said. It was a comfort for me to think my mother would return. A few months later, after being brutalized and abused by Nana, I realized I was lying to Vicky. Mother wasn't coming back. Mother and father had left us-forever. I couldn't find the words to tell my little sister. I knew it would break her heart. I held on to her little hand and kissed the fat little dimpled knuckles, while my heart burst inside and I cried silently as we watched the airplanes together.

Years later, Nana had broken my permanent teeth, my nose and allowed her boyfriend to beat me and molest me. I became withdrawn. I survived, but I was broken inside. I had lost myself and most of all lost any and all hope to be loved. Nana died when I turned seventeen. I suddenly had to be a normal person. I found a job, went on my first date and married that man a year later. He said I was the most beautiful woman he ever saw. I believed him and loved him. We had children together and I found love overflowed in my heart with every cry from my baby, every smile, every little giggle. I had more children and I hugged and kissed my children and supported their efforts at home and in school. I read books about children with hopes that I would be a good mother. I swore to do the exact opposite of what Nana did, I would love and cherish my children and grandchildren.

Years later, my children told me I was the best mother ever. They gifted me with the best gift possible, grandchildren. I became-Nana. I wanted that name to mean something special to not only me, but to every one of my grandchildren. Each child has been a blessing to me and I fawn over them and love them so they know their Nana is there for them. Today, I stare at the tiny face of my grandchild and thank God for the chance to be in her life. I feel sorry for my mother, father and Nana. They had no idea that a blessing was given to them, a blessing they threw away, a blessing I was given, the blessing of being a mother and a grandmother...

#parenting #abandonment #childabuse

# LIFE

# #LIFE

### the simple things

# Jeanne A. Dexter

Florida, United States of America

## *Finding JiJi*

I loved sitting in the carport when I was six, cooking out, singing songs and making funny faces with my dad. We both loved talking like Gomer Pyle, making faces like the comedian Red Skelton and just laughing and entertaining each other. I loved that I could make dad laugh. I am sure the rest of my family was there, but I only remember dad and me.

I was the middle child, nicknamed JiJi by my older brother who, as a toddler, couldn't say my name. A little girl with no formed expectations of anyone or anything, accepting and loving of everyone and everything, I had it all. My mother would later say I tolerated her and then she would chuckle. I was all "daddy's girl" and I loved it.

When I was 8 years old, it all changed, suddenly. At least it seemed that way: out of nowhere, dad coming home late every night, the drinking, the fighting, vicious fights, slow at first, more and more regularly as time went on. Night after night I cried myself to sleep. My little sister, always reaching out to me as we lay there in our little twin beds, feeling like something tragic was about to happen. I wondered why I didn't hear her crying, only to find out later, how scared of our Dad she was. She was probably holding her breath, trying not to make a sound. I know I was and at the same time trying to listen. How could things be so bad? I just couldn't understand being scared of my bigger than life, fun loving, playful dad! Even with the fighting I was not ever scared of him, only what might happen.

One day something was very different. You could just feel it. Most of it's a blur. I remember more fighting and dad and me. I know everyone was there, my mom, my brother and my sister, but I only remember my dad, in full stride, headed toward the front door of our house. With all the force and might I could muster, I was clinging to my dad's pant leg, holding on for dear life, crying and begging him not to go. I knew I could keep him there if I could just hold on long enough. I knew he wouldn't leave me here, his little girl; the one he would sing and laugh with and make all those funny faces. He just kept saying; "I have to go". "I have to go". "What you mean you have to", I cried out. "What about me? What about all of us?" The door slammed shut. I just stood there crying for what felt like days!

I had no idea of the impact that day would have on my life, even into my adulthood. A huge part of me, JiJi, the happy little girl, was gone forever. Life would never be the same, or so I thought.

Enter: "The Pioneer of Divorce". Remember mom, the woman I "tolerated". I call her, "The Pioneer of Divorce", because in the 1960's, no one in my world had divorced parents. We were the only kids in my elementary school with divorced parents, we were the kids from the "broken home".

My mother wouldn't have her children labelled. She was a powerhouse of reality and determination. Mom was the "great communicator" and an even better listener. Mom was the woman who ultimately became my hero. She was now my mother and my father and she was good at it!

So, our new life began: mom pulling from her own family foundation began laying the bricks, building our new life. One which was loving, solid, secure and filled with humor. She created a foundation which allowed each one of us to learn who we were, to decide who we would become and what we wanted for ourselves in this life. She did it with passion and connecting, laughing and talking and always being real, especially when times were tough.

Then, there were her phrases, a collection of gems all her own, or so we thought, that would always bring you back to earth. Don't tell me you don't have a few of your own? My favorite, the phrase that pulled us through thick and thin: "this too shall pass, if you live long enough". Little did I know how often I would need that phrase throughout my life?

With mom's grounding I, JiJi, found myself again and we found each other. I would need this foundation way beyond anything I could even imagine.

Life smoothly continued through the teenage years into adulthood. I had many successes in life with some big failures blended in. My first marriage came and went. Thinking this was how life was supposed to be, after all, my parents were divorced, I never really worried too much about the marriage or the divorce. It was 1978. I remained single for 6 years and started to learn who I was, who I had become.

I remarried. Never really thinking about having children, I became a mom in my second marriage, my greatest accomplishment in life. I love being a mom. I don't think anything is more challenging or more rewarding than bringing life into the world, especially when it looks and sounds just like "you".

Just like with my first marriage, I once again found myself getting divorced. It was 1997. I was beginning to feel like I was part of the lost and found. Every time I found myself, it seemed something traumatic happened and I felt a little part of me disappear. A little more chipping away at who I thought I was or who I wanted to be. Did I ever know who I was? How could I keep getting so lost?

On good days, I realized the power I had as a mom. I felt like a mother lioness, loving and protecting my children. This was the happiest time. I know many women who say they are afraid of being a single mom. I found this one of my greatest times of self-discovery. I was afraid of nothing and nothing was going to keep me down. I didn't know it at the time, but my roller coaster ride was just beginning. I was at the top of the track about to take a hundred mile an hour ride to the bottom.

I began to write during this divorce aftermath. The divorce had created frustration and separation between my two kids and me. I needed a way to communicate with my daughter and my son, who was particularly angry. It broke my heart that they wouldn't talk to me even though I understood what they were going through, being a child of divorce myself. I had thought I was much like my mother, that her lessons were ingrained in me, that I was a great listener and connector.

Communication had come to a halt and the silence was killing me. Where had I gone so wrong?

I had an idea to write questions about difficult topics. If I wasn't asking the questions directly, maybe they would talk. I went to the counselor at my children's school, Paul Schweinler; and enlisted him as my partner. Together we created "third" party questions which opened up dialogue and helped us all talk about the difficult times, as well as, the good times. We put the cards into Jars, like a game. The topics would be endless, just from my own experiences and Paul's expertise. The first two titles were, The Talking Jar and The Anger Jar. My son, 12 years old at the time and an excellent artist, drew the first two labels.

I used The Anger Jar at home with my kids. We laughed, we cried and we connected. It worked.

If this worked for us, why wouldn't it work for others who were going through similar experiences?

We then created *The Marriage Jar* and put all three titles in a catalogue. They began to sell. My daughter, then nine years old would sit on the floor with me for hours and put decks together so I could pack them in jars and ship them out. We were helping others and helping ourselves at the same time. I had found myself again.

Years passed and I was in my 40's, perfectly content and happy with myself, I found the man of my dreams, my gift from God, my Prince, Doug, my superman. He was so handsome and kind, so soft spoken and logical. Yes, it can happen. This time I knew who I was and I would never lose "me" again. Right? Wrong.

**Neither one of us would know the journey ahead of us, which was to begin only months after finding such unspeakable happiness!**

We married in March 2001. Remember the one hundred mile an hour trip to the bottom I was speaking of? Two months after the wedding, my 47 year old brother passed away, totally unexpectedly. We were devastated and in shock, pain so unbelievably great. He had been my best friend through childhood and our teenage years. We played baseball and basketball. He taught me how to play guitar. We had even been roommates in our early 20's, after my first divorce. We had so much in common, including the same sarcastic sense of humor. Now he was gone.

My life has never felt the same. I changed that day more than I realized. I became someone totally different. The only thing I could feel was pain, anger and loss, of my brother and myself. It was like I was living in a tunnel and could only see light, way at the very end, but, would never get to it. I was so lost. Years later, my mother would tell me "you gave up when your brother died". She was so right.

In 2002, my 13 year old nephew took his life. He was being bullied in middle school. In 2003, I lost my dad for the second time, only he wasn't coming back, he passed away suddenly. In 2004, one of my best friends also suddenly passed away. After that, it was one funeral after another, until I was literally begging God: "please don't put me through another funeral. I cannot do one more". 15 funerals in 9 years, I thought I had all I could handle. I didn't stop crying for 9 years. During this time, we wrote The Grief Jar, The Teen Jar and The Bully Jar.

Then a two year reprieve and we found out my mom had terminal cancer. She chose not to have treatment. Mom lived 6 months of the 2-12 month sentence she was given and passed away. Those six months were the most painful time and yet one of the greatest blessings of my sister and my life. We talked, we laughed, we cried and we created a new normal for a time. Mom was so funny and so playful just like we remembered her as kids. She was amazing. She even wrote her own obituary. Who can tell your story, your legacy better than you? We even laughed at some of those possibilities. Imagine what you would say about yourself if you really chose to have the final word. It really can get quite funny. We'll save that conversation for another time.

A year and a half later I found out I had cancer. I made it through with the help of my husband, my sister and great friends. I thank God every day my mother was not around for "my turn". While recovering, I wrote the Cancer Jar questions, empowering families to talk about Cancer. The hardest part is to know what to say in difficult times, whether grief, illness or divorce. To find the answers, we must ask the right questions. I continued to write.

My life had been so up and down like that game at the carnival: Whack -A-Mole. Every time my head popped up, I felt like someone took a mallet and hit me back down. Little pieces of me being left behind; scattered through every portion of my journey.

It took years to be able to see it. Now I realize I was losing a bit of myself with every emotional trauma in my life. My happy life was becoming more and more difficult to enjoy. That happy little girl from my childhood, JiJi, kept coming and going. For the first time in my life, I felt like I didn't know who I was nor did I care.

Unless... I was creating, writing, helping others through and so I write... it heals me. I write questions and statements which help others to connect, to find common ground, build lasting relationships and solid foundations and to heal. Writing is so powerful.

Remember the movement; "Look out for number one? If you don't look out for yourself, no one else will"? I don't believe that. I believe if we look beyond ourselves and look out for others, if we create something that speaks to others, we are looking out for ourselves.

It's so simple. It means just talking, listening and connecting with your kids and your spouse every day, meeting your neighbors, reaching out and sharing your story to help someone else. The world is not just about "me". It's about the big picture. We are all connected. We hold so much power to right the wrongs and to create a world of mental health. "Reaching out is Reaching Inward". By reaching out to others, you will find yourself, as I've found myself (JiJi).

And as for the trauma..., "This too shall pass..." and it has, well most of it. I've finally found me and I love who I am. JiJi

# Roshanda E. Pratt

South Carolina, United States of America

## *Finding Your Voice*

### "You Have the Right NOT To Remain Silent"

One of my favorite things about our home is the beautiful flower beds out front. At first glance, I was intimidated by the beauty because unlike my mother and father, I don't have a green thumb at all. Somehow I have managed to keep things looking decent enough for the rich bounty of butterflies to grace the assortment of gold, fuchsia and white flowers. The butterflies are amazing to see. The garden attracts big and small; all elegant, light and carefree as they take flight around each flower.

It's hard to imagine this beautiful creature once spent its time wrapped in a tough, multi-layer protective shell, hidden from the world. It has been said, *"Butterflies can't see their wings. They can't see how truly beautiful they are, but everyone else can."* Interestingly enough, this is my life's journey. Many times, I felt like I would never emerge from the cocoon as the butterfly I knew in my heart I was destined to be. I desired to soar, but my wings felt clipped. Have you ever felt that way? You know you have something impactful to say, you can feel the words bubbling up on the inside and yet you don't give voice to it? In fact, when you yield to the urge, which is not often; people tell you how much they are touched by your words. Others can see your beauty, but there is still that struggle of life inside the cocoon versus life outside of it.

Now, as a storyteller strategist, I help businesses and non-profits find their voice and release their message to impact the world. When I consider my life, I was always a talker. In elementary school my father and I had a discussion about my progress report, which stated I was a good student, but just talked too much. When my dad asked me about it, my response was I had something to say. I advocated for the underdog. I was named the "Dear Abby" of my class, Best All

Around, Senior Class President, Homecoming court, Student Council and the list can go on. I ALWAYS knew my words mattered. Then life happened, somewhere between middle school and college, I lost my voice, not literally, but figuratively.

Life choked my voice. Tragic events stifled my voice. Disappointments, depression and low self-esteem spoke louder. Hurt dominated my vocal cords. When I did speak, my words seem to cut like a knife to those who mattered most. When people hurt, all they know how to do is hurt those closest to them. I was a broken butterfly. Have you ever seen a butterfly that can't fly? You want to help, but you can't fly for them. Unfortunately, for many years that was my story.

The process of reclaiming my voice began in college. The process began with me giving "voice" to the truth. John 8:32 in the bible states, "*Then you will know the truth, and the truth will set you free.*" For the first time in years, I confronted the pain I never wanted to speak about. It was paramount for me to speak the truth in love. I discovered speaking about the hurt of my childhood, the rejection and the shame was not about hurting or shaming my family, but it had everything to do with taking what once was in the dark and bringing it to the light.

The heart transformation that happened next, only happened because of my life was surrendered to Christ. Prior to receiving Him as Savior, I never knew the God who created the world wanted to hear from me. Until that point, I felt like a raindrop in a bucket, nothing really special or out rightly unique. I had the facade down. Smart, boisterous, popular, hard worker, but my heart was broken. I remember the literal pain I would feel from what I called a wounded heart. The love of Christ changed all that and continues to woo me daily.

Since the day, I gave my broken heart to Jesus. He is continuing to update my picture of myself from analog to high definition. I've always loved the power of the pen; journaling became therapeutic for me. The words on the page allowed me the ability to speak without opening my mouth. Words are powerful! I know it all too well working as a television news producer for more than a decade. In my position I worked daily to tell the stories of those in my community and beyond, yet as I became more comfortable with telling my story, I stopped.

The reason I told myself was I was too busy with life, motherhood, ministry, wifedom, business and everything else. Honestly, I was helping craft the stories of those around me, but once again questioned my own. The blatant truth, I questioned not the importance of my story, but the importance of me. Would anyone really want to hear from me? I learned the answer is yes. The bible says, "*For the creation waits in eager expectation for the children of God to be revealed* (Romans 8:19). The world is waiting on your story, your voice. Could it be that you are the answer to what ails your community, nation or world?

Like the butterflies in my garden, I had to learn that in the mess of my life there is a message. It is what I like to call a beautiful mess. I am learning in the midst of chaos and in trouble, God hides beauty. Your voice is beauty. Now, you must understand just like the butterfly there is a process and I must respect the process. I had to be content with the negative thoughts I had about me and those imparted to me by others. I had to be content with the competing voices and by God's grace I am winning every day. The process is just that, a process each of us has to go through. You cannot skip the process. It's in the process that your voice, your story is created. Trust the process.

**Here are three steps taken on my journey:**

1. **SPEAK:** Realize the power of your voice. To do this I had to say what my creator said about me. His word had to shape my words. One of my favorite scriptures, Psalm 81:10, *"I am The Lord your God, who brought you up out of Egypt. Open wide your mouth and I will fill it."*

2. **Know the Value:** Treat your story like fine china and not a Walmart plate. This means your story is valuable. Don't cheapen it! For every mess in your life, there is a message. When you understand your value, you will never play small again. I went from not knowing this, to now being a highly paid speaker. Amazing!

3. **Take the Risk:** I know risk can be scary, but it's necessary. Joyce Meyer says it best, "Do it Afraid." If you are waiting for fear to leave before you take that speaking engagement, tell your story or write that book, you'll never do it. I remember the anxiousness I felt sharing my story for the first time, but I knew those feelings were part of the process. But here is the exciting part, when I did share my story the amount of women who felt empowered to do the same was well worth it.

**Here's the bottom line:** the one thing you have which is unique to you is your voice, your story. Stephen Covey says *"Find your voice and inspire others to find theirs."* The most powerful thing in the whole process of embracing your voice is you get the opportunity to open up the door for others to share their God-breathed story. Let's start a revolution of fearless messengers armed with the weapon of their story. You can no longer remain silent.

# Michelle Gardiner

### Victoria, Australia

## *The Quiet Achiever*

It was a cold, dreary and grey Melbourne day, not so different to any other in the thick of winter. My grandmother, with her dark sense of humor, would have called it a "cut your throat" kind of day. It was a Monday morning and I was sitting on a crowded tram on my way to work in the city. I was surrounded by professional workers dressed in grey and black suits, scattered with the odd white shirt. I wore a red scarf, matching red vintage hat and carried my favorite red floral tote bag. My bag overflowed with a bright green drink bottle, two pairs of dancing shoes and costume items. I rummaged through the bag and took out a needle and thread along with a red lace bodice that would form part of my burlesque dancing costume.

My week prior had unfolded with the ending of a fresh relationship. My newly repaired bike had failed and skidded in the middle of a busy intersection and a large four wheel drive had run into the rear of my little car. I held a belief that things would be better this week. I put my headphones in my ears and pumped up The Beatles "Here Comes the Sun" and tuned into my own inner world. Somewhere along the way, I looked up and took in my surroundings.

I then looked down at the red lace I was sewing in my lap. I felt I had two options, to care that I was the point of difference in my environment and change in some way, or to continue on as I was. I smiled, chuckled to myself and carried on sewing.

While growing up, I was an incredibly shy child, yet I had plenty of friends. I was the "Quiet Achiever" and made conscious effort to live in the background. While my parents were ecstatic about me finishing high school, a University education was beyond their vision for their children and they were baffled when I told them about my application. My mother experiences significant mental and physical health issues and has spent seemingly endless stints in Psychiatric wards since I was 17 years old. In 2014 alone, my mother spent several months between intensive care and a locked Psychiatric ward. For many years I feared I would have similar struggles in my life and set out to build a safe and protective life to buffer me. My family's experiences had made me feel somewhat ashamed and I had resisted sharing the impact I felt from this with others when I was growing up.

I moved out of home with my first boyfriend shortly after turning 18 and we got married when I was 20 years old. My husband and I came from families who experienced social, emotional and economic issues and we grew up very quickly. Often, we were better positioned to support our families, than they were to offer support. We were both raised with an incredibly strong work ethic, resilience and care for others and held high, but relatively safe aspirations for our life together. We faced a number of challenges and had odd bouts of depression, anxiety and for five years, I failed to sleep more than half of each night.

As a fresh faced and newly qualified Social Worker, I began working in Child Protection at the age of 22. I visited families in crisis and made assessments about the welfare of their children. At times, I attended the Children's Court and I presented in the witness box on several occasions. I truly believe the work Child Protection do is one of the most important roles in our society. Personally, the extent of pain and anguish I have felt over a stranger's life and for their children has at times been overwhelming. The ecstasy over positive outcomes was also often overpowering and amazing.

By the time I was 26 years old, I felt like a shell of a person and I felt suffocated. I was exhausted from my work and life; as well as socially isolated, constrained and frustrated. I felt overloaded with responsibility and had a strong desire to express who I really was and to live for myself. My marriage ended and our house was sold. Over a twelve month period, I essentially walked away from my life, from many of my social connections and in addition, I experienced three family members passing away.

As I contemplated the next phase of my life, I channeled a belief that nothing could hold me back from to seeing and experiencing the world in a whole new way. For the next three years, I took on life in a whirlwind. I was like a child with big wondering and curious eyes. I travelled, I volunteered with an art therapy program in Thailand. I left my outer suburban job and moved to the city. I explored my city, my country and the world. I explored me. I tried everything that came my way from meditation, to scuba diving, sky diving, theatre and art. I dated. I shared houses and I lived alone.

I found my greatest inspiration in dance, movement and an endless curiosity about other people, their perceptions and how they live their lives. My life and I grew exponentially and I came to love the thrill of positive personal challenges.

These experiences have brought me to a new space where I am seeking to combine my sense of individuality and independence with my love of community. I spend my time working in the community, dancing, writing, doing yoga, exploring, travelling, socializing, spending time outdoors and experiencing art and culture. I live each day, aspiring to be more loving, graceful, strong, energized and expressive than the last. I work with young people who have lived complex lives. I am inspired by their courage and resilience as they develop a voice about their experiences, make sense of their story and work out what they want for themselves. I love working with people who are bright and creative and I feel joy when I assist them to see how they can use their experiences to draw strength for their future.

I turned 30 in 2014, and I can truly say I've arrived. I have no interest in living like a cardboard cutout of perceived perfection. I only seek to live in a way that has meaning for me and this is what I also want for others. There is immense power in standing strong in ourselves and following our true north. Our reward is a blossoming, adventurous and illuminated life of color, with plenty of opportunities to express our energy and presence. I value diversity and I see few things in life more beautiful than the willingness to expand our world and perception to include those who live differently to us. It is in bringing our boldness to the world, that we have true opportunities to connect with ourselves, others and our community.

There is a lot of grey in life. We see it, we experience it and we move through it. It is the grey that gives color such richness. It is the falling away of the old that allows space for the new. There is a time and a season for each life experience and all are valid and meaningful. We have the choice of what we want our experiences to mean and how we want them to shape who we become as people.

It is nearing the end of winter in Melbourne and as I sat on the tram that Monday morning, sewing my costume, in my bright red clothes surrounded by grey, I looked out of the window, thinking about the clearer skies to come and the days where I can ride my bike as opposed to catching the tram. I love the excitement and sense of possibility, creation and expression that resonates with Spring. Just like my coming future, I know I will have the opportunity to deepen my roots and grow a firmer foundation than ever before.

The most authentic thing about us is our capacity to create,
to overcome, to endure, to transform,
to love and be greater than our suffering"...Ben Okri

# Hillary Foster

California, United States of America

## *I Hired A What?! Why? It Let You Do What? Ah, Passion!*

The first time I remember someone suggesting a doula was during my first pregnancy. There I was - 26, pregnant, unmarried, barely employed and living in the third floor of someone else's beautiful historic home in downtown Providence, RI. It was beyond a wild ride to get to that point; never could I have imagined. These people were so meant to be put on my path, but I had no idea why. Why I had to go through all that heartache and turmoil just to get to that moment: the very first time my roommate Quinn asked if I had thought about hiring a doula. I could never have known just how much that one word would shape, and impact my birth, my views on motherhood, and so very much of my future.

I'm pretty sure I went upstairs to my room and did what most of us do when we don't know much about something. I googled, and then googled some more. If you ask me what page I landed on, or even what it said, I couldn't tell you. I have some educated guesses but nothing definite. I was at least 7 months pregnant, so I'm going to chalk it up to foggy pregnancy brain. I do know that it sparked something inside my core, and enough that I began on this discovery.

What I discovered was that, like a lot of first time mothers, I was unsure, nervous, and really anxious about what was going to unfold during labor. I was terrified that my mother wouldn't hold it together well, despite having had her own two natural home births. That wasn't it though; it was more about our dynamics, and the pressure of seeing me in pain, or not tolerating the stress and chaos I so feared labor would be. I was a first time mother, young and feeling essentially alone. The idea of having someone there that I knew would stay calm, and wasn't going to yell at me for being a wuss about the pain was appealing to me. Someone that was a trained, professional, and had tricks and tools to put me at ease during labor, and that could be there unwaveringly because it was her job.

I took the next logical step and asked someone actively involved in the birth world for a reference. I was taking a childbirth education class per my midwives recommendation at my local hospital, so after a break in the class I asked my teacher if she could recommend anyone. Of course she did;, she gave me several names on the back of a business card and I was on my way..., or so I thought. A couple weeks later I had still not found anyone that was available, so back to my teacher Tina I went. She agreed to take me on being a doula herself; I believe I was almost 38 weeks at the time. I was a true testament to the belief that it's never too late!.

We dived in and scheduled a prenatal appointment right away, especially since she would be on call for me immediately. We spent that time talking about my pregnancy history, who would be joining me, and what my wishes were for my birth. I was closed off, and probably not the most forthcoming. I was in a dark place despite being at the preface of one of the most pivotal moments of my life. I put on a brave face and kept on going, because I was pregnant and I felt I didn't have a choice.

Fast forward to 40 weeks plus two days:, Tina had been checking in regularly via email. I had just received an email from her that morning. I didn't want to respond;, I was tired and feed up, and I was frustrated and scared my baby was still not here. I was sick of telling everyone I was still pregnant, and yes I could pop any day. I was an emotional rollercoaster sobbing on the bottom stairs, going back and forth with my mother on whether she should go home and get some clothes and rest. We ended up going for a walk to get the essentials (toilet paper and ice-cream) on the way home, and so began my birth story. There was a project, a shower, timed contractions, packing of the bag, and then my mom and I headed slowly down three flights of stairs.

When I got to the bottom I needed nourishment, so I grabbed a banana. While outside discussing with my roommates whether it was time to go to the hospital, I leaned over the banister and threw up that banana. Off we went despite my midwife's insisting I should wait at least another hour. We called my doula and a family friend and they meet us there. When my doula arrived I was already quite loudly insisting I could no longer do this, and would need the drugs now! However I was still in triage, and my doula gently reminded me I had to be admitted first and would be more comfortable once I was in the birth center.

I spent most of my labor in the tub, and really didn't want to get out. When the time came, everyone tried to get me out, my midwife, my mom, my family friend, but in the end it was Tina. She came in and she guided me through a few contractions, wiped my head, made sure I had water, and encouraged me. I trusted that she wouldn't steer me in a direction I wasn't comfortable or wasn't good for me. A small whirlwind later she was there to share in the moment my daughter was born;, she took pictures and helped with my initial breastfeeding. I was on top of the world--, I felt like if I could do that without drugs, well then I could do almost anything. It renewed a strength and confidence that was a great way to begin the journey of motherhood.

Two point nine months later, I was at it again. This time in a different state, with a toddler, and my girls' father. I knew I would hire a doula again, and I did, but I hired two! We interviewed with several doulas, and agencies, but when I met Cheryl and Jordan I just knew. They were amazing and worked in partnership, and the bonus was that they offered both birth and postpartum doula services. This time around wasn't all peaches and cream. We were adjusting to life living together instead of oceans apart, we were both back in school, and we had a wild toddler like you wouldn't believe.

When we finally decided it was time to leave for the hospital we called Jordan and she meet us there. I have to say I'm not sure what I would have done if she hadn't been there both during my labor and then for the next 3 months that followed. She was my rock! She encouraged me and reassured me when I was feeling defeated and beginning to waiver. She gave it to me straight when I lost it completely, and at the time it was just what I needed to get over that hump in transition. She took turns with Brendan literally holding me up. She was amazing at gently encouraging him to meet my needs and give him other jobs when he seemed overwhelmed. When Maya was born and she had to be taken to the NICU she stayed with me for hours as I screamed and cried for my baby. When I finally got the green light to go see my baby, she even gave me her shoes because they were easier to slip on. (In the haste of heading for the hospital , I hadn't packed another pair of shoes; I only had my snow boots!) . She went above and beyond the call of duty, and for that I will never be able to thank her enough.

When we finally got home that continued. She started postpartum work the morning after Bren had flown out to California to start his new job. She anticipated my needs, she made sure I ate, showered, got extra rest, and she even helped with Lilah. Most importantly, she listened. I needed to process so much that happened and that was still happening, with my birth, breastfeeding, parenting, and the future of my family. As we went on, I began to ask her more about doula work--, and what it was really like, and how she got into it.

I didn't know for sure then, but the seed was definitely planted, and so began my own journey into doulahood. I read, I researched, and I bounced the idea off many people over the next year and half. I was home visiting my mother with my girls, and back to contemplating my life. I asked myself those tough questions:, what was I doing, what I was teaching my girls, what was I giving back, what was I missing, what was my passion. The next thing I knew I was looking up doula trainings in the area; I told my mother about one that was coming up not too far. She said jump and gave me a little push and so I jumped. Here I am today, now a trained birth and postpartum doula and in a thriving doula partnership myself, actively involved in my community and local hospital.

The sky is the limit when you follow your passion.

# My Ly

London, United Kingdom

## *The Shed of Hope*

Living in a shed at the bottom of someone's garden, a stone's throw away from East Finchley tube station didn't exactly appeal to me. The sentence "Why don't you come round to my shed for dinner?" wasn't something you wanted to drop into a conversation with family or friends. But let's face it, I was utterly desperate and in my head, I was convincing myself this shed was no ordinary shed.

No, no, quite the opposite. It was the crème de la crème of sheds.

Yes, from the outside, it looked like an ordinary shed, but once you stepped inside, it was more than just a place where you stored your Wellington boots, golf clubs and garden chairs. The ditsy blonde letting agent had left me alone for a few minutes whilst she popped out to find the owner. Looking around, I could see it was extremely compact. There was no room to swing a mouse, let alone a cat.

However, it did have everything I needed. Albeit not everything was in tip top condition. The tiny bathroom had a broken sliding door which got stuck halfway when I closed it too quickly. The shower cubicle made me face one way only. As I turned towards the broken door, my knees brushed against the lumpy looking day bed. The dirty brown chair had three working legs. The flimsy looking cardboard box turned upside down and used as a coffee table had a million random words scribbled on it, begging for a story to unfold. The shaggy turquoise rug propped up the teetering kitchen table. Despite the obvious flaws, it seemed like pure luxury compared to what I had been accustomed to. This might be a place I could proudly call my home.

What a lovely street name 'Cherry Tree Road' was. With two winding pavements full of delicate cherry blossom trees and houses in pristine condition. Surely people would want to visit me if I lived on a pretty street?

Thinking it through, I could handle the 'interior design' of the shed, but the safety aspect unnerved me.

The shed was located at the bottom of a five-bedroom house's garden. An alleyway ran alongside the garden leading into a dimly lit car park with the top of the shed visible to passersby. Strangers, drunks and thieves walking through with darker intentions could easily clamber over the rickety low wooden fence to have a good nose around.

*"So Lucy, I would like you to meet the owner, Derek."* shrilled the letting agent behind me interrupting my thoughts. I turned round to see 'Barbie' flirt with 'Ken' for a minute before stepping aside and revealing a tallish forty something man with blonde hair, a wonky nose and muscles which resembled a Roman Gladiator. *"Would you like me to tell you more about this palace?"* Derek quizzed. In my head I was thinking "No, and 'palace' is really pushing it." but the sensible and polite part of me said out loud *"Yes, that would be great." "When I first bought the main house, I rented out all the rooms so I needed somewhere to stay myself. I turned this shed into the little beauty you see today. It's got trashed a bit over time, especially with the last tenant who had no respect for possessions or property and I am looking for someone who isn't going to cause me any trouble."* I could see he was quite proud of his shed, so I nodded in agreement.

*"You can use anything inside the main house, just treat it like your home. I know this shed only has the basics so for example you can use the washing machine and tumble dryer. I just ask that you respect everything you touch and tidy up after yourself."* I perked up when he said this. Ah ha, so I would be living in the best of both worlds. Little did Derek know I had actually been inside his house before. I could curl up with his sleek black cat on the red corner sofa and watch some trashy television on the third floor. I could wash my own clothes using his Persil Non-Bio and borrow his iron tucked away in the small airing cupboard on the second floor. I could wash my own dishes in his kitchen on the ground floor whilst overlooking the garden, deciding where to plant my beetroot seeds. I did love a good beetroot and chocolate cake.

Although the shed was less than perfect, I could at least dip in and out of luxury; returning back to the 'South Wing' every night.

Derek was deep into his sales pitch of how the shed worked (or didn't work from what I could see), other house rules and how much he loved his neighborhood, tenants and precious cat. I continued to pretend to look intrigued by his enthusiastic spiel. And tried not to smirk too much.

As the weirdest of coincidences goes, I dated a guy many years ago who lived in this very house with the tiny shed sitting at the bottom of the garden. A charming IT geek called Michael, who caught my attention with his big blue eyes, humorous one-liners and constant chit chat of Windows XP. At the time, I never had an opportunity to see inside the shed because I was always in the main house. But isn't it funny how surreal life can be? I debated if I should interrupt Derek to tell him, but just let him rabbit on.

My focus was to negotiate hard. I was usually a good judge of character and Derek seemed like a fair man. Strictly speaking, if I was going to be living in this shed, it was *my* garden as much as his. I just needed a decent patch of his soil. At least, this way I could grow a few fruit and vegetables to save on the expense of food shopping. Along with other short cuts, if I was savvy enough, I was sure I could live on only a few pounds a day.

If you are wondering whether I've always had to scrimp and save, you would be wrong. There was a point when I was a normal person with a normal job and salary. I worked as a normal secretary for a normal (and rather boring) high-flying businessman in the dizzy heights of Canary Wharf. I lived in a normal house in a normal part of London with a normal dad. I had normal friends, work colleagues and neighbors. Life was as normal as it could be.

That normality was turned upside down with the rug pulled from underneath me when my dad unexpectedly passed away three years ago.

It was after his death when the real fun and games began.

I will never forget the day when I forced myself to go through all of my dad's possessions, and the moment I stumbled across a red and black patterned suitcase which would change my life forever.

The suitcase was well hidden to say the least.

My dad had buried it deep inside the base of his king sized bed. Somehow he had managed to cut an opening to fit the exact size of the suitcase. Using his carpentry and tailoring skills, he had put together the base so professionally, no one ever suspected anything sinister.

Once I had pried out the suitcase, I opened it to find something more than just a couple of duvets and blankets being tucked away.

It was the biggest gasp of breath I had *ever* drawn.

Staring at me were bundles and bundles of rolled up fifty pound notes, wedged in from left to right and neatly stacked on top of each other in multiple layers. Only the initials 'D.T.K' sewn onto the inside lining of the suitcase seemed normal.

It was like one of those scenes you would see in a film. Nothing you would ever associate with the lives of a poverty stricken family like ours.

And lying on top of one million pounds, to be precise, was an old photograph of a young man and woman standing outside East Finchley tube station. On the back of the photograph, in my dad's distinct and neat handwriting was a short message:

*'Dearest Lucy, one day, please return this suitcase and its contents to the rightful owner for me. And then I shall be at peace. Love you always, Dad.'*

Snapping out of my deep thoughts, Derek looked at me sternly as if he was going to ask the most important question ever. I knew time was running out. It was either this shed or being left out in the cold, damp and wet streets of London. Again. Naturally, this latter option didn't appeal, but did I really have the guts to sign on the dotted line?

My thoughts focused back to my dad's wise words. He had always taught me to persevere through the tough times and to never judge a book by its cover. He often said to me *"Lucy, you just never know what treasures you might uncover at the end of a dark tunnel."* So with his words ringing in my ear, I knew this odd little thing that I was standing in had its faults, but ultimately it's my shed of hope. And it was up to me to ensure that my dad's legacy carried on.

Somehow. Someway. Some day.

# Diana Schreiber Murdoch

Ontario, Canada

## *Finding Diamonds on the Road to Happy*

### "Hearing a Still, Small Voice"

If someone had told me on my forty-ninth birthday I would be happily single in my late fifties, enrolled in University, and a powerful positive influence on many young lives, **I wouldn't have believed them**. In the past eight years, my life has gone from the wretched depths of depression to a joyful anticipation of what each new day can bring.

For years, my marriage had been crumbling under stressful encounters, frequent deception and sarcastic, aggressive words. I was living with a perpetually angry man. Though I had often used humour to diffuse touchy situations, I couldn't find anything to smile about anymore.

On that fateful birthday, I started a journal. I decided that by my fiftieth birthday, I would be happily married or happily single, but I was determined I would be happy again. The journal and a wonderful counselor helped me through many fervent efforts to create that happy marriage. But when I turned fifty, I found myself only single. It took years of tearful soul-searching, huge life changing decisions and just plain hard personal work to reach a state of happy. This is my story.

The day my daughter approached me saying, "Mom, don't sleep with Dad anymore. You might get an STD" I was shocked. I knew things were bad, but I had no idea he was getting intimate with strippers and hookers. After a confrontation with a storm of questions from me and a wall of silence from him, we agreed to separate and divorce.

Since I had a family history of depression which had already taken two lives by suicide, I found myself in bed for almost a year. If you aren't familiar with depression, this will sound ridiculous to you, but those who know this demon are nodding now.

In my journal, I wrote: "I want to scream. I want to die. I want to sleep and never wake up again. The agony of rejection and adultery has hit me square in the face as I find his car at our favourite anniversary motel. He's having sex with her. Devastating physical pain ripping me apart. Nausea wrenching my gut. My chest feels like a thousand pounds are on it. Oh God, my God, why have you forsaken me?" I cried out loud, howling like a wounded animal.

I believe God answered me with diamonds I held onto for dear life. They were powerful thoughts that flashed into my mind when I needed them most.

The angry man lived in our house for four more months. There was no place for me to escape the cause of my pain. Every time I heard footsteps, I cringed. I desperately wanted to get away from him. But, how? *Your room is your retreat. A retreat is a safe place to regroup and get nourished for the next battle. This is where you prepare for victory. Open the door only when you choose.*

My fiftieth birthday came and went, and there was no happiness. The first Christmas without him was really awkward. It felt like he was missing everywhere. In reality, I only missed the man I thought I married. I was mourning the loss of a relationship I never really had.

After months on mental health leave, my doctor had to send me back to work. But I couldn't get up. The alarm went, and my body didn't move. I would cry into the pillow, and call in sick. I had to resign my lucrative job because my mind just couldn't think clearly. I had no motivation. There was no reason to get out of bed. *Try to get up. Set the alarm clock, late if you want, ten or eleven a.m., but when it goes you need to try to get up.*

Income on "sick leave" was minimal, so I took in renters to try to keep the mortgage paid. It wasn't a steady income and I had to sell the house. As we packed and moved, my youngest told me she was pregnant. She hadn't finished high school yet. We took an apartment and her little boy joined us by winter. I was living on welfare and help from the food bank. I had hit bottom.

I hated going out. People were always asking about him, but I couldn't tell them, over and over. It hurt me every time I had to recount what he had done. Talking about it would just throw me back into the depression I was trying so hard to climb out of. How could I avoid repeating the ugly truth? *Press Release: a short statement that discloses facts without making you re-live every detail. "He has decided he no longer wants to live the life of a Christian husband and father. His new friends are strippers and prostitutes."*

Forgiving is hard when the pain is fresh, but I was determined not to hold a grudge. I monitored my thoughts and quickly re-phrased anything that could trap me in a cycle of bitterness. I listed all the things I chose to forgive him for, like staying away all night playing poker with the boys without calling home and leaving me wondering if he was dead at a roadside, or taking our daughter to a strip club for a beer on her birthday, going on about what a good profession stripping could be. The list was long, and I verbally forgave him for every item. I had to ponder a few, but they had to go, for my sake, not his. Many times, when I was tempted to take back my right to be angry with him, I repeated aloud, "I choose to forgive him. I will not hold a grudge." *Forgiving is not for him. It's for you. You do the forgiving, so you can be free. He can receive forgiveness if or when he is sorry.*

I also had to forgive myself for all the foolish mistakes I had made, all the times I had left our family vulnerable to his selfish ideas. That list was long, too.

I had many sleepless nights. My future was a blank. I lived in constant fear that I would lose the apartment, couldn't pay the phone and hydro bills, or buy baby needs. But the biggest fear was maybe he never loved me. Maybe I wasn't loveable. Maybe no one would ever love me again. Maybe nobody cared if I could make it through this financially or emotionally. *Always challenge every negative thought.*

So I made a list of the people who would open their doors to me if I needed them. I've always had a policy of sharing anything we had with anyone who needed it more than we did. I had to believe people would care for me in return. The list of people who cared about me and what happens to me grew every time I read it for encouragement.

I knew if anything was going to change, I would "need to be needed." I thought if someone needed me, I would have a reason to get out of bed. I prayed someone would need me, even if it was just for the morning coffee run. *Try to get up, every day. Try for at least fifteen minutes. Some days, you'll make it!*

Then it happened. I started doing administrative work for a team of educational therapists. I worked with Learning Disabled children who could rejoin a regular classroom after doing our program. I saw miracle after miracle change the lives of children and families! My brain got clear, and I was able to focus again.

Depression is like a nasty little dog. Once it gets hold of your ankle, it just won't let go. What is considered a "normal" workload for others can look monumental for someone with depression. I found myself unhappy in spite of the many wonderful outcomes at work. I slept poorly, worried I wasn't doing a good enough job because I was so slow and detailed. I was often nauseous in the mornings. I cried a lot and couldn't seem to get happy. I was exhausted and wondered if I had reached another turning point. *You are not like everybody else. You are unique. Not slow, just different. And you are allowed to dream. What have you always wanted?*

It was nice to be needed at work, but I had to pay attention to my own needs now. A dear friend pointed out, I always seemed to "light up" whenever I jokingly mentioned going to University someday. She challenged me to take it seriously and I left my fulfilling job risking everything to find my happiness.

Motivated by the incredible changes I had seen at my job, I chose to major in Psychology. I LOVE being in University. I am in third year and I get mostly A's.

Embracing my pace, and accepting my limitations has allowed me to live a peaceful life. With scholarships, bursaries and student loans, I manage finances carefully. I monitor my schedule to avoid overload. I hope a degree in Psychology will make me more credible when I write and speak on the topic of the amazing brain that can change. Then I can work at a pace which is healthy for me, as I share what I know with those who need to hear it.

If someone had told me I would be an author and an encourager, living in Student Housing at the age of fifty-seven, happily single, would I have believed it? **I believe it now, because it's true!**

# Chocolate & Diamonds

# Deborah Naqvi

### Florida, United States of America

## *Introduction to Apple Seeds of Faith, Hope and Love*

An Introduction to Apple Seeds of Faith, Hope, and Love

Everyone has a story and everyone has a destiny. I believe the secret in life is to learn how to walk out of one's story and into one's destiny. This is my journey.

My name is Deborah Ann Naqvi, known professionally as Debbie Appleseed. I was born in and raised on a Mennonite/Amish farm in Northern Indiana in 1970. I grew up with three brothers, one older than myself and two younger than me.

My grandparents were Amish, however, my mother never became a member of the Amish church. She turned her back on the traditional "Rumspringa" which is a period of time after becoming 16 years of age where Amish young people experience different lifestyles not embraced by the traditional values they hold. Instead, she chose to become a member of the Conservative Mennonite church at the age of sixteen.

My dad, originally from Austria, was adopted at the age of ten and raised in Ohio by a French Catholic family. He stumbled onto the Mennonites at a Mennonite Mission and was taken in by a Mennonite family. He left behind his catholic roots and chose to become a member of the Mennonite church which is how he met my mother.

The transition for my father was difficult. He often felt like an "outsider" and had a hard time adhering to the many rules of the church. Admonition from the elders was not well received as it took him back in time to his boyhood years when he was rejected by his adoptive parents. He would often bring his frustration home, causing chaos and unrest. That is…when he was home. For most of my growing up years, my parents were separated. Divorce for my mother was never an option even though they lived apart. After we children had grown, my parents did eventually get back together and are currently both active members of the conservative Mennonite church I grew up in.

During the times my father was gone, we shared a big, two-story farm house with my mother, brothers, grandparents and aunt. This gave me the unusual opportunity of experiencing both worlds of the Mennonite/Amish traditions. While one side of the house was wired for electricity and phone, the other was not. Television and radio were not accepted by either religion.

In the evenings, I would often watch as my grandmother would light the kerosene lamps. Although the Mennonite church allowed cars, I often rode in my grandparents' horse and buggy on the old country roads. Today, these remain to be some of my fondest childhood memories.

My mother was a perfectionist and I learned a lot from her as a child. She was well known in our community for her hospitality and enjoyed entertaining guests on a regular basis. She decorated cakes professionally out of our home for fifteen years and taught me the art of baking when I was only five years old. When I was thirteen, she held a decorating class which I was a part of. I remember hating it. I vowed I would never bake another cake until I was married. That vow was short-lived as my mother had other intentions.

I had a very creative mind as a child and would often daydream. I started reading at the age of five and remember reading a story about a magic ink bottle and how letters magically came together to create wonderful stories and poetry. This inspired me to write my first poem when I was six years old. When I was in seventh grade, I wrote my first song and have been writing songs ever since. To this day, my songs are the windows to my soul.

Selling came naturally to me at a young age. We had a milk house that was no longer in operation for its intended purpose. One day I asked the neighbors to donate any ice cream bars or popsicles. I convinced my mom to help me set up a "Dairy Queen" of sorts. A window on the side of the milk house by the sidewalk, became my drive through window and I was in business. Shoe string potatoes in Styrofoam cups were my "French fries" and my toy cash register actually added up totals, even printing out a receipt. I invited the same neighbors that had graciously given their frozen treats to come to my "Dairy Queen" to buy with real money what they had donated earlier!

I attended private school for eight years. My mother allowed me to go to public school for my high school years. Soon after I graduated high school, I left the Mennonite church. It was during this time I met my first husband. We became engaged after knowing each other only a couple of months. Shortly after the engagement, I became pregnant. I was four months pregnant when we got married in 1992. My precious son, Matthew Eric Geiger, was born five months later in 1993.

Along with the challenges of marriage, my husband's best friend passed away. He became distant and we fought a lot. He left me for his high school sweetheart one month after our son turned one and I filed for divorce. Our divorce was made final in 1995.

Matthew's father did not exercise his weekend visitation rights in the early years after the divorce, therefore the courts allowed me to move to Sarasota, Florida for healing and a new beginning in 1998. Matthew was five.

When my son was seven, I found out I needed surgery to remove a tumor in my right breast at the Moffitt Cancer Center in Tampa. I hate the idea of anesthesia, so on the day of surgery, I asked the doctor if I could stay awake during the surgery. She agreed and I was able to watch the entire procedure. One week later, they found the tumor to be benign which I thank God for. The year was 2001.

After the surgery, I started thinking about how I wanted to leave a legacy for my son. I was trying hard to do something with my music, but felt I was hitting a brick wall every time I tried. Around this same time, I was offered a job at an alarm company which was financially beneficial for me. I accepted the offer and soon I started bringing in Dutch Apple pie to the potluck lunches. My friends asked me if I would consider starting a pie business and I emphatically replied "Absolutely not!" One of my friends refused to take no for an answer and created an order sheet, and brought the orders to me. The management agreed to let me process the orders, and soon I was making more money baking pies than the job I was hired for.

In 2003, Debbie Appleseed Homemade Pies was born, although I was not discovered till 2007. My signature Dutch Apple Pie received much publicity through the media in the latter part of 2007 as well as 2008 on the West Coast of Florida. In February of 2009, I put my web store on hold to earn an Associate's Degree at Florida Culinary in West Palm Beach.

It was here that I met the love of my life...my husband Rashid Naqvi. He has continually inspired me to pursue my dreams, encouraging me to overcome my fears and exceed my self-imposed limitations. Together, we have added a full catering menu to Debbie Appleseed as well as specialty items, such as our version of Amish Peanut Butter. In addition, he has given me the gift of my beautiful step-daughter Sophia whom I cherish deeply.

A little over a year ago, we also added another precious addition to our family...our little "furry daughter" Bella. She is a Yorkie mix rescue dog, five pounds of absolute delight! She has melted our hearts and is the best example of unconditional love... Our journey has not always been easy but we have learned together, as a family, that love and forgiveness is the key to unity for our mind, body and spirit. We are grateful for the daily opportunity of sprinkling apple seeds of faith, hope, and love into each other's lives and around our world!

Debbie Appleseed is not just a melt-in-your-mouth good pie. It's that...and much more. It depicts how one tiny apple seed creates ten thousand apples. It is a beautiful example of how we are all connected. Everyone's story is important. No dream is too big or too small. When you seek, you will find what you need to walk out of your story and into your destiny...it's time. It's my time. It's your time.....take a step of faith and walk with me...your destiny awaits you.

Love, Debbie Appleseed

# Jennifer Seminara

Florida, United States of America

## *I Put Me on My To-Do List*

I met my husband (Joe) at a party 24 years ago. I walked down some stairs, tripped and literally fell directly into his arms! Joe refers to it as "catch of the day." We were married 18 months later. And I got lucky! As young and as dumb as I was, I married a great guy. After we married, I was desperate to become the "perfect" wife. I compared myself to the other women in his family and became consumed by the fact I didn't seem to be measuring up. The problem was I was not a good cook and I was not organized. In a large Italian family, the inability to cook or be organized can be considered two of the original sins.

In my eyes, I was failing miserably! But, the fact of the matter is, no one was judging me. I was judging myself. I was 24 years old! What could I possibly know about running a household or making my own spaghetti sauce? And what's wrong with Prego anyway? 12 years and three kids later, I finally began to loosen the reins on my need to be perfect. To be honest, I didn't really have a choice. Who the hell can really be perfect while chasing after three children? I didn't have the time or the energy, but thanks to my mother-in-law's training, I did make a mean spaghetti sauce.

I was a perfectly content stay-at-home mom. I had an amazing partner and three great kids. Anyone who looked into my life might have been envious.

But, the death of my mother at the age of 61 changed everything for me. I came face-to-face with my own mortality and this burning question invaded my thoughts … *"if I only have 20 more years to live, what would I do with my life?"*

I began to realize I had lost myself because I was too busy taking care of my family. I placed so much effort on being the "perfect wife" and the "perfect mother" that I lost sight of being perfectly myself.

But, the nagging feeling and my desire to want more, left me feeling incredibly guilty. Then these awful questions came in:

*Why wasn't I satisfied?*

*How could I possibly want more?*

*What gives me the right to want more?*

I knew I needed help with these terrible questions and I decided to take part in a personal growth program at my church. Our first task was to share why we chose to attend. When it was my turn, I started to choke up and then it turned into the full-on cry. You know the cry that causes you to hyperventilate? I believe it was Oprah who labeled it "the ugly cry." Yup, that was me, performing the "ugly cry" in a room full of complete strangers.

I have no idea what I even said or if it made any sense, but I can tell you I never felt any judgment. Rather, I felt love, connection and understanding. It was then I realized it was completely normal for women to lose themselves in their families, to want more than just a family life and to feel guilty for wanting more.

This program stretched me because I went to that uncomfortable place called "self-discovery." During this process, I learned I needed to take care of myself. I spent so much time taking care of others, I hadn't even considered the importance of taking care of myself first. Imagine that?

I consciously began putting myself on my to-do list and as a result and I realized by filling my soul, I became more patient, more curious and more understanding of everyone around me. Plus, I let go of the need to be perfect. I actually knew in my heart I was perfect just the way I was. As a result, I began to fall in love with a "me" I didn't even know existed.

I was able to take this newly found freedom and be totally present in my life. I was no longer worried if I was doing things right. It didn't matter anymore. I was living a life of joy and freedom. And, get this – not only did I become a better wife and mother, I actually became fun!

Imagine, putting yourself first and feeling neither selfishness nor guilt, but feeling happier and as a result, seeing a happier family? What a concept! It sounds so simple and yet, most women aren't' doing it! I knew I was on to something and I have made it my mission to help other women! I was later invited to join the leadership team of the ministry. Before I knew it, I was building workshops and retreats which were empowering women on a National Level!

I now feel my gift and purpose in life is to empower women and encourage them to place themselves on their own to-do list. Who knew a complete breakdown and an "ugly cry" in front of a group of complete strangers would lead to a powerful form of self-realization which would have a ripple effect on thousands of others?

I was so excited I decided to become a certified life coach. I am now a wife, a mother and I am known as the "Wisdom Within Coach." I chose this name because I believe everyone has the wisdom within themselves to make changes for a fuller and happier life. I am living proof of this fact. I am no longer the young girl who wants to be perfect. I am perfectly - imperfect. Through my coaching, I am able to live my purpose of serving others and sharing my gifts. Nothing brings me more joy than to see clients leave my office feeling the same love, acceptance and empowerment I felt the day I let out all hang out in front of a group of strangers. So, you read my story! What are you waiting for? Put yourself on your to do list! You deserve to have fun!

# Vicki Tongeman

### Dorset, United Kingdom

## *Daphne and the Smiley Shells*

This time, I think I can do it", said Daphne the little dolphin, to herself, trembling with fear. She tried to steady herself on her surfboard as the next wave rolled towards her, bigger, and bigger... "Here goes", Daphne thought nervously as her surf board began to wobble, and then, like so many times before... sploosh!... she fell in the water again.

As she came up to the surface, Daphne could hear some of her friends laughing at her whilst her teacher, he simply shook his head. Daphne headed for home. "I am confused," she muttered to herself, trying not to cry, "I thought friends were supposed to be kind". She was so deep in thought that she almost swam into the mouth of a great big basking shark and jumped out of her skin! "Why is the world so scary?" Daphne groaned, and swam on home as fast as she could.

A few days later, Daphne's Mum was fed up of her moping about, so she sent her off to see her Grandad.

"Now, what's all this I hear about you getting under your Mothers fins and being miserable?"

Daphne looked down at the seabed.

"Come on," said Grandad "it can't be that bad".

"Yes, it can! Said Daphne defiantly, "I am no good at school, I am too clumsy to learn to surf so my friends all laugh at me, and well, I am frightened in case the big creatures pick on me as well!"

Grandad thought for a moment.

"Well," he said at last, "I used to feel a bit like that when I was your age, but then I went to see my granddad.

"What happened?" asked Daphne.

Grandad smiled "he taught me a very useful trick and I still use it, even today"

Daphne felt herself cheering up. "What is it? What's the trick?"

Grandad pointed to a shelf, where he kept a glass jar with shells in it. No ordinary shells, but shells with smiley faces painted on them. Daphne had often wondered about the smiley shells, but never had the courage to ask about them. They looked so pretty and lots of fun!

"That's my "bank a smile" jar" said Grandad. Just hearing the name made Daphne smile.

"This is how it works," said Grandad lifting the jar down from the shelf. "Every evening after tea, I sit down and think of at least five good things about me. It could be things I've done, or it could just be something I like about myself"

What five things will you think today Grandad?"

Grandad looked at Daphne for a moment - "Well, today I am enjoying spending time with you. Ooh, this morning I helped old Jimmy Jellyfish get untangled from a plastic bag that some human being had thrown into the sea. Remember, you can include things you would like to come true too."

Daphne's eyes grew wide, "really, you can wish things to be true?"

"Oh yes," said Grandad "you see, it's a question of learning to believe in yourself" Daphne trusted her Grandad, so she listened carefully to what he said next.

"Just say "I am happy that" about something you want to be true. That's not so very difficult is it?"

Daphne looked across at the jar again and giggled, because all the shells were smiling back at her.

"What do you do when the jar gets full? Daphne asked. "Recycle my girl, recycle! I take them out and I start all over again. Daphne laughed out loud "I love you Grandad!" "Quite so, and I love you too. Now, it's time to celebrate. How about one of your Grandma's seaweed muffins?"

Back at home with a pocket full of smiley shells her Grandad had given her, Daphne asked her Mum if she could have an empty jar. Her Mum didn't ask what the jar was for, she was just happy that Daphne looked less down in the dumps.

The first shell was easy. "I am so happy that I told Grandad how I was feeling" Plink! The shell hit the bottom of the jar. She pondered for a while "I know! I am happy that I painted a smiley face on my "Bank a Smile" jar". Plink! Another shell landed in the bottom of the jar. Then she tidied her bedroom and put another shell in the jar. That felt good!

The next day at school Daphne felt a little bit more confident and she didn't even mind too much when her friends laughed at her as she tried to surf. That evening, Daphne thought about why she was feeling a bit better.

"I am happy that I am not so scared of the shadows" she began and put a shell in the jar. After a few more moments she picked up another shell. "I am happy that...I've got nice flippers!" Plink!

Then she remembered about saying things she would like to be true. She carefully chose a big shell with a very happy smile on it. "I am happy that I am brave and I am happy that I can surf!" And she thought how wonderful it was skipping along on top of the waves.

Daphne carried on with the smiley shells. She had good days, and days that weren't quite so good, until gradually she noticed the dolphins that she thought were her friends didn't come to play with her any more but she had new friends who were much more fun to be with. Her teacher told her he could see she was really making progress and even the bigger dolphins and sea creatures...they just didn't seem scary anymore! Daphne was even happy spending time on her own surfing the waves and collecting more shells to take home. Daphne realised, just as Grandad had promised, that by believing she could be happy she really was happy!

### Be your own Cheerleader!

Have you ever been told you did something well, or looked nice, and said "thank you" but secretly couldn't feel good inside? Do you have a "successful" life or career on the outside, but have times when you just feel so small on the inside? Like many of you, I have had those experiences in the past many times, and I have heard from many others who have shared that experience.

In a bid to help change people's lives, whatever their background, I studied counselling, NLP (Neuro Linguistic Programming) and many modern day philosophers and have learned these feelings often result from the way we were brought up as children. We were brought up to "behave" and to gain our parents, teachers and other authority's approval. But we were often not taught to approve of ourselves. This leads us and our children to seek external approval throughout our lives and can leave a big hole of low self- esteem where self-love and self-affirmation should reside.

I believe our children should learn at an early age that we are the only ones that really know what we have achieved, how hard we have tried, and that each and every one of us has many beautiful qualities. Therefore, we are the best cheerleader we can have. I also believe that as children, or for that matter adults, the greater our self-confidence, the better our life will be around us – we will attract nicer, more positive people and things into our lives, and more easily shrug off the negatives like grumpy bosses or a classroom taunt.

In this story I have embedded some simple NLP techniques to help you and your children increase your inner feelings of self-worth, and attract more positive experiences into your life. Please do try following Grandad's instructions for yourself and/or a child you love, and notice as you practise this technique regularly, how both your inner and outer worlds become brighter, happier and more fulfilling!

An inspiring audio of this story is available at www.smileyshells.com, beautifully narrated by my editor and "Arts as Wellbeing" consultant, Cathy Elder.

# Chocolate & Diamonds

# Tara Pritchard

Mississippi, United States of America

## *Life after College*

We all grow up with the aspirations of being something great. We make straight A's throughout high school, receive all the prestigious awards and join all the right clubs in school to set us up for a bright future. We get accepted into the college we have always wanted to go to, and before we know we it, are out in the world.

We soon begin a life without our parents watching our every move and we accept more responsibility. When you graduate college, every responsibility that was once taken care of becomes your own. Welcome to your early twenties; where you have no idea what you are doing.

Should I go to graduate school? Did I choose the right major? These are examples of the many questions which will flood your mind as graduation nears. College is one huge party that requires many decisions to be made. I changed my major three different times before finally deciding to stick with Psychology. I have always been fascinated by the human psyche and what makes people do the things they do, so I was relieved when I finally made the switch.

However, I was unaware of the limited options I would have for a career with only a bachelor's degree. It wasn't until the semester before I graduated that I took a class which laid out all the paths that could be taken with this degree, but I was in too far to turn back. So now I am a college graduate with very little options as to what to do with my life as a professional in the workforce. I feel as though my options are limited due to the fact I've followed all the criteria, yet find myself somewhat lost with what to do with myself. If I choose to take a particular path, am I choosing the right one?

Even though deciding what to do is a very stressful process, I am fortunate enough to have parents who supported me through my college career. I am very thankful to be debt free, which is a pretty rare thing these days for graduates.

This allows me more options, since any money I make is going straight to current bills and not to the last four years of my life.

I currently work as a waitress/bartender in Starkville, Mississippi at a sports bar. I have worked here since my sophomore year at Mississippi State. The service industry is a tough one to get out of due to the fact the money is great, the food is really good, and the hours are very flexible. Not to mention, you leave every shift with cash in hand. All the jobs I apply for offer salaries much lower than what I am currently making. This is very disheartening, because you grow up believing a college degree is the answer to your future. So the question now is whether to sacrifice more money for more experience.

We are all familiar with the phrase, "it's not what you know, but who you know". This phrase will have a whole new meaning to you when you begin searching for jobs after college. You will begin to see your highly under-qualified friends working jobs simply because of who their parents are or who they know. Meanwhile, you are applying for the same job actually qualified for, only to be slapped down because you don't have experience. How are you supposed to get experience if no one will hire you in the first place?

According to a study from the Federal Reserve Bank of New York almost half of all recent college graduates are working jobs which don't require a bachelor's degree. Unfortunately, a Master's degree is the new bachelor's. Going to college used to set you apart from other people not too long ago, but now everyone does it.

One way to counteract this is to get internships during the summers when you are off of school. Unfortunately, most of these are unpaid. Although my parents covered my tuition and rent, I had to have a job for any spending money I needed, so an unpaid internship was not an option.

A very good thing about being in the service industry is you will never really stress about the job economy. You can pretty much get a job anywhere, anytime. Plus you meet new people every day, so you never know who you might run into and who may be able to help you out with a job.

I am a very routine person, so the crazy hours and working late is not really the greatest plan for me, but for now at least I know I am able to have a stream of income. So to anyone struggling to find a job like me, I would highly recommend getting a server job. The experience is good for you, but an added benefit is you will meet some lifelong friends who you will share these years with.

To anyone out there going through this exact same thing, know you aren't alone. There are many options to get yourself and your resume out there for people to see. You can sign up for online websites such as Indeed, LinkedIn, and Monster which will allow people to see your profile and they can contact you for a job if they feel you are a correct match for what they're looking for. Most of these websites also allow you to search for desired jobs and you can simply apply through the website where your resume is already uploaded. They will also ask you to fill out certain things about yourself, such as strengths and weaknesses so potential employers can see these. Be sure to monitor your Facebook and other social media to make sure nothing inappropriate is on them. When you apply for jobs, they may run your name, and the last thing you want a future employer to see is you getting wasted with your friends. The struggle is already real enough, so you don't want to make it any worse!

# Mandy Straight

Colorado, United States of America

## *Life is Best Spent Naked*

It started off innocently enough—all very PG-rated. I clothed myself respectably, like a good girl. I did everything the way you are supposed to: I joined clubs, marched in the band, and got good grades. In high school I was voted "Most Likely to Live a White Picket Fence Life," and from the outside, I think that's how it all seemed. But in the end, that was part of the problem.

From the very beginning I had depression. One of my earliest memories is sitting cross-legged in a circle in kindergarten feeling like I looked fat and all the other kids were staring at me for it. I grew, but my depression never left. It was like some mopey travel companion, my twisted version of an imaginary friend who wouldn't leave, a squatter on my mental futon throughout adolescence and beyond. It taught me so many lessons—one of the biggest being how to insulate myself from the world so it didn't hurt so much.

I learned to pitch my own little tent along the bank of my personal Walden Pond and struggle through my emotions in isolation. The idea seemed good at the time. It was so much safer and meant I didn't have to risk judgment from everyone around me. But this was just the pretty packaging. My cocoon worked so well those around me didn't get the whole me, only got little pieces small enough to fit through the holes in my shell. I stayed safe. I also stayed alone. My layers were like the Emperor's clothes, they falsely convinced me I was insulated. The more layers I thought I wore, the more deluded I was in thinking no one around me saw what I looked like naked.

It would probably be easier to tell you I got married at 19 to avoid being alone or because I thought it would fix my depression or because we wanted to have sex (ok, it was a tiny bit of the last one). If so, it would be easier to write off the tragic ending. But life isn't neat and tidy. We got married because we were in love, because I wanted to spend my time with him, share my life with him, and because we saw past each other's layers of insulation. We were naked little jaybirds, stripped down to our raw selves and flitting around our 20s together, convinced love was uncomplicated and life offered happily-ever-after's to good people. My depression was still there, but my husband held me when I cried and helped me tread water when I was exhausted from drowning in my own head.

Learning to be naked with him (in every sense) was so wonderful I didn't have enough motivation to push past my fears and try it with anyone else. We had very nice friends, but I never felt connected to any of them, with few exceptions. I thought they distanced themselves because they saw the flaws I saw and didn't want to deal with them. In hindsight, I see it was me that was the problem. Projection is a powerful manipulator (a favorite tool of my old friend depression). If I had stripped off my own layers and risked the judgment of letting them see me naked and real, I know now that most of them would've been ready to do the same. We could have stripped off the veneer of pleasantries and simulated perfection and actually loved one another for all the flawed, vulnerable loveliness that we each contain.

I will spare you the details of the disintegration of my marriage—this journey is bigger than that. I will just simply say that truth is just as hard to connect with as people when buried under layers. It is difficult to get to the naked, raw core of a matter when we project our own assumptions on top of it. Over time, this buried truth inevitably changes both the relationship and the people in it. The foundation that was once solid is now built on assumptions (not great foundation material) and there is a point when the structure must be condemned as uninhabitable.

Any breakup can be gut wrenching, but ending a marriage carries the added bonus; mounds of paperwork, legally hashing through and mapping out the shrapnel from the bombs you have thrown at each other and tons of distress. The state doesn't care who ends up with the big purple sofa—but they make you tell them anyway. I would add to it in this case, I was mourning the loss of a true love, of an amazing person who would now no longer be a part of my life. In addition, and just as painfully, I was mourning the loss of my white picket fence and my happy ending. All the layers I had carefully clothed myself in were suddenly hanging off me in tatters. I was emotionally evicted, exposed to the elements. Who I thought I was and what I thought life was had been shattered. I was left naked, surrounded by people pointing, staring and laughing.

I won't say this was a blessing in disguise—that trivializes the situation. What I will say is that we, as humans, ***seem to need dire conditions to find the motivation to reprogram our flawed circuitry***. Until it is required of us, we don't know what we are capable of.

I began to re-build, but not to re-dress.

I was so overwhelmed by facing each day I had no effort left in me to re-construct my protective layers. I found comfort in the pain. I was an emotional cutter, diving deep into my psyche, reveling in the agony, and watching the blood ooze from my soul just to verify I was still alive. I didn't try to avoid, to cover up all the emotions, instead I bathed in them and faced all the awful parts of me I didn't want to look at. I nursed a manic need to push my own boundaries and expand my comfort zone. I began a mental search party for all the things that scared me, and did them anyway.

Slowly, I began to examine the mutilated me that remained, and I realized I kind of liked her. I stopped staring at my fat, my knees, and my nose and saw the simple beauty of a being that is present, honest, and trying. I felt like a phoenix. I was rising from the ashes. You would think the bonfire had burned me, my life, my being, but you would be wrong. The fuel was not myself. It was my layers, it was my assumptions, my projections, and my self-judgments. The little fledgling who crawled, renewed from the ashes was (the me) who had been underneath all along.

My depression was pivotal in my personal development, as was my divorce, but they didn't make me what I am. One would think so, but as it turns out, they were just roadside attractions on a much bigger journey. One that requires me to strip down to self, to forego the layers and the safety. I am learning to live in my new skin, learning we are all supposed to live naked, but we let fear convince us to hide. I've come to see the protective clothes were all in my imagination anyway. In my new nakedness, I find myself better equipped to help others with their load, especially now I am no longer carrying my own unnecessary baggage.

And all those people who I thought were pointing and staring? I looked again and saw they were naked too. Some of them knew it. They weren't laughing, they were inviting, calling to me to join in a different way of being— one who shares real shape and true color, who stands in nakedness and encourages the same in others, who finds more satisfaction in the chill breeze on the bare skin, than in the safety of layers and layers of clothing.

Did I mention I was also voted "Most Likely to Become a Lounge Singer"? This stripping lesson is my life journey. It is ongoing and never-ending, but I am committed to the challenge. I've stopped looking for a destination or a solution and try to simply focus on the next step and the gorgeous view. I try to find comfort in navigating the road with less and less clothing. It does become surprisingly freeing.

P.S. I am always up for traveling companions. Life is best spent naked with people you enjoy.

# Brooke Ochoa

Texas, United States of America

## *Confidence and the Game*

I walk up to the table, take a breath, chalk my stick and shoot. A game of 8 ball starts with 15 balls on the table racked all together in a particular set up. However, nothing is determined or begins until all the balls are scattered with hopes at least one falls into a pocket. I remember a time when I thought I had everything intact, but it also felt like my life was going nowhere. In just one moment's stroke, all was scattered. I couldn't keep anything together. In the game of pool, your best chance at winning is when the balls are spread around enough to leave yourself an open shot every time you shoot. In life we strive to keep our composure, to hold it all together even when all we want to do is fall apart. Ever wonder what it would be like to just take a breath before you act and have the confidence to know that even when things are scattered, the outcome for you will be success? When I figured that out it absolutely changed my life.

When I started playing pool one year ago, I just played in the moment. It was the rush of the game that kept me going. I shot at anything that looked easy, and hoped that every ball would go in. I was pretty good, until I started to actually learn the game. I wanted to be a great player, not just a lucky one. I admired many that had been playing for years and could do such amazing things on a pool table. So, I started watching videos, reading books, and practicing endlessly every chance I got with anyone who was willing to help me.

Then the game got complicated. Because I took in so much knowledge, I couldn't just shoot anymore. I learned very quickly about speed, angles, banking, etc. I started doing extremely well in a short period of time. Unfortunately, with that came doubt. From people who said it was a "man's game", who kept telling me to just have fun, you can't make anything out of this, or laughed when they thought I was lucky, but I knew I was going to make that shot. I let it get to me. It changed my perception of the game and of myself. It reminded me of the person I had left behind not too long ago.

When I was younger, I was very angry at the world. I blamed anyone and anything every chance I got for why I wasn't all I had hoped to be. I had the talent and the opportunities to make something of myself, but I always chose otherwise. I looked for happiness in every single temptation which came my way. I couldn't understand why I was treated so ugly or why people doubted me so much. It wasn't until recently that I realized this was because I felt that way about myself. I didn't think I could be successful or that any of my work was good enough. I allowed the people and situations in my life to determine how I felt. I chose my circumstances. I believed everything was true.

It was easy to let the negativity bring me down because I have struggled with weight and body issues all my life. I was bullied at school. All the diets, work outs, and makeup couldn't change who I was or how I felt on the inside. I wanted so badly to be someone else. When I was 26, I found myself and accepted the beauty of who I truly am in this world.

I remember being told, "Your reputation follows you for the rest of your life." Psalms 23 says "Surely goodness and love will follow me all the days of my life." It doesn't say, "My mistakes and blunders." Our problems, our past have a tendency to rob us of hope, but, it's when we have hope that we begin to walk by faith and not by sight.

I can proudly say I've been a plus size model, walked in runway shows, been in music videos, on covers of magazines and online, etc. These opportunities gave me confidence. In the game of pool, you have to know that you know that every shot you take is going to go in. You have a chance to win, so walk up to the table like you own it, even when playing the better players. I believe you have to be confident in everything you do. Trust you have what it takes. Take a moment to look at what you have overcome and watch your confidence rise.

I received my Bachelor's Degree in Mathematics, but in college I never listened carefully. Every page of my notes has drawings in the margins. I did everything just to get by. I find it humorous now that I work in an attorney's office and have an art business. I am actually living the pages of my notes.

I started my business, Arts of Utopia, two years ago. I offer Photography, Face Painting, and Acrylic Art. The game of pool taught me to be attentive. If I take my eye off the table, listen to the whispers, or watch what others are doing, I no longer see my next move or what might affect my game. The same concept applies in life. If you don't stay focused then it becomes easier to stumble and fall.

Within 6 months, I turned 10 jobs per year into 10 jobs in one month. I took control of how I feel, and where I want my business to go. I work all over Texas now, and my art and photos are displayed abundantly throughout Texas as well. I donate my time and art to many fundraisers. I love that my efforts make a valuable impact on other people's lives.

When you take your success, your goals, and your feelings and put them in another person's hands, you create boundaries that keep you from your full potential. It's YOUR potential! You have control over yourself, the way you act, how you feel, and most of all, how you RE-act to what happens in your life. Find what you are passionate about, what compliments you most and stick to it.

Be proud of who you are, the talents you were given and keep moving forward because you cannot change the past. It took me a while to smile and learn from my mistakes at pool instead of being angry about them. It also took me a long time to accept who I am. The fear of rejection while sharing things about yourself that you are so passionate about can be really scary.

I love the scriptures that include, "And it came to pass." Just imagine a life where mistakes are forgiven, where everything you do, right or wrong, makes you a stronger individual. The possibilities are endless. It's achievable. You just have to make the change.

It's a great feeling to be treated like an opponent and not just a girl playing around on a table. I've gained respect because I play the game with my heart. I've also gained respect and admiration as a business woman. There's a quote I love, "I know what to do, but I just won't do it…so I guess I am right where I should be." Change can be intimidating, and from time to time we feel the need to fight it. But, sometimes you cannot fight change because you are simply a part of it.

What if we said, "I am going to take better care of myself so I am treated better" I am going to create opportunities in everything I do. I am going to eat better, work out, and walk out the door every day with my head held high, my eyes wide open and take every opportunity to make this world a better place."

When you take control of you, all the stress, problems, drama, and reasons why you can't do what you want to do slowly, but surely become easier to manage. That will leave more room for growth and positivity in your life. So, next time you feel doubt or feel like you are not good enough, remember you control who you are today, and who you can be tomorrow.

I would like to share one last story I saw on the internet. It was an interview with an 80 year old woman and her family. She decided when she was in her 70s to go to law school to be a lawyer. Her family laughed at her. Her daughter said to her in the interview, "You will be 81 by the time you become a lawyer." She said, "I will be 81 anyways, I might as well be a lawyer." It's so important to remember it's never too late. And if it's too late for new beginnings, create new endings.

# Rose M. Tuttle

### Florida, United States of America

## *Diary of a Bossy Little Girl*

I am one of those women who was born to be a mother. When I was a little girl, other children call me "Bossy". Ugh! I shudder to this day. Personally, I think the label has a bad rap and needs some rebranding. "Bossy" little girls, or BLGs, are really just natural born mothers. This bossiness most often, does not stem from a mean spirit or from the need to control others. It is the resulting stress caused by a compelling sense of responsibility and empathy for the surrounding world.

Now, if someone happened upon a small child playing in the middle of the road, oblivious to a car rushing toward them, they would urgently get the child out of the street and out of harm's way. Correct? It is a similar sense of urgency felt by the young BLG, who directs a fellow kindergarten classmate on the "right" way to handle scissors, lest a finger be cut instead of the paper. Thus the label BLG is the result of a soft hearted nurturer who through clumsy inexperience, is simply trying to avert several hundred potentially harmful situations every day. The stress of this urgency can be very uncomfortable for a rejected young BLG.

So I confess, I am a BLG or born mother, as I prefer to think. I had difficulty picking a major in college, my interests were varied and nothing struck a chord true enough to indulge my life's work. As my friends were planning careers, what I kept to myself, buried deep inside my heart, was my yearning to build and nurture a family as my life's work. I had lost my mother at age thirteen and I deeply wanted to build a close relationship with daughters of my own. Nary a class, was listed on the college rosters in that field of study.

So what do BLGs do? They make things happen. I married and was soon a young mother. My first daughter was quickly big sister, as a second daughter arrived. Before too long, a son joined the crew and then identical twin girls. I had forgotten to be careful with what I asked for. And the old adage, God doesn't give you more than you can handle, well sometimes it feels pretty darn close!

This BLG found her niche raising five young children; exhausted, challenged, joyous, heartbroken, loving every minute of it and often all at the same time. I leaned heavily on my faith in God as a young mother, making my daily prayer, "God, please help me to be the mother You want me to be."

There is great joy in standing as witness to a child's journey from infancy to independence. While children are little, a BLG mother is the perfect fit, a loving drill sergeant of sorts, as hours seemingly stretch endlessly. A born mother recognizes, sometimes slowly, the necessity to rein in BLG tendencies to make room for a child's own character and identity to take shape and be nurtured.

The first day of Kindergarten is momentous for a BLG, forced to share responsibility for the first time. Just resting my eyes for a moment too long, I open them to graduation day with all its pomp and circumstance. Time seems to have been stolen from me, though the thoughtful thief leaves behind precious memories of first steps, birthdays, family vacations, band and chorus concerts and college visits.

Recently this BLG celebrated the last high school graduation and I won't lie, it was bittersweet. I felt a sense of a life's purpose fulfilled, one of them at least. I proudly patted myself on the back for a twenty-eight year job well done and responsibly relaxed, but not over.

In the hospital after the birth of my first child, a nurse related her opinion on the post-partum period stretched to age eighteen. I have thought often of this nurse and her comment through the years, especially as my own darlings reached this milestone. The BLG in me disagrees. Not to depress anyone, but I believe, post-partum lasts the remainder of the mother's and the child's lives, though this shared connection will ebb and flow throughout the tide of life. Contrary to popular belief, a BLG is completely capable of encouraging and sharing responsibility in a supporting role.

Now facing a new chapter of life, what does a BLG do? She makes things happen once again! After nurturing five creative souls to adulthood, mothering is my expertise, and has quite often stretched beyond my children to their classmates, to adult friends, family and co-workers. These outlets remain, as does the innate BLG sense of responsibility for those around me. At some future point, I look forward to being a Grama, but right now, this is MY time and I am excited to explore new ventures.

My dream of building a family has been fulfilled, my dream of walking into a bookstore to see my book on display is in progress and there are new dreams I am just starting to nurture. The ending of one chapter in life only signals that a new chapter begins and I am looking forward to writing the rest of my story!

I am proud, at this point in my life, to be a BLG. The very character traits that earned me the label, "Bossy" as a child, led me to nurture others, fulfill one life purpose and I am sure, avert untold hundreds of potentially painful disasters for those around me. I nourished a family that continues to grow together, while still encouraging each member's individual growth.

Most importantly, God is not finished with me yet and I look forward to continuing to become the person I was meant to be. I invite others to embrace their own BLG that may be lurking inside. Give her the freedom to become all she can be as the born mother she is. There is no pre-requisite to have birthed children; only to look beyond the obvious and be creative with new ways to inspire and encourage other travelers sharing this journey of life. So BLGs of the world unite, let us go and make things happen!

# Mehnaz P

### Ontario, Canada

## *Enough is Enough*

I don't know how I got here, I don't know what was the exact moment in time, which had driven me to this unshakable feeling I had lately; all I felt lately is hopelessness, despair, and doom.

I felt like a failure as a woman, human being, mom, wife, daughter and sister. The same week I was approached to share my story was the week I decided, "Enough is ENOUGH!! You can either keep feeling sorry for yourself and the little you do have left will wither away as well, or you can get yourself up each day and say it's going to get BETTER! It has to get BETTER!! I had also declared on Facebook, that as bad as things feel right now, I know I will have a story to share someday and this is just the obstacles I have to overcome till then.

I am not usually the type to post things about myself, so this post was more as a reminder to myself than getting anyone else's attention. I had to believe things would get better, because no one could make it better for me, but me. Even if there are kind souls out there who would try to help the best way they can, they also have their own life and hardships that they are busy with.

At first when I started writing, I really didn't know where to begin, but I just knew I always wanted to help people somehow. So I decided to turn on my laptop today and simply type away and empty out my heart onto this keyboard. A few months ago, as I was sitting on the comfortable recliner in my naturopath's office, with soft relaxation music in the background and a tissue box in my hand, crying and sharing with her my past from what I can remember from my childhood at the exact moment I was sitting in her office.

That AHA moment was that in my deepest corner of my heart, I wasn't happy. The same day I was listening to an audiobook in the car, where the speaker again said what I realised earlier that day, that when your inner blueprint doesn't match your outer world, then it never fully functions to its fullest potential. It's like a glitch in the computer system.

My glitch was I kept living my life for everyone around me, but me. I was used to being extremely hard and unforgiving to myself, except the husband, I had chosen in life wasn't really the guy I wanted be with, there were many signs he wasn't the right one for me, but I kept ignoring them due to guilt. Growing up, I was what people called a "goodie-two-shoes", who had set some rules for herself, I said I would never sleep with anyone before marriage, and the first guy who I would have sex with would be my last guy. So that was it when things moved too fast with my then boyfriend (future ex-husband),

I couldn't forgive myself, I was no longer the shy girl who couldn't even say the word "sex" out loud and what my friends thought of me. I know I convinced myself he was the one for me and I was in love with him. I prayed every day that God would let me marry him. Be very exact with your prayers and requests you make to God/Universe, if it's vague, then you'll receive a vague version of it too. The term self-fulfilling prophecy then began to take a new meaning in my life. The relationship had gotten so out of hand that before I knew it, I was pregnant out of wedlock. This pushed me over the edge, now I was determined, if he wasn't going to marry me, I wasn't going to ever marry anyone else and just raise my child alone.

I had begun my 8 long years of marriage where I was verbally, psychologically and emotionally abused. I felt once again unloved and neglected, I started to lose myself and couldn't recognize myself anymore. I had given up on hopes and dreams and accepted I would never mount up to anything, but failure. I failed to stay a virgin, I failed to keep my parent's honor, I failed to complete my university studies and I failed to be a good wife. My husband only treated me this way because I deserved it. Soon into our marriage, he went back home where his family had a bride ready for him to marry. He didn't tell his family about me. He hid our child and my existence.

He made me wait months before he finally came back. When he did come back, I was sure I would leave him, but when he cried, holding our baby in his arms for the first time, I somehow couldn't ask him to leave. It was a love-hate relationship; I love to hate him and I hate to love him. I was always confused how I knew I didn't want to be with him because I was miserable, but somehow losing him seemed scarier than putting up with his abuse.

I always described it like a bad drug addiction, as much as you know it's slowly killing you, you still can't quit it. Then I found out he was expecting a child with this other woman. My heart simply was shattered in pieces beyond repair. I think after that moment I no longer felt committed to the marriage. As he mistreated me, the love and respect slowly disappeared. I was only staying in it for my kids. I never realized how it was unfair to my kids to make them responsible for my unhappiness.

Leaving a long relationship you have been in for so long, a habit sets in, so leaving that routine lifestyle is not easy to begin with. What you experience when you come out of an abusive marriage is you start having the well-known symptom called Stockholm syndrome, which makes the departure much more difficult. Here I was, I finally had the courage and determination to leave him; all the while still uncertain. I thought I had set my expectation of backlash and difficulty. I had asked help from friends to mediate my conversation, I had started looking for an apartment to immediately move out, hide my children, my passport and strategized an escape plan. Nothing prepared me for how my own close friends and family wouldn't support me and change their tune.

I took a deep breath, my knees felt weak behind the strong front I was putting up for everyone, I told myself I have 3 beautiful, healthy kids who need me now more than anything to make sure they have a better life than I did. They are young enough that their resilience will help them get through this, but I also need to show them resilience and perseverance today. I want to be the best person I can be and that resolution hasn't changed since I initiated my separation from my ex. I remembered two things that were said to me, "the only way to help yourself is by helping others" and "there is no such thing as a good or bad experience, but simply a learning experience". So I told myself my story will be an inspiration to others if I overcome this experience and help as many people as I can. My hope is this story will reach people and make them feel like if "she can do it, why can't I?"

Let the universe feel your vibe, I knew I had a story to share and I believe it's not a coincidence, I was asked the same week to share it. God created us to be the best version of us, we simply have to believe it first and then work towards the results that you will then be able to see. Even as I write this story my hurdles aren't yet over, but I am realizing what needs to be done and if I overcome my mind junk, I have no doubt my dream life is waiting for me to unleash my full potential.

# Karen Alleyne-Means

Florida, United States of America

## *Let Your Essence Speak Truth to You*

When did you first realize you weren't alone in this spiritual thing called soul-journing? Was it when you started talking to others like yourself–fierce women who had gone through battles, storms, triumphs, letdowns and everything in between? Who still smiled, dreamed and dared to make incredible plans for their futures. What makes one woman lay down and never get up again, and another woman be determined to never give up?

The more I speak to others in an authentic way, stripped bare of pretense, attitudes and premeditated expectations, the more I understand we are all linked on many levels. We need each other physically, mentally, emotionally and spiritually. We need to hear one another's stories of sorrow, resilience, perseverance and hope. Too often, particularly with women, we only want to put our best foot forward. We want to present our "I've got this, girl" face to the world, all the time, even when things aren't going right. And when we do, we miss the opportunity for growth to occur. Not only is there a woman like me who desperately wants to share her story of triumph and continued self-actualization, but there's a woman who desperately needs to hear it. But if we all keep hiding our truths, then no one knows. I am here to make it stop.

Let's stop smiling when we feel like crying. Let's stop putting up with less than we deserve. Let's stop accepting the leftovers in life. Let's stop making our sisters feel "less than" because they aren't skinny, pretty, smart, accomplished, rich, married, raising children, whatever. We need to stop forcing women to have these expectations placed upon them of always having to DO something. We are called human BEings, not human DOings. One of the first things I've realized in my journey is when I stop focusing on what I expect others to be, it leaves a lot of time and space for me to work on myself. When I stop pretending, about everything, my authenticity guides me like a river to the ocean. It's not forced and it's not fabricated. Honestly, it's quite the opposite.

When I started just doing ME, it was like, "Whoa, watch out!" I am discovering along my soul-journ that as long as I am doing things from a place within my core that's true and passionate, life holds no boundaries. I am literally set free to be the woman I was designed from birth to be. I believe our essence–our authentic self–resides in us since birth, and waits for us to have life experiences before it presents itself. Being YOU takes time, patience, maturity and a willingness to accept its revelation. You have to let it marinate before it's ready for all of its layers, flavors and nuances to unfold. You have to be ready to live it as your truth.

I consider myself lucky. When my inner essence called to me, I listened. Oh, I am not going to lie. It didn't happen at first. I was busy being a wife, mother, salesperson extraordinaire and entrepreneur. And I am still all those things. But I had to learn to let that enchanting voice of truth whisper to me, then guide me along the path in all of my affairs. It is like my own inner North Star which I've carried all along.

So when you think of your own travels as a soul-journer–your own truth as it's unfolding inside you–what are you learning about yourself? Maybe it's that you are not working in a career that generates passion. Or maybe you are not in a romantic partnership that brings the love you deserve. For me, I had to walk through seasons of heartbreak in my marriage and mothering. I had to watch my body attack itself and become my enemy. I had to struggle financially in an economy that was a devourer of dreams. All these things threatened me and my beliefs in who I was as a woman.

Yet I had something to sustain me through it all. I had an irrepressible desire to be true to myself, and the power I knew I carried within me. My will to persevere was uncontainable, so much so I couldn't keep from sharing it with others. The more I divulged, the more I realized how interwoven our lives are on this planet. I became amazed as I listened to stories from strangers who, just like me, had come through incredible, sometimes horrific, circumstances, and were still able to be brave and daring.

So what makes one woman able to walk through fire and still carry on? From everything I am hearing and learning, and in knowing my own truth, it's this—we are confident in our abilities to survive and thrive. In your lifetime, many things build your confidence but there's nothing like surviving adversity that sharpens steel. Jay Z once said, "I've learned more from failures than success. I don't know how you learn from success. I haven't figured that part out." Life is a series of trials and errors, falling down and getting up, two steps forward and one step backward. No one has a charmed life all the time. Conversely, no one has a cursed life all the time.

We must learn to accept the fact that we are all called to do something great, and this calling lies within us, if we will only listen. However, we spend too much time getting bogged down with life's minutiae, wringing our hands over bad things that have happened to us and fretting about the future (according to Abraham Hicks, "Worry is using your imagination to create something you don't want."). Instead of focusing on things that have already come to pass and are behind us, or circumstances that are beyond our control, what if we focused on following our passion? What if we listened to the voice that keeps urging us to follow a different path than the one we are on now? What if we were true to ourselves, and not to the voices of the world telling us to be something we are not?

Ask yourself this question: If I could start being exactly who I wish to be today, what would I look like? And I am not talking about a physical manifestation of yourself. I am talking about your SOUL, your ESSENCE. If we were all viewed by the content of our character, the significance of our spirit and the earnestness of our essence, how would we shine? Would others be drawn to the beauty of our substance? Would we be the kind of person who could make another emulate us and want to know us deeply?

My hope for myself, and for everyone I meet, is that we continue to go deep into our true selves. By doing so, we will develop relationships which are intimate, profound, life-affirming and far-reaching. We can change the world with relationships like this. Hearts get healed, spirits are soothed and we are all transformed into an authentic version of who we were designed to be. Your essence will speak truth to you.

# Chocolate & Diamonds

## Terry Neabel

Saskatchewan, Canada

### *What If?*

At times I wonder how different my life might have been if... These questions come to mind most often when I am fearful, sad or hurting. Each hill and valley, each twist and turn, each choice has brought me to where I am today.

Still I ask myself, h*ow would my life look today if...?*

There are many *what ifs* in everyone's life. My first "what if" is what my life would have been like if my family hadn't moved when I was eight. That move marked the beginning of a very difficult period in my life that is never far from my thoughts, filling me with sadness. We arrived in our new town filled with both anticipation and trepidation. It didn't take long to find out I wasn't welcome. I was devastated by the harsh reception. I was in grade four, I was bullied by my classmates and by one of my teachers. For two years I was lonely, scared, confused and hurt, never knowing what to expect from my peers. As an adult I can see the actions of my teacher for what they were – something I hadn't understood at the time.

It was a relief to leave that community behind, never to look back. We continued to move frequently and in each new community I feared the worst while hoping for better. Sometimes I was pleasantly surprised by kindness and friendship and other times I was again tormented by bullies who were getting bigger, stronger, more intimidating and cunning. Efforts to end the bullying resulted in change – change that allowed the schools to pretend it wasn't happening anymore – out of sight, out of mind. I learned to stay to myself, distrusting people and situations.

When I wasn't withdrawn, I tried too hard. Today people appropriately express sadness and horror at news stories about the horrific life damaging and life stealing results of bullying, but still there is no answer. No parent wants to believe their child would cause such pain to another child. When I was young, a common response from adults was "kids will be kids, they'll work it out". It didn't stop with my generation; as an adult it broke my heart to watch my own children suffer at the hands of bullies – kids were still being kids! I had a parent say that same thing after a very serious incident that I believe changed the course of our lives. A hand shake, a forced apology and all was believed to be better! I am a mother, but I feel powerless to change what I experienced and what I saw my children exposed to. I learned that despite the passage of time, still no one wants to hear about bullies – not the bullies or the parents of bullies or even my own family members who I trusted with my heart and soul. Time changed little.

*What if?* What if that little girl hadn't moved, would she have grown up in a different social environment? What if that girl hadn't been bullied? What if she hadn't married? What if she hadn't had children? What if... If these events hadn't unfolded making me who I am and my life what it is, I wonder what my life would look like. Without my children, I would be heart poor. Despite successes, I still doubt myself and fear the disapproval of others – both family, friends, and strangers. I distrust easier than trusting. I continually second guess my worth and my value. My views of society are oppressively negative. Truly, what if...

For years I've asked myself "what do I want to be when I grow up?" What do I really believe I could be? I cannot change the "what if's" of my life. For a long time I believed I could change how people see me and how I feel about myself by finding that life fulfilling career, proving to them that I am capable – that I didn't deserve to be bullied. I've accepted that I cannot replace my poor self-esteem and self-doubt with any career.

My 52nd year has been a year of acceptance and in some ways resignation. After many years as a stay-at-home mom in rural Canada, growing my family and searching for fulfillment and answers, I have gone back to full-time work testing out whether or not I can earn an income to sustain myself should I need to as well as contributing to my children's post-secondary education. I live in the city during the week and drive home for the weekends. I am elated - my job is on the same university campus where two of my children are studying and where I started working in 1984. I've reconnected with some people I knew in the 1980s. Sometimes I still ask, "what if?"

What if I had never left this campus, city, and province in 1989? Finding a job and living in my own suite has been such progress. I am trying to look after myself, but I've tried to do it without tearing my family apart – or not completely apart. I never understood women who reached this point in life and felt the need to "find themselves", but ironically, now I do. I desperately need to find myself and for the first time since that little girl experienced the cruelty of her peers and elders, I know I need to learn to trust and love myself because I am loveable. It's no longer about "what I want to be when I grow up", but it's about "who I want to be". It's finally time to "grow up" and leave that damaged little girl and woman behind. To learn to embrace the life and blessings that I deserve, instead of desperately wondering "what if".

I have taken a journey down memory lane on the campus where I work and in the city I used to know so well. I cannot go back, but how will I move ahead. Leaving everything behind is not the answer. I cannot undo what has molded me into the woman I am today, nor do I want to.

The negative things in my life have to be replaced with positive things, the fear has to be replaced with confidence. I have to learn to embrace the kind words from friends, colleagues and employers. I used to be passionate about so many things when I was young. I used to be creative. I loved to paint and create. The passions of my youth are high on my list of things to revisit and explore – not as they were, but through the eyes and heart of the woman I am today. I am a lifelong learner looking for my next opportunity. Being independent without feeling selfish is a tall order; it's a balancing act. It will never all be about self-care because I have a family I love and I am committed to.

What if? I can't help, but wonder if those "what ifs" would have changed anything. I will never know. Maybe this journey was mine to take regardless of the actions of others. Nonetheless, it's time to take the control away from those that have held it for so long. It's time to treat myself as I deserve to be treated for the rest of my journey. A good friend recently told me life has to be lived one day at a time, recognizing how far I've come while being kind to myself – that's my goal.

# Michelle Flagg

New Jersey, United States of America

## *From Death to Life*

Some dates weigh more significantly to us than others. Typically we associate fabulous or equally frightening events of our lives according to a date, etching them into our memory banks. From the broader world view perspective on occasion, some even serve as markers. Indicators of definitive change from what had become accepted standard to what had yet to be imagined by many. Dates such as the connection of the Transatlantic Cable, creation of the iTunes music service platform, and the crossing of precedent and present day to create "a first" in the political landscape for the highest held office in the country.

From the micro view of my personal life experiences, 2003 was a pivotal year. Everything I thought I knew, believed, and valued came under immense scrutiny and hellacious fire. Unprecedented loss and change became unyielding anchors ushering in a heaviness within the depths of my soul.

Definitely, September 16, 2003 and October 11, 2003 are dates that will always be a part of me. What they mean will always remain the same. How I would come to relate to them represents a major transformation which I never could have foreseen. By this point in time, the house I had obtained by standing in faith had foreclosed. My new plush mode of transportation had been repossessed.

The pension payout received due to involuntary separation from my 15-year stint at a Fortune 500 corporation had dwindled into nonexistence. I couldn't get a job washing dishes, scrubbing floors or collecting trash — how "over qualified" do you have to be for that — really!? Conditional friends scattered like roaches exposed to the light. Close relatives treated me as if I had brought shameful reproach on the family at large. While in the midst of having become broke, busted, and utterly disgusted, my father and mother died, respectfully on September 16, 2003 and October 11, 2003. To say I went from being broke to being broken is the proverbially understatement.

At this juncture in my life I am more convinced death is not final, it's transitional. It is part of a cycle that moves us from one state of being to another. It's non-negotiable, irrespective, and constant. I still don't know if there is any significance in the fact my parents died twenty-five days apart, in different states, living totally separate lives. I do know their deaths impacted me in ways that haven't been comparable to any other thing which I've known within life and living. Material and status losses can be regained. Fortunately, the demise of superficial relationships can give place for cognizant efforts to be practiced so that true, meaningful relationships can be built.

Although we expect our parents to precede us in death, when they die "abruptly" twenty-five days apart, where does that leave you? Where do you stand in the world? Was I an adult "orphan" now? The two people responsible for my physical existence were gone. In the immediate months to follow, shock subsided just long enough to make way for the flood of questions that managed to seep through the cracks of my splintered mind. I couldn't escape them. I couldn't avoid them. Each showed up commanding attention be given to discovery of an answer. It was in the aftermath of their deaths where learning took on a new dimension. In the place and space of time of examination of their lives, I couldn't help, but be drawn into looking at myself in the process.

My parents endured childhoods tainted by prejudicial restrictions and limiting perceptions. Lack of unified commitment to themselves and their family, alcoholism and infidelity were instrumental in their actual living three-quarters of their marriage apart. If the "Great Migration" from the north to south had played a role in their planned dreams to seek a better life, fruition of those dreams where snuffed out by survival mode living and a lack of understanding universal laws pertaining to living.

Until they died, I hadn't even considered the "fact". Two individuals came together, each with a combined set of everything they possessed whether good, bad, or indifferent. I am thankful though for them. My existence or more pointedly lack of existence could have stemmed from a very different decision. Instead, they gave me every measure of good they had known and possessed. Quantitatively, their misses may have outnumbered their hits.

I wasn't the beneficiary of material possessions or generational wealth. Qualitatively, the legacy they left me though is priceless. It continues to stand the tests of time, experience, and death. Their lessons came through sometimes seemingly miraculous and contrasting volatile means. But they came.

As weeks and months continue to roll into years and decades, I carry the lessons to *fear God* and *fear no man* within my heart. In modern terms, fearing God does not mean you cower throughout life under dread, judgmental religious traditions, and legalism as if you are waiting for lightening to strike you or hell to just open and swallow you up. Fearing God is a lifestyle of protective submission in relationship to God and His everlasting, never wavering love and wisdom. To fear no man means you first examine that "man in the mirror"; it's your internal compass which points you toward an external destination. It requires honesty with one's self and soul.

It requires critical thought be given to what you know, believe, and value. It requires eliminating the things (and relationships!) that ill serve, dis-ease, and rob you from being the best you are capable of being. And the forces of the two lessons together have proven to be unstoppable so far in my life. I've gone through times of loss, heartache, devastation and the like. I cried tears, fought depression, and have had to refuse to lose my mind. Nothing and no one has penetrated or defused the power inherent to the legacy left to me. Even in death, meaningful life prevails if you choose it.

# Natalie Gentry

Colorado, United States of America

## *Dancing My Way to Freedom*

I need to dance like I need to breathe." My movement instructor spoke those words at the beginning of a free movement/dance workshop I attended a year and a half ago. I immediately burst into tears; this instructor echoed a truth for me that I felt on a gut level, but didn't acknowledge consciously until that very moment. It was a simple moment of grace! What I didn't realize in the workshop was that I was beginning a continuation of a long journey that was "bringing me home" to myself in deeply profound ways or that dancing was going to play a pivotal role in my personal evolution and in how I serve my community.

### A little backstory…

My dance journey began when I was four years old. I studied ballet for 11 years. As I got older, I began to realize that, in spite of all of its beauty and grace, ballet necessarily imposed judgments regarding height, weight, body proportion, "turn-out", flexibility and appearance which created self-doubt within me. I didn't "fit in". I was struggling to keep up with classmates who were older and, technically, more advanced than me. Although I quit ballet, I grappled with my self-image and an imaginary weight problem for many years. At age 28, 115 pounds, and at a clothing size of 0-2, I realized I was too thin. I needed to cultivate a healthier relationship with myself.

In a subconscious effort to connect more deeply with myself, I began to play with other dance forms. I "clubbed", as most 20 somethings do. I also attended classes in African dance, belly dancing, and tango. I even got certified to teach Nia, a movement form which blends dance with martial arts and the healing arts (like yoga and The Alexander Method). I was drawn to each of these different movement forms because, in addition to being fun, they each awakened a deepening awareness in relation to how I experienced my body.

However, in spite of my growing awareness, I could see how reliant I was on looking to others to tell me how to move. Additionally, I found myself swimming in that old poisonous sea of self-judgment from my childhood; I needed to "get it right" and look good while doing it. And as my eventual need for perfection increased, my connection with myself, and my love for dancing, decreased. I had gotten out of my body and firmly entrenched in my head. So, I stopped.

**The wake-up call...**

Somewhere in my journey, I attended a concert of one of my favorite artists—Taj Mahal. My presence at his concert was a divinely timed intervention. As Taj Mahal played his dynamic blues set, the area in front of the bandstand teemed with revelers dancing their hearts out. Those revelers bopped and swayed, dancing on beat and off, and they were loving every ecstatic minute of it! I sat toward the back of the audience, staring at the dancers. I longed to join them, but I couldn't will my body to move. I was too afraid to dive in. I was jealous of the revelers' freedom.

In that moment, I realized I had, unknowingly, become painfully self-conscious about dancing in public and of exposing myself to judgment. (I believed others were judging me as harshly as I judged myself.) I also realized my hiatus from dancing had exposed me to struggles with depression. Furthermore, I was able to see and feel that moving my body helped me to process emotions and memories. I had turned away from the one thing which had fed my spirit, in addition, to my body. That realization broke my heart. I sat there and cried. This event also proved to be a wake-up call regarding how important dance is in my life. I need to honor my desire to move for my own sake. My body and spirit both need it; it gives me life! Moreover, when I ignore what my body's needs, I pay on an emotional level.

**The gift that appeared at the perfect time...**

Shortly after the concert, I attended my first free movement class with Vin Marti. It brought tears to my eyes...I had finally found my dance home! There were no instructions and no requirements; only an invitation and a willingness to say "yes". I loved being invited into movement that felt good to MY body! I loved that my dance didn't have to look like anyone else's. No one had to "fit in"; we were all unique, beautiful, and perfectly imperfect in how we all expressed ourselves through dance.

I am a big advocate of free movement. HUGE! Why? Because as we become adults, get educated, take on ever increasing responsibilities, and become increasingly rational and mature, we sometimes ignore or forget our childlike, playful nature; the very things in life that "juice us" and make our hearts sing. Many massage clients I see echo this truth. They lament how busy they are, how they don't feel joy and are "living on autopilot". They are numb to their lives. Or they share that they have achieved everything they wanted in their lives, but feel that something deeper is missing. We can actively dismiss playfulness as mere childish antics. We can also become uncomfortable with others who display an openness to connecting with that whimsical part of themselves, which is unfortunate.

A friend of mine, who attended an event a couple years ago which included an opportunity to dance, shared with me that someone in her party had remarked no one over 40 years old should dance. As a 40 something, I was dismayed! I recalled my Taj Mahal concert experience. I could only imagine how someone who might have wanted to dance but, upon overhearing her comment, might have reconsidered the wisdom of being playful.

Free dance and movement are important to me because dancing is a way of expressing myself in ways that are full, open, expansive, raw, and honest. The students I facilitate in dance (Yes, I now teach, Gratefully!) leave my classes feeling just plain joyful, playful, even a bit more sassy and daring! There are few things more exhilarating, freeing, and enlivening than whirling, stretching, contracting, exploding, stomping, shaking, and gliding in playful dance around a dance floor (or kitchen, or outdoor space…)!

### What we can learn from children…

Think back to when you were five years old…did you care about how you looked when you listened to music you liked? Did you fret over getting your dance steps right? Did you stop to question whether your dancing was "appropriate" for your age? Or did you just get out there and dive into pure sensation? Guess what? You don't grow out of the desire to express yourself in movement. It's still there! It's just waiting for you to notice it again.

Children possess an inherent wisdom; they know we are meant to dance and play. That's why they have such difficulty keeping still. Dancing and playing are what help us to ground and center ourselves. It helps us maintain our youthful vibrancy. They help us to tap into our creativity, our imagination, and our natural ability to relax and be open. They also help us to problem solve because we are more intellectually and emotionally available to increased possibilities.

When I move, there is a point where I stop being the dancer and become the dance. I am completely immersed in movement and feeling. My dance becomes my voice. I dance my happiness, my sadness, my anger and my fear. I dance my hopes and my dreams. I dance my longings and disappointments. I dance my desires and my connection with space and community. I dance my gratitude that I can feel myself and feel my life fully! I just leave it on the floor. And in so doing, I learn more and more about who I am and I love who I see! I love the ME that is evolving; I feel more colorful and expressive. I am more willing to be vulnerable and am more accepting of my imperfections. I am even speaking up more and am feeling more comfortable with what I have to say, with no apologies. I am also much more open to seeing and experiencing what more is possible in my life. THAT is what the gift and power of dance has given me!

Martha Graham once said, "Nobody cares if you can't dance well. Just get up and dance. Great dancers are not great because of their technique; *they are great because of their passion."* Preach, Ms. Graham!!! We all carry our own unique, beautiful representation of that passion within us. I am proud and grateful to bring that message to my community. I invite us all to connect with, reveal, and fall in love with ourselves through dance, in all of our beautiful freedom, our awkward grace, and our perfect imperfection. C'mon…let it out!

# Chocolate & Diamonds

## Mariane Barakat

New South Wales, Australia

### *In Blindness there is Vision for Life*

No, no *I don't want to go to hospital*, there is nothing wrong with me" I cried, with my arms wrapped around my father's neck, kicking and screaming. My mother proceeded to pay the Doctor's bill as she and my father tried to calm me down. I was only four years old at the time, but 31 years later I remember it like it was yesterday.

*I had just been diagnosed with Type 1 juvenile diabetes. What was diabetes to a four year old?* It meant nothing. "I have no cuts or bruises and I am not bleeding, so why do I need the hospital" I remember thinking. I felt so confused and scared. None the less, straight to the hospital we went. My mother didn't leave my side the whole time I was there. After what seemed like months, however, it was only a couple of weeks. They sent me home with my overnight bag filled with a life time of diets, daily insulin injections and blood glucose tests. Leaving the hospital, I was otherwise oblivious to the life that lay ahead.

Growing up as a child, life was beautiful. I was happy. I had the amazing love and support of my parents, older brother, wonderful family and friends. I enjoyed school. I spent a lot of my time with my two closest friends who conveniently lived across the street. My weekends were spent with cousins. Summer holidays with family were always a highlight. I did the usual thing as a teenager including leaving school early to sit and watch the boys drive by at the local McDonalds. I left high school knowing I was to be a pre-school teacher. With my love and passion for children, I knew working with them was the only thing I wanted to do. My best friend, since the age of ten, became my high school sweetheart. We ended up getting married in July 2003. Life couldn't have been better, it was as close to perfect as it could get.

That was until one Friday on a sunny October morning in 2003, I had just returned to work after my honeymoon break. Everything had been running smoothly as usual at the preschool; the children were all outside. All of a sudden

'POP'! Something was wrong, something was terribly wrong. It was like the blood trickling down a wall in a horror film, but this wasn't a horror film…. Oh how I wished it was.

That was all I could see on the inside of my right eye. It was morning tea time. I was walking through the empty classroom to the balcony with the tray of cups in my hands, to where the children were waiting for their morning tea. My right eye had suddenly started to hemorrhage and was filling up with blood. I froze; all I could do was stand there. My legs lost all feeling. I couldn't move. My hands began to shake almost dropping the tray. I was petrified. Little did I know leaving work that day I was closing the classroom door behind me forever?

"Mum I can't see". I was trying to sound composed over the phone. Straight to the hospital we went, my husband meeting us there straight from work. I was still waiting when the chill in the night air revealed how late it had become. After seeing several doctors, I was sent home and told to return on Monday as there was no one there at the time to help me. I left the hospital with my eyes filled with tears, unable to speak.

Monday came and a diagnosis was finally confirmed: Diabetic Retinopathy. What does this mean for me? I remember thinking. Two days had passed since that horrid Friday and my body was still feeling numb. I wanted to sleep, thinking maybe when I woke up this terrifying nightmare would all disappear. Instead I heard "there is a long road ahead, this isn't going to be easy". The calmness and gentleness in the doctor's voice was soothing to me. Arrangements were made to start intense laser treatment immediately. I was booked in for surgery in the following month.

Two months later I was at home when POP! The image of dripping blood was now familiar to me. A hemorrhage once again, but this time in the left eye. A sense of panic shot right through me like a wave of electricity. I knew what this was and again I was frozen. "You are very unlucky, I've never seen a case so severe in someone so young and definitely not in both eyes" the sound of the doctor's voice echoed in my ears as he spoke to me in his office the next morning. I had become accustomed to his calm and gentle voice, although, unlike the last time it wasn't soothing. This time I couldn't be soothed. I was booked in for surgery, something else I was getting familiar with since this would be my third one in two months.

Soon enough another familiarity was the wheeling in and out of the operating rooms. For a few years, I found myself staring up at the operating theatre roof every couple of weeks. Recovery left me positioned either flat on my back or flat on my face for weeks on end, usually until the next one. Over 60 surgeries and procedures and still counting. They aren't as often, but they still continue today.

After the loss of my eyesight, my life as I knew it came to a complete halt. I instantly lost my career, my independence, and my car. Three years later, I also lost my marriage. The biggest loss of all was myself. All that was certain became uncertain and the familiar became unfamiliar. It was as if suddenly the lights were switched off, not only to my physical sight, but also to my vision for the future and everything that lay ahead. Everything became wrapped in darkness. Who was I? What was happening to me? What now? Where do I belong? What is everyone going to think? Am I going to make it safely into the next room? Is this the sugar or the salt? I knew nothing. ***The overwhelming fear was intense and all I knew was that the darkness was here to stay.***

The life events that followed were anything, but easy. I quickly learnt to embrace the uncertainty and the "ok" of not knowing. The choices I made and what I chose to believe played a huge part in overcoming the challenges and becoming who I am today. Think about this; would you rather sit in a room and allow fear to take over or would you rather face the world and live life on your terms? I could have chosen the path of isolation and led myself into a state of depression. I chose to laugh and to live the life I've been given. Everything we do is a choice and it's these choices which create the life we currently live. ***You see, it'is not the situation itself, but rather how you choose to deal with it.***

Moreover, this journey has also taught me the power of acceptance, not just in overcoming adversity, but in everything we do. I reached a point of total acceptance of my entire situation and to what was happening around me. Only then was I able to let go of all the negative emotions and see things for what they really were. I truly welcomed and embraced the experience and only then did real growth begin. I gained a deeper understanding about life, others and myself. Who I really was, who I was becoming and what I wanted out of life became so clear and so certain and my life came alive once again.

My already strong faith has become even stronger and the presence of God has become paramount in my life. My faith has given me an inner strength and purpose that is unlike anything I have known. We often search for external things to find what we are looking for whether it be happiness, love, peace or freedom, not realizing what we are searching for is right there within ourselves.

For so many years of feeling pain I chose happiness. I have learnt with certainty LIFE is an EXPERIENCE, not a circumstance. Accept it. Embrace it. Have faith. Choose what you make of life and believe anything is possible. I believe in you.

# Kerri Dohring

Florida, United States of America

## *My Ambidextrous Life*

I was a left-handed little girl born into a right-handed family. I am hoping this analogy says it all since my family may actually read this story. But, I will expand on a few points.

### The Right Side

I have never seen anyone in my family show emotion. My aunt had the potential during the funeral of her late husband of 40 years, but she was so jacked up on Xanax, I am not sure she actually knew where she was. I say this because as we sat in a silent prayer to honor my deceased uncle, my aunt literally yelled at the top of her lungs *"Wow, that pill really works!"* That was the first time I actually laughed at a funeral.

### The Left Side:

I am sensitive, emotional and intuitive. I love to talk about my triumphs and tragedies. Crying comes naturally to me. Though I am building a strong case that I may have been the milk-man's kid, just one moment in time created what I like to call my Inner-Bitch-Critic. My Inner-Bitch-Critic (or IBC for short) was born in 1978 at the tender age of 5 and I remember it clearly....

The incident occurred in our navy blue Monte Carlo with tan seats which smelled like a strange combination of popcorn, mildew and Old Spice. I climbed into the backseat and immediately began to stake out my territory. Back in the 70's, parents didn't worry much about safety such as car seats or seat belts. In fact, I am amazed I am still alive.

Without seat belts, the back seat was a wide-open space with a subtle stitched line that appeared from top to bottom on the seat. This small stich became our Game of Thrones and the person that was able to secure just one inch over the center- line could feel like the victor of the trip.

On this particular day, my brother was nine. Being four years older than me gave him the advantage of being faster, stronger and smarter *(but that only lasted for another month or two)*. On our way home, my brother swiftly pushed me over the line and began making faces at me. Not knowing how to defend myself, I did what any 5-year old would do – I began to scream and cry. This defense technique caused me to appear as the "troublemaker." After all, I was the only one flailing, crying and yelling. His mere "faces" kept him under the radar.

Since my plea for help only got ME in trouble, I launched my own campaign for redemption, revenge and that inch of backseat space that was swindled from me. I raised my game by quietly leaning towards him and biting him on the arm as hard as I could.

And then it happened...he wailed in agony. The one and only time I had ever seen my brother cry! He cried not to show emotion, but as a knee jerk reaction to pain. My parents lost it. My father came to a screeching halt in the driveway as my mother yelled in her Italian/northeastern/ JFK voice: *"Hun, she put a hole in his ahhhm!"*

My brother acted as though he had just returned from Vietnam and I was in disbelief. My one attempt at instilling justice was foiled by a small, red mark on his arm. It was hardly a hole, but the family's reaction suggested my brother needed to be plunged onto a gurney and rushed to the nearest trauma unit.

My reasoning for self-defense all went ignored. My father scooped me up from the back seat, stormed into my room, threw me over his knee and smacked me into what he thought was submission. That was the first and only time I was hit by a parent. *(It left a mark and not just on my ass.)*

### The Inner-Bitch-Critic is born

That moment convinced my younger-self that I was the black sheep in my family, my brother was the favorite and I was not loveable. The only way to cope with this tremendous sadness was to develop an Inner-Bitch-Critic who knew no boundaries! *Why would one moment in time cause such strong misguided beliefs?*

That's just how we roll when our first experience with injustice snatches us from our *Lucy In the Sky with Diamonds* youth. Without knowing it, when attempting to do something that will expand or challenge us, our Inner-Bitch-Critic comes out of nowhere to keep us safe. *Wait, we create the bitch to protect ourselves?* (Yep, aint' that a bitch!)

My IBC was like an ESPN highlight, repetitively popping in unexpectedly when I wasn't paying attention. And her voice strangely resembled that of Rizzo from the movie Grease...

*"Do not even bother, you will fail!"*

*"You are not smart enough to take that on."*

*"You cannot afford another mistake."*

### Ambidextrous Takes Hold:

The next 30 years were an attempt to fit-in. I attached myself to every non-emotional person who came within a five-foot radius of me. I never learned to fit in with my family, but I did become a pro at people-pleasing and at creating my own Xanax'd future.

But, the Universe had another plan for me. In 2012, I went through a yearlong certification process and became a Professional Life Coach. After level-setting my own perceptions, I've been assisting women of all ages and stages with their own IBC challenges. I am not alone *(or crazy... huh, who knew?)* It's incredible when we can pinpoint not only the exact language we hear, but the exact moment in childhood when our IBC was born. Just last week, I had a client (let's call her Mary) whose critic told her: *"You look awful and you are fat."(It should be noted that she's far from overweight)*

When prompted, Mary recalled the day her mother stated... *"You are getting fat, stop eating the junk food and eat something healthy!"*

Mary was 7. To preserve our sanity, we must believe our parents did the best they could. My father's motivations, I am sure, were a valiant attempt to end my Hannibal Lector tendency. Truth be told, I never bit anyone again. *But, why did that moment leave a lasting mark on my life?*

### It's simply a survival mechanism...

Every time my Inner-Bitch-Critic would pop in with a negative comment, I would people-please to avoid being "smacked on the ass." This protective IBC voice is virtually impossible to eradicate. But, I did make it work for me by listening and looking for patterns. By asking the right questions and employing some empowering visualization techniques, I was able to tame mine. I also began to review the areas in my life where I was people- pleasing and while this is still a work-in-progress, I now ask myself... *"Do I really want to do this?"*

If I determine that I am attempting to help someone because of my inherent desire to fit in or a fear of abandonment, I gracefully bow out. Another big step was giving my Inner-Bitch-Critic's voice a make-over. She now has a gay man's voice. Yes, the tone of Rizzo was no longer serving me so I have replaced her with Curtis. Curtis is slightly sarcastic, gay man, with a touch of loving caution. "Uuh, uh, guuurl," he says. "Are you sure you can do this?"

I tell him to "f-off', imagine him smiling and continue on my task. As I progress on my journey, my family is still right and I am left. Most importantly, I've learned my left handed-nature can live successfully in the right-handed world. And I am proud of that!

# Jennifer Adrienne

Ontario, Canada

## *Dreamer*

**"No matter how many mistakes you make or how slow you progress, you are still way ahead of everyone who isn't trying." – Tony Robbins**

I am a dreamer. I always have been. Blame it on Walt Disney, Fairy Tales, or the perfect family shows I watched growing up – I've always dreamed. Of what? Well, of being super successful, falling in love and having a Prince Charming, having a wonderful family with kids that listened to my every word (I didn't say my dreams were realistic), being famous, having the perfect marriage, being Miss America – I loved to daydream as a kid.

However, life has a funny way of throwing some curve balls in there. As we get older, we forget our dreams and get into survival mode. You know survival mode – just trying to get to the next day. But what I want to take some time to discuss with you right now is something that many of us, especially women and caregivers, forget – the *In between*. See, I know, and I know I am not alone in this, I've taken for granted that I open my eyes to a new day every day and I've somewhere to lay my head at night.

What I want to focus on right now, is what happens in between the time my eyes open in the morning and my head goes down at night. It's the in between where the most precious, beautiful, and significant events occur. It's where we laugh and cry; interact with others; build relationships, fall in and out of love, learn and share skills, experience our firsts. For example, do you remember your first car? The feeling of having something to call your own? The smell of that new car. Well, my first car was obtained in 1999 and it was a 1985 burgundy Honda Civic. It smelled of cigarettes and the brakes were shot. BUT IT WAS MINE. And I treasured it for the time I had it. It's the in between where life happens.

When I was growing up, I was raised in a small mining town in Northern, Manitoba – 8 hours drive north from civilization. My major influence to the outside world was the television. My favorite show was the Cosby Show because I was able to identify with the characters. I was a young black girl growing up in a middle class home in a city of 26,000 and there were probably 50 other people in the city that looked like me. So the Cosby show was my reality to what black people were like in the "real" world. In this show, all problems and issues were solved within 22.5 minutes excluding commercials. The parents, raised their kids similarly to how my parents raised me. The belief and the goal was to go to school get good grades, graduate, go to post-secondary school, get a job, meet a boy, get married, buy a house, raise kids, launch the kids, retire and then enjoy the fruits of your labor in retirement. Is this familiar to you? I personally hate it because it takes way too long to have to get to the part where life is enjoyed.

The problem for me was I wasn't raised learning about *how* to enjoy the process of life – the in between moments. No one taught me about or told me how challenging relationships could be – marital relationships, parent-child relationships – remember, my reality was Cosby Show. I am not saying I needed a step by step guide or a prescription on how to live life. But I've learned there is a need for us to model to our children, friends, and family how to enjoy life. *For years my life has been in a pattern*.

Wake up, feed everyone, dress everyone, pack lunches, go to work, come home, try to get some rest, run a small business, go to sleep - and so on and so forth! Do you see a pattern?

Do not get me wrong, there is beauty in raising children and watching them flourish. There is joy in success at work, especially if you are fortunate enough to work in a place where you are appreciated and you love what you do. But for me, it was the repetition I found stifling. It felt like life was living me instead of me living life. In the beginning I said I was a dreamer. Well, I've also always been goal oriented and a planner. So much so, I was always focused on accomplishing the next goal as opposed to enjoying where I was in the moment. I was missing out on what was happening in my life 'NOW'.

In my journey to accept and enjoy the now, I've developed three principles I think we should all adopt and adapt to suit our own lives.

*Lose the fear.* Do me a favor and think of all of the things you think you may have failed at. Think of the experience, how you felt, and what came out of the experience. The saying is so true, it is better to have tried and failed then to not have tried at all. Because it is in the failing where we grow, learn, and adapt so that the next time we are wiser in our decisions. Ultimately, as long as we have tried, we can never truly fail.

*Appreciate where you are and how you got here.* The road isn't always nice, clear and easy. Mistakes happen and hurts happen. Trust me, I've made some big ones that are more dramatic and convoluted than the most popular soap opera. But the lessons I've learned from those times are invaluable. I now know that no matter what I am going through, there is a lesson to learn that will propel me further than I ever imagined in the first place.

***Be totally and unapologetically selfish***. Take care of you first. There is a reason when you are in an airplane, that they tell you in case of emergency put your oxygen mask on first, before helping the person beside you. You cannot help someone if you cannot breathe! Fill the inner you. You cannot bless or serve someone else with your cup that "runneth" over if your cup is empty! You are the most important person in your world. Take care and love you.

"Forever is composed of NOWS" – Emily Dickenson

"Life is a journey, not a destination" – Ralph Waldo Emerson

Enjoy, respect, and appreciate the in between. It's where life happens.

# SPIRITUALITY

# #SPIRITUALITY

the soul within

# Kate Bares-Cochrun

Texas, United States of America

## *Take It To The A.L.T.A.R.*

If you follow my work or my writing, you are likely familiar with what I call "A.L.T.A.R™" practice. A.L.T.A.R™ is an acronym for **Ask. Listen. Trust. Act. Repeat**...a simple, *powerful* practice that instantly moves us out of our own stubborn way and allows for Higher Guidance/Consciousness to direct our life.

I think of it like a GPS for my Soul. When I am using my navigator in my car, I put in the destination **(Ask)**. Wait for it to update my location **(Listen)**. Follow directions **(Trust)**. Push the gas **(Act!)**. Wait for the next step **(Repeat)**. As anyone who knows me can vouch, I am *terribly* directionally challenged and depend completely on my GPS when in uncharted territory. No shame here...it WORKS! That's how the A.L.T.A.R™ works for me, too.

I received the process while on the brink of my wit's end, feeling "lost" in an already too-long term relationship, crying my eyes out in the shower yet again. I wanted so desperately to fix what (I believed) was broken in me that wouldn't allow me to simply *be happy* in what appeared on the outside to be a perfectly good relationship. It was maddening to feel so discontented, yet there was something in me that refused to let me settle. It was exhausting and painful for both of us and I had resigned to the fact I was the problem.

I was so frustrated, not knowing how to get all the way in or all the way out, and I was pleading for an answer when I heard the crisp, clear words, "Take it to the ALTAR". I knew immediately Spirit was nudging me to *go pray about it.* These were the words a dear friend had offered through the years as a gentle reminder to pray my way through a struggle or problem. I smiled at the reminder and felt relieved for the nudge, but then there was more! Before I could wash the shampoo out of my hair, the entire A.L.T.A.R™ process literally *downloaded* in my mind, right there in the shower. The answer to my plea for an answer was...there is no answer! I was being asked to Ask. Listen. Trust. Act. Repeat. What? I was *already* asking, wasn't I?

Oh, I had been asking, alright; I had the *praying* down pat. But I wasn't really listening, or trusting. I wasn't *doing* anything other than keeping myself in my own miserable rut! I scrambled out of the shower and dripped to my little altar, sat down, and asked for more. This is what I received:

1) Ask God to guide you in the *highest* good, in all ways, in all circumstances and decisions. Ask for right action. 2) Listen for the first answer/guidance you receive. 3) Trust it. You will NEVER be guided to harm yourself or someone else. This is not the same as others' disappointment. Not everyone will understand you are acting in alignment with higher consciousness, but they, too, will ultimately benefit from the results. Trust. 4) Take action immediately. Don't delay or seek to understand. You will understand the purpose in time. 5) Repeat the process. Ask for the next step.

I was instructed to practice these steps every day, *all* day for one month, in all decisions, great or small. I already felt a renewed peace I had not felt in so very long; not only did I not have to know, but I couldn't *possibly* know, and that in itself was a huge relief. I made the decision that night to surrender the relationship to the highest good, which meant I would no longer push, prod, fix, control, or otherwise act according to my own *perceived* needs or wants, but would take my cues from God. I committed to use the A.L.T.A.R™ as my only compass. As uncomfortable as it might have been for my partner, he was supportive and agreed to trust my process. We both knew this would potentially shift *everything*.

And it did! Not only did it shift the relationship, but my entire *life*! **Engaging in this practice forced me to ground zero**, where I had to humbly admit I had no idea what was or was *not* in my own highest good, much less the relationship. I was most definitely in uncharted territory, but as I acclimated in those first 30 days, I was genuinely the most free I had ever felt! Rather than feeling responsible for everything and everyone, my only *true* responsibility was to trust God and do my best to do my best, without excuses or exemptions. I didn't need to control outcomes, or people, or be afraid of others' reactions. I only had to listen, trust and follow guidance. When I was nudged to reach out to someone, I followed without knowing why. I would simply say, "I was guided to reach out to you," and watched as synchronistic connections and events unfold again and again.

When it came to the partnership, A.L.T.A.R™ allowed me the space to slow down and respond where I might have otherwise reacted, bypassing so many of the old codependent paradigms we had been stuck in. If I wanted alone time but was guided to connect, I connected. If I wanted to connect but was guided to take time for myself, I sat still. No excuses. No exemptions. There were plenty of times I struggled through the pangs of instant gratification withdrawal, but the energy shift was so palpable it kept me willing. One month morphed into two, then three and before I knew it, A.L.T.A.R™ had become my walking/waking meditation; my living mantra.

Amazingly, within six short months, the nearly ten year struggle came to a graceful, peaceful close which we both knew was right. We had been here before, but this was different. God had done what neither of us had been able to do on our own, or together, and we were changed for the better. I continue to be grateful for the profound role that dynamic played in my healing and for my own tenacious Soul that never let me give up on BIG LOVE! I am happy to report I am genuinely, blissfully married to the truest love of my life to this day; living proof my Soul did indeed *know* all along.

A.L.T.A.R™ (i.e. my relationship with the Divine) continues to be my Soul compass, consistently guiding me to the places and people and experiences that encourage and allow me to unfold in all that I am; lovingly and gently bringing me home to my Self, again and again.

# Katherine Amber Murray

New South Wales, Australia

## *My Healing Journey*

Looking back, it's all a bit of a blur. As it can be, when life change suddenly, almost seeming to compel us, in a new direction.

For many years, I had held a desire to do my own work. I wanted to help people overcome their challenges and to heal. I had been through difficult times and found gifts in the challenges, healing and growth. I wanted to play a part in assisting others to do this. Yet, I told myself it wasn't the right time and I wasn't ready. I just needed to study one more course, wait till my children grow up, and get ahead financially....There was an inner desire, yet it wasn't strong enough to overcome the obstacles that I saw.

In the meantime, my work in a local resort, was becoming increasingly unbearable. There was a sadness in my heart and soul, which was getting harder to ignore. I was doing what I thought was necessary, to do what I needed to do....someday. Yet, it was getting harder to wake up each day and go to a job, which gave me so little opportunity to truly help people in the way I wanted to.

I remember going to work, and the day beginning, just like many other days. The resort was full and I seemed to be running more than walking, to get everything done. I was moving a table and my back went into spasm. The pain was intense and it hurt to move. I felt a twinge of fear in the pit of my stomach. I had experienced lower back pain before, but not like this. I finished work, went home and had a warm bath.

I woke up, hopeful my back would feel better after a night's rest. My back twinged and spasmed as I got out of bed. It felt better after warming up a bit. So, off to work, with an intention to take it easy, until my back is better.

I continued to work, in a physically demanding job, while in constant pain. As I don't take pain medication, I used herbal pain tablets and liniments to lessen the pain. One of the worst things, was feeling I didn't have a lot of choice.

Apparently, I have a high tolerance for suffering, as I went on like this for several months. By the end of the day, I would often be crying from the pain. It became clear I couldn't sustain this. Without proper rest, my back was getting worse, not better. I was overdue, for some self-care.

I called my manager and told him I was in intense pain and needed to take a week off to rest. Then, I went to the doctor and applied for worker's compensation. At this point, I saw this as my best option. This was the beginning, of what was to be in many ways, a long and tough journey. I felt exhausted, from months of working, while in pain. For the first time, I was scared about my future and that my back wouldn't get better.

I found myself navigating a system, designed to return me to work as quickly as possible. This meant consulting with doctors, who seemed to see their role, as assisting me to reduce the pain with medication, so I could get back to work.

One of the things I remember about this time was how invalidated I felt, by the doctors. I was told my back injury was minor, that many people live and work with such injuries and the pain was in my head.

It was much later, I had an accurate diagnosis, which explained one of the vertebrae had slipped out of place, causing the pain and nerve pressure.

Life has taught me, to stand up for myself and listen to my own counsel first. I knew the pain was there for a reason and masking it would not assist my body's healing process. That, if I continued to do physical work with a back injury, my back wouldn't fully recover. I had made up my mind to heal my back and get my life back. What I most needed was rest, as I was beyond exhausted. I said to the doctor I need 6 weeks off work and to my surprise, he agreed.

Injuring my back was a huge wake up call. I remember, during this time, asking myself: **"What did you think you were doing?"** The answer was, I was working too hard, for long hours, to earn a few extra dollars. I was not respecting myself or doing what I knew I was meant to be doing. It was time for a change. Something deep inside me called, to choose a different path. A path of joy, of doing what I really wanted to do, instead of what I thought I had to do. Enough! I made a commitment to do my own work, and started looking for new ways forward.

During this time, I became an avid researcher of chronic pain and back injuries. What I found, was most people do not recover, to live a full life. Instead, they live with significant limitations and pain for the rest of their life. I was determined to find healing and solutions. I had things to do, important things. I wanted to travel, to run, to dance, to do my work, to live my life fully, once again.

It's funny, it's often not until we lose something, we have taken for granted, that we come to truly value it. After a few hours in bed at night, I would wake up in too much pain to move. It hurt to walk, to sit, to stand. Running, dance and bushwalking, my favourite hobbies, were not something I could do, as it hurt to walk a few metres.

At times, I experienced intense fear and hopelessness, that this would be my life. My pain fluctuated from low level constant pain, to intense pain and spasms, during which I couldn't move. I don't like hospitals. I object to being pumped full of drugs, having tubes in my arms and being confined to a bed. So, I stayed home and found my own ways to deal with the pain. Meditation and relaxation helped. Deep breathing and warm baths brought relief. I tried everything from herbal liniments to a pain liniment for horses, to stop the spasms and be able to sleep.

My gift to myself during this time, was a 10 day healing course. An opportunity, to immerse myself in a healing environment and to find physical, emotional and spiritual healing. I needed to rekindle my belief I would recover.

I returned home after 10 days, feeling renewed and optimistic about my future. I had cleared some of the emotional patterns and cellular memories which were contributing to the pain. The pain was considerably reduced and I no longer experienced back spasms or immobilising pain. I felt reconnected with my sense of purpose and the faith I was now on the road to recovery.

My treatment continued with a physiotherapist and exercises to strengthen and release tension in my back. It was important to do things which brought me joy and helped me to feel good. I walked in nature and danced again, every day feeling my strength returning, slowly.

Managing my mental and emotional state was just as important as the physical recovery. I had seen how easy it is to get bogged down in hopelessness and depression and how this exacerbated the pain. I practiced focusing my mind positively, on goals which were important to me and inspired me with a sense of purpose. I visualised myself, living the life I wanted to be living and doing the things, I wanted to be doing. I saw it, felt it and imagined it with all of my senses.

I knew part of my healing was to start doing my own work. It was time. Nothing had changed and everything had changed. I was a woman with a mission. I wanted to assist others to overcome their challenges. I had experienced what it is to live with constant pain, which stopped me from doing the things I love and enjoy. I was on my road to recovery and I wanted to assist others to have both the belief in themselves and the tools, to move forward, to heal and live their life fully.

There were so many wonderful blessings during this time. Money came to me from unexpected sources, allowing me to do, what I needed to do, to move forward. I was blessed with wonderful friends, inspiring teachers, coaches, mentors and earth angels, who showed up at just the right time.

And so the journey continues.....I am now a qualified life coach, hypnotherapist and NLP practitioner. My personal journey of healing, intertwines beautifully with my work. I get to assist people to overcome their challenges, using my skills and training, as well as what I've learned on my own healing journey.

I feel blessed to have my life back. I dance, run and bushwalk. I feel grateful the pain no longer governs and controls my life. I have a sense of purpose that inspires and drives me to do and be all that I can be.

# Sheila Krichman

Florida, USA

*Finding God: a 50 year Journey*

"Existence – in itself
Without a further function –
Omnipotence – Enough –
To be alive – and Will!
'Tis able as a God –
The Maker of Ourselves – be what –
Such being Finitude!"
  -Emily Dickinson c. 1863

I talked to God today. I do that quite a lot now. When my eyes flick open in the morning, I say, "thank you, God for the gift of today." When I spot birds soaring invisible air currents. For me this is spirituality. And it feeds my soul. I've come to realize that every moment of life is a surprise. That I am wealthy beyond calculation. That you and I contain a spark of God's infinite light within us.

If it sounds like I get an A-plus in life, I confess in advance: spirituality is a new and welcome addition to my life.

When I was a copywriter on Madison Avenue, I wasn't spiritual. All my energy went into being clever and creative. When my fist-swinging, knock-'em-down brother didn't wake up one morning at the age of 38, I felt secretly glad. Guilty, too, but I didn't talk to God about it. I'd wished for faith so many times. But it eluded me. Years later, when I noticed my husband behaving strangely and the test results proved early-onset Alzheimer's disease, God wasn't part of my vocabulary.

I went to a caregivers' group and the more courageous attendees pointed out how angry I was at God. My parents tried to comfort me, but our roles had already reversed. I was taking care of them as they grew more infirm. Yet I was afraid, angry and I couldn't go "off duty."

Alzheimer's disease is a powerful teacher for the healthy.

I kept my husband at home for as long as I could, until he became combative. I had to search out Alzheimer's assisted living facilities. I found one nearby, and on the staff's recommendation, I brought him there and left him to "adjust" for five days without visiting.

Once I could visit, my six foot two inch husband would start crying and beg me to take him home.

I had to learn phrases like, "I'm working on that honey," and, "let's give it another day or so." I'd hug him and tell him I loved him so much and get an aide to open the locked door to the building for me. Once outside, my tears would explode. Could I do this one more day? How? God never entered my mind.

I visited every day at first. The facility had a rotation of activities. Not-so-great singers would come to entertain. There would be parties and dances for every possible occasion…bizarre affairs where the healthy visitors would help their loved ones eat and drink festive colored juices. Therapy dogs would visit. Some patients cuddled dolls. Others clutched teddy bears with age grizzled fingers. My husband was so much younger. How could I imprison him like this? There were coloring books and puzzles and games. But the only people who touched the patients were aides and visitors.

One of the "inmates" was a woman with stick-straight white hair chopped off above her ear lobes. Her clothes reminded me of the home-sewn dresses my grandmother wore when I was a little girl. They looked foreign and indeed they were.

All of the patients wore identification bracelets, and one of them always seemed to be pulling at hers. I was sitting on a couch and when I saw her arm, it had neat black numbers on the skin just above her wrist. I realized that she had been in a concentration camp. That is a cruel enough fate. She had lived through horrible atrocities, no doubt, lost her loved ones and now as an old age "bonus," she had Alzheimer's disease. God was nowhere in the picture.

I learned that her name was Molly; that she'd been born in Poland; had been fluent in numerous languages; and that Alzheimer's took away all but Polish. In a houseful of English speakers from all over the world, no one could miss Molly.

Every time she could get close to the piano, Molly tried to play it. She belted out Polish numbers I'd never heard before. Day after day, she was a one-woman show, always singing. Her joy was so infectious, I'd find myself humming along with her.

One day Molly was singing away, and a male patient dropped his tightly-belted trousers and started swinging them over his head like he was roping a steer. In seconds, another patient grabbed one of the trouser legs and started dancing around the tangled trousers legs like a Maypole while Molly sang away. I had to smile. A solemn dance, a half-clothed man, the lilting song. There was a dignity to the moment.

My husband lost the ability to walk and talk about a year later. Two years in, he didn't always know who I was. I began visiting every other day. Hosted solo pity parties for myself. And then I hauled myself back over to the facility to check on him. We married too late in life to have children and I was his sole caregiver. I had to be "there" for him.

I would hold my husband's hand, kiss his face, his hands, his hair, and be his human security blanket when he got anxious. At least I felt like I was getting through to him. And oddly, I began noticing that I was feeling grateful for how caring some of the aides were. One chunky woman would slip my husband an extra dessert after dinner. The elixir of sugar would bring pleasure to his tongue. Another aide would comb his thick, wavy hair just so and tell him how handsome he looked for his "girlfriends." How kind of them, I'd think. And good old Molly was still crooning tunes with a semblance of melody.

I was watching my husband disappear more every day. A very sad and lonely feeling. Yet, I was also more aware of the little kindnesses that came his way. When I went home, I would make note of them in my diary. He got a close, cut-free shave one day. His clothes would make it back from the laundry to his closet. His shoes were on the correct foot instead of the left shoe being jammed onto the right foot and vice versa.

Molly was becoming happier and more animated every day. She was living every minute of her life with all the energy she had to give that moment. It was transformative for me. Yes, my husband and many of the other patients I knew were declining daily. But Molly was still a songstress. And I was becoming one too, recognizing that every time I sang, I was feeling a touch happier. A tad more alive.

God re-entered my life through Molly's songs. Bits of appreciation were rising up in me like dandelions growing through the concrete cracks of city sidewalks.

My husband died four days after his seventieth birthday. I was at his side, whispering that it was safe for him to let go of life. Safe for him to let go of me.

Several months after he died, I heard a female barbershop quartet performing at my library. What a joyful sound. Four voices in harmony were rekindling my spirit like Molly had.

I will always miss my husband. Often have something to tell him. And I tell it to God. On paper. In person. Outside. Inside. Today, I am a Sweet Adeline. I sing in a chorus of 55 women who sing barbershop harmony. It takes work. And growth. I still thank Molly for her songs. And at long, long last, I have spirit and source. What a lesson.

# Mandelyn Reece

## California, United States of America

### *Falling Down the Rabbit Hole*

It hit me out of nowhere like a sledgehammer: I had to go out on the streets with posters about kindness. I blurted this revelation out to my friend Claire, whom I had known since kindergarten.

She looked at me like I was nuts. But that's how my life purpose struck me, like lightening. A few months later, after some rigorous planning, I stepped out onto a street corner shaking like a leaf, dressed like an angel in the City of Angels, and holding a poster saying Be Kind. The LA Street Angel was born that day. It has taken more courage than I ever thought I could muster, and more will-power to keep going than ever before. Life seemed like it just kept getting crazier on me, like I had literally fallen down the Alice in Wonderland rabbit hole. I even began telling everyone it felt like Los Angeles was a mixture of Wonderland, Neverland, and Oz. My life was like a Rubik's Cube, and God was crank-shafting it around in all directions to test my strength, wit, and faith.

When it comes to life, I don't think anyone would argue with the fact life has its challenges and obstacles. Unless you live out your entire existence in a padded room with little stimuli or interaction with the outside world, things are going to happen to you in your life that shake your foundation, change your path, and maybe even alter your reality. Sometimes in life things happen that can just feel so gut-wrenching or stressful, that you find yourself wondering what to do next, or even how you'll go on.

One of the most powerful things you can do in an intense moment which has brought you to your knees, is to pray or chant positive words. Many great philosophers of the past have said it's these defining moments in life that are actually catalysts for growth. Everything is in constant growth, change, or evolution. Even if you are an atheist, praying to whatever you believe in or chanting positive words or affirmations can help you get through the tough times. Shifting your mind to anything higher on the positivity scale can save you from drowning in sorrow, fears, self-sabotaging thoughts and actions, or even lift your mood when you are sick.

The mind can be like a downward spiral if you are not cognizant to the fact that you can stop it and turn it around. Research shows positive thoughts are much more powerful than negative thoughts. One of the easiest ways to shift into positive thinking are to give thanks for all of the things you can be grateful for. No matter how bad things get, you can find something to feel grateful for. I try to remember to thank the universe daily that I have my basic senses: I can see, hear, taste, smell, and touch. I have all of my abilities and can perform some tasks above average. I recognize beauty fades and the body deteriorates over time, so I try to remember to be grateful for each day that I am functioning at my prime. When you set the intent to have an attitude of gratitude, via the Law of Attraction you will experience more positive things entering your life. It's true that what you put out there comes back to you, sometimes immediately, and sometimes after some time. Relationships can be like our mirrors, showing us areas to work on where we can be more patient, understanding, tolerant, be more kind, and show unconditional love.

Based on how things have gone in my life, I've learned to look at each day as a birth and death. Some days have been so bad, that it's felt like I could die from the experiences of the day. What has worked for me is prayer, finding hope, having courage, and just making it all the way through the day into going to sleep, and usually by the next morning, I feel better or things feel different after the "dust has settled" from the upheaval. When your life takes a turn for the worst, take a moment to visualize yourself as a strong, graceful lioness, with the strength to tackle and get through anything. Finding that inner flame that burns strong with courage can give you the will to go on. No matter what you are going through, you don't have to go through it alone unless you choose to. If you desire it, you can reach out and find someone who would be willing to help you cope and work through a traumatic or stressful experience.

Hope is another important facet to find in any difficult situation. If you find yourself at one of your lowest points in life, maybe a devastating end to a relationship or the sudden loss of a job, look for that glimmer of hope to keep you going. Find or create something to look forward to, something that makes you smile or excited to plan for. There have been times in my life where I was debating whether or not to go on with life, because I was just so heartbroken and drowning in sorrowful emotions. And yet, despite all the heaviness I was feeling, there was this little speck of hope that remained inside of me that gave me just enough strength to not give up that day, and to make it through another day.

If you can hold on long enough, eventually you will come out of the clouds and see the sunrise dawning of a new chapter unfolding before you: a blank canvas you can create new experiences on. I am such a different person now. Things that used to scare me are now viewed more as a challenge to overcome or a lesson to learn. People underestimate the power of their thoughts, which can ultimately shape and decide the quality of their life, moment by moment. Now I've gained a higher awareness of how my thoughts and feelings directly affect my life experiences, I put more effort into being aware of what I am thinking and do my best to wrangle my mind more often to be more positive, fear less, be more grateful, have more tolerance and patience towards others, and have more courage.

Once you are cognizant of your thoughts and how your negative self-defeating thoughts can bring you down into an emotional tailspin, you can work towards *releasing* and counteracting them as best you can, so they don't continuously build up and create more heavy energy in your body that weighs you down and weakens your immune system. Are your thoughts positively serving you or making you feel bad? Notice how your thoughts and emotions are affecting you physically.

Is your chest tight? Shoulders tensed up? Eyes squinted? Focus on relaxing, finding inner peace, and letting your tensed up body release into a state of calm. Release the worry habit, have faith, and let go of your cares to the universe, God, Angels, or whatever higher power you believe in. Picture a young baby: the glow of innocence, curiosity, and awe that's in their eyes. Be like a child again, imagine yourself cradled in the hands of Mother Earth, being nurtured and stroked with unconditional love. This feeling is your natural state and birthright. Try to think of how it would feel to be enclosed in the soft comforting feathers amidst the wings of an angel. You can experience this feeling anytime you need it by simply remembering it and tapping into it mentally.

I hope these tips will provide you with some tools and comfort to navigate your most challenging times that life may bring. Just remember, you have all the strength, light, and potential inside you that you could ever need.

You are your own untapped resource. ☺ Namaste

# Janelle Hoyland

### Texas, United States of America

## *Unlock Your Soul's Radiance*

### "A True Story"

I want to take you on a journey of a state of being. So as you read this, let your eyes softly drift from one word to the next. Let this chapter guide you on an adventure into divine being through imagination, curiousness and open heart. Remember, this is a true story about my life of learning. Off we go…just let my words take you into this adventure.

**Breathe, imagine with me.**

The scene is simple: a place where there are people flowing in and out a front door. A gentle breeze rolls in, moving your hair. A relaxed smell of flowers and incense fills the breeze in the room. It's a sunny day…the sun fills the room with rays.

Some people are seated, engaged in deep conversation with one another. Others are looking around this small shop full of crystals and books. This shop is a place you have to know how to get to – it's definitely off the path. It's tucked away in the corner of a center, next to a local flower shop.

At the store, I sit at a small card table covered in a turquoise and purple cloth mixed with gold specks. A sweet smelling candle sits next to me along with crystal. This is the kind of place where you could just sit and put your feet up, losing track of time. The store was called Crystal Odyssey – the perfect name. This store is where I started to do readings for clients.

There was no air conditioning, which is unusual for Texas heat, but it worked with all the doors open. There was a small sign outside with the name on it. At certain times of the month, they had psychic fairs, and this is how I began to play. When I sat down, I would see my energy radiating out – attracting all the things I needed for each person I come in contact with. I would feel my radiance going out into the street as a golden light, pulling everything in.

A couple of hours into my day, one client came over for a session with me and the first words out of her mouth were, "I was drawn to you. You are a bright light in the room" I laughed, saying, "I work on it!" joking around. She laughed too, saying "Well, it worked!" From that point on she has become a close friend.

**For weeks I had been playing with my own energy – my aura – learning how to clean it with my hands.**

I started with my hands just about one foot away from my body, trying to get a sense of something. A subtle feeling of what I feel like – what my energy or aura feels like. My question was simple: What do people feel when they stand next to me?

I started by running my hands around me, like feeling an invisible layer of skin. My hands floating around my skin, I began to focus intently on each movement. I would focus on whatever feelings I felt, not making any exclusions on any one feeling – just noticing different parts. Did my energy feel cloudy, heavy, or light like air?

Slowly, my hands became like cleaners, wiping away debris like soot and revealing a shining new exterior. In my mind with my eyes closed, it looked like I was pushing dark energy down my body – starting from my head to my toes and into the earth below.

In doing this, I became sensitive to my core, as well as, my aura. My core energy began to shine with white light while my aura began to shine with a golden light, radiating out. I began to feel more peaceful from within. Shortly, I felt like when I was walking it was like I was floating or gliding with each step. Every day I would work on feeling more aligned with inner radiance.

The aura is usually about five feet around you; it is what people come into contact with first. Really, you don't even have to shake hands with someone – you can simply just stand next to them. Your aura is also responsible for attracting what you need like a magnet. Imagine it's like a signal or antenna that you put out into a room. It extends out all around you.

I began to sense every single person's energy without even touching them. This also included me. I began to see how I felt in different places and people. So as I would enter a room, I would start playing with my energy, trying to see how radiant I could become. In my mind I saw myself in the center as a white light with a golden light radiating out far beyond where I happened to be.

Eventually people began to say to me, "I feel so comfortable around you". When I started this it was only a game wanting to attract what I needed at the moment. The second part was to feel as clear as I could for me.

In the moment of radiance, you are abundance, pure love, infinite possibility and nothing at the same time. It's still motionless like time stops. Your breath slows. Your eyes become half gazed. You are not focused or intentional. You are just gentle like the breeze. You are one with everything you could be aligned with. I began to realize, the more I see myself in the radiance; the more I am radiant. People around me are feeling loved as I love myself enough to stand shining my radiant golden aura for all to see so everyone can be empowered to do the same.

**I uncovered this prayer.......**

*I stand in the radiance that is you as you hold me in your hands, brilliantly created for all possibilities to unfold in my life. AS you are pure love and abundance so am I. I unlock all of the doors and windows to divine flow of radiance to anchor within me. Shall I forget, gently push me back to center. It is so...*

The key is your imagination with a touch of open heartedness. It has to be said though, this was my process. Yours is within you. The discovery is radiance. Only you can feel it for yourself – my goal in sharing this with you is to help you add another piece to your abundance. To help everyone understand this place is not just for those connected, so to speak, but for everyone.

We all share in the same energy, connected to one presence within our center. To step into your radiance allows for everyone who comes in contact with you to be filled with love and radiance. I say it is like a bubble – once you enter into this space with another person all things are possible. Life flows

**The tools I use are simple ones that worked well for me.**

- The first tool is: Begin to feel your own energy (aura). I started with asking, "How do I feel?"
- The second tool I used was: Wiping my energy clean
- The third tool I used was: Focusing on what I was feeling without judgment.
- The fourth tool: Imagination and an open heart.

So how do you feel?

# Dionne Thomas

California, United States of America

## *Beautiful Women Should Not Look Sad*

Beautiful women shouldn't look sad. She said she was SAD because society says beautiful women shouldn't look sad. Well society says self-image is everything because I don't have anything else going on.

Beauty begins on the inside. Belle has four children, her hair has fallen out and body won't snap back after this last baby. I realize society says if you are thin with no belly, you are beautiful. If your legs are long and you have big boobs or booty then you are beautiful. You don't have to be thick, or thin to be beautiful.

Her skin color is not dark nor is she light. Belle believes if you are brown, red, black, yellow, and purple with polka dots you should be proud of your self-image; nor should the color of your skin dictate your self-image. Don't allow this world to dictate what your self- image should be.

She has been through molestation repeatedly and "they" told her she was nothing. Chelle had been on drugs because of the molestation and had no self-worth or image no matter what you have been through in life whether you were raped, molested, battered. Sugar, don't allow the chain of events you have been through stop you from moving forward. So many COOs, attorneys, physicians, all colors, shapes, sizes of women have been through this and much worse. You can and will survive this and much more. You are strong, powerful and you have the drive to make it. Even if you were on drugs or sold them or sold you.

Why should one forgive the person or forgive myself? Why shouldn't we look back and hold on to these things we have been through. You must forgive them and yourself. When you walk in forgiveness this allows you to free in your mind body and spirit. When we forgive then we can be open to be healed. Forgiving others and yourself allows good things and people to come YOUR way. Forgiveness is the ultimate healing tool. Forgiveness is the ultimate action to many positive things. If you continue to look back at all of the things of the past you cannot move forward. When our mind is focused on those things of the past we are closed. Our body doesn't open up. When the mind is open the body follows. When we let go we can receive. Example when our hand is closed, we can't receive. When our hand is open, we can receive all things that are to come. Most of all it starts the healing process in the body and mainly the mind.

Belle now possesses a college degree and her self-image is still not where society expects it to be. Most importantly self-image should not be predicated upon looks, but, if you have a brain and use it. Oh my goodness nothing burns her up more than a man or woman thinking because of the way we look a certain way we don't know a thing. People think we are just uneducated. She knows personally from experience and had conversation with folks and they were shocked because she can talk about the stock market or any other subjects of importance, politics, religion, even the drop in the housing market. Her personal cliché is "I am cute not stupid". People have the tendency to undermine women because of their looks. They don't realize they can do anything.

How does Belle know she can make it after having been through all of this? I get what you are saying, but, am I capable. As women you must know you are empowered to conquer anything and tell about it. How we think shows up on the outside. Self-image starts on this inside with your attitude and demeanor. No amount of wigs, braids, extensions, or makeup or designer clothes will improve your self-image permanently. Self-image is something which must be nurtured on the inside first. Your perception of yourself is what's most important. One day Belle, took a long look in the mirror and realized she was nothing that the other people said she was, beautiful on the inside and out. She knew that because God tells us and speaks it in His word. She believed, accepted and knows it. Learn to love yourself. Love the curves that God has given you. Whether your lips are full or thin, love you. Love the earned fat that you have since bearing children. Love the fact you are uniquely shaped. God made each of us different, no two people in this world are exactly like.

As a child Belle was considered the dark one until her father corrected the issue. As a teenager, she was called ugly horse head, all kinds of names. One Day the guys started telling her she was pretty and her family would say you look just like your mom. Her mother was tall, articulate, and smart. She has gaps in her teeth, shapely body, and nice hair. One day Belle looked at my mom as a young girl and she was her twin just a lighter version. That same day she took a long look in the mirror and realized she could wear anything and do anything.

God made her different than others and she needed to embrace who He made and what He made her look like. Psalm 139 13-14 "for you formed my inward parts; you knitted me together in my mother's womb. I praise you, for I fearfully and wonderfully made." Belle confessed, "He broke the mold with me. I reminded myself who's I was. I began to change because I speak life into myself daily in the mirror." She was not a young lady who stayed in the mirror, except to curl my hair. She looked into the mirror at herself and realized she was gorgeous on the inside and the outside.

# Kisha Johnson McRae

New York, United States of America

## *Delivered From Suicide*

My life got worse before it truly began. I think of all the times I've tried to process the things I've endured and all I come to is this: That which doesn't kill you makes you stronger.

There were many times when I wanted to do just that, kill myself I mean. The first time occurred in 1989. I had left school thinking I was in love and on June 4 1989 I gave birth to my first child—a baby girl, just what I wanted. She was so beautiful and perfect. A year after she was born I suffered with not being able to swallow and my face blew up like a balloon. I was so disfigured I was unrecognizable. I remember being in the middle of the examination room while doctors crowded around me trying to figure out what was wrong. I felt like an item on display that no one wanted. During this time in my life I smiled a lot, but silently I didn't want to live. Although I was only19 years old with my whole life ahead of me, my life seemed empty—there was no meaning. Before my mystery illness could kill me, *I* wanted to kill *myself.* My emotions were all over the place, but no one knew I was falling to pieces.

After feeling like the walking dead for months, I was finally diagnosed with pneumonia. Even after being treated for it, things didn't seem to work in my favor health wise. One morning I awoke and found a pimple on the side of my nose. I was disgusted because I never got pimples. I tried to put band aids on it to keep it flat, but after a few days I noticed it had begun to change its shape and was spreading over to the right side of my face. That day I wanted to end my life then and there. Thoughts of suicide filled my soul. Don't worry! I am just fine now, blessed and thriving.

The sound of my daughter crying made the idea an impossibility. I knew it was wrong. I knew taking my life was something Jesus would not forgive me for. *I am not gonna play with Jesus*, I decided.

My physician referred me to a dermatologist at Columbia Presbyterian in NYC. When the dermatologist asked me about family illnesses I told him about Lupus. I explained my aunt and maternal grandmother had it. He took a biopsy of the ugly pimple on my face and asked me to come back in a week. During that week, all I could think of was I might have Lupus. I started wondering what I would do if it was confirmed and how I would live. I contemplated my life being different upon returning to the dermatologist. I was afraid. Although the pneumonia was subsiding, my soul felt like death. I think subconsciously I already knew the truth. When I returned to the dermatologist's office, I walked in feeling like a dark cloud was lingering over me. My body felt like it was going to shut down.

The doctor walked in slow motion as he approached me to share the results. I remember his exact words. "I am sorry but you have Lupus." He said it like it was something he was used to saying daily—with no feeling, no compassion.

My heart stopped. All I could think about was me looking like my grandmother whose skin appeared to be burnt as a result of Lupus. Frantically, I called my mother and step-dad to pick me up because I couldn't move. I literally wanted to lay on the floor and die right there. The doctor told me the life span of Lupus patients was about ten years. Upon hearing this, I prayed for my heart to stop, but God wouldn't let it happen because I had a beautiful daughter to raise.

As if my body hadn't endured enough trauma, I later suffered through a woman's worse nightmare. I was raped. I remember him saying to me, "You can trust me," as he preyed on my naivety. Bits of me were chipped away as he pinned me down and violated my body and crushed my spirits. Even years later, I never told a soul. Thereafter, I began to hate my own existence. I was disgusted with the image of the woman I perceived as weak who stared back at me pitifully every time I looked into the mirror. With her eyes filled with despair and her torn soul lingering in a debased body, she often pleaded with me to explain to her how we had gotten to this point. Again, I found myself wanting nothing more than to vanish from this life.

I tried to pull it together and maintain a positive outlook. I received my G.E.D and went on to college but soon after I got really sick and was hospitalized. This was the biggest Lupus flare I had ever experienced. My body was tired of being strong and my mental faculty was totally exhausted—I wanted out. I had so much support yet I felt alone, so I allowed my weakness to take over. As I slipped away, God spoke to me. "I am not ready for you," he said. "You are not done here." It was HIS will that I survived.

With God's grace, I carried on. In 1999 my son was born. Later, I graduated with a Bachelor's of Arts degree in social science with social work being my major.

In 2001 my grandmother died from Lupus complications. She was the love of my life and was a fighter. I knew she would have wanted me to be the voice of a lupus thriver because she was a firecracker herself. In 2012, my grandma Lula died before my very eyes. I literally watched her slip into peacefulness. Six months later I was called by the nursing home where my maternal grandfather,

Lula's husband, resided. They were resuscitating him. I was the first to arrive and there he lay peacefully dead. He died in his sleep which was what he wanted. He had lost the love of his life, but now his heart no longer had a void because he was with his wife in heaven. My soul cried out in agony. *Lord, I am sick! I cannot take any more deaths,* I prayed through the tears. I began to imagine my own death even more. A manic depression plagued me. Prodigiously, I saw death where ever I went, especially my own.

Therapy helped me tremendously, particularly with the panic attacks I had begun to experience. Once I got myself together mentally and began doing what I loved again, like mentoring women with Lupus whose low self-esteem kept them from thriving, I felt like a new person. Then on March 4, 2013 my mother called me to say the hospital had contacted her. My dad had been there for a while and they were encouraging us to come see him immediately. I knew from the call that his condition had worsened. I jumped in a cab because the lord said to me, "Go now."

I arrived to my father's bedside alone. As I walked in, I saw the angel of death upon him. What a sight to see! Dad looked beautiful, but I knew he was barely alive. I stood by him and as I rubbed his head I told him he could rest. I promised him Mommy would be taken care of. "Daddy, it's okay," I said.

Immediately after hearing my assurance, my father slipped away. I harbored a little guilt over those words, but I knew he was at peace and it was his time. God makes no mistakes.

After every storm I've weathered, from health issues, rape, suicidal thoughts, and coping with death, I know there is nothing I can't get through with the guidance of my Savior. Over time my diagnoses seemed to pile up— Hypothyroid, Shingles, Manic Depression, anxiety, herniated disk, Vitamin D deficiency, Arthritis, down to Attention Deficit Disorder at 44 years-old. I currently take over fourteen medications. Despite all of this, I still give God praises because I understand my tragic testimony may very well be someone else's intervening inspiration. Sometimes you have to go through hell before you are able to thrive.

There's someone who needs to know they aren't alone and suicide isn't the answer. To that person I say, ***remember you are God's creation.*** It's amazing what the power of faith can do to restore you physically, emotionally, and mentally. I never thought people would depend on my strength for survival, but that's how God works. He places you where you need to be in order to make the greatest impact within his kingdom. Through it all, trust in him to carry you through. If he can do it for me, he can definitely do it for you.

# Dianne Reilly

### Florida, United States of America

## *Who Are You, Anyway?*

What's in a name? When people ask you who you are, you may start with telling your name and then perhaps go on to say what you do, who you work for or about one of the many hats you may wear. Our name becomes one of the most basic identifiers of who we are, when we are asked.

Yet, what happens when we change names, for one reason or another? Have you ever wanted a different name or perhaps a different spelling of the name you have? My first name is Dianne and it is spelled differently than many I know with the same name. I never thought too much about it until I was about ten or eleven years old and had my first taste of wanting to conform. In my class, most of my friends had names that were five letters long, names like Susan, Linda, Renee, Cindy, etc. My name was six letters long, so guess what I did?

I started writing my name with only five letters - Diane! I don't know if anyone noticed as my teachers didn't say anything and I don't remember it being a family discussion. It didn't change anything, no one treated me any differently. Thankfully, I outgrew this within a few years and went back to spelling it properly. My early conformity had no real payoff for me! This, however, was not my first exposure to a name change.

Many who are reading this have had name changes due to adoption, marriage and/or divorce. When I was born, my mother was happily married to my father, but within the first two years of my life, she made the courageous decision to leave and I never saw him again. This is something I didn't know about until I was in my teens, when I was snooping around some papers. I had been brought up to believe he died when I was a baby. The truth was, he had serious issues with drugs and alcohol and my mother wouldn't allow me to grow up in that environment, so moved back to her home state with me.

When I was about 4, she remarried and had my name legally changed to her married name. Interestingly, my step-father did not adopt me, something I didn't consider until well into adulthood. She had two more children and we all had the same last name. Sadly, this marriage was not long lived either and she was once again, a single mother, struggling to make ends meet. I still had the name of my step-father until I married, yet felt very disconnected to that last name. It was just a name, not one to be ashamed of, but not one to be proud of either.

I want to tell you that your name is not your identity, it's only an identifier, a description. Like many children from broken homes, I had some inner emotional issues which needed to be dealt with, but I covered them up. I wanted to be strong for my mother. She had enough to deal with without having to worry about me. As a teenager and even well into my young adult years, I didn't have a strong sense of my own identity, about who I was at the core. I saw myself as a product of a broken home and envied people who were from intact families.

When people have inner wounds it affects their choices in life as well as how they see the world. Healthy people make healthy choices. People who have damaged emotions don't make healthy choices until they deal with the issues at hand and experienced healing. As an adult, I came to understand I had neglected myself in several important ways, not just emotionally, but spiritually. You see, people are basically spiritual beings having a human experience! At the core is our spirit, we have emotions and we live in a body.

Most of us pay the most attention to our bodies by what we feed it, how we take care of it, how we clothe it, etc. Secondarily, we experience a wide range of emotions every day, and it is important to learn to identify our feelings and express them in a healthy way. Yet, when it comes to our spiritual nature, many put it in last place. My friends, I want to tell you, we have it backwards! We need to feed our spirits from within which will cause us to have healthier emotions which will motivate us to take care of our bodies! It really is an inside job.

As a child, I was brought up in church and had learned about God. Children think as children. This is a part of my life I cut off in very formative years, which, I believe, is a major cause of my confusion about who I was. And it all happened very innocently. When I was about thirteen, I had friends who were of a church denomination who met on Saturday. Sunday was their weekend day off. During the summer, they would go to a great swimming area about an hour from where we lived. I went to church on Sunday. When they invited me to go with them, I went to my mother and asked her and guess what-she let me make the decision. Can you guess what kind of decision a wounded thirteen year old girl makes when left to her own? Yes, I decided to go with them on Sunday instead of to church. The problem is, like everything in our lives, we operate out of habit. Once one gets out of the habit of doing things good for you, a new habit is formed and usually not changed until a catalyst for change occurs.

It wasn't until I was about thirty that a big catalyst occurred in my life. I was at a very low place due to some problems in my own marriage and I felt like I was about to fall apart. Thankfully, everything I knew from my earlier years came rushing back to me and I realized I was operating in a big spiritual vacuum. No wonder things had gotten so out of hand in my life! I had neglected who I was at the core. My spirit was parched dry and I needed to get back in touch with the only One who could help me, and that person was my heavenly Father. I reached out and He was there. He said, "Welcome home, my daughter". I submerged myself in reading my Bible and slowly but surely, the life came back into me. People around me could see something was different and you could see the sparkle in my eyes, once again. You see, He can make all things new, and He did that for me. He showed me who I had been all along, a child of God, created to do great things.

It has been amazing walking with the Lord. I came to experience the love of the Father in a way I had never known. You see, our earthly fathers are supposed to demonstrate God's love by how they take care of us, protect us and love us. I had never experienced that and it had made it difficult for me to comprehend the love of the Heavenly Father. As healing began, I began to trust the people in my life and became open to dealing with those wounds from childhood so I could heal properly. Remember when I mentioned my step-father hadn't adopted me? That was a rejection I had never faced, but I was able to forgive and move on.

Fast forward about twenty years, I had to deal with the name issue once again. After my divorce of more than two decades of marriage, I was faced with the last name I would use. Many adult women go back to their maiden name, but what name was I to go back to? I surely wouldn't go back to my father's name, whose family I knew nothing about. I didn't want to go back to my maiden name, the name of the stepfather, who caused so much pain to my mother and myself. I decided to keep my married name, because I had come to realize my identity does not come from a name. My identity comes from who God says I am and what He did for me through His son, Jesus. My faith gives me all the security I need, no matter what I am called! My name is Dianne, with two 'n's!

So, who are you, anyway? When you know who you are, nothing can tear you down. Strength is an inside job. I pray you find yours today! Blessings!

# Caroline Angell

Queensland, Australia

## *An Angell's Gratitude*

I had read that a Gratitude Journal could help make me happier. Boy, did I need to feel happier about life! I had acquired a severe Traumatic Brain Injury (TBI) along with other physical injuries when I fell from a horse in 2003. I was feeling pretty down and confused about not being my 'normal' old self.

To start with I really had to discipline myself to write down all of the things I had achieved or was grateful for in my journal every night before I slept. Some days I just didn't feel very grateful at all, but after a few weeks this became part of my routine. I found I really did look forward to writing down these things every day.

My Gratitude Journal really showed me I did have lots to be grateful about - not just my rehabilitation. I definitely was improving in lots of ways as the list kept growing! I also used to cut out pictures and colors I was attracted to from magazines and catalogues. I would stick them in a large scrap book so I could look over them again to refresh my memory. Unknowingly, I was creating Vision Boards as I defined my new likes.

These tools allowed me to focus on possibilities and opportunities in a very positive way. It was the foundation I needed as I rebuilt myself around my new boundaries. I am not an expert on Traumatic Brain Injury (TBI). I am only an expert on what *my* TBI has done to me and what strategies I have used over time to make my life seem as close to 'normal' to others and comfortable as I can for me into the bargain.

With my parents looking after my two daughters (then aged 3 and 9), I had decided to take a horse for a 'test' ride to weigh up whether he would be suitable for my needs. I had ridden him in his home paddock already with one of his paddock mates and his then owner accompanying us. He seemed to be quiet and easy to handle. He was a Percheron X Shire Horse - he was 18 hands

(182.88cms) or slightly taller - and his hooves were the size of dinner plates! I am a fair amount shorter at 157cms. My boyfriend at the time came along with his horse to accompany me.

I only remember parts of the day leading up to the time when we left the paddock on horseback and were walking up the driveway. This next bit is made up of what friends and family have told me about the actual fall and the time when I started being able to remember and understand things again.

We were only a few hundred meters from the home paddock of this horse when a bird known as a Willy Wagtail sat spinning around and chirping on the top wire of a fence close to us. It gave the horse a fright and he reared up and headed for home. He galloped with his reins and stirrups flying all over the place.

It all happened so quickly. As the horse reared up, I slipped off the saddle and over his rear end. I landed on my tail bone and then smacked my helmet covered head on a rock. I was knocked out straight away. In total the fall would have been around 3 meters. Quite a height when the landing point on my body was to be my tail bone closely followed by my head!!

Initially it was thought I may have been brain dead as there was absolutely no reaction from me at all. Levels of consciousness are assessed by something called a Glasgow Coma Scale which tests eye, verbal and motor responses. I was initially thought to be very close to the brain dead level. This would mean harvesting my organs for transplant to save another person's life.

I don't know if I was given mouth to mouth (CPR), but I may well have been. I know my boyfriend at the time saved my life with his knowledge of first aid. I know I was airlifted to the Cairns Base Hospital (which was approximately 2.5 hours by road). Of course, by then it was known I wasn't brain dead, but that I had a very bad Head Injury and I was in a Coma. In total, I spent nine and a half months in hospital in three different hospitals.

Everyone who has a TBI will be affected differently so what happened to me will certainly not be the case for everyone but the symptoms maybe similar. A clear vision of what my injuries and TBI would hold for me took some time to develop and understand. My TBI was considered very severe. I still had a very low Glasgow Coma Scale score upon my admission to hospital. It took almost a month for anything sensible to come out of my mouth! This time is known as Post Traumatic Amnesia (PTA). I had been given a lot of medication to keep me calm so my brain could heal and I could rest.

At the very end of the first month I started showing some signs of recognizing people, understanding and remembering what was going on. This was the time I consider is a little bit like a rebirth. I finally emerged from PTA. From this point onwards I am able to tell you from my own memories what happened.

I became aware that the professional, qualified, trained staff at the hospital were preparing for the worst. Of course, they were overjoyed to see the milestones of my recovery and celebrated with me along the way. This gave me the motivation I needed to keep trying and to never, never, never give up!

Things such as being wheelchair-bound, not being able to look after my children, being unable to drive the car, being unable to look after myself in both practical and physical ways, were all under the microscope. The list of things that were on unknown was long. This was very difficult to deal with. I had no understanding of TBI so I found all of this very upsetting and frustrating and no doubt everyone around me did too!

Finally the day came when I could go home. I called this day my 'get out of jail free card'! I know hospital wasn't a jail and if I hadn't had the opportunity to go to this Brain Injury Recovery Unit there could have been many dangers that would have remained unknown.

It was pretty exciting to think that after nine and half months staying in three different hospitals and undergoing daily tests and feeling like I was under constant surveillance, I was finally free to go home. My parents were very generous with their time and stayed with me until I was well enough to cope on my own. *As soon as I got home I started setting myself goals and tasks I thought I needed to complete for the household to run smoothly. I was the queen of lists!! Lists of tasks and goals everywhere!!*

Slowly, but surely I didn't need to rely on the lists as much as things became routine. I was my own worst enemy sometimes as I would forget to take my 'shopping list' to the shops with me and we ended up with more than one badly put together grocery shop - courtesy of me guessing what we needed – that's for sure!!

I was very happy to be home with my daughters. I was and still am absolutely determined I would be a good Mum. I have put both of my daughters as priority in my life. I was and continue to be a single mum. I have tried as hard as I could over the years to offer my daughters the best opportunities, fun, laughter and love I could possibly muster for them to take through into their adult lives. There have been lots of things that didn't go according to plan, but we all let go of what other people thought things should be like and worked together as a team.

We always had what we needed and the rest, well, that was just something that we didn't really require: an optional extra. Overall I came to realize we only needed a simple life. The simpler, the better! With a positive outlook, my Gratitude Journal and Vision Boards, I've learned to embrace my life, follow my dreams and not take things for granted. I have also stopped concerning myself with whether what I do, or achieve, in my life is 'normal' for others.

After all, is what they think is 'normal' really 'normal'? Or is that just their point of view?

# MILITARY WOMEN

# #MILITARYWOMEN

stories of courage

# Rita Wiggins

## Texas, United States of America

### *A Military Story*

I realize how fortunate I am to have had the childhood I did. My parents were truly in love with each other. They shared that love with my brother, sister and me.

My father was in the United States Air Force. My mother was a loving stay at home mom which was common in the nineteen sixties and seventies. As an Air Force "Brat", I had friends from all different races, religions, and cultures. I delighted in each new adventure we would undertake, knowing how special the opportunities were. My love of travel was born during those days.

All of the military families supported each other. There was a bond of trust between them. As "Brats" we all benefited. I remember my parents taking one of my best friends with us to explore castles in Spain. I learned to water sky with another best friend and her family on the Chesapeake Bay. The families supported each other in tragedy too. It was the Vietnam era and unfortunately some neighbors were lost. My sense of trust, honor and respect were instilled not only by my parents, but through each of the families I was blessed to know. My sense of community, respect, honor, love of country and trust were instilled as core life values during this time.

My father retired in 1973 and we moved to Illinois to be closer to my mother's family. I attended high school there. I had the best time getting to really know my grandparents, aunts, uncles and many cousins. While I really enjoyed being around my extended family, my friends, and the community, I still had that burning sense of adventure running through my veins. After all I had lived in Spain, Italy, California and Delaware to name few of the places. I enrolled in  the Community College near our hometown but after having difficulty with the nursing program that first year decided to join the military. The GI bill would help pay for further college and I really hungered for adventure. I wanted to enlist in the Air Force but they would not guarantee a medical positon. The Army however offered me every enlisted medical job they had available.

I enlisted in the United States Army as a Combat Medic and Behavioral Science Specialist. I was so thrilled with the idea I was going to be able to help Soldiers and their families. In basic training, I loved the sense of comradery and accomplishment we Soldiers shared. It was like what I remembered as a child. My basic training class was the last to receive the Women's Army Corps Crest (WAC). We were inducted into the WAC and Army at the same time. The WAC was in the process of being disbanded but had not been officially disbanded. It was a rather confusing time for the military and some of the men had the mentality that women shouldn't have been integrated into the Army.

I was apprehensive and excited when I received notice of my first duty station. I was going to Germany! I arrived ten days before Christmas in 1978. The post I was assigned to was in a beautiful, quaint little German town. The post was surrounded by concertina wire, up a cobble stone road at the top of a hill. The clinic I was assigned to was near the middle of post between a laundromat and the gym. The Drug Abuse Prevention and Control Clinic was a small white building with cream colored walls. The main entrance entered into a small waiting room.

The hall was in back of the receptionist desk and lead to the counseling offices on the left side and a conference room on the right. At the end of the hall was another conference room which was converted into a two person office for the Officer in Charge (OIC) and the Non-Commissioned Officer in Charge (NCOIC). The office led to the storeroom where the furnace was located. The storeroom was small with a window on the same wall as the furnace, some shelves for supplies, a few file cabinets, mops, the old metal wringing mop buckets and brooms. There were six inch pipes along the walls connected to the heater. The other female Soldier assigned and myself would turn the heater up each morning as we arrived to heat the building.

From the beginning my assignment was interesting. We counseled Soldiers with some serious problems, some addicted to heroin, many self-medicating with alcohol to forget the horrors of war. My teammates and I supported, respected and worked great together. We were one team one fight as they use to say. That all changed when we received a new NCOIC. He was married but was on a short tour so his family was in the states. He constantly asked me personal questions of a sexual nature. I would not reply and asked him to stop. He was talked to about it but really didn't stop. Little did I know this person would be the one to destroy all the beliefs I had developed about the military and its community.

On the day of my assault, I arrived to the building about 6 am and was turning up the heat in the storeroom. I suddenly heard footsteps behind me. I turned around and my NCOIC was there. I started walking out of the room but he blocked the entrance. He asked me for a piece of gum and I replied I had just ate my last piece. He then said "I will take that piece". He pushed me against the wall and held me against it. I could feel the hot steam pipes through my fleece warm up jacket. He proceeded to stick his tongue in my mouth and keep it there. I was in shock. This man was to be my battle buddy, he was to lead me, protect me and if it came down to it fight for my life as I was his. Instead he was assaulting me.

I could feel him getting hard as he pushed himself against my body. His hands were all over me. Everything was happening so fast. I was finally able to use my knee to get away from him and hit him with a mop. I ran to the front reception area where another Soldier staff member was coming in the door. He saw how distraught I was. I couldn't talk at the time. After I calmed down I was able to speak to him and our OIC about what had happened.

Unfortunately, at this time the Army was still a very much male dominated organization and they really did not have a system in place to report such incidents. I had talked with my chain of command which supported me, but no charges were filed and no report written. I was told it would be my word against his and he out ranked me. When they found out he had been harassing the civilian secretary they made sure no females were left alone with him. They finally found him another position on another post in Germany. However in order to move him they had to give him a glowing performance appraisal. So he received no punishment and greater potential for promotion due to the appraisal.

Although this incident changed some of the way I viewed the military, I always tried to remember this was one bad person, not all male Soldiers were that way. I went on to become a Sergeant promotable and helped many alcohol and drug addicted Soldiers throughout my career. I was able to form a women's counseling group which gave women soldiers a safe place to discuss their issues. I however never shared my story. I tried to forget what had happened and see the good in people. I tried to see those values I had learned as a child in each individual. I tried really hard to not let the destructive behavior of one man destroy my happiness. Even when my oldest daughter joined the military I didn't talk about what had happened. I just talked with her and told her not to take any form of sexual harassment but to report it right away. I tried to raise three independent daughters.

It was not until I had an incident in an Army mandatory training class on preventing Sexual Harassment almost 30 years after the incident I realized I was effected by that long ago incident. Some of the males in class were making comments that sounded like the individuals in the scenarios were lying. I didn't have the nerve to speak up, but came away crying from that class. It was then I decided there were two people I know who would listen to me and it could change the way they lead. My two son-in-laws were Officers in the Army. I told them my story and asked them to always investigate when someone relates an incident of sexual harassment, assault, or worse. They were shocked at what I had been through and I believe they looked at things differently because of it. I have shared my story with a few senior leaders and female Soldiers since and know it has made them better leaders. It was not easy, but as a senior, respected civilian and former Soldier my story is taken to heart and people listen. Maybe they change the way they lead, if so it's worth the pain of relating what happened. Through the support of them and others I have regained what I lost those many years ago.

Am I effected by what happened to me in 1979? If I am honest, yes. I have been divorced now for almost sixteen years and have had close friendships with males, but no partnership. I am truly happy alone, but sometimes I wonder if fear is really the answer as to why I am alone, I have friends, but I stay alone. It has only been in this last decade of my life I have been able to talk about it. It has taken me way too long to realize this incident while not as devastating as some have experienced, did change my life.

This is the first time I have shared my story in a public format, there are many people who know me that do not know this part of my life. Writing this has given me a sense of freedom and relief. I encourage you to speak out to those that love you and let them know what you went through. Someone will listen!

# Denise Joy Thompson

Texas, United States of America

## *How Quickly Life Changes*

The day began as an "ordinary" travel day, 3 am wake-up, packing, last minute computer work, double-checking of details, copious amounts of coffee, quick drive and drop-off at the airport to wait in line for luggage check-in and then security.

I do this about 20 times a year, so everything was moving along as normal. There is not a thought of when arriving at my destination there is a phone call from my brother, with the words "it's bad, it's dad." As a social worker and a crisis response instructor, my words were short and to the point, "is he dead?" the answer "yes, a heart attack". It is 12:15 pm Eastern, my crisis response and military training kicks in, I get my bag from the baggage carousel of Southwest, I tell my friend Carolyn, who had traveled with me from San Antonio to Orlando (she was a blessing,) I have to go to Delta (I know Delta flies closet to my home town) and get a flight to Iowa, my dad has died.

I was in shock, but I knew I had to get home. I wasn't overly coherent or patient with the Delta attendant, at times it was difficult to talk and my tears would well-up, again my training took over and I focused. Luckily a supervisor assisted me and through booking and re-booking I received a mid-afternoon flight and a price which wasn't outrageous, although at that moment, price didn't matter anyway. This was on May 26, huge storms were rolling across the US, leaving that morning we had severe flooding in San Antonio, Houston, and most of Texas, flying to Detroit then into Iowa, I knew there may be some challenges. Even with flight delays, ground closures, re-booking to a morning flight, just in case of a total cancellation, I arrived home the same evening after a 17 hour day of flying and being in airports.

My dad, as are most of our dad's, is a very important person in my life. My dad was a hard-working man, raised by hard-working parents. I know my dad loved me, and all the family very much. We had become closer after he retired and we spent many weeks of vacation together, with my parents visiting me in which ever state I lived (thought they wouldn't visit me in Turkey).

We laughed, my parents had the best of both worlds between vacationing with me and my husband, and then with my brother and his family. I like cruises, the beach, wineries, while my brother and his family like camping, nature and hiking, my parents were able to enjoy all the things they liked by spending time with both of us. Holidays are important and as much as possible we all try to be home for Christmas, if not we Skype and share the opening of presents. In October 2014 while in St. Maarten, my parents even lived through their first hurricane thanks to vacationing with me.

The waves were really exciting until they continued to grow and we realized it was not just big waves ascending on our resort, but it was a first and being from Iowa, they had not imagined ever being in one. Of course my parents agreed one was enough!!

It's the memories of our time together which allowed my family to spend time celebrating the life we had with Dad. Yes, we cried, yes, it was frustrating and tense at times deciding on the funeral details, but we CELEBRATED we had him in our life. We joked as we would do something like Dad, he was "channeling" through us. I joked one night as I got up 5 times to go to the bathroom that it was Dad. I measured something the other day 3 times with the measuring tape and I told mom, it was Dad channeling (his attention to detail is notorious amongst our family and probably to his friends and co-workers also).

Don't get me wrong, we miss him terribly, what gave us comfort was the fact we could celebrate him. We talked about the fun times, laughed about our times together, cried together, but we didn't focus on what we wouldn't have, we focused on the blessing he was to all of us. My mom, after almost 61 years of marriage, will have a significant adjustment, but we also can talk about anything, the good, the bad and the "I don't know(s)".

There is no one way to grieve; there is no one model to follow. What I do know is being grateful for what a person has been in your life, for the time shared, for having love, and celebrating the life lived can help ease some of the pain. As I am beginning to write this, we just celebrated the first Father's Day, 25 days after my dad's death. On July 1st we will celebrate his first birthday after his death.

The firsts are often times the hardest, but also the realization of how life has changed. Change may be painful, but it isn't impossible. We are not yet "moving on". We know as a family we have each other to talk to, to share with and to seek comfort from. Our family growing up with Dad as an EMT, a firefighter and my work as a therapist, crisis responder and a military member is a bit unique. The way we may view death differently, knowing more about death and accidents than most families, perhaps we were better prepared, but we also supported each other and knew we had each other.

We will all face the death of a loved one, I wish for you to find comfort in what the loved one brought to your life. Celebrate their life and love. Let the tears flow both in sadness and appreciation for your loved one. Embrace the memories, laugh and cry at the same time. Know even though they are gone, you are still here and you can get through this, with no expectations or time frames in which to do so. During this time though, remember to take care of you, it's what our loved one wants us to do.

I cherish Dad was part of my promotion ceremony. Dad, along with Mom, was and still remains one of my biggest supporters and encouragers. I started writing my chapter on June 23, not even a month from my dad's death, but didn't finish it until July 31. I had lost some of my motivation to write, to share my feelings, to be happy. I also know I cannot stay in this part of the journey. I, as do the rest of the family, need to move forward a little each day. To continue to create our lives, to accomplish goals and live up to everything Dad knows we can do. I can be of more support to my mother and the rest of the family by taking care of myself.

As I finish writing this, I know Dad is smiling down on me and my family; I know he loves us.

# Lindsay Kinslow

Odenton, Maryland

## *The Resilient Soldier*

As long as I can remember my parents told me I was special and God made me especially for them. I believed that for a very long time. As a little girl I was proud and told anyone I could that I was special.

Then I was introduced to society. I was teased and made fun of because I was not like the rest of the kids. My parents didn't birth me. As time went by and I got older I started to feel like I was different than my family. I felt lost on this place we call earth. I started to think, who am I? I really wanted to know so I searched. Not for my birth family, but for my individuality. These years weren't easy on my parents, but they never gave up on me. They knew I was destined to be a star. After all my years of aimlessly wandering through the world, I decided it was time for a change. I did what only 1% of America would do. At the age of 21 I enlisted in the military, the Army to be exact.

The day I left for Basic Training was one of the happiest days of my mom and dad's life. I could see the happiness beaming from their eyes. My days of purposelessly running the streets seemed to be over. As for me, I was ready to start a new book and close out the old one. As I raised my right hand to be sworn in I felt like a different person. The joy that overcame my body was like nothing I felt before. It truly was more exciting and more intense than the day I graduated high school.

I was finally gaining my independence and joining something greater than me. This was the start of my first chapter in my new book called life. As the van drove away from the Military Entrance Processing Station (MEPS) I looked out the back window and saw my mom and dad standing there waving like their hands were going to fall off. My mom had tears of joy in her eyes. It was in this moment that it really hit me I was leaving everything and everyone I knew and loved. As I fought back my own tears, I waved back.

When I got to basic training I had no idea what to expect. It didn't take long for the Drill Sergeants to give me a glimpse into what I was about to experience. *My class was one of the first classes to start basic after the United States invaded Iraq.* At the time, I was unaware of the details on what unfolded in the world. It didn't hit me until the day the Drill Sergeants were livid because they thought we weren't taking training serious at the time. To be totally honest, I wasn't. Rolling around and running from tree to tree was not what I wanted to do. One of the Drill Sergeants actually stopped us and told us "look to your left, now look to your right. You are going to Iraq and one of you won't make it back".

It just got real and from then on I took everything we did serious. I managed to keep my bad attitude somewhat under control and I graduated. As always my parents were at my graduation to support me. On to the next step: Advanced Individual Training (AIT), training for the job I was to perform in the Army. I chose to be a Human Resources Specialist. I thought the days of yelling and screaming were behind me.

After the short drive to the school, we pulled up and the Drill Sergeants got on the bus and repeated what I previously went through for nine weeks. This time I was prepared and ready for whatever they were going to do. As it turned out AIT wasn't as brutal as Basic. I learned enough about my job to get me started at my new duty station. When graduation came my parents were not there as they had been all my life. I was heartbroken. It wasn't until I came home on leave before departing to go to Germany I learned the reason why they weren't there; my dad had stage four lung cancer. Not only was I heartbroken, but I was devastated.

Moving across the world knowing my father's days on earth were not guaranteed was not a good feeling. I had to put it aside the best I could and be a Soldier. This assignment is what paved the road of my now twelve year career. I had excellent leadership. I was shown what I needed to do to excel in my job and as a Soldier. I did what was asked of me and more. I was starting to love being a Soldier. Despite all the advance promotions, kudos, coins, and great job I still wasn't great. The fact my dad was dying from cancer had me broken. After the passing of my dad, I was never afforded the opportunity to truly mourn my dad.

The day after I returned to Germany from his funeral, I immediately went to the field. I remember crying while trying to get through training. I was told by my squad leader to suck it up and drive on. That is exactly what I did. My attitude was completely different as you can imagine. I relied on alcohol to get me through one day at a time. I was crying out for help but in those Army days you just didn't seek help. It was frowned upon and your career could be cut short. I did what everyone else did in those days. I dealt with it on my own. Two years later my cousin and second father to me passed away from a car accident. Once again, I was unable morn his death due to high demands at work and history repeated itself.

Fast forward four years. Life for me in the military was going extremely well for the most part. I advanced rather quickly for my occupation, but up to this point I was missing something. This something was a deployment. Rest assure I was headed there. In November of 2007 I left for my first deployment to Baghdad, Iraq. I was sent to Kuwait earlier than the majority of the personnel to ensure everyone was properly accounted for as they entered into theater. I can never forget my first day in Iraq. We got mortar attacked approximately 30 times in a row.

I knew for sure Iraq would be my final resting place. The 15 month deployment took a toll on me mentally, physically, and emotionally. Even though I didn't go out on missions there was always a possibility I could get blown up just walking to the gym or getting something to eat. I remember a year into my deployment calling my mother to tell her I loved her and I was sorry, but I didn't think I was going to make it back home. That's what I felt in my heart. I was tired of getting attacked on a daily basis. I wanted out, but there was no way, I was trapped.

After my 15 month deployment, I returned home, however, I felt like a stranger in the world. Until this day, I still have issues within myself which I deal with on a daily basis. Being from the era I grew up in the Army, I haven't sought help yet. In my opinion, no one comes back the same person they were when they left. I deal with it the best I know how.

Currently, I've been serving our great Nation for twelve years and my life in the Army hasn't always been exciting. I've been under investigations for various unfounded reasons. I've had people not like me because of my success or for no reason at all. In the end, everything I have experienced in the Army rather good or bad has contributed to the person I am on and off duty. It has taught me how to be resilient and hunt the good stuff. *Finding the good in what you think is a bad situation will open your eyes and make you realize things aren't as bad as they appear.* Always look forward to a brighter day and a much better future.

# HEALTH

# #HEALTH

the core of existence

# Barb Davies

## Ontario, Canada

### *Your Health is Your Wealth*

*"It is not what we get. But who we become, what we contribute, that gives meaning to our lives."*
Anthony Robbins

As a childless woman approaching 50, I often wonder what kind of legacy I will leave. How will I know that my life mattered? As I reflect upon the first half of my life - the disappointments, mistakes, and the blessings, I am determined to make the rest of my life the very best it can be.

I have come a long way, although I believe anyone of my age would feel the same. As we grow and navigate through life's challenges, we gain wisdom and an appreciation for what is really important. Material possessions are losing the appeal they once held; and shared experiences with loved ones bring me the most joy. Yet, I am also driven by a need to make powerful contributions to the lives of others in my professional life. I pursue these ambitions through my work, both in the social work field and in my business ventures, with a focus on helping others to achieve wellness. It doesn't feel like work when you are pursuing your passion. Mine is educating others about health and nutrition.

My own health trials have provided valuable learning experiences that have shaped my mission in life. I was diagnosed with fibromyalgia in 1998 after a severe flare-up which kept me off work for two years. The specialist who confirmed my severe sleeping disorder (a classic symptom of fibromyalgia) opined there was no way I could work and that my condition rendered me permanently disabled. I was 29 years old. I will be eternally grateful for that little voice in my head which said quite clearly, "I don't think so".

And so my journey began. I began eliminating the processed foods I had been using for the first time in my life, as I had been too fatigued to cook from scratch. Intuitively I knew they were making me feel worse. I stopped using artificial sweeteners and drinking soda. I made some big changes in my personal life to reduce stress. Over time, I have transitioned to an organic diet which is largely plant-based; and I started using organic and chemical free products in our home and for personal care. What a remarkable shift in health I experienced just by making these simple changes! I have been off all of my fibromyalgia medications for over 10 years now, and I've never felt better. My lifelong struggle with severe allergies has ended, and my chronic headaches and sinus issues have resolved. My only regret – and it's a big one – is that I didn't comprehend sooner how toxic my lifestyle was, as it was likely a major contributing factor to my infertility. I suffered two devastating miscarriages in 2012 and it has taken me a long time to heal. Perhaps I will never fully recover from the loss, but I can share my story in the hope that it will help others.

The most important thing I have learned on my journey is that reducing our toxic load can have a profound impact on our health. One only has to view a YouTube video such as "10 Americans" by the Environmental Working Group to realize that you cannot unlearn what you have learned; and changes are desperately needed. I was shocked to discover that the average woman who uses a dozen personal care products in the morning has applied over 160 chemicals to her skin before she leaves home. Your skin is your body's largest organ. You may be surprised to learn that whatever you apply to your skin is absorbed into your bloodstream within twenty six seconds! Studies have shown that many of these toxic chemicals can be absorbed and held in the body's tissues for years, and no one knows what the effects are from combining them. I know what you are thinking. *What harm could possibly come from using products with such tiny amounts of chemicals?* This is the most dangerous misconception of all. The common belief that low doses of chemicals don't matter is completely false. Consider this: numerous pharmaceutical drugs are effective at a few parts per billion.

Many of the chemicals you likely use every day are associated with health effects such as hormone disruption, allergies, skin irritations, infertility, birth defects and even cancer. I grieve for the young girls and women who don't realize how their reproductive systems are being compromised by all the chemicals they use in the name of beauty. It drives me to speak out and to share what I now know.

It's not only personal care products that contain toxic chemicals. They are also found in your carpets, home furnishings, home cleaning products, plastics, and conventional food.

Knowing this, I have prioritized buying organic food. I can no longer obliviously enjoy eating food which has been genetically modified, sprayed with toxic pesticides and herbicides, and/or enhanced with artificial chemical flavorings engineered to make you crave more.

Some people find making these changes much more difficult than others. I am often asked for advice from people who are desperate to start feeling better. Many of them refuse to give up the unhealthy foods they love because they are addicted. I agree with David Wolfe's philosophy that it is easier to start adding more of the good foods than to reduce the unhealthy ones. Eventually, one will find a new healthier balance. It's very interesting what happens when you eat organic, nutrient dense food. You require less to feel full. Your cravings for junk disappear, and you begin to crave fruit and vegetables. Weight is released effortlessly and people begin to compliment you on your youthful appearance. What's not to love, right?

How can you make these changes too? I encourage you to take control of your own health. Educate yourself about ingredients and begin to read labels. Become aware of what is really in the products you use every day and the food you purchase. Use the databases at the Environmental Working Group's website and/or download their app to research your favorite brands, investigate individual ingredients, and to find safer alternatives. If you need help, please visit my website at www.barbdavies.com for a list of other resources to assist you on your journey to toxin free living.

If my story has helped even one person evaluate their lifestyle and make positive changes, I have succeeded. And if you, too, cannot unlearn what you have learned, share the wisdom you have gained to make somebody else's life better. There is hope.

# Rosie M. Preston

### Alabama, United States of America

## *Living with an Autoimmune Disease*

It's my first day of vacation. The perfect place for inspiration. It's definitely picture card perfect as the waves are calm. The sea is blue as I sit on the white sand of an Alabama Beach. There is a gentle breeze blowing. It is so relaxing as my mind absorbs the nature around me. I lie back and let the lazy waves wash over my feet.

Suddenly I hear thunder in the distance as the dark clouds are gathering several miles away. The waves change quickly as if dancing to rock and roll music with the coming windstorm. The bottom falls out of the clouds as the rain begins to pelt my skin causing a burning sensation. Within minutes the wind becomes so powerful. It's taking all my strength to force my body backwards, to keep from being washed out to sea. It occurs to me the sea is a symbol of eternity and I have to make a conscious effort to save myself; to save my soul.

The wind whips and wraps my towel around me. I am fighting the sand blowing in my face almost blinding me. With the wind at my back, I am thankful to be slowly approaching the hotel. It is a refuge where everything is conditioned for comfort and safety.

After changing into dry clothes, I decide to relax with a Dr. Pepper and a box of chocolates. The description on the box says: Dark chocolate with Caramel and Sea Salt. I laugh at myself thinking it's the perfect time to skip lunch and indulge. I savour the candy as I relax to read a book until the storm has passed. Later the tide now moves slowly against the sand as the ebb flows away as mysteriously as it came. Now the ocean seems pleasantly free of the wind and the large waves. My body has settled into a stress free zone. Feeling drowsy I fall into a light sleep.

Upon awakening, I walk to the patio which faces the sea. It's very clear to me after spending hours watching the ocean perform and be changed by nature, it has offered me a better understanding of how the ocean scene represents my journey. A story of how a devastating virus of which I had no control over, changed my life forever. As the ocean moves with the simplicity of nature, I've flowed with the path-breaking phases as the sun, the moon, and earth are in their eternal cycle. Looking up at the sky still masked with different colors of clouds, I ask God for guidance to write about this illness, hoping it will open the eyes of others who may not know the diagnosis of living with an autoimmune disease. I focus on the past thinking of nothing, but when my world changed,

It was 1993 and I was 41 years old. I remembered it just as if it were yesterday. It all started with me being exhausted for several weeks. This wasn't a normal tired, but an exhaustion so overwhelming I didn't feel like I had any energy and wanted to sleep all the time. I was sick for several weeks before going to a doctor. It started with me taking a nap and going into such a deep sleep, my daughter couldn't wake me. It would be several minutes before I could move. I began to cry because I knew I was very sick.

In fact, I had to be helped to the car by two people. After being examined by the doctor, my diagnosis was a viral infection. I had contacted Epstein - Barr virus, also known as Mononucleosis. The blood test showed a very high titer. The normal level is 100 and mine was 900. He advised me to quit work and go home and go to bed. There is no medicine or cure. He also said it would remain in my body and lie latent until I experienced any type of infection and then it would reactivate. This couldn't be happening! I had always been the picture of health. My day care had survived the difficult years. It was as if a rug was pulled from under me and I hit the floor with such force I felt I couldn't breathe. I had no choice, but to close my business as I was told if I continued to push my body, I could damage my heart, lungs, and liver.

My doctor explained it was if my body was at war within, fighting an autoimmune disease. This was serious because it can be a catalyst for several other serious ailments; such as Lupus, MS (Multiple Sclerosis), RA (Rheumatoid Arthritis), and several hundred types of cancer. The natural rhythms of my body were just as the ocean with the underlying currents. Neither could be observed by the naked eye. As I struggled with emotional and physical pain accompanied by depression. The trip to the E.R. changed my life just as the ocean waves had been disturbed by the dark sky.

Several months passed before I had some days when I had a few hours of energy. Since that time, I've never had the normal energy I had before EBV. I was lucky to have days where I had a 'window' of energy. I fought my way out of the darkness and felt the sun upon my face. I took the good days and began a new path. I had always wanted to write. I had kept journals for years and wrote poetry and short stories, but had never thought about being published.

Many people told me when one door closes, another will open. The more I thought about writing, I had a story in my mind. It was about my MawMaw. When I was young she took me to the theater to watch the Elvis Presley movies,

I thought she did it for me. I didn't realize she was still young and could be attracted to Elvis, also. So I sat down and wrote a humorous article, "MawMaw Loved Elvis". I sent it to the local newspaper and to my surprise, it was published! This gave me the confidence and inspiration to send articles to other publications.

In 1998, five years after I was diagnosed with EBV, I was writing a weekly column titled, "Keep Smilin' with Rosie". Ideas seemed to flow and I couldn't write them down fast enough. After being published, I felt blessed as my inspiration came from the readers. They began to let me know how much they enjoyed the stories from my heart. There was a relationship between us that lifted me so high. I met people everywhere I went who recognized me from my photo in the paper. Many would even recall an article that had personally touched their lives. This was an emotional connection that was wonderful and it was if I had new friends through doing something I loved.

Looking back, there is gratitude for my past experiences, both good and bad for they are what made me who I am today. I am strong. I know the mornings will always bring a new day. The sun will shine or the clouds will bring the rain.

My vacation is ending as I walk along the beach and allow the waves to splash my feet, knowing I am not alone I have faith, hope, and love and the greatest of these is love. My journey has opened my eyes and is comparable to nature's core. I am like a tiny grain of sand, exactly like the small bit of carbon which forms a diamond over a period of time. So was I... being transformed from being dull and lacking brightness to feeling a new joy for life.

Over a period of time the diamond is cut and polished to reveal its splendor. It will never again lose its inner shine. It is filled with beauty and nothing can crush its inner clarity. The future unfolds as I move forward, I will be content knowing it's natural to return to my resting place with the moon. There is a vast ocean of peace and consciousness that surrounds my body as a shield of protection and love. I will hold on, just as the air surrounds the earth, I am surrounded by the light of the sun which brings life from God. I will hold on with my enlightened spirit each day as a present never to be taken for granted again.

# Chocolate & Diamonds

# Cyndi Stewart

## *Root Causes*

### Colorado, United States of America

While addressing the importance of lifestyle and emotional aspects of healing, I became intrigued with the signs and symptoms on the physical side as well and uncovering the underlining root causes to one's health. I hope my story inspires you to get your power and life back, however that looks for you to rewrite a chapter of your life.

Because I've been on a health journey since an early age, getting to the "Root Causes" is my lifelong passion. A life that started filled with fear to leave my home, debilitating panic attacks, constipation, constant cravings for sugar and low energy all of the time. Of all the fears, the worst one was throwing up, particularly in public; turns out it's actually a common phobia and now has a name, Emetophobia.

Mind and mood challenges, even in adolescents, now commonly recognized, but weren't in the 70"s when I grew up. Between the fears and phobias, digestive issues and child obesity, obesity also not common in the 70's; I was known as "the disturbed girl" from those who didn't know me. During this time my parents were going through a divorce, so that satisfied most as to why I was acting that way.

Indeed, I may have been disturbed, but I was fully aware of how I felt. Embarrassed by the looks from the teachers when walking down the halls and the way the school counselor spoke with me, I knew something had to change. I saw two choices; play into this or fix it. If I played into this, I could get away with everything, including homework, like the other disruptive kids.

My other option was to become unnoticeable, today it's called mainstream. I would have to cover up the anxiety, do all the activities other kids do regardless of my fears, ignore my digestive issues and lose weight. Many with anxiety don't like to be a bother or embarrassed, i.e. throwing up in public, therefore, my only option was to hide my signs and symptoms and become a really good chameleon.

Life turned into a series of various diets that didn't seem to work. Unbeknownst to me, they didn't work because I was missing the root causes to my food craving, anxiety and digestive issues. By middle school, it was diet of Tab and lean cuisines, and I took the weight off. Then I became lightheaded with very low energy, and was diagnosed with hypoglycemia. The good news is I had to learn how to eat three balanced meals a day, drink water and exercise. This worked well through high school, but once in college, the yoyo dieting started with poor self-image, negative comments about my body and fearful relationships with food.

Towards the end of high school, I moved in with my dad, my step-mother and step-half-brothers. I started dealing with bouts of depression, which I assumed was due to my home life. I began to gain weight, have acne outside my monthly cycle and urinary tract infections. This transition to live with a new family was difficult. I just couldn't shake the emotions. A few years later, college years were filled with happiness and health.

After college, I started working and met someone whom I married. My best assumption, it was time to get married. I like to follow the rules. During the engagement and into marriage, I started having chronic sinus infections, PMS with menstrual cycles which lasted two weeks, and again urinary tract infections. I was treated with antibiotics, but without relief. Eventually I found an urologist who diagnosed me with Interstitial Cystitis (IC). My first diagnosis of an autoimmune, although, it was not a known autoimmune at the time. I started medication, which helped a bit. A few years later I divorced, the IC pain went away. There is a common phrase regarding urinary challenges, what or who are you pissed off about?

In my 30's, I moved out West. My career was flourishing. I met a wonderful man, now my husband. Life couldn't be better, but my anxiety and panic attacks have taken over. I was exhausted all the time with constipation so bad it required supplements and colon hydrotherapy sessions to have a bowel movement. A holistic practitioner diagnosed me with Candida, I followed the Candida diet and supplements and the Candida was cleared. This was the start of the best and most challenging 10 years with new signs and symptoms to uncover and getting to the root cause of my health and purpose.

How can I have all I wanted for my life i.e. career, weight was down, hikes in the mountains, exotic vacations, a wonderful relationship, adopted two beautiful girls, loved my house; but yet, still unfulfilled? I spent most of my life managing my mood and mind, so it was natural for me to seek energy work. This physical side of my health, although likely triggered by the emotional side, was real. It required a lot of my own research, intuition, putting the series of events together and finding the right practitioners. My symptoms required more than a pill to avoid what I was feeling.

Even on Lexapro or Zoloft, I was still experiencing panic attacks. The doctors said take Ativan, take a higher dose of Zoloft, switch to Lexapro, and see a therapist, but never a discussion on what physically could be causing this. Turning to energy workers and healers finally lessoned the anxiety and panic enough to start, what felt like my second job, of uncovering what was going on in my body. Coincidently, this lead to my next career.

The doctors discovered my thyroid was low and I had a goiter. I was prescribed Synthroid, a common thyroid medication. Turning to a second opinion with a known endocrinologist who also checked my thyroid antibodies and adrenals, I had Hashimoto's. My second autoimmune, and needed support for my adrenals. Information on Hashimoto's was limited, so taking Synthroid, was cutting edge. Today, it's estimated more than 94% of hypothyroidism is actually Hashimoto's. There's a lot more information available now, but still most don't know that Autoimmune has a connection to the health of the small intestine (SI) and common foods are irritants to the SI, such as gluten, gluten free products, soy, dairy and eggs. It's common to have more than one autoimmune. Here is where signs and symptoms and listening to your body really matters.

Within the year, some new symptoms appeared, regular spells of dizziness on and off. I recall I had this once for a few weeks in my teens, and was told it was related to a sinus infection dripping in my ears, eventually it stopped. At first I thought this new dizziness occurred from going off the anxiety meds. Dizziness is a common side effect, but something inside felt this was different. With no sinus infection at this time in my life, I referred to Louise Hay's probable causes in her book, You Can Heal your Life, it reveals "refusal to look". I've been thinking about my life purpose and a career change. Could the dizziness be triggered from fear of leaving job stability for my purpose, or even discover what a purpose was for me?

Not interested in going to a medical doctor, I found a wonderful chiropractor who practiced kinesiology. Right away he tested and treated me for Ménière's disease, a disorder of the inner ear. It took almost a year to stabilize. The research on Ménière's is very scary. Many report after years, still no relief and completely debilitated. I felt a sadness in my heart for them, wondering why they don't have the resources I have found. After a year I experienced some hearing loss, which is common with Ménière's. My medical doctor agreed I probably had Ménière's, an autoimmune, and suggested to go back on Lexapro. I guess being numb to symptoms solves everything. I was even more determined to stay off those meds and uncover the root causes, now I'm at autoimmune #3.

After spending a month in the Ukraine to adopt our girls, during the worst bout of dizziness and with my gut health compromised from two autoimmunes; I found myself constantly nauseous, or extremely hungry when back in the States. This was different than the nausea from being dizzy. I had no interest seeing the doctor who wants to always refer Lexapro, so decided to continue with my chiropractor. Parasites. What is challenging about parasites is if your gut bacteria is compromised, it's very difficult to get rid of them. Just when they appear to be gone, they reappear.

Overall, my digestion was getting worse. The constipation, constant nausea and now gas after eating. My chiropractor felt it was my gallbladder. I tried some supplements, but didn't follow the dietary changes also required, so no relief. Went to a gastroenterologist, she said it definitely wasn't my gallbladder. After months of every other test, including scopes for cancer, the diagnosis; a low functioning gallbladder which had to be removed. The gallbladder has an important job, it stores cholesterol-rich bile secreted by the liver. Bile helps your body digest fatty foods. Without it, your liver continues to manufacture bile, but there is no longer a place to store it or concentrate it, so bile continually slowly trickles into intestines. Now healthy fats aren't absorbed, vitamin D absorption decreases, and brain, digestive and issues with your liver increase.

Over the next few years and in my 40's, it felt like all of my symptoms reappeared, and they brought new ones with them. Most challenging was the brain fog, I had this with Ménière's, but now I also had headaches and chemical sensitivities. Brain fog can be caused from food intolerances, overgrowth of bacteria in the gut, leaky gut, hormone imbalances, candida, and a low function liver. In addition, every digestive symptom was on the table; constipation and with diarrhea, cramping, acid reflux, distended stomach with bloating so bad my clothes were tight by the end of the day and multiple food intolerances.

Things that used to be easy to deal with at work and home, now overwhelmed me. So stressed all the time with fatigue, coffee was king. My monthly cycle was erratic, I never knew when it would begin and end or how heavy it would be. I assumed I was in perimenopause. The worst was I was eating and excising the same amount and gaining weight. Some days I was eating less because I wasn't as hungry as I used to be, although, I increased the wine because the stress was not relieved anymore just from being home after a day at work. Not only was I gaining weight, I was in weight loss resistance. I knew it was time for a complete overhaul and it started with food. I followed the Paleo autoimmune diet. This relieved many of my food intolerances. Some food I now eat again, and some I don't have the desire for anymore. My monthly cycle went back to normal so I don't feel like I'm in perimenopause, the brain fog lifted, energy increased and I started to take some weight off. Still, I had digestive symptoms and chemical sensitivities.

Through my own research, I tested for MTHFR which was positive and the root causes finally all started to make sense. MTHFR is a genetic liver dysfunction which can be common with autoimmune. I have the gene on both sides of my family, so my liver only toxifies at 30%. Everything we eat and breathe has to be processed through the liver, so a lot is being compromised in my body. When the liver is congested, the gallbladder becomes overloaded and low functioning. When the liver and gallbladder aren't working at their best, your stomach acid isn't at full capacity to kill off critters, such as parasites.

When your liver, gallbladder, and stomach acid are compromised and you have parasites, your gut, specifically your small intestine is compromised and you have what is called leaky gut.

Leaky gut can trigger an autoimmune response. Leaky gut is irritated by food, especially sugar, processed and diet foods. Gut and hormones imbalances are closely tied together causing inflammation in the body. Constant fatigue and low energy is related to thyroid, which impacts the ability to balance blood sugar and adrenals become zapped from years of inflammation and an increase in gut bacteria.

What was most interesting about MTHFR, it causes anxiety. Wow, I finally understood why the anxiety started at such a young age and why it was so intense. Most recently I learned I have one more digestive imbalance, it's called small intestine bacterial overgrowth (SIBO). It causes constipation with diarrhea, cramping, distention, bloating and different food intolerances than leaky gut. These symptoms are the last pieces to the unresolved puzzle and I'm currently under treatment for it now.

I've come to understand how important all symptoms and possible connections to one's health are needed to address the root causes, versus mask the symptoms. For years I sabotaged my recovery because I wasn't taking my food selection seriously. It took until I felt sick all over from almost anything I ate, that I started to trust what my body needed and leave a diet of processed-GMO and sugary foods. My hope is everyone takes seriously what they eat and uses it as a way to sustain health versus numb our pain. I understand how frustrating and scary this can be when you don't feel well and don't know what to do.

After years of suffering, I finally made the decision to take control of my life, regain my health through addressing the emotional and physical root causes and integrate a holistic approach to my healing. My journey included education on nutrition, but specifically, which foods worked best for me, considering; autoimmune, leaky gut, low functioning liver, inflammation, SIBO, hormones imbalances and blood sugar imbalances. In addition, and most importantly, how my body felt after I ate specific foods. Basically, I had to create a diet that worked for me versus based on what the experts recommend. Expert advice is needed to spearhead the journey, but we want to stay connected to our bodies and focus on what works for us individually.

# Laura Gray

North Carolina, United States of America

## *Overcoming Autism*

What is the first thing that comes to your mind when you hear the word "Autism?" Is it the picture of sensory issues, social issues, or maybe a child struggling with a meltdown? Or, is it kindness, compassion, or humor?

My name is Laura and I am sixteen years old. I was born three months early and in the NICU for 53 days before I finally arrived home with my parents. Both of my parents have backgrounds in computer engineering. My father is still a computer engineer, and my mother is a full-time manager and entrepreneur with her own businesses. When I was born, I had a slew of health conditions to overcome including pneumothorax, anemia, and ROP (retinopathy of prematurity) Stage 1. None of these conditions, fortunately, caused me long-term health complications. My parents knew I undoubtedly had, or was going to have, some form of a developmental disorder and possibly be somewhere on the spectrum.

They were correct about this. I was only barely starting to talk when I was about two years old or two and a half, and I was still hardly speaking by the age of three. At the age of three, I was diagnosed with Autism. I had extensive speech delays and motor delays. I was supposedly not on track to make it very far cognitively. However, neither of my parents, especially my mother, would take "no" for an answer.

I started kindergarten on time and was on target academically, including reading, by the end of it. Through most of elementary school, I was pulled out of the class most of the time for support. I don't remember struggling all that much with school. As far as I was concerned, I participated with everyone else just the same way, got the same homework, went come to complete it and had extra-curricular activities and a sport or two just like everybody else. I never paid much mind to whether or not I even had Autism in the first place until I was about ten years old and in fifth grade. For me, the two biggest aspects that did, and still do, affect my everyday life, are sensory issues and social issues.

As far as sensory issues go, mine are certain textures of food and clothing. Large, crowded social events are a nightmare, including dances, the mall, and the school cafeteria. I am sixteen, and I am not incredibly picky about food, but there are some things I will not eat, like steak. I am fine with onions taste, but because of their texture, I prefer to have them in my food. I do not eat steak. As far as red meat goes, I enjoy an occasional Reuben, burger, or taco, but I do not like steak filets. The texture is overly chewy and grainy.

I have acquired a taste for other foods, such as cucumbers and tomatoes. Your sensory perceptions can taste over time, and your body is always changing. I used to hate cucumbers, lettuce, and tomatoes. Cucumbers and lettuce seemed bland, and cucumbers slightly slimy. Tomatoes to me were, with the combination of the skin, slimy and squishy. To me, the textures of tomatoes clashed. Now, I love salads with cucumbers and tomatoes. Cucumbers add a certain element of crunch I love and are slightly more flavorful than lettuce. I would eat those raw with a little bit of dressing regularly. ☺

It has taken me a long time to learn appropriate social cues, and I am always learning. My parents have worked with me a lot on this. I have learned by being instructed directly on what is appropriate, or observing how someone acts, or just guessing what is right, and learning from it. If I am correct, great; if I am wrong, okay, I won't make that mistake again. Either way, I learn something.

The biggest way my awkward social tendencies affect me now goes about as far as engaging in a conversation, in a group, and then maintaining it. This is an ongoing process I am learning, but I have learned to go up to someone at school and strike a conversation with them, maybe about how the day is going, what their plans are, food, the weather, or just about anything. I have learned to start somewhere and take it and run with it. Now, it is very difficult for anyone else to tell I even have autism. Not because it presents any fewer challenges for me than it does for any other individual with Autism, but because I have learned to adapt and develop coping strategies, whether I realize it or not.

It is very typical for an individual with autism to have a very narrow, but highly focused, interest in activities. Currently, I am a registered Girl Scout, a varsity rider on both teams at The Grier School, and a recreational archer. I also enjoy running. Considering I am an introvert and everyone should find something they are passionate about, my parents pushed me to step out of my comfort zone and try new things, but she let me learn what I like on my own and make some of my own decisions.

For several years, I was an active gymnast, and I liked it just fine for several years, but I was not enamored by it. When I was nine years old and in fourth grade, I decided i was done with gymnastics. Later, I also tried ice skating. However, horseback riding is my passion. I began riding when I was about six years old, and the riding habit stuck.

I was in public school up through my first year of high school. My ninth grade year in public school brought it to an abrupt halt between huge classes, an immense school size, and various social issues and on the target end of repeated bullying.

At the same time in public high school, I began my Girl Scout Gold Award, a leadership award that is among the highest awards in Girl Scouting. I got through the paperwork I needed to do before completing it, including the proposal. I completed my project, a sensory garden, at Horse and Buddy, a therapeutic riding barn over the summer of 2013. Following that was a mass of paperwork that took me a year to complete.

By the end of the first semester of high school in public school, my mother and I hit a wall and decided we were done with public school between the social and academic issues at the time. The adventure of looking for the right boarding school began. Now, I am a student at the Grier School.

I absolutely love the experience, have a lot of fun, and refer to Grier as my second home. I completed my Gold Award almost immediately following my first year at Grier. I have a group of people I am pleased to call my friends, especially Jamie, a girl who is to be my roommate. I am an honor student, a varsity rider on both teams, a recreational archer, and a member of the yearbook staff over the 2014-2015, and potentially over the 2015-2016 school year. I also have a horse, and his name is Nash, and he is my partner. ☺ I am going into my junior year of high school.

My parents always make a point of letting me make my own decisions and be my own person, but they also will push me out of my comfort zone so I learn what I like, but without forcing me into anything. Throughout the past several years, I am within the top three cookie sellers in the area, from 2008-2013. I set my own goals, and met them, with my parents more than happy to support me in pursuing my own interests. I have Autism, and it does not have me. It is a mere part of who I am, and not the sole defining aspect of my character.

# Susanne Ridolfi

Queensland, Australia

## *My Body and Me!*

I remember when I was trekking up the very last bit to put my flag down on the Mountain, over 5,700 metres above sea level in the Mount Everest region, being extremely sick and the only thought I had in my mind was 'I am not giving up, I WILL put this flag down'! I did put it down and then ran off to throw up behind a nearby rock. Yep, altitude sickness, it was and not a very nice experience either.

Life is Journey and my story about *My Body and Me* has been a huge part of my Life Journey. A Journey about love and acceptance, about trust and believing, about walking your talk and never giving up. Today I am happy to say, I love myself for who I am and I love my body for what it is. Yes, I can honestly stand in front of the mirror, naked or dressed, and say 'Hello Gorgeous' - and mean it!!!

Now, this is not how it always was - as a teenager, I hated, more than loved myself and my body. I was teased and bullied, for the way I looked and for being different. Whilst everybody else enjoyed playing handball, I chose gymnastics and I was good at it. I also did well academically and I was liked by the teachers - well that wasn't popular amongst my friends either. So I was a very happy camper, when it was time for me to leave my 'pals' and move on to college and later to University, where I could build up a completely new sphere of contacts and friendship.

We are all spiritual beings, having our Human Experience here on planet Earth. Our body is the vehicle we have chosen for this Journey, so why don't we look after it and listen to the needs it has? Well, maybe you do - I certainly didn't at all to start with. I thought I was indestructible, like many other teenagers in this world. I never asked permission from my Body doing what it did. I just went ahead and did stuff and sometimes suffered badly in the process.

Our body is such an amazing vehicle! It tells us what is working and what's not - on a daily basis....my mistake was I didn't listen!!! All the little sign and symptoms my body gave me, I dismissed. Sometimes it screamed loudly and you would have thought I learned the lesson....hmm. It took me a long time and it wasn't until I started to study Oriental Medicine and the Power of Touch through a beautiful Japanese form of healing art called Shiatsu, that I started to 'wake up', listen within and view ME differently.

So when I talk about my body and me, I don't mean just the physical me - I mean the Entire Me - The physical, emotional and spiritual Me all together. I don't think we can separate these parts. In the end, we are all energy and part of the whole, so we need to take all parts into consideration. Our energy vibrates in relationship to what is within, as well as without. A sense of **Balance** is the key!

Think about it - What's your body made of?

- 9 systems comprise the Human Body including Circulatory, Digestive, Endocrine, Muscular, Nervous, Reproductive, Respiratory, Skeletal and Urinary

- What are those made up of? Tissues and organs

- What are tissues and organs made up of? Cells

- What are cells made up of? Molecules

- What are molecules made up of? Atoms

- What are atoms made of? Subatomic particles

- What are subatomic particles made of? ENERGY!!!

You are, we all are, PURE ENERGY-LIGHT in its most beautiful and intelligent configuration. Energy that is constantly changing beneath the surface and you control it all with your powerful mind!

Through Shiatsu I started to understand the importance of looking after my mental, emotional and spiritual health, as a crucial part of my physical well-being. If you are not happy, it's really hard to achieve any goal, especially health goals and many of us go to chocolate, for comfort! ***Chocolate for the Soul!*** Yeah, some of the content in chocolate has physiological effects on the body and are linked to serotonin levels in the brain. Serotonin is known as the 'happy transmitter'. So we chose chocolate to feel happier...it is all about CHOICE!

I made my choice - I started to invest in my own health and well-being and have done ever since. Shiatsu taught me that energetically we are all connected to the environment around us and to each other. Energy circulates through our body, as the river of water flows in nature, along pathways we call energy channels or meridians. So, the studying and practicing Shiatsu brought me back to Nature and the wonderful healing power nature provides. This wonderful healing power of Mother Nature is referred to as Biophilia. Biophilia has become a favourite word of mine and if you think about it - when you are in nature and around other living organisms, you feel connected, you gain perspective and life seems simpler.

This in no coincidence! Nature has a positive effect on human's well-being. We thrive physically, mentally and emotionally when we are exposed to nature. The energy from Mother Earth helps with 'grounding', the Sun brings nourishment absorbed through the skin and helps balance your hormonal levels. Being in the Rainforest or on the beach, close to the Ocean provides us with negative ions, which is great for calming and stress reduction. All this is there for you, in Nature and the great news is - it's all for FREE and you have unlimited access to it. It is your choice and such a beautiful gift to give yourself - just get back to basic and back to Nature!

I grew up in Nature myself, in the countryside of Sweden and I remember the times my mother sent me out to the veggie patch to dig up potatoes for dinner. Did I enjoy it? No, not at all and I admit, I loved the fresh boiled potatoes served at dinner, especially the very small ones with just butter and salt on top. Yum! I equally enjoyed the fresh fried up mushrooms picked in the forest at autumn time and the various berries we ate. Yes, I am born a Natures Being and my parents brought me up in accordance with nature, that's for sure.

My life Journey brought me to living in big cities like Stockholm, New York, London and Sydney. What I came to realize is the further away from Nature I found myself, the more I did seek to connect with Nature's energy in various ways. Shiatsu, Tai Chi, Yoga and other modalities have been fabulous vehicles for me. Today I feel I have embodied Shiatsu - it's part of my body and soul. I live Shiatsu on a daily basis and move as gracefully as I can through the different energetic movements.

My Life Journey did finally bring me back to Nature and I now find myself living in Paradise! - on the canal, close to the beach on the magnificent Gold Coast of Australia. I chose to live according to Natures Laws and Rhythms. I get my food from the local Farmers, enjoy exercising outdoors practicing yoga and running. I chose to wake up every morning with a smile on my face and I write in my Gratitude Journal before going to sleep. I listen to my intuition and hang around with like-minded people that lift me up. I run a business from home, built on these very principles, I believe in simplicity and I feel passionate about LIFE!

There has been a lot of self-talk over the last years and I can honestly say I have a great relationship with My Body. We have done a couple of half Marathons here on the Gold Coast, we go to the beach every morning to breathe the fresh air and run in the sand, we take ourselves to the valley and the mountain to relax and enjoy pampering ourselves with massages and facials in between working our business from home. Self-belief is about being the best version of you and inspiring yourself to be more! Many times have I been called 'stubborn' - another way of looking at it, is being persistent and consistent....never give up on You!

*If there is light in the soul,*

*There is beauty in the person,*

*If there is beauty in the person,*

*There will be harmony in the house,*

*If there is harmony in the house,*

*There will be order in the nation,*

*If there is order in the nation,*

*There will be peace in the world.*

# Liz Sutton

Texas, United States of America

## *My Path to Wellness*

As a nurse, I tried to teach patients simple actions to change their health. Nurses are not allowed to do this. Especially if we write it down. It must coincide with the doctor's actions. After many years and much delusion with nursing and western medicine, I simply had to retire. It was hard at first with the change of income, but I just didn't have it in me anymore.

From all my nursing studies, I knew of NO avenue to help myself and others, so I got busy, researched many resources, and attended workshops and schools. I had been searching for a way to live, eat and be. I attended a Natural Hygiene seminar in San Antonio one day. Wow! I loved the energy of the presenter – a Dr. Petrano who was 78 years old and she jumped off the stage! This was it! This is the answer to my search! I met David Wolfe, Dr. Andrew Weil and attended small group sessions with all of these amazing teachers. Then I went home and applied everything I had learned. I started eating raw food every day and making green juices. I became known as the Juice Master at work. Eventually, though, I fell back into my old ways of eating, with occasional juices sprinkled in. I gained weight and I was not healthy or happy.

Finally, I found the Institute of Integrative Nutrition. It was awesome and their teachings resonated with how I felt about how our relationship with food should be. I also attended massage school to renew my license. I was excited to be learning and growing again! Then life took a dive. I was on the way to the "Hotter than Hell" bike ride in Wichita Falls, Texas when I discovered I had a urinary tract infection. I stopped into a clinic, and peed in a cup. I was expecting to leave with antibiotics. When the doctor came in with my results, she asked me if I was a diabetic. I said NO. She says YES. I cried for three days. I didn't go to Wichita Falls. I didn't bike in the race. I ended up on insulin almost immediately.

I became a full-fledged diabetic. I screamed "No! This can't be happening to ME"! Not a phi slamma jamma nurse like me! If you know anything about nurses, you know there are certain health problems we all swear will not happen to us - diabetes, cancer and back surgery. All the things I swore would not happen to me, did!

So, I got busy with learning how to heal myself. I attended the American Diabetic Association classes to learn more about diabetes and how to manage it. Oh my goodness, what a crock! They taught us a can of peaches is the same as a fresh peach. And I could eat whole wheat bread. And many more things I knew in my bones were just not right. However, I still needed to increase my insulin intake.

I clearly remember the day of January 13, 2012 because it was the last time I was able to run the trails with my dogs. During an appointment with an alphabiotics practitioner, which I had heard would balance the left and right sides of my brain (which, if you know me, you might agree I need!). He pulled on my leg three times and BAM! My sciatic nerve was impinged. I need immediate emergency back surgery. My life took a dive. My whole world changed! I was in constant pain. I was on numerous pain medications which left me feeling drugged, but still in pain. The ceiling was falling. Fear was everywhere.

I lived in pajamas. I had to go with my hubby when he traveled to Colorado for work because I couldn't take care of myself at home alone! After seeing a neurologist, I was loaded with gabapentin, narcotics and muscle relaxers. On my way to addiction. Soon I could only crawl to the bathroom. If it hadn't been for my husband's dedication to me and my daughter's devotion, I would have chosen to pass to the other side. (The Grass is always Greener theory). Keith would build pipeline all day, then sleep on the floor all night so as not to disturb me and cause me pain, and wake me to do exercises when I was crying in my sleep. Wow. Guess I have to do his laundry FOREVER! After months of this, I was making small improvements and finally driving.

One day I went for a drive and it was raining. I was so sad. I couldn't see the path to take. As I was passing Wal-Mart something told me to pull in. I followed my inner voice, parked and got into an electric cart. Inside, someone was giving away free ten minute massages. I said, "I could use that". Then God, the Great Spirit, whatever you call your higher power, told me to stop. I spoke with this beautiful woman, with green eyes, full of life, light and love. She even shared her lunch with me. She helped me to the massage chair. I was so scared!!!! I really couldn't take any more pain! As soon as she started the massage, I burst into tears and couldn't stop! The Clouds opened. The Waters parted. Then I left Wal-Mart.

She suggested I go to a Rocky Mountain chiropractor. I decided to take her advice and after the first visit, I had finally found my path. I received immediate relief and felt my energy was moving through my body for the first time in a year. Keith and my daughter Shannon helped me wean off all medications. After only one week of chiropractic treatments, I drove to the beautiful Lake Loveland. Got out of the car, and didn't fall. I grabbed a tree and walked all the way around it. Got back in the car and drove back to the hotel. I repeated this every day, increasing the distance a little each time. One day I went a whole mile! I called my husband and excitedly told him I walked a mile. He, of course, being the cautious man he is, told me he wasn't close enough to save me. While I waited, I sat looking over the lake and a peace came over me as I had never experienced before. I saw EVERYTHING in this beautiful space with clarity and brilliance. I chose to stay on this side. I had hope... just a bud, but hope and it was blooming.

Today, I have immense hope! After my back was on its way to health, the next issue was the diabetes. I researched my options, and settled on the Institute of Integrative Nutrition College. I knew in my heart there was a cure for diabetes. I discovered we have been lied to about diabetes. After this revelation, I was hooked! I immersed myself in learning 100 different diets, lifestyles and what real health means and how far western medicine has moved away from this. I found that it isn't just about food! It's about our relationships, our spiritual care, our movement, our careers, and what we eat.

Our jobs here are to care for this planet, care for our bodies and souls and care for each other. We each have an important role to play on this planet. If we choose to do what is right, what is good, what is helpful, and always align with Spirit, we can WALK anywhere!

This story isn't really about me. It is about Love. It is about persistence and courage. It is about not giving up and not taking no for an answer when your soul is calling for one. It is about listening to the spirit that speaks within each one of us.

Now, I am training for the ""Hotter than Hell" 100 bike race in Wichita Falls Texas this August! I found my health, my energy and my purpose. I wish the same for you!

May the Force Be With You.

# Dr. Rosetta Lee

### Texas, United States of America

### *I Believed!*

It was Tuesday morning and my doctor's appointment was at 10am at the hospital's Family Medicine Clinic. I had made the appointment because I felt a lump in one of my breasts. I didn't know what it could be but I did know I wanted to live a healthy blessed life. The clinic was located 4 blocks from my home. I left my home at 9 am and slowly walked to the hospital's Family Medicine Clinic.

I arrived at the hospital's Family Medicine Clinic just before my scheduled appointment. I checked-in with the Family Medicine Clinic's appointment desk before taking a seat in the waiting area. It was ten minutes later when I heard the door to the examination area opening. As my eyes gazed at the opening door, a tall slender nurse appeared. As she looked around the waiting area, she called my name. My heart seemed to skip a beat as I rose from my chair. I looked at the nurse and slowly began walking toward her and the opened door.

The nurse escorted me to the examination room. It wasn five minutes later the doctor lightly knocked on the examination room door. He asked if he could come in and I responded 'yes'. When he opened the door, both he and the nurse came in. The doctor proceeded to ask me questions about why I had come to the clinic. During the examination, the doctor felt the lump in my breast which was the reason I had come to the hospital's clinic. After the examination, he wanted me to be admitted into the hospital on Monday for an operation on Tuesday. He explained that the operation was to remove a piece of the mass to do a biopsy. Well, that really scared me, so I told him I wanted a second opinion!

Then he asked the nurse to make an appointment for me to go to the Surgical Clinic. The nurse escorted me to the appointment desk and explained to the clerk that the doctor wanted me to be seen in the Surgical Clinic as soon as possible. The clerk made an appointment for me to be seen in the Surgical Clinic on Friday. I received a Surgical Clinic appointment for 9am on Friday morning and left the Family Medicine Clinic.

As I began to slowly walk home from the clinic, I started thinking about my children, a one and a half year old son and a 13 day old daughter. I felt that when a woman has a baby, she loses a lot of blood and if I had surgery, I would not survive. As I walked, everything I saw, thought and felt was vividly imprinted in my mind.

After walking for about thirty minutes, I entered my home quietly. I walked slowly to the living room and sat on the couch. My mind was filled with the words of the doctor, the hospital and surgery. My mother, who had been caring for my children, walked into the living room from the kitchen. As she looked at me, she asked "What's wrong, you look so sad". I looked at her and said, "The doctor wants me to be admitted into the hospital on Monday. He wants to remove a piece of the mass to do a biopsy. I asked for a second opinion and he scheduled me to go to the Surgical Clinic on Friday." My mother said, "Did you tell them that your baby is only 13 days old?" I replied, "Yes, but he said he still wants me to have surgery".

On Friday, I went to my appointment at the Surgical Clinic. The Surgical Clinic doctor examined me and agreed with the Family Medicine Clinic doctor that I be admitted to the hospital for surgery. The nurse escorted me to the admission's desk to schedule my hospital admission on Monday morning. The admission's clerk completed the documentation for me to be admitted into the hospital on Monday morning. She provided me a copy of all of the admission documents. I left the hospital clinic and slowly walked home.

As I walked on the sidewalk, I felt the warmth of the sun on my face and felt the gentle breeze of the wind. The sky was light blue with a few scattered white fluffy looking clouds. The streets were lined with big green trees. I looked up at the trees and said, "This time next week, you will be here, but I won't." As I continued to slowly walk home, I began to examine the look of each home. The shape of the homes, their driveways, whether the structure was brick or wood, the house color and whether they were one story or two. It seems like it took forever to get home. After walking for about thirty minutes, my home was in view.

When I entered my home, my mother met me at the door. She was anxious to know what the doctors had said. I said, "They still want me to be admitted into the hospital on Monday for surgery on Tuesday." My mother immediately said, "That's just a milk clog in your breast." She then left the room and returned with a small bottle of oil. She called it "Blessed Oil". She handed me the Blessed Oil and asked me to rub it on my breast. I accepted the Blessed Oil, then asked if I could wear one of her dresses. My mother was a woman of a large frame and I had a small frame. I went to my bedroom and changed into my mother's dress so I could put the Blessed Oil on the mass without clothing restrictions. Afterwards, I returned to the living room, sat in the recliner, picked up the bible on the end table and started reading a bible verse. During the weekend, I continued to sit in the recliner, reading the bible, and massaging the mass with the Blessed Oil.

On Monday morning, I prepared to go to the hospital. Before getting dressed, I decided to give myself another self-breast exam to check the mass. The mass was gone! It was not there! Thank you, Jesus! My prayers had been answered. I put on my robe and ran and told my mother. I told her that God had answered my prayers! I did not go to the hospital! I did not have surgery!

"And I will do whatever you ask in my name, so that the Father may be glorified in the Son." John 14:13

*Remember to learn more about our co-authors visit*

*ChocolateandDiamondsfortheWomansSoul.com*

# Pat Duckworth

Cambridge, England

## *Hot Women Rock!*

The first time I heard the word 'menopause' I was about 13 years old. My brother, four years older, said to me, "I hope I've moved away from home before Mum goes through menopause!

I had no idea what he was talking about but I registered whatever this menopause thing was, it wasn't good. Subsequently my mother had a hysterectomy while she was in her early 40's, but that's another story.

Fast forward many years and I was at a committee meeting for a local business event. I suggested we should not just market the event as a 'Family Day Out' as it might exclude older people. The response from a male member of the committee was 'Oh, so now we need to market to menopausal women do we?'

Sadly, it has been my experience of the way menopause, and women going through this phase, have been talked about ever since. Men and women talk about it in a very negative way if they talk about it at all. It's almost like a dirty secret rather than a natural phase in life which all women experience.

I am passionate about bringing the fun back into this subject which is why I prefer referring to us as Hot Women. Who doesn't want to be a HOT Woman?!

So let's explode some of the unhelpful myths around menopause.

**Myth #1** 'My mother's menopause was miserable so mine will be the same'. Not true.

Every woman's experience of menopause is different and as individual as she is. Your genetics are only one indication of your possible menopause experience. Your mother's menopause can give you a clue to the timing and symptoms you might expect but remember you only share 50% of your DNA with your mother so your experience may not be the same.

The quantity and quality of your nutrition will influence the nature of your menopause and it is likely to be very different to your mother's diet. There are also a number of lifestyle factors which have been shown to affect menopausal symptoms including exercise, smoking, and drinking alcohol.

All of this means you do not have to be a victim of your genes. The decisions you take all through your life about your diet, exercise, and lifestyle will have an equally significant effect on your experience of menopause and your health in later life. It's never too early to plan for a healthy menopause and it is never too late to have a healthy lifestyle.

**Myth #2** 'I will put on weight during menopause'. Not true.

Just as during puberty, hormonal changes during perimenopause bring about changes to your weight and body shape. At this stage of your life, your metabolism will be slowing down and you may be naturally losing muscle which helps you to burn off fat.

During this phase of your life your ovaries produce less oestrogen and your body tries to compensate by manufacturing oestrogen elsewhere to protect your body against osteoporosis. The fat around the middle of your body is one of the sites where oestrogen is produced.

As you have grown older you may have become more sedentary. Regular exercise and maintenance of muscle mass supports insulin sensitivity, boosts your metabolism, and stimulates your body's natural appetite-control signals. This makes it easier to manage your weight. Aerobic exercise, such as jogging, cycling or dancing, targets abdominal fat, and resistance exercise helps preserve lean muscle tissue, especially during weight loss diets. Finding the time for regular exercise benefits your physical, mental and emotional health.

There are other factors which can lead to weight gain such as stress, poor sleep, low thyroid function and insulin resistance. These are not a consequence of menopause and are issues you need to discuss with a medical practitioner.

**Myth #3** 'Women over 50 are invisible' Not true

Visibility is all about attitude and there are many more positive examples of powerful, visible older women. Just ask Madonna, Helen Mirren or Goldie Hawn! It's often a case of your self-esteem.

A woman's experience of this stage of her life will be strongly influenced by her beliefs. Beliefs about menopause come from a variety of sources including our mothers, friends, society, the medical profession and media. This doesn't mean they are true.

We look for evidence to prove the things we believe to be true. If you have grown up believing nobody will pay you any attention as you move into middle age, you will find evidence it is true and you will behave as if it is true too. If you want to be noticed, believe it and you will be.

If you have a negative belief about menopause which is holding you back from enjoying your life, challenge the evidence that it's true. Think of a more positive belief and find the evidence for that and I bet you will find it.

**Myth #4** 'Menopause will be the end of my sex life'. Not true

A study in 1986 (Masters & Johnson) found women have no decline in orgasmic potential during their lives and may become more orgasmic. Remember, sex is good for you. Sex stimulates the hormones, releases tension, boosts the immune system, relieves headaches and is a great form of exercise.

This stage of your life could be best time for your sex life. The sex may be as whizz bang as it has always been but slower can also be more sensitive and intense. You have more experience now and you have learned more along the way. You may not have to wait for the children to go to sleep or worry about interruptions any more. This can be a time for exploring and enjoying without bother of periods and the fear of unwanted pregnancy.

This is not only about penetrative sex. There is a whole range of foreplay and intimate touch which will stimulate the production of positive hormones, improve your mood, and tone your body.

You can get back in touch with your own body and your partner's body through massage. Massage is always sensual and does not have to be the precursor to sex if you don't want it to be. It can be a way of finding out more about what parts of the body are particularly sensuous for you and your partner. You can experiment with different types of oil and creams and lubricants and with different textures to heighten the experience for example feathers, fur and ice.

**Myth #5** 'If I don't take HRT for menopause symptoms I will just have to suffer in silence'. Definitely not true!

Some women tell me as soon as they get their first menopause symptom they are reaching for the HRT (Hormone Replacement Therapy). I understand, but HRT is not suitable for every woman and many women do not want to take it. That doesn't mean there is nothing you can do. There are lots of options.

Reviewing your diet, exercise, and lifestyle is a good start. Complementary therapies can also offer relief from symptoms and support for wellbeing. These include hypnotherapy, homeopathy, Traditional Chinese Medicine, acupuncture, reflexology, Reiki and herbalism.

It is important to talk about what you are experiencing. This is not a forbidden subject. Women who feel they are supported during menopause feel they have a better experience. Talk to your partner, your female relatives, and your friends. If your symptoms are impacting on your work life, talk to your manager or your welfare officer or Human Resources. Silence is not an option!

So what has been my experience of menopause? I had no idea what to expect because of what had happened to my mother. But it has been one of the most exciting times of my life. In my early 50s I decided not to wait any longer to find out what I was going to do when I grew-up! I left my job as a senior civil servant and retrained as a cognitive hypnotherapist. In the last five years I have set up in business, written three books, given numerous talks, and delivered lots of workshops. I have specialized in helping women experiencing menopause symptoms and I have talked about it on radio and written articles for newspapers and magazines.

I have found my women friends who are going through this phase are caring, supportive and experienced. They are willing to share their knowledge and stories and provide a listening ear. They are also ready to laugh and help me to laugh.

Most importantly I have helped lots of women to talk about this subject and to celebrate being Hot Women. Let's rock!

# Denise Harris-Heigho

Surrey, United Kingdom

## *My Life So Far in a Nutshell*

We were a family of six. My parents and four children under the age of 10. My Mum was a great Mum who worked whilst bringing up the four of us. My dad was a business man. To me, those days were good. I recently had the privilege of seeing a 1969 S-Type Jaguar owned by one of the parents at my son's school.

As I lovingly stroked the smooth curves of his British racing green car and inhaled its smell, wonderful memories came flooding back to me. My Dad had a light blue one.

I vividly remember sticking my head out of the sun roof when he got out the car to go to the shop to ask him to buy me some sweets since my Mum didn't allow us to have any. I later made up for my considered loss to my detriment. I remember snuggling into the leather seats feeling so happy that I had my packet of Spangles.

Apart from my youngest brother, we all went to the same school. I remember one particular parent's evening. We were leaving the classroom and the teacher said to my Mum, "you don't have to worry. Denise is capable of being or doing anything she wants to." I decided when I grew up, I would be married, a great Mum with 2 or 3 children and be a business person just like my Dad. I even imagined how I would look. Well dressed like my Mum always was, even down to wearing tights. As it turns out, I cannot stand wearing tights and rarely do so.

So at the tender age of 9, I had my life mapped out. Then things went wrong between my parents. Home life was no longer happy. By the time I reached 10 years, my parents were divorced, we had a new home, a new school and my Mum was bringing us up alone. I don't remember ever wanting for anything other than maybe more ice cream on our days out.

I am eternally grateful for all those things she instilled in us during those years of our upbringing. The best thing (apart from loving us all so much) was she kept telling us that anything is possible and to follow our dreams. The world was my oyster. But I was not sure exactly what field I wanted to be a business person in. Teaching was something I was drawn to, so I embarked on teacher training specializing in Science and Math's for 7-11 years olds. After a very short time of realizing that it wasn't for me I dropped out of University, which was then Kingston Polytechnic.

My Mum was supportive as I was going to take a year to figure out what I wanted to do. Suffice to say it took longer to work out than I thought. In my early 20's, I worked for a company where my husband and I ran it during the week and the owner would pop in at the end of the week to see how things were going, meetings, etc. This is where I got my first taste of business and I liked it.

To cut a long story short, pretty much since that job I have hardly ever been employed as soon after I began my own entrepreneur journey. I followed my dream did fairly well. By my mid 30's, I had became successful at it and even had my brothers in the business who helped make it a success. From the outside looking in, we had it all. We had a beautiful home, the cars, a child and several long haul holidays per year. I should have been really happy, but I wasn't.

At work having sold the business, but being retained, I was miserable. My creativity was stifled and I no longer felt secure. Being a then control freak, I no longer felt in control. I felt like a bird locked in a cage. I felt resentful. I had sabotaged my own experience of so-called "SUCCESS"

So what had happened? I followed my dream, what on earth was making me so unhappy.

In a nutshell, my needs were not being met and it manifested in constant sore throats and tonsillitis. I had been tolerating a lot. Not only in work, but in my personal life to keep the status quo. I stopped saying what I really wanted or felt. This was fine for me until my eldest began to get sore throats. If you have ever had sore throats or tonsillitis, it isn't a pleasant experience to have them constantly. I definitely didn't want my child to suffer any more. At that point, I made a decision. I said 'No'. I will no longer have sore throats ever again. That is exactly what happened. From that day forth I have never had a sore throat. Whenever I get a tingle of a possibility of one, I know there is something that I am not communicating. It took some getting used to, but it was easy and instant.

Through the journey of building my businesses, I also built up a lot of deep seated emotions and anxiety in an industry where there were very few women at the top. I was completely stressed out. However, it was my perception that that is the way it had to be in order to be where I wanted to be. I couldn't have it all and I had to give my power away.

Being so stressed caused me to eventually lose focus and not think clearly or spread my attention in all the places it was required. My marriage was suffering too. Something had to change. So I went within and took a real good look at what was going on. It was this, in my model of the world I had to be the best mother I could be like my Mum was to us and be a good entrepreneur. Love with a partner didn't come into the equation. It was just a given.

Being the amazing wonderful mother that she was, my Mum taught me to be independent women as she was. So guess what I subconsciously did? I thought that that was what I was supposed to do. I worked hard and believed I had to provide it all. Even though my husband worked with me, I didn't believe he really was supposed to or allow him to provide for me.

At the time, a track called "Independent Women" by Destiny's Child was popular. That was me to a T. I would turn the track up full volume every time it came on the radio and dance around the house singing my heart out. So guess what message I was sending to my husband.

There I was the woman he loved, singing out loud constantly. "Don't buy me anything, I depend on me, I buy my own diamonds, for my own fun ...." There was no incentive for him to work hard because I was telling him that I didn't need him.

I was constantly worrying about my survival. As it turns out, my Mum did exactly the same with my Dad. Being an extremely independent woman she was not prepared to settle for less than her dreams. Since she is a 'Super Manifestor', she always got her dreams and more. But it wasn't working for me and I was repeating the same pattern as my Mum with my husband. Subconsciously, I was pushing him away.

So I got the call. Stop self-sabotaging yourself and live in resonance with who you truly are and all that you desire. I knew I didn't want what it resulted in. I became really unhappy, lacked confidence, I felt small, my hair began to fall out and I lost a lot of weight. Whenever returning home, I remember feeling the anxiety increase within me. My heart would start to race the closer I got to home causing shortness of breath. I dreaded walking through the front door. I knew it was ending.

I made a decision. I knew I could manifest anything I wanted, so why wasn't I manifesting it all. I decided that I would do whatever work is required to get there. So I went on a transformational journey. At this point, I was ready to get divorced. Thankfully I met a lady who opened up a new world and changed my life. I have much to thank her for. I didn't think that all that was happening was my fault. Yes, I know I was naïve. She began coaching us. One of the first things she told me was that everything going on in my world I had created. On hearing this I thought "Why on earth would I do this to myself?"

Okay I eventually had to admit that she was right. Along my journey I also had been blessed to have moved on to an amazing friend, teacher and mentor Tom Evans who also taught me advanced tools and techniques to help me evolve and support me and to whom I am eternally grateful. I did "the work" and so did my husband. We ended up being much happier than we had ever been and rode the waves of life together with greater ease. There were further twists and turns which I may share in another story and we still have what I call our 7 year hitches. Having been together nearly 30 years, I am however working on making those a thing of the past too.

I wanted to evolve, love and be loved, achieve prosperity, accelerate my learning so I could live a full life with integrity and wisdom. Knowing it would result in me being at peace and embody who I truly am and share what I have learnt with the world. So as a Transformational coach, which I really can't call work because I enjoy doing it so much. I help people to stop self-sabotage, live in resonance with who they are, so they can fulfil their dreams in the shortest possible time. I got there, I am fulfilling my dream.

I am not done yet. I am a constant work in progress. So many more exciting and possibly challenging things to learn. As a consequence, I am much happier and attract more clients and opportunities. So many doors started opening. My wish is the same for you. Anything is Possible if you Believe and do "the work" and keep doing the work.

# Marsha Lecour

### Toronto, Canada

## *Rise Up and Reclaim Your Health*

How many of you have ever been emotionally or mentally beaten down? How many of you chose to rise back up? Do you feel that you are just surviving and not thriving? My mother would experience a great shock when she learned that I was born with a hole in my heart.

"Mrs. Lecour. Your brand new baby daughter has an opening in her heart. She will require open heart surgery around age 4," said Dr. Charles Wall, our family doctor. "Oh no, Dr. Wall, will she be all right? What will we do? Asked my concerned mother.

"I am going to refer your little daughter to Dr. Fraser Mustard who will perform open heart surgery on her at the Hospital for Sick Children in Toronto when she is about 4 years old. In the meantime, I will monitor and care for your daughter closely Mrs. Lecour." "Oh thank you Doctor."

In February 1957 during the heart surgery a blood transfusion was required. A blood transfusion was administered and the surgery was a complete success. I grew up with minimal health issues or concerns.

I moved away from my small hometown to the big city of Toronto to pursue a career as both a teacher and a guidance counselor at the high school level. I found a family physician who was compassionate, articulate and had a good bedside manner in my opinion. During one appointment, he requested that I go for routine blood work at a local lab. I completed the blood work, got the results from my doctor. He noticed something unusual with the results, so he referred me to a liver doctor (hepatologoist).

"Marsha, your blood work results indicate that you have non A non B hepatitis," stated the hepatologist. I was stunned and asked all kinds of questions about this new diagnosis. One part of the entire conversation really left a lasting impression on me that day. He told me that I would require a liver transplant later on down the road. This form of hepatitis is a virus that causes deterioration to the liver over time.

I asked to go into more detail about the possible liver transplant. He told me that his research team was conducting research on pigs' livers for transplant purposes.

I am a committed vegetarian. The thought of having a pig's liver inside me made me gag. There was no way this was going to happen to me. I know that it could possibly save my life, but there had to be another way.

At this point, I was not a candidate for conventional treatment as the damage to my liver was not that serious at this point. I made up my mind right then and there that I was going to become proactive in my journey to either slow down the progression of the damage to my liver or remove it altogether. I was on a mission.

Over the course of many years, I spent thousands of dollars out of pocket in an effort to actively slow down the damage to my liver or to reverse the damage as a result of the hepatitis C virus.

I decided to make a conscious decision toward natural/holistic methods of healing including: Ayurvedic approaches with shirodara and full body abhyanga, acupuncture, chiropractic, naturopathy, yoga postures, Transcendental meditation, breathing routines, macrobiotic food routine, raw veganism, wheat grass juicing, green juicing, exercise, positive affirmations, massage therapy, homeopathy, silent retreats, meditation courses and prayer. I wanted to try everything I could without the necessity for a transplant.

At one point in this journey, Dr. Jenny Heathcote had become my hepatologist for many years. During one routine visit, she asked me what I was doing from my side to be proactive my diagnosed illness. I told her about my efforts. Her immediate response was not to change anything in my routine because the damage to my liver had slowed down for the time being. This was wonderful news to hear.

In 2000, Dr. Heathcote recommended that I actively engage in conventional treatment of double therapy of interferon and ribavirin as routine blood work and ultrasounds showed more damage to my liver. Yet the progression of damage was still slow as compared to the general population with hepatitis C. After 6 months of this treatment, I was a non-responder, so I stopped the treatment. This treatment consisted of self-injections of interferon and ribavirin in pill form.

Despite this attempt with conventional treatment, I still remained proactive in my efforts to continue on my health journey. Despite the slow progression of the liver damage, I was still feeling positive, had great energy and remained active.

Dr. Jenny Heathcote had actively moved into fulltime research at the University of Toronto and I was now under the care of Dr. Jordan Feld.

I had heard about the Hippocrates Health Institute (HHI) under the leadership of Dr. Brian Clement) in West Palm Beach Florida. There had not been any reported cases of someone being cured of hep C with their alternative approaches to various health issues. But I decided that three weeks of following a dietary routine of raw food, wheat grass and green juicing would have positive benefits in the grand scheme of things. I did not have any expectations to be cured. I wanted to improve the general health of my liver. This was October 2012.

I spent three glorious weeks there in the sunshine enjoying a daily schedule of infrared saunas, the whirlpool, a regular pool, meditation, raw vegan diet, activity in the gym, lectures with assorted faculty and staff of HHI and making new friends. I really came to enjoy the sun.

I really thrived here with the daily warm sunshine, being outdoors, fresh wheatgrass, green juicing, raw diet, and meeting wonderful people.

While I was there, my desired weight goal had been reached effortlessly – a dream come true. I had wanted to reach my weight goal for many years and it finally happened here in such an uplifting positive environment.

Upon my return to Toronto in November, I felt great and optimistic moving forward. I had my regular appointment with my hepatologist Dr. Jordan Feld at the Toronto Western Hospital.

I had the routine blood work and ultrasound for this visit. But this routine visit was different. Up to now, he always mentioned that he would continue to monitor the functioning of my liver. This time he told me in no uncertain terms that I had basically had two choices: immediate conventional treatment or the worst case scenario (the end of life).

I chose conventional treatment which consisted of 48 weeks of triple therapy with three different medications with a number of side effects like hair loss, depression, nausea, hacking cough, irritability, etc. I had them all. I spent every week in therapy as I didn't want to have another medication in my system like anti-depressants.

Prior to treatment, I had four major goals:

1. To enjoy a complete 100% cure
2. Listen to the music of The (Canadian) Tenors daily during the course of treatment
3. Maintain my goal weight (had a previous weight issue).
4. Be independent as much as possible.

I found the music of The Tenors to be very healing and soothing for me. I love the sound of their voices. I repeated these goals aloud and I told a close friend of mine about my goals. This made me "accountable" to someone. It was a lighthearted approach to have something to look forward to.

One of the important pieces for me was the support system that I had created around me – family, some close friends, pharmacist, homeopath, therapist, chiropractor, massage therapist, my hepatologist and private Facebook groups for people with hep C.

There were days that I could barely manage to get out of bed. There were days where I felt better and could go for a short walk.

I can remember having days where I felt I could not take another Ribavirin tablet. I was so sick of taking these tablets every day. It was a drag at times.

I was very irritable and I would call the liver clinic from time to time to rant about how I had just screamed at someone for no apparent reason. The doctor (not my hepatologist) at the other end of the phone would remind me once again that this was really not me and that it was the effect of the drugs on me. It was challenging to go out in public for this very reason. I kept to myself a great deal for those 48 weeks.

As I reflect back on this journey, I am deeply grateful that I somehow found my grit to persevere throughout the tough times of the treatment. If I had quit, I would not have been cured. One year later after treatment, I am cured of Hepatitis C.

I have worked hard to rise up and to reclaim my life. I started over one step at a time to eat nutritionally and skillfully, to exercise regularly with joy and to thrive with ease and joy.

I am about to set out for a week to experience a 20-mile hiking and camping adventure in the Grand Canyon. There is definitely life after an illness.

Live your life by design not by default. If you have endured the condition of HEP C and feel that your energy is low, take a moment and just go for a walk. Maybe a short walk to start with, but a walk will help your health. Always believe in life and know that you don't have to just survive – you can thrive.

# Debbie Rapport Pickus

Illinois, United States of America

## *Cut the Crap Now*

What does health and fitness mean to you? This is a question recently posed to me. I had been talking with my fiancé about this exact subject and the broadness of this topic. He turned around and asked me the same question. To me it means being able to do all the things I want to do physically without pain. It means feeling strong. It means I am able to do the work necessary to run our business which delivers fitness based, corporate team building and self-defense events. It also means continuing to teach high-intensity group fitness classes weekly. It means the ability and energy to travel to see my grown children who are scattered around the country. It means FREEDOM.

Health and fitness is not about the perfect body. (Don't get me wrong. I would kill for a perfect body.) I like being in good shape but at 57 years old, the perfect body can be elusive. In a post-menopausal stage, there is some serious commitment and sacrifice involved, the kind I am less willing to take with all the other demands in my life. I do think it's important to feel strong and energetic. What it's really about is a lifestyle.

Here are some of the stats on my own family. My father lived a nice long life until the age of 89, but my mother died from breast cancer at the age of 62. My oldest sister died at the age of 60 due to stroke. My other sister is a breast cancer survivor. On top of all this, my fiancé's brother just suffered a hemorrhagic stroke at the age of 54, the same age my oldest sister was at her first stroke.

My fiancé had spent all his adult years being obese, diabetic, depressed and gout ridden. He was overall an unhealthy, unhappy person. He has lost 70 pounds in the last seven years and now works out with me several times a week to keep himself in good shape. His brother's stroke was a reminder as to why he is doing what he is doing to keep in shape. He feels so sad his brother never took his advice to decrease stress, eat better, and move his body. We aren't sure what the prognosis is right now. But we are more determined than ever to keep ourselves as healthy, strong, stress free and happy as possible.

So what type of lifestyle is important to you? Do you want to run a marathon or just crawl around on the floor with your grand kids?

Do you want to travel around the world or just travel around the block hand in hand with your partner or spouse? Is it looking incredible at that 30th or 40th high school reunion? Or is to dance at your son or daughter's wedding? It doesn't matter if you haven't been an athlete all your life or even if you haven't done anything before now. It's never too late. It's not about a gym membership it's about being able to do what you love with little or no physical limitations.

As a veteran group fitness instructor and former owner of a fitness boxing club I often hear from people who are brand new to the gym. They are embarrassed because they may not be able to keep up or they are afraid they will look stupid. First of all, everyone is busy thinking THEY ARE the ones looking stupid, so they aren't looking at you. They are way too concerned about themselves and not about what anyone else is doing.

However, a good rule of thumb if you are walking into a new place or class is make sure the instructor knows your background and any physical limitations you may have. If the instructor doesn't make you feel welcome, then that class is not for you. No one should ever make you feel small or bad about what you are not able to do. I always make sure to show modifications and to help out people who are new to my classes. If someone feels unsuccessful in a class, the INSTRUCTOR has failed.

Another thing I hear is people don't have time to work out. No problem. If the gym is not for you or you don't feel you have time to work out here are a few tips:

There are so many options for quickie workouts or "bursts of energy" as I like to call them. If you can do high impact exercises: Do 15 jumping jacks, 15 jump squats, walking lunges and 15 pushups. Repeat as many times as you have time for. Or jump rope with a real or imaginary jump rope for 2-3 minutes. This will boost energy and get heart rate up. Take 3-4 deep breaths and then march in place vigorously. Gets heart rate up and helps circulation. Incorporate some yoga and stretching with 5-8 sun salutations. These are good for digestion and upper body strength. People get stuck in thinking they have to do an hour or even 30 minutes. I can show people how to do bursts throughout the day and burn calories and recharge energy, or calm down if that's what is required. It can be done with little to no equipment or cost. It just requires a little "out of the box" thinking.

Now let's talk mindset. Not only is it one of the biggest factors I find to be so limiting, but it's also detrimental to your health. Did you know you can actually make yourself sick with negative thinking? I didn't mention this above, but depression runs in my family and my mother and sister were both victims of it. My mother was an unhappy woman who didn't live out her own dreams because she married young in a day and age when women did what their husbands wanted. My oldest sister was reclusive and anti-social. She smoked, ate terrible food and was overweight, and had no peer group or close friends at her own choosing. These are the types of people who often die alone and aren't found for days. This is exactly what happened to her.

Are you a victim of your own limiting beliefs? Most people think of fitness as just what your body looks like but what does the inside of your head look like? Is it cluttered with negative thoughts? Is it telling you 'you are fat, ugly, old, stupid, not talented, not good enough'? Or any of another slew of negative self-defeating phrases? The first step in any health plan is cut that crap out now!

A few years ago I came up with a solution to that issue within myself. I looked in the mirror after showering and verbalized some pretty harsh words to the woman in the mirror. You might think why would someone who's been in fitness for 16 years bad mouth the way she looks? We can be our own worst judge quite often. At that moment I visualized the look on my then 17-year-old daughter's face had I said those things to her. I saw her face completely crumble in my mind and of course, I lost it. To this day, I cannot even tell the story to others without shedding tears envisioning her face if I spoke so horribly to her. I realized back in that moment that if I couldn't say it to her, why was it ok to say it to myself? My life changed forever that day because I stopped the language and the personal verbal abuse. Now admittedly there have been occasions where some of those thoughts try to creep back in, however, I nip it in the bud quickly.

One of the most attractive and fit things I find in people is great posture, confidence and a positive attitude. Walk in a room like you own it. Dress yourself in clothing which makes you feel beautiful. Once those negative thoughts are gone and the positive, confident mindset are in place, you will soar.

So, regarding your personal health and fitness I encourage you to do these things: Think long and hard about what's really important to you, then get your body and mind prepared to do it; if need be, hire a trainer or expert to help you get there but realize you may also not need anyone at all. There are tons of online resources available to you. Just remember, think "out of the box" Check the negative thoughts at the door, smile, stand up tall and own the room.

Be healthy, be strong, Love life, Live Long

# Becca Jane

Alberta, Canada

## *My First Mammogram*

I found a lump. In my breast. I was in the shower, minding my own business, and came across something just not "right". Did I panic? No. Did I worry? Sure. You see, a few years ago I found a lump in my breast and was quickly sent for an ultrasound. The radiologist told me the good news: my tidy little nugget of concern was just a deposit of fatty tissue. I know right? There's nothing quite like being told by a doctor I've got fat boobs. It was a pretty proud moment, I must say. So I didn't freak out, but I did contact my family doctor and get scheduled for an "Emergency Mammogram". Nothing scary in that term. It's *possible* I start to freak out a little bit.

Fast forward a few days and I am off to the truest rite of passage to becoming a woman, my FIRST MAMMOGRAM...

I am sitting in a wee change room, with a bench and a door, and I am waiting to be called for my turn. It's a bit strange, like sitting on a toilet in a public bathroom waiting for permission to wash my hands. I wait with the door ajar as sitting behind it shut is plain awkward. But, just my luck, the door directly across from mine is open, and the cubby hole is occupied, with its patient looking for new friends. She's barking up the wrong tree here, Sister. I am not the type of girl that picks up at the Breastorium.

My name is called and a very gentle woman leads me into a typical X-ray room. Dim lights, soft hum, pleasant temperature for those of us dressed in a stylish paper gown. Like a princess. Since she's about to ask me to disrobe, I think the addition of wine and candles would only be appropriate.

I am asked a myriad of questions, several focusing on whether I am pregnant. I find it interesting my first, perhaps overly enthusiastic, "NO" wasn't enough. The questions are tricky too, all worded differently as though trying to catch me in a fib. Then I have to sign the affidavit swearing I am not pregnant. Geez, maybe they should just let me pee on a stick and eliminate any doubt!

(Pun intended)

So it's tops off and tits up time for me! For the first time...ever...I am actually cold. And it's obvious. I am okay with it though. This gal's seen 'em all I am sure. Deep breath. Act natural. Like a moderately dedicated nudist.

The Squisher asks to approach the machine. Which I do. Warily. Now I am the one with questions. Is a mammogram an x-ray? An MRI? A CT Scan? Whatever, as long as the machine has superpowers like that dude in the red tights. Am I right? BUT it kind of resembles a drill press. A really clean, totally tricked out drill press, but a drill press just the same. Minus the bit.

The machine is adjusted to my height. According to The Squisher, I am shorter than I look. You would think I would be nervous, but I am way too distracted by the pretty lights and shiny bits. The "Squisher" by the way, is the person who squishes your tits while you are getting the procedure.

My right breast is scooped and heaved and placed carefully on the secure, non-stick Plexiglas surface of the shelf. Pull and stretch and turn and hold. And turn. And hold. Okay, no more breathing. Good thing I chose to wear yoga pants. It's when you least expect it you'll be asked to pretzel yourself into the 'Humbled Warrior' pose.

An identical top plate slides down to rest upon my skin and is then tightened by hand. It crosses my mind I took a wrong turn and wound up in a Panini press. My girl skitters off behind her protective barrier and away we go...take a breath, hold, buzz, buzz, flash flash, and one is done. Wham, bam, thank you ma'am, "git yer" butt out the door.

A few more yoga poses, a few more shots and I pull it off without a single snare. Literally. Which is good. Boobs can be delicate. She checks the tape and...SCORE! No retakes for this girl. This technician is good. Maybe she should think about branching out into school portraits.

I re-dress in my gown and am led back to my Cubicle of Change. I am told the radiologist will take a look and then someone will fetch me for an ultrasound if need be. No worries. I could use the rest after that workout. Great news! Little Miss Friendly from across the way is back. Greater news! I was smart enough to close the door this time. I can hear the rustling of getting dressed, the squeak of her shoes. Am I the only one that's creeped out that she's lingering despite being released into the wild?

The Squisher comes back and tells me the doctor took a look and it all looks pretty good, but I will still have to go for an ultrasound of the lump for a closer look. Sounds good to me, baby! These breasts haven't had nearly enough manipulation yet, they are still attached after all. As the Squisher steps back to leave me in my cubicle, she whispers, "Watch your gown there," and gives a wee nod to the south. Say whaa...? I look down and discover, to my obvious delight, the gown has fallen open and my right breast is smiling hello as people walk by. Another proud moment. At least we are back to temperate conditions. And here I had never believed in wardrobe malfunctions.

Soon another voice calls my name and, gown tied tightly, I open the door to find my sweet little ultrasound tech. Ultrasounds are pretty routine for me, I had a ton back in the days when my organs were hell bent in mutiny, not to mention the pregnancy peeks. Basically speaking: same sound waves, different room. With dimmed lighting, of course, but still no music, candles or wine. I am pretty sure these should be mandatory at the boob gym.

I hop up on the table and the tech and I start poking away at the specimen (aka my right breast). "Can you feel it?" "I think so. Can you feel it?" "Yeah. It's right there. Here try it with your arm up. There! Found it!! It's way easier with your arm up." Happy to oblige, ma'am. I live to serve.

More questions about the girls and their love child, the lump. When did you find it? Did you find it yourself? Did your doctor find it first? At this point it occurs to me the fact my doctor has never actually physically touched me might be cause for concern. Note to self: find a new doctor.

The specimen (R.B.) is slathered with lubricant, and we are off to the races! It's easily the warmest lube I've ever encountered, almost like hot wax. Did I take another wrong turn somewhere here? Beep beep boop boop...pictures taken (very artistic natch) and back to my cubicle to wait for the doctor. With a fish for a handshake he assures me I am just chock full of scar tissue. Hmm...better than fat, I guess. He's "incredibly confident" there is nothing wrong.

With my breasts. Oh, if I had a nickel...But that's another story.

# Catherine M. Laub

New York United States of America

## *My Healing Journey*

In 2011 I developed a strong relationship with Angels. Now that I know they are around me I love telling people about how Angels can help you through some pretty tough times in life.

Up until now my life has revolved around my health, but my angels are changing that. I have multiple illnesses, but here are the ones that are prevalent. I always base where I will be taking trips on whether or not a bathroom will be available because I have "lived" in the bathroom since October, 2012. I say up until now because I am finally, at the age of 57, *on my road to recovery*.

When I was growing up, my family travelled from Long Island, New York to Callicoon Center, New York every summer to visit my grandparents. We always had to stop for me to pee at least twice and it was only a three hour ride. There were many times on those long rides, I would have to go off into the woods because there wasn't an exit nearby. Today I always have a potty chair with me just in case of an emergency. Once we were there I saw spirits often, but didn't know they were angels then.

In fifth grade I had to go to the nurse's office every time I had to go to the bathroom. So I had to raise my hand, which drew attention to me, plus I needed a partner to walk with me. This was very embarrassing since I went very often. I associate most of this beginning in fifth grade because my teacher was the first male teacher I had. His name was Mr. Roughness (slight name change) and he was also rough like his name. I remember him yelling at me to stop "playing" with my earrings the week after I had my ears pierced. Another time my violin teacher came to get me and asked why I missed my lesson. I told her Mr. Roughness said "no" when I asked to go.

Every time I was at a concert as a child, I got nervous and had to constantly make trips to the bathroom to pee. When I was in eighth grade I was in a play.

Every time my turn to be on stage came up I had to run to the bathroom to be sure I didn't have to go while I was on stage. It took away the fun for the play.

I quit high school when I was sixteen because of my frequent bathroom trips and the embarrassment around it. After a year I returned and graduated with my class. I had special permission not to have to draw attention to myself and just leave the classroom when I had to.

I was diagnosed with Interstitial Cystitis in 1998. It is like always having a urinary infection. It is very uncomfortable and also keeps me in the bathroom. I have pain, frequency, and other symptoms from it. I began on a medication, Elmiron, and took it steadily until just recently. It helped, but not enough and I took several other medications throughout the years. In 2014 I had an Interstim device implanted to help send messages to my brain saying my Bladder spasms were not causing pain. It has helped enormously, but not on a constant basis.

I had Irritable Bowel Syndrome all my life and in 2005 during a routine colonoscopy a pancake shaped precancerous polyp was found. The only option to remove it was through surgery. So I had one third of my large colon removed. I came through the surgery fine, but after I was home a few days I ended up with an infection. My recovery was about six weeks and I had to miss a previously planned trip to Florida to visit my son, Richie. He lived there for about five years and I didn't get to see him often. So I missed him and was upset I couldn't put off the surgery. Anyway, this caused my diarrhea to get worse because I now had less intestines to do the work.

In 2007 I had pain on my right side which seemed to move around. It turned out to be a hernia on the section that my large intestines were reconnected to my small intestines. Again, I needed surgery. That was November 2007. There were no complications with this one. I just had to be careful how I moved around for about three weeks.

In 2012 I began feeling better, and it was great to say so. I told my gastro doctor about it and he was thrilled to hear it. THEN, I had my routine colonoscopy!! He found hundreds of precancerous polyps and said I need the rest of my colon removed. I was diagnosed with Familial Adenomatous Polyposis. It is usually hereditary, but my family members test negative. It is funny, though, because my step-daughter and her son both have this disease.

My angels had something different in mind when they orchestrated the need for surgery. I had complications during the surgery. My doctor came out after an extra 3 hours and told Tony (my husband) he just saved my life. He said if he didn't do the surgery now I would have developed an infection that the cause wouldn't have been found and caused death. You see, the previously implanted hernia mesh was now strangling my small intestines and the tacks were starting to puncture through. I was anemic so this explains where I was losing blood. My belly was cut open about 8 inches vertically, instead of just a couple laparoscopic holes.

They had problems stabilizing me and in recovery Tony was worried because the problems continued. Thankfully, he donated blood just in case, and I needed it that night. The doctors were asking me why I kept shaking and if my blood pressure was ever that low before (90/60). I said I think my body is in shock because I didn't expect to have a "major" surgery as it became. I came home the night before Hurricane Sandy in New York and after the nurses not being able to get to me, I ended up with an infection and went right back into the hospital for another week. The recovery was long and exhausting.

So, along with my IBS, Interstitial Cystitis, and only having about 10 inches of colon, I practically lived in the bathroom.

My gastroenterologist didn't know what to do for me. I was taking so many medications already and there weren't any more to give me. I have taken Lomotil steadily since 1993. Then there is Librax, which I took on a regular basis until about 2010 where I now take it as needed. There is a medication I took since I was about 37 called Lotronex. I had to sign a waiver because the side effects could cause death. I didn't have a good quality of life so it didn't matter to me. It helped me for many years until I had the polyp. I took a couple different cholesterol medications where the side effects were constipation. They helped me on and off. Recently, after my last surgery, I was giving myself injections of Octreotide, a medication used for cancer patients that have diarrhea. It was helping me, but when I changed insurance companies they wouldn't approve it anymore. The cost was $2000 a month!!

I say I am on the road to recovery because I prayed to God and my angels in August, 2014 to help me get off some of the 22 medications I was taking and to help me start to feel better. They answered me in their own way and three days later, I attempted suicide by trying to take pills. Tony managed to stop me and I was hospitalized for a week. Finally, someone listened to me that I am a package deal. I suffered from depression/anxiety and had all these other ailments that nobody wanted to look at together. I was actually interviewed in front of 15 students by a psychiatrist because they realized how much my packaged situation can help them learn. I got put on the right track with some new doctors who were now coordinating with each other! But I still wasn't getting better.

In April, 2015 my angels guided me to a Holistic doctor, Dr. David Pollack, in Commack, New York. After working with him for only a week I started to feel better and I no longer "live" in the bathroom. Plus, I already lost 16 pounds. I am eating the foods that are specifically good for me and taking supplements that are doing the work of my body to digest my food until I am healthier to have my own digestive system work on its own.

I am excited to say I am starting to feel better and plan to totally heal myself with the help of my doctor.

# Cindy Clendenen

Texas, United States of America

## *I Wanted to Die – My Personal Battle with Candida*

It's almost midnight on January 2014 and I am still wide-awake in my bed with my laptop doing Google searches, feeling determined to find an answer to my problem. Doctors always told me my anal itching was from allergies. I had managed with it for over ten years. It wasn't bad until 2013. I am searching and searching, but couldn't find anything. Then, by the grace of God, I find a conversation on Yahoo. Everyone is saying the same thing, "They all have anal itching." I stumbled upon something very interesting I hadn't thought of or knew anything about, which is called Candida.

Throughout the last ten years of my life, I had several different symptoms. I couldn't believe my eyes! I wondered if some of my symptoms were from Candida. I had about 40 of the 60 symptoms listed. You might be wondering, "What on earth is Candida?" According to Dr. Amy Myers, Candida is a fungus, which is a form of yeast, a very small amount of which lives in your mouth and intestines. Its job is to aid with digestion and nutrient absorption, but when it is overproduced, it breaks down the wall of the intestine and penetrates the bloodstream, releasing toxic byproducts into your body and causing Leaky Gut Syndrome. This can lead to many different problems ranging from digestive issues to depression.

Every Internet site stated I would need to start an anti-fungal diet. I had never heard of this before, but I am desperate and willing to try anything at this point. Every diet was different and this left me feeling extremely frustrated and confused. Not knowing which diet was the best, I started with what I thought made sense. Immediately, I stopped eating all wheat, processed food, bread, sugar, fruit, dairy products, beans, grains and starches. The itching went away about a month after I started the diet. So I knew I was on to something. It wouldn't be long though before my weight dropped from 126 to 109 pounds. I wasn't trying to lose the weight, and it was scary, but I knew it was from my change in diet.

Being on this diet meant I wouldn't be able to eat like everyone else. I love to eat! I didn't know how I would survive. I've been so used to eating any and everything I wanted all my life. My life was turned upside down. I became very depressed. I explained my situation to some friends and my family. Some understood and others gave me the deer in the headlight look. I don't blame them. I probably would have done the same.

After you start the anti-fungal diet, yeast cells are rapidly killed, a die-off (Herxheimer reaction) occurs and metabolic by-products are released into the body. As a result, I started having horrific die-off symptoms. I wanted to die! I let out a blood-curdling scream and prayed to God on two occasions to please take me, as I couldn't go through this anymore. Feeling like I was chained to my bed, only getting up to take care of my doggies, cat and to eat, I knew I had to take action. It was bad enough I had die-off symptoms, but also had a nasty rash on my buttocks so broke down and made a doctor appointment.

My regular doctor wasn't available, so I saw someone new. She walked in and I told her, "I know what I have and here's the list of symptoms I have had for over ten years." She told me Candida is another name for yeast. "If I was a suicidal person, I'd be dead," I said. She just looked at me. After showing her the rash on my buttocks, she says, "Oh my God, you poor thing, you're all red and inflamed." I asked if I could be tested for Candida. "There isn't a test for Candida," she said. She's wrong and I knew she was wrong! Feeling helpless, and with only a referral to Dermatology and a prescription for Diflucan (an anti-fungal drug), I left. I could barely see to drive home from all the tears that filled my eyes. I felt like no one had any knowledge about my condition, nor did they care.

Lying on the table in the Dermatology clinic with my buttocks up in the air for all to see was quite embarrassing. I didn't care though. I just wanted the rash gone. It was so unbearable, I couldn't sit for more than 30 minutes at a time. I could tell they actually felt sorry for me. They told me if it didn't get better, to come back. They did indeed confirm I had Candida. I don't know how as they didn't take a skin scrape. I didn't argue, as in my mind, I already knew what it was. They sent me home with a prescription for an anti-fungal cream. It did clear the rash up.

A year went by; I was still on the anti-fungal diet. I felt much better, but decided it was time to seek help from someone with knowledge about my situation. I needed a doctor willing to run the test for Candida. I also wanted to know if I had any other conditions hindering my getting well. I had attended the Health and Wellness Expo in San Antonio, Texas the year before, I listened to a Functional Medicine Doctor by the name of Dr. Lara Sweeney of San Antonio Family Integrative Medicine. Functional medicine looks at the whole body including all of its major functions. I made an appointment. My first appointment was with her husband, Dr. Jay Sweeney. We went over my entire medical history. The next step was to run tests. They collected urine and stool samples, a swab from inside my mouth and ran 85 different blood tests. Boy, did I ever feel like a lab rat that week!

Walking into Dr. Sweeney's office, I am both scared and excited for my results. I needed answers and I knew she would be the one that could give them to me. After our three hour meeting, I suffered from brain overload. So much helpful information and the best part of it all, was now I had answers. The best news she gave me was the Candida was gone. I do have a Leaky Gut Syndrome (from the Candida) with a long list of other conditions. Had I not gone to her, I wouldn't know what other ailments I had, nor would I know the Candida was gone.

I cured my Candida mainly by being on a strict Phase One Diet. You can find this diet at **www.knowthecause.com**. Not only will you find a list of foods that you can and can't eat, there is also a lot of information and recipes. Once you start the diet, you can't cheat at all. If you do, it will take you back to day one and you'll have to start over. I took herbal supplements Caprylic Acid, Olive Leaf Extract, a good multi-vitamin, Florify (probiotic) and drank Pau d'Arco tea. If you're taking medication, please consult with your physician before taking any herbal supplements.

The Die-Off may be bad. Unfortunately, it will get worse before it gets better. You will more than likely feel like dying. Every person is different, so no one can tell you how long it will take for the Candida infestation to be gone. It depends on how long you've had it and how faithful you are to the diet. Once you're back to feeling healthy, it will all be worth it!

Throughout my research, I found out you can get an overgrowth of Candida from too many antibiotics, birth control pills, a high-stress lifestyle and diet high in refined carbohydrates and sugar.

Dr. Amy Myers states the top ten common Candida symptoms are:

- Skin and nail fungal infections
- Feeling tired and worn down or suffering from chronic fatigue or fibromyalgia
- Digestive issues such as bloating, constipation or diarrhea
- Autoimmune disease such as Hashimoto's thyroiditis, Rheumatoid arthritis, Ulcerative colitis, Lupus, Psoriasis, Scleroderma or Multiple sclerosis
- Difficulty concentrating, poor memory, lack of focus, ADD, ADHD, and brain fog
- Skin issues such as eczema, psoriasis, hives and rashes
- Irritability, mood swings, anxiety, depression
- Vaginal infections, urinary tract infections, rectal itching or vaginal itching
- Severe seasonal allergies or itchy ears
- Strong sugar and refined carbohydrate cravings

If you suspect you may have Candida and your doctor won't run the appropriate test, see a Functional Medicine or Holistic doctor. I was told allergies were causing my itching and I am stuck with it for life. One of the wisest decisions I ever made was seeing Dr. Sweeney. When you get sick and tired of being sick and tired, get help! Don't suffer over ten years like I did. After all, if you don't have your health, what do you have?

# The Talking Jar Series

A Game Changer in Talking; Connecting the Disconnect; through Questions that heal. I am Jeanne A. Dexter, Speaker, Author, Family Advocate, and the Co-Creator of the Talking Jar Series, along with my partner, Paul J. Schweinler LMHC.

The Talking Jars are a game changer because they give everyone a voice, open dialogue through Conversation Starters on Focused Topics, connect people together by allowing them to find common ground, build lasting relationships, instill self-confidence and heal the hurts, all in a fun, surprising and non-intimidating way.

All of our questions are written to inspire dialogue, to give voice to the voiceless, to express thoughts, hopes and dreams, like in our Talking Jar, to share challenges and needs, like in our Anger, Bullying, Grief, and Cancer Jars or to talk about family and traditions, as in our Family, Teen, Marriage, Dating, Life and Legacy or Christmas and Hanukkah Jars. Our Dialogue Journals, which I call "Share" Journals, allow written conversation between two or more people within a family, along with the questions from our jars; giving voice to conversation in the most difficult times, when communication has hit a wall.

Ever been misunderstood? Seeing the Bigger Picture Technology has connected us together in the world in so many ways however, in this world of technology, of social media, video, games, groups, circles, events and chats; we have become more disconnected than ever before in our own personal lives. We think we no longer have time to gather at the kitchen table, or the family room, to sit and eat, to have a conversation, face to face with our families, to hear the stories of our parents and grandparents, to learn the lessons of generations before us, to pass on the family history, to give everyone a chance to share and ask questions, to empower each other by just talking and listening.

There are many ways of having a simple conversation, by talking, through personal journaling or through our own stories. Don't we all just want to be heard, whether in our own family, a networking group, on social media, in a job or in our belief systems? We just want someone to listen, to allow us a voice, to matter or make a difference, to be connected to something. We cannot be heard, if no one is "Listening", not just listening, but actually "Hearing" what we are saying and understanding what we are sharing. That is how the connection is made. There is so much healing power in this process.

Visit our Website! www.thetalkingjars.com

# Conclusion

Chocolate & Diamonds for the Woman's Soul is an anthology featuring over 100 women who all worked together in a unique program to strengthen writing skills and build emotional strength. By releasing their legacy, each writer became a diamond. Our programs allow for *emotional and writing coaching calls* each week during the development of the book. It's far more than just a story; it's an experience.

Carla Hall and Laurie K. Grant have successfully helped over 250 women become bestselling authors through the **Hot Pink Publishing Anthology Program**. The Hot Pink approach is to help women get published, regardless of their writing ability, education or experience. She has worked one on one with several authors who have disabilities to help them have the same opportunities to have their story told in writing.

If you would like to write with us, please email **carla@hotpinkpublishing.com** and let us know. We will try to fit your story into one of our ongoing anthologies.

**www.ChocolateandDiamondsfortheWomansSoul.com**

"I have had the best time working with these women from all over the world. Their stories made me laugh and cry" – Carla Hall

**Hot Pink Publishing is a member of the International Women's Day Event and is a proud supporter of the Breast Cancer Association.**

Hot Pink Publishing at Be the Change Event in Orlando, Florida

Great Meeting the UK Writers

Joshua (L) Carla H. Gwen C. and Michelle L.

**http://www.hotpinkpublishing.com**

All Rights Reserved ©

***Co-Compiled by Carla Hall & Laurie Grant***

**http://www.anthologcreation101.com**

Become a Compiler in our Premier Anthology Program

**http://www.hotpinkmembership.com**

Join our membership program for $27 a month

Made in the USA
Charleston, SC
19 November 2015